Searching For Sugar Man
Sixto Rodriguez' Mythical Climb to
Rock N Roll Fame and Fortune

Searching For Sugar Man
Sixto Rodriguez' Mythical Climb to Rock N Roll Fame and Fortune

Howard A. DeWitt

HORIZON BOOKS
PO BOX 4342
SCOTTSDALE, AZ 85261

Horizon Books
P. O. Box 4342
Scottsdale, AZ. 85261-4342

E Mail: Howard217@aol.com

First Published 2015

ISBN: 1511419288
ISBN 13: 9781511419284
Library of Congress Catalogue Number: 2015904759
CreateSpace Independent Publishing Platform
North Charleston, South Carolina

TABLE OF CONTENTS

ROCK N ROLL BOOKS BY HOWARD A. DEWITT

Van Morrison: Them and the Bang Era, 1945-1968 (2005)

Stranger In Town: The Musical Life of Del Shannon (with D. DeWitt) (2001)

Sun Elvis: Presley In The 1950s (1993)

Paul McCartney: From Liverpool To Let It Be (1992)

Beatle Poems (1987)

The Beatles: Untold Tales (1985, 2nd edition 2001)

Chuck Berry: Rock 'N' Roll Music (1981, 2nd edition1985)

Van Morrison: The Mystic's Music (1983)

Jailhouse Rock: The Bootleg Records of Elvis Presley (with Lee Cotton) (1983)

HISTORY AND POLITICS

The Road to Baghdad (2003)

A Blow To America's Heart: September 11, 2001, The View From England (2002)

Jose Rizal: Philippine Nationalist As Political Scientist (1997)

The Fragmented Dream: Multicultural California (1996)

The California Dream (1996)

Readings In California Civilization (1981, 4th edition revised 2004)

Violence In The Fields: California Filipino Farm Labor Unionization (1980)

California Civilization: An Interpretation (1979)

Anti Filipino Movements in California: A History, Bibliography and Study Guide (1976)

Images of Ethnic and Radical Violence in California Politics, 1917-1930: A Survey (1975)

NOVELS

Stone Murder: A Rock 'N' Roll Mystery (2012)

Salvador Dali Murder (2014)

SPORTS BOOKS

The Phoenix Suns: The View From Section 101 (2013)

The Phoenix Suns: Turnaround (2015)

PREFACE: WHO IS THE SUGAR MAN?

When I walked into the Harkins Camelview 7 Theater to see **Searching for Sugar Man**, I had no idea who Sixto Rodriguez was or why he was important. I was in for a shock. The documentary by Swedish filmmaker, Malik Bendjelloul, analyzed everything that was wrong with the music business and everything that was right with Rodriguez. This documentary presented a person who is truly amazed at his success. For his entire seventy plus years, it has been about the music. Along the way, myth and reality clashed in such a way that his records were confined to Woolworths' cut out bin in the U. S. Some were pulped, that is destroyed.

At the same time, record sales in Australia and South Africa went gold or platinum. How could a singer songwriter who was bigger than Elvis Presley or the Rolling Stones in South Africa not make a dent in the American market? How could Rodriguez sell records in large numbers in Australia and tour the country to adoring crowds?

When the Light In The Attic head honcho, Matt Sullivan, purchased the **Cold Fact** album at a Seattle record store, he was amazed at the Dylanesque lyrical maturity, the accompanying music and lilting vocals. A record storeowner in Cape Town, Stephen "Sugar" Segerman, began to search for Sixto Rodriguez. The **Cold Fact** album intrigued him. He couldn't find a single word written about Rodriguez. There were rumors but few concrete cold facts. He wrote the liner notes for a South African record label that re-released a Rodriguez album. Then a South African journalist, Craig Bartholomew-Strydom, came aboard and the Great Rodriguez Hunt was underway.

Segerman was obsessed with Rodriguez and his music. He was determined to find every fact he could about the Sugar Man. The hunt turned up one dead end after another. None of this deterred Segerman. He knew that there was a story. He would find it.

While ignored in America, Rodriguez' music was the marching tune for the young, politically conscious anti-apartheid South African's. Rodriguez also represented the birth of the Australian counterculture. Australia's mega hit rock band, Midnight Oil, claimed Rodriguez as a mentor. In America, no one had a clue neither about Rodriguez' music nor the man's extraordinary intellect.

There are many other ironies to the story. Sixto Rodriguez has a family. He graduated with honors from college. He raised his daughters. He recorded two albums that failed to sell. He left the music business. He didn't receive royalties. He continued to sporadically perform. He followed **Billboard** and other music magazines. Rodriguez had a life. It was a good one. He wasn't bitter. "It's the music business," Rodriguez told an interviewer when asked about lost royalties. Then acclaim and financial success from **Searching For Sugar Man** provided a new life. Guess what? Rodriguez didn't change. He is the same person. When **Searching For Sugar Man** won the Academy Award, he was home relaxing. He told a reporter: "It's Malik's work. Let him bask in the glory." How do you spell humble? How do you spell appreciation? Rodriguez did by continually praising filmmaker Malik Bendjelloul.

He seldom displayed the hubris of a high profile artist. Rodriguez has neither excessive ambition nor unmitigated pride. He wrote songs. He recorded songs. He didn't agree to appear at teen dances, to lip sync his songs on television or to answer to inane disc jockey questions. He often performed with his back to the audience. That way his music was featured. His drop-dead good looks, cool clothes and shimmering sunglasses made him a ladies favorite. He was bewildered by the acclaim from the worldwide popularity of **Searching For Sugar Man**. Rodriguez preferred to be at home with his family or hanging out at the Motor City Brewing Company, the Cass Café or the Old Miami Bar. These establishments in Detroit's Cass Corridor are walking distance from Rodriguez' two story Avery Street home. They also define his persona.

While **Searching For Sugar Man** displays his sex appeal, his songwriting genius and mercurial performing talent, there is more to the story. Ironically, much of what has been written about Rodriguez makes virtually no mention of the women in his life. There are important women in his life, his three daughters. He raised them doing backbreaking manual labor. He also has two wives who he remains friendly with in Detroit.

Rodriguez' blue-collar work ethic led him to employment in home repairs, casual maintenance, heavy construction and remodeling. This is the type of work that no one would hire on to do in the crumbling Detroit housing market. He loved the work. He said that it: "kept him in shape."

His first wife, Rayma, lives near the Detroit airport, and his second wife, Konny, resides in another Detroit suburb. Her given name is Constance Mary Rodriguez.

For Rodriguez some relationships are complicated. This is the nature of the artist. During interviews, he thanks both wives for helping his music evolve. There is a tranquil nature to Rodriguez that is essential to the myths surrounding his life. He is a person who is so centered that he often serves food to people who come backstage during his concerts. He thanks them for coming. The audiences and those who meet him love his gracious manner and unswerving humility.

Rayma met Sixto when they were in high school. She is part Cherokee and her intelligence, as well as her beauty, early on attracted Rodriguez. When Rayma got pregnant they dropped out of school, they had two daughters Eva and Sandra. To support the family, Sixto worked in a steel mill, an auto plant and a linen factory. He had diverse skills working as a bricklayer, a construction worker and as a trench digger. The Detroit housing industry offered continual rehab employment.

He married Konny. In 1979, they had a daughter Regan. Somewhere along the way they separated. Konny, who lives in St. Clair Shores, remains friendly with her ex-husband. "I never believed in marriage, so I sure as hell don't believe in divorce," Konny said.

Konny Rodriguez studied at Wayne State University from 1969 to 1975, where she received a B. A. in psychology. When she married Sixto, Konny went to work for the Children's Hospital of Michigan. From 1984 to 2005, she worked with three administrators running the hospital, and her skill in managing people is unparalleled. Then she moved to senior housing and assisted living, where she worked for the Presbyterian Villages of Michigan.

The Presbyterian Villages of Michigan are faith based retirement homes. There are twenty-five in Michigan, and they serve 4,300 seniors. During numerous interviews, Konny said that Rodriguez' Detroit house is too primitive. Konny remains a bit of a mystery. She was with him sporadically in 2012, and it appears that the financial success brought about by **Searching For Sugar Man** changed their lives. For some time, Konny has lived near her work in St. Claire Shores, Michigan. This is a part of the Metro Detroit area, and this comfortable suburb is home to rock singer Patti Smith and Fred "Sonic" Smith of the MC5. She remains married to Sixto, but they have an understanding. It is private. It is personal. It is no ones business.

Konny Rodriguez: "He's a dyed in the wool Detroiter. He's comfortable there; he's a happy camper and at peace."

She points out that the Avery Street home is lacking in key comforts. It is now being slightly renovated. Rodriguez is not spending his money making the Avery Street home look like a mansion. There is a brand new fence that hides the side of the house from the street. There are signs of the front cement steps being improved. A large, orange cone blocks a portion of the steep cement stairway leading to the front door. The homes on Avery sell from $55,000 upward. There is an increase in young families. There is a slow, but steady, gentrification-taking place. One neighbor said: "We are experiencing a flight from the suburbs to Woodbridge."

This book will not deal with Rodriguez' personal life other than what he has said during interviews. There will be a second volume **Rodriguez: Coming From Reality.** It will explore the exploding phenomena surrounding the Sugar Man, as well as the production of the second LP. He deserves his privacy. The purpose of this volume is to provide as much detail as possible, to quote Stephen "Sugar" Segerman, on "the artist known as Rodriguez." This information will be used to showcase the phenomenon that is Rodriguez.

In an interview with Eric Lacy in January 2013, Konny explains why she lives in St. Claire Shores. She also reflects on her marriage. She calls it a complicated, yet loving, and highly personal relationship. Konny remarked of her husband: "We do get along, we love each other very much; I just can't live with the man."

The subject of **Searching For Sugar Man**, Sixto Diaz Rodriguez, is a part Mexican, part Native American musician who grew up in the shadow of poverty. He developed an affinity for songwriting. His lyrics are that of an existential poet. He listened to Bob Dylan, and, like Dylan, he has an original writing touch. His subjects are the working poor, the politically disenfranchised and those who view the system from outside the mainstream. It is the songwriting of an existential contrarian. The lyrics are beautiful. The music is soothing. It looked in 1970 like Rodriguez was destined for stardom. Then something happened. He fell into obscurity. He raised a family. He went to work every day. He earned a college degree. He was off the music business radar.

As he grew up in the shadow of Motown, the nascent Detroit music scene influenced his developing talent. In 1967, as Rodriguez recorded his debut single for Harry Balk, Detroit experienced a five-day riot that killed forty-three and destroyed more than 200 buildings. He was deeply touched by the violence. Rodriguez was concerned about police brutality. School funding, community outreach, union rights, public commissions to oversee the police and economic development were issues that brought Rodriguez support in the Cass Corridor when he ran for public office.

It is in his writing about the crumbling layers of Detroit that gives Rodriguez' music its edge. He describes in copious detail the flourishing music scene, the lower middle class family problems, the decline into abject poverty, the changes in political attitudes and the youthful rebellion of the late 1960s and early 1970s. He is a musician who writes prophetically about the Motor City. How he perceived his surroundings, and how he experienced an epiphany that few people understood is an integral part of the Rodriguez story. What he witnessed in the world around him translates beautifully into song. No one understood it in 1970-1971, when his two albums were released, Rodriguez' message was lost in the shuffle. When his music finally surfaced in 2012, thanks to Malik Bendjelloul, Stephen "Sugar" Segerman, Craig Bartholomew-Strydom and Brian Currin, the Rodriguez phenomenon burst onto the cultural scene.

When **Searching For Sugar Man** debuted on July 27, 2012, no one realized that a few weeks later Rodriguez would appear on these Late Night Show With David Letterman. It was mid-August and Rodriguez walked out on the Letterman stage with a set of symphony string musicians backing him on "Crucify Your Mind." He acquired skilled management. It is his daughter, Regan, who took over his career. She hired a professional road manager, she signed with various booking agencies, and she coordinates with groups around the world that back up Rodriguez. He was buried once by the industry. It won't happen again. He has a vast music-business empire in place that is well organized and looking out for his best interests.

A part of Regan's management formula is to limit interviews. This keeps the Rodriguez mystique alive. She realizes that too much press coverage provides negatives. Her skilled management has led to continual concert sellouts and a lucrative income. Rodriguez is really running the show with his daughter's expertise. He had trouble with the industry during the first go around. This time Rodriguez and his family are calling the shots. It is a smart move.

He is a lyrical and musical genius. He remains humble, unaffected, and he wonders what all the fuss is about. He lives his life through his music. Looking back upon his career, Rodriguez remarked: "I just wanted to sell some records and play bigger rooms." Once the New York premier of **Searching For Sugar Man** hit the big screen, he was in demand. The interesting part of his career is that he is compared to Bob Dylan. Listening to Rodriguez, his lyrics are as brilliant, as colorful, and as philosophical as Dylan's, but he has his own imagery and style.

Why write two books about Rodriguez? That is the question. The first volume runs through the **Cold Fact** LP and the second begins with Steve Rowland's **Coming From Reality** and ends with the fame and fortune resulting from the documentary. Sixto Rodriguez is articulate. He is intelligent. He is one hell of a writer. He is also a great performer. It has been a joy to interpret his journey. The Rodriguez biography is one about the phenomenon and not the man. It is also a project where more than one hundred people talked to me about the Sugar Man.

The Rodriguez story is not only heart wrenching, it is a look at a man who overcame adversity to record some of the best music that no one listened to in the 1970s. In 2012-2015, he was one of the world's best selling artists. Rodriguez' talent needs a careful reassessment.

When Stephen "Sugar" Segerman began his search for Rodriguez on the Internet, he set up the Website: "The Great Rodriguez Hunt." One of his co-conspirators, Brian Currin, established the "Climb Up On My Music" Website. This began the search for Rodriguez, and this incredible story took shape.

This is a tale of a humble man with a genius songwriting talent. It is a tale of humility that is second to none. As he eases into his seventies, fame and fortune are present, as talent triumphed over adversity. The Sugar Man is back, enjoy the ride.

Obsessive-compulsive record collectors largely fuel the Sugar Man story. The Stephen "Sugar" Segerman and Craig Bartholomew-Strydom tandem brought him back. In Seattle, Light In The Attic, a small record label, under the stewardship of Matt Sullivan, reissued the Rodriguez material. A young filmmaker from Sweden, Malik Bendjelloul, created the documentary that made America fall in love with Rodriguez. His producers Dennis Coffey, Mike Theodore and Steve Rowland spoke of his legacy with reverence.

The Sussex Record chief, Clarence Avant, is put through a grueling, and at times unfair, interview in **Searching For Sugar Man**. For years, Avant allegedly collected royalties for Rodriguez' sales in Australia and South Africa. He may not have collected these royalties. The truth is that Avant has always been a Rodriguez supporter. In 1997-1998, he quietly funded what would have been a third album for the Sugar Man. Rodriguez gave up. Avant reluctantly commented that he is innocent of withholding royalties. The people who have done business with him to a person remarked that, as Mike Theodore said: "Clarence never screwed anyone." It is Avant's story that is as interesting as Rodriguez.'

There are highs and lows in Rodriguez' career. He has recorded for some of the best producers in the game. Such names as Harry Balk, Mike Theodore, Dennis Coffey and Steve Rowland suggest the legendary music men who have been a part of his career. There are many players, many subplots, and many main points. It is a great story of redemption and rediscovery.

The Rodriguez story does not take place in a time warp. It is part and parcel of a larger history of the music industry. His music was subject to the times and the trends. These factors didn't always help him. He lacked the business skills to prevent industry insiders from taking advantage of him. Many of the contracts were legal ones that were worded to provide songwriting and publishing royalties to the record company. The artist was billed for record storage, publicity, advertising, publishing costs, photography, graphic design and miscellaneous expenses. The artist receives what is left. There is normally very little in the way of royalties left.

What happened to Rodriguez? The story is a familiar tale of music industry greed. When music mogul Clarence Avant appeared in **Searching For Sugar Man**, he said that he didn't know about the royalties. He had no idea what happened to the money. That appears to be the truth. When Matt Sullivan's Light in the Attic licensed Rodriguez' albums, they secured the rights from Avant. Light In The Attic said that they had good dealings with Avant, and he has paid royalties to Rodriguez since 2008.

That Rodriguez was bigger than the Rolling Stones or Elvis Presley in South Africa is an important point. His debut album, **Cold Fact**, outsold all other South African artists. But along the way the artist known as Rodriguez got lost in myth. There was no reality. Thanks to Stephen

"Sugar" Segerman for finding Rodriguez and pitching his story to young filmmaker Malik Bendjelloul.

It is as a writer that Rodriguez excels. He is primarily a singer-songwriter, who is also a talented performer. The words, the images, the subtle nuances, the observations and the humility make Rodriguez's music unique.

By 2013, the Rodriguez phenomenon was in full bloom. He was touring non-stop. The South African tours were bigger than ever, and at the 85th Oscar ceremony there was talk of a third album. The Sugar Man looked tired and drawn, but he was enjoying every minute of his improbable fame.

Rolling Stone reported that Rodriguez stated: "that once he breaks from touring in June he will explore the possibility of recording a third album." Rodriguez mentioned **Coming From Reality** producer, Steve Rowland, as a potential partner in this endeavor. "He told me to send him along a couple of tapes, so I'm gonna do that," Rodriguez continued. "I certainly want to look him up, because he is full of ideas." **Rolling Stone** got hold of Rowland who responded: "We both have ideas on how the album should go…We both want to work together again, but it is really up to others that are involved in his future."

As I followed Rodriguez' journey, I was amazed at his resilient personality. Nothing bothers him. It is this stoic demeanor that brings out the existential philosopher that is Sixto Rodriguez.

I didn't interview Sixto Rodriguez for this book. I was backstage with him for a brief moment when he appeared at California State University in the Luckman Auditorium. I was with Steve Rowland and they had a brief, but intimate, discussion. I was amazed at his kindness, his discretion and his humble nature. He also looks healthy. There is no trace of bitterness. He has worn well considering the sheer intensity of his past life. When I talked to his daughter, Regan, she ducked most of my questions. It was a comfortable time backstage with Rodriguez. He is shy and prefers to maintain his privacy. He has been ripped off by too many people and lied to by many others. His daughter, Regan, is the perfect manager. She is smart, she is knowledgeable about the music industry, and she knows how to hire and direct the best people for Rodriguez' concerts.

Ruben Blades, the Grammy Award winning singer from Panama, said it best about Rodriguez when he responded to a **New York Times** review of Clive Davis' autobiography. Blades wrote: "record executives do not discover artists they stumble upon them." Then, as Blades suggests, the executives and the label collect more than their fair share of the royalties. Blades wrote of Janis Joplin that she probably never collected her fair share of royalties. Blades continued: "These usually go to people who can't sing, who can't write, can't perform and yet end up millionaires, while true artists, like Rodriguez, end up broke and ripped off." Thank you Ruben Blades for this letter to the **New York Times** Book Review.

Rodriguez is a poetic genius. He was ignored for more than four decades. His quiet gestures and discreet life obscured his talent. Then **Searching For Sugar Man** brought him the acclaim that he deserves.

When I sat down with the print interviews, the people who were central and peripheral to the story, the albums, the press material, the tapes of his concerts, the back stage stories, the Detroit neighborhood material and the documentary; there was a mountain of evidence. Much of it was conflicting and a great deal of it was mythical. How to separate myth from reality? That was the key question.

Surprisingly, it is not music that is most important to Sixto Rodriguez. It is his humanity. It is his political activism. It is his family values. To tell the story properly, it is necessary to highlight the people around Rodriguez, the influence of Detroit, the impact of Stephen "Sugar" Segerman, Craig Bartholomew-Strydom and the other South African Rodrigologists and the manner in which the entire music industry reacted against and then for the Sugar Man. It is a never-ending story.

This is a biography of a great American singer-songwriter who has written less than thirty songs. This is not a vast output. His life is partly a story about lateness-patience, fortitude and waiting. In some ways, he is like other forgotten singer-songwriters who simply vanished into obscurity. He began as a brilliant twenty-eight year old recording artist. By thirty-three he was working a series of dead end jobs that occupied his life for the next forty years.

His first album, **Cold Fact**, came out in 1970 when he was twenty-eight. He achieved stardom in 2012 when he was, as he said, "a solid seventy." That is what this story concentrates on and in this first of two volumes the Sugar Man emerges as an ethereal, mystical, almost mythical, person with a talent that few possess. This perception obscures his talent as myth triumphs reality.

His personality quirks are well known. He is drawn to lost causes and personal failures. These themes impact his songwriting. The Sugar

Man's voice is exceptional when dealing with feminist issues. In telling his life story, it is important to remember that he describes hypocrisy, cruelty, dishonesty and malevolence in his songs. These tunes argue that there is a relationship between the soul and the intellect. Rodriguez likes to deflate hypocrisy. Yet, his personal beliefs are mildly stated, and he has guarded opinions. There is a sense of control and a restraint in Rodriguez' personality. He has a lifestyle that is subtle and economical.

There is no glamour to Sixto Rodriguez and no self-advertising. He is the ultimate existentialist. He is also evasive and reserved. He writes in a quiet voice with a blend of darkness and humor.

The story of a musician who triumphed over all odds is a unique one. But he is also a person rooted in Detroit, close to his family, helped by his producers, rediscovered by Matt Sullivan and his Light In The Attic label and then the general public fell in love with this humble and uniquely talented performer.

There is no adequate description of Sixto Rodriguez. We know he is humble, he has little use for money, he is an existentialist, he is a committed intellectual, he is family oriented, he is a writer, he is political and he is a strong supporter of Detroit's political-social-culture. To understand the Sugar Man it is necessary to examine those around him, including family, musicians, producers, industry figures, Detroit's influences, his peripatetic employment and his education. These forces describe the Sugar Man and his strange journey to fame and fortune.

As Rodriguez' music unfolds, a line from one of his songs suggests why he is an important biographical subject. Rodriguez wrote: "Climb up on my music and my songs will set you free…."

PROLOGUE: WHY THE MUSIC INDUSTRY DESTROYS ITS OWN

"I'M HARD WORKING AND PROUD OF IT. I DIG BOOKS AND LIKE TO READ, I'M INTO COMMUNICATION," RODRIGUEZ IN CONVERSATION WITH AUSTRALIAN JOURNALIST GLEN A. BAKER

"I CONSIDER MYSELF SOMEBODY WITH AN UNLIMITED AMOUNT OF CURIOSITY IN AN UNLIMITED AMOUNT OF DIRECTIONS." REM KOOLHAAS

"ART IS NEVER FINISHED ONLY ABANDONED." LEONARDO DA VINCI

Sixto Rodriguez remains a one-man argument for the notion that biography is a tale of singular individuals and shining deeds. There is an eccentric personality to Rodriguez. His gregarious countenance allowed him to survive from his last album, **Coming From Reality,** in 1971 until his reemergence as a superstar in the 2012 Oscar winning documentary **Searching For Sugar Man**. The contradiction is that the Sugar Man, despite his winning personality, is quiet and private. He is the ultimate contrarian.

MAINTAINING AN ARTISTIC VOICE IN POPULAR MUSIC

The ability to maintain a continual voice in popular music with any level of intelligence is a difficult task. The critics laud Bob Dylan, Leonard Cohen and Kris Kristofferson for their songwriting. Others like Patti Smith, Jim Morrison and Kurt Cobain influenced their generation. Still others, like Van Morrison, ooze artistic integrity in lyrical and musical form. The mainstream artist is often a bore like Sting, a musician full of himself like Bono, or an artist who won't get off the road like Bob Dylan. It is rare to find a talented, humble and analytical rock artist who is influential, while writing lasting, intellectually based songs. Sixto Rodriguez is the exception. He is not a megastar on the concert circuit. He is not a superstar among songwriters, but with almost thirty excellent rediscovered songs, he is a legend. Once you hear Rodriguez' music you wonder how he got lost in the rock and roll scrap heap.

The confluence of myth and reality made many of those who heard the Sixto Rodriguez story a tall tale. There is no artist who has had more tales of excess and mystery attached to his career. Ironically, many of the stories have little basis in reality. When Rodriguez recorded his second album, its title **Coming From Reality** was apocryphal.

The tales of musicians who are cheated out of royalties, who fail to find the proper label, who are unable to sustain more than a five year career and those who fall by the wayside is a big part of rock and roll history. There are only a few artists who find redemption after years in the creative wilderness. When Sixto Rodriguez emerged from the creative dungeon that the music business cast him, he demonstrated a unique and original talent. He would not have come out of the wilderness had it not been for Malik Bendjelloul's documentary.

Once the New York premier of **Searching For Sugar Man** hit the big screen, he was in demand. Listening to Rodriguez' two albums, his lyrics are brilliant, as well as colorful and philosophical. His descent into obscurity is a window into what is wrong with the music business.

Stephen "Sugar" Segerman and Craig Bartholomew-Strydom kept the story alive. They told anyone who would listen about Rodriguez. Segerman refused to accept the lack of information. This led to the documentary, and an extraordinary popular culture tale. It also paved the way for **Searching For Sugar Man's** Oscar.

THE MYTH AND LEGEND OF THE SUGAR MAN

The Sixto Diaz Rodriguez story is one of myth and legend. Somewhere along the line the two concepts meet and the real Rodriguez emerges. The Rodriguez phenomenon is one that tells us a great deal about the record business, education, personal choice, family values and a commitment to ones craft. It is a tale full of interesting characters; think Rodriguez and good guys, think Dennis Coffey, Mike Theodore and Steve Rowland. There were also wizards of detection, production and information, think Stephen "Sugar" Segerman, Brian Currin and Craig Bartholomew-Strydom, record company owners, think Harry Balk and Clarence Avant who discovered Rodriguez as well as Matt Sullivan at Light In The Attic, who is a music mogul determined to pay royalties, as well as the people at Sony and a documentary guru who never gave up, Simon Chinn. He is the fiscal angel. Lastly, think Malik Bendjelloul for his documentary genius. Finally, Roger Armstrong, founder of Ace Records, was the quiet informational force behind the story. Armstrong and Ace Records has done more than any label to resurrect talented, but forgotten, singer-songwriters. Armstrong is London's hidden detective as Ace Records opens the vaults to historically significant material.

Not only is the Rodriguez story one of redemption; it is the recognition of his talent, his humanity and his gentle nature that makes the road to fame so important. The only person who seems unaffected by the story is Sixto Rodriguez.

Searching For Sugar Man made Rodriguez a phenomenon. Genius is often accompanied by eccentricity. No one displays this trait more than Rodriguez. The genuine brilliance in his music is testimony to his genius. He remains eccentric.

It is unusual for an artist to have a second chance at fame and fortune. As Rodriguez' rebirth unfolded in 2012, it was plagued by myths that often obscured reality. Even Rodriguez' daughter, Eva, suggested that perhaps the myth was better left alone.

RODRIGUEZ' TALE OF ENORMOUS TALENT

The staid, almost sedate, daily ritual that Sixto Rodriquez lives is interrupted by fame and fortune. By examining the myths, one can see his musical impact, his personality and the manner in which his story highlights everything that is right and wrong with the music industry.

There is depth and creative intrigue to the Rodriguez story. The Oscar winning documentary **Searching For Sugar Man** is a brilliant look at his South African fame. He had another career in Australia that is credited with helping to establish the counterculture down under.

The story of Sixto Rodriguez is buried under a great deal of conflicting history. While his music didn't receive a mainstream American audience until 2012, he was a star in South Africa and Australia for decades. He was also a cult figure in the U. K. long before **Searching For Sugar Man**.

Many of the details in Rodriguez' life have been either ignored or casually reported. He is a brilliant philosophy student who has a degree. He performed internationally before captivating South Africa in 1998. His career in Australia and New Zealand has drawn little interest. Now in his early seventies, he shows no signs of slowing down. The other side to Rodriguez is his personal integrity, his championing of the underdog and his ability to analyze and dissect social-economic issues.

Steve Rowland described Rodriguez as the finest songwriter he has ever worked with. Then Steve thought for a moment and said that he is one of the best studio artists that he has ever produced. That no one knew who he was for more than forty years is a paradox. As stadium rock grew, the singer-songwriter syndrome floundered. The emergence of large-scale concerts and festivals dominated the rock and roll box office while Rodriguez was home raising a family.

The Oscar winning documentary covered Rodriguez' triumphant South African 1998 tour. There were many parts of the story that Malik Bendjelloul ignored. In his defense, there was too much material to include everything associated with Rodriguez. The missing material is included in this volume, as well as the second book, **Rodriguez: Coming From Reality**.

There is a debate on how much influence Rodriguez had upon South Africa's apartheid movement. My research indicated that he was a major figure in developing protest attitudes. When Stephen "Sugar" Segerman pointed out that South African musicians took their cues from Rodriguez' lyrics, he was correct. When the Voelvry Movement began on April 4, 1989, it brought white South Africans into a movement to end apartheid. It also benefitted from indigenous musical influences.

There was a U. K. career for Rodriguez. He performed in Sweden, and he had a minor presence in the U. S. before the documentary. The irony is that while he didn't record, Rodriguez never stopped performing. Then he quickly returned to his day job doing backbreaking manual labor. He invariably showed up for work in a three-piece suit complete with sunglasses, a cool haircut and an imperial presence. The Sugar Man has style as well as intelligence, grace and integrity.

When Stephen "Sugar" Segerman remarked in **Searching For Sugar Man** that Rodriguez' music inspired civil rights, he was correct. But it was an inspiration that crossed racial lines. He influenced all aspects of South African political life.

There is an influence from Detroit that formed Rodriguez' character, shaped his songs, led to his political activism and prompted him to major in philosophy. He loves the Motor City. He does everything in his power to bring the city back to prominence. While Eminem and Jack White have fled Detroit, Rodriguez hangs on helping to build the new Motor City. Ironically, producers Dennis Coffey and Mike Theodore have returned to live in the Detroit suburbs. They remain strong supporters of the attempts to return Detroit to its previous glory.

The Sixto Rodriguez story is much more than a musician who gets a second chance forty years later, it is the tale of a brilliant talent who would be just as content doing construction. He still leads a simple life.

He just does it on stage, and in front of the media. One wonders if Rodriguez views this as progress. Maybe! Maybe not!

What is obvious is that the Sixto Diaz Rodriguez story is about much more than his record sales and triumphant concerts. The story also demonstrates that Detroit is the fountain of wisdom for Rodriguez' talent. The Sugar Man's tale is as much about the Motor City as it is about Sixto Rodriguez. The inseparable and continuing influence from the Detroit landscape upon the Sugar Man's art remains the end all and be all of his intellectual development.

"The intellect of man is forced to choose perfection of the life or the work," Eugene O'Neill wrote. Sixto Rodriguez chose the work.

RODRIGUEZ IN CONCERT AT THE
NEPTUNE THEATER, SEATTLE

chapter

ONE

RODRIGUEZ: THE ENDURING MYTH

"MY INSPIRATION COMES FROM THE ENVIRONMENT AND PERSONAL ANGST...EACH SONG IS WRITTEN TO A THEME." RODRIGUEZ, MARCH 1998

"THE AGONY OF BREAKING THROUGH PERSONAL LIMITATIONS IS THE AGONY OF SPIRITUAL GROWTH." JOSEPH CAMPBELL

"EVERYTHING SPEAKS IN ITS OWN WAY." ULYSSES

You were a bigger recording star than Elvis Presley. Your popularity was greater than the Rolling Stones. Your mystique was a romantic one. You reportedly died on stage shooting yourself after a mundane show in a nightclub, or perhaps your death resulted from a drug overdose. You were a ghost vanishing into the obscurity of the musical wasteland. Your records went platinum. You were an influence upon the white supporters ending South Africa's apartheid. The soundtrack of South African liberal politics marched to your songs. Your words created a liberal reaction in a country noted for its conservative, right wing politics.

Yet, Rodriguez was a mystical figure. The myths surrounding his life endured until 1998. Then he emerged to perform to capacity crowds in South Africa. After these concerts, the Sugar Man returned to Detroit to the backbreaking work in the rehab home industry that he had been doing since the mid-1970s. He didn't talk about his 1998 South African triumphs. He was simply Sixto Rodriguez father, family man, musician and local character. He was a mythical figure who reclaimed his legacy. No one knew it. He was private. He didn't talk about himself. He simply went about the task of being Sixto Rodriguez. As Malik Bendjelloul demonstrated in **Searching For Sugar Man**, Rodriguez was quiet and unassuming.

JOSEPH CAMPBELL ON MYTH

Joseph Campbell points out that every society needs myths. Myths often have a way of becoming reality. In 1970-1971, the singer known as Rodriguez spun his myths in two musical albums that didn't impact American popular culture. Then the Oscar wining documentary **Searching For Sugar Man** catapulted Rodriguez into the spotlight. Fame and fortune arrived unexpectedly.

Rodriguez appears in **Searching For Sugar Man** for only eight minutes. His daughters, Regan, Sandra and Eva, dominate the film. They tell the story in great depth. When Rodriguez finally opens a window on his Avery Street house, it is a magic moment. The rumor of Rodriguez' death is echoed in Joseph Campbell's remarks on the power of myth: "Mythology is the penultimate truth." That statement suggests the power of the Sixto Rodriguez story. By leaving out Rodriguez' Australia stardom, the film ignores another side of his life. That is to be expected, as Malik Bendjelloul couldn't place his entire oeuvre and life within the context of a ninety-minute documentary.

In Australia, Rodriguez' lyrics defined the counterculture. His records were popular down under, and the 1977 LP **Best of Rodriguez** sold well before he toured there. In 1979, a live Australian LP brought him to the attention of a future worldwide mega hit act Midnight Oil. They became fast friends with Rodriguez. There were no rumors of death, disappearance or any such weird tales. Reality triumphed over myth.

When Midnight Oil became an international hit record sensation, they credited much of their success to Rodriguez. He provided the inspiration, the on-stage formula and the writing-production direction that made them successful. Looking at graffiti, as well as conversations with Rodriguez, inspired their platinum album, **Redneck Wonderland**. They had known the Sugar Man for almost twenty years when Midnight Oil drummer, Rob Hirst, remarked that the band played Bruce Springsteen, Billy Joel and Rodriguez records when they wrote and recorded.

THE RODRIGUEZ MYTHS PERSIST AND GROW IN STATURE

The power of myth often shields reality. Not coincidentally, Rodriguez' second album, **Coming From Reality** is a paean to the forces of myth. Myths are stories and legends that people use to define their culture. The use of myths to educate the young is important to all societies.

On the Sugarman.org website there is a section "Rodriguez-The Myths and The Mystery." This section does a wonderful job separating fiction from fact. The mysteries remained into the 1990s. In the June 1996 **Q** magazine John E. Gainney writes: "Any info on U. S. singer Jesus Rodriguez, who had a large cult following…and shot himself on stage after quoting from his song?" That same year the South African **Sunday Times Cape Metro** observed: "Even the fate of Rodriguez is unclear and no one seems sure what has happened to him?"

Stephen "Sugar" Segerman's liner notes to **The Best of Rodriguez** speculated on his music in October 1996. He wondered where Rodriguez was if he was not deceased. Segerman pointed to the strong demand for Rodriguez' music in South Africa. For this reason alone, he believed that he should continue his search for the elusive singer-songwriter. He pointed out that the album's sales validated Rodriguez' legend. Earlier in 1996, the release of Rodriguez' CD **After The Fact/Coming From Reality**, along with **Cold Fact**, provided a complete Rodriguez musical collection. Segerman could not believe that Rodriguez was deceased. He had to be out there somewhere. He was going to find him.

THE PERSISTENT "SUGAR"

What is important about Segerman's research and writing is that he pointed out the history books, the music reference tomes, and the journalistic sources had no reliable information on Rodriguez. Like many record collectors, Segerman could not let go. He didn't believe the myths. He knew that there was a reality. He was determined to find it. When he began a website dedicated to finding Rodriguez, the myths that had persisted faded into obscurity.

Segerman wrote: "Who Rodriguez was or is remains a mystery with even the record companies still religiously paying royalties to an unknown source or recipient somewhere in the USA." This sentence was a portent of things to come. Segerman discovered that Clarence Avant, an African American record executive, allegedly collected the royalties. He also learned that virtually no one in America had heard of Rodriguez. His records were not available in the U. S. Segerman asked people to listen to Rodriguez and judge him on his music. That, as Rodriguez said, is "a concrete cold fact."

The search for Rodriguez began in March 1996 when Segerman established his website: "The Great Rodriguez Hunt." There was a faux milk carton on the website asking if anyone knew where Rodriguez was at the moment? When they found him there was euphoria. There was a degree of disbelief, as the artist known as Rodriguez stepped from obscurity into the South African limelight.

To South Africans, who witnessed his concerts in 1998, it was much like a dead man coming back from the grave. The story is so intense, so uplifting; it feeds the force of myth. Reality dulls the tale.

THE CRITICS OF SEARCHING FOR SUGAR MAN

The critics of **Searching For Sugar Man** came out of the woodwork early. In London, Peter Bradshaw, writing in the **Guardian** commented: "We came to the flaw in the movie. It gives the audience the impression that after Rodriguez was dropped by the label, he simply collapsed into non-show business obscurity until his South African fan base was mobilized." This is, of course, unfair criticism. While Bradshaw accuses Malik Bendjelloul of being "guilty of the sin of omission," he doesn't recognize that the documentary was not a full-fledged biography. This pithy criticism does a disservice to Rodriguez. It is also unfair to Stephen "Sugar" Segerman. The idea that Segerman could have found everything he desired about Rodriguez on the Internet is preposterous. This is not just unfair criticism; it is contrary to the facts. There was virtually nothing about Sixto Rodriguez on the Internet prior to **Searching For Sugar Man**. But Bradshaw wasn't done with his uneven and heavy handed criticism.

Bradshaw writes: "This movie might itself make a modest contribution to rewriting the history of white South Africa." He misses the point. **Searching For Sugar Man** is about the trials and tribulations of a singer-songwriter who didn't get paid, didn't get recognized and then suddenly came roaring back to commercial prominence. It is also about a voice for racial equality that is unrivaled.

Almost everyone who reviewed **Searching For Sugar Man** got it wrong. Stephen "Sugar" Segerman got it right. He pointed out that young Afrikaners battling against apartheid were Rodriguez influenced. When Stephen "Sugar" Segerman discussed how influential Rodriguez was on South African rock, he was right. Rodriguez influenced the Voelvry Movement, which began in local universities in 1989. This was a coalition of young, white musicians opposing apartheid. The native population had opposed apartheid in song since 1948. The white South African support from 1989 to 1994 helped to tip the scales of racial injustice toward a society that slowly became more equitable.

Another critic, Bill Cody, skewered Bendjelloul's documentary. In the process, he demonstrated his lack of knowledge of South African history, Rodriguez' music and the record business. **Searching For Sugar Man** is not a complete biography of Sixto Rodriguez. It is a look at a phenomenon.

RODRIGUEZ' UNEXPLORED NATIVE
AMERICAN SHAMAN SIDE

As part Native American, there is a Shamanistic side to Rodriguez. "The Shaman is a person who in his early puberty has cracked off, broken off and gone into what we would today call a psychosis," Joseph Campbell wrote. What Campbell meant was that when a person does this they begin a journey of rebirth and redemption.

The Shaman is a healer, taking the broken parts of society, explaining them and resurrecting them. "I've always concentrated on social issues, because I've always found it easiest to write about things that upset me...." Rodriguez, commented in March 1998. In a number of epic narratives, the hero begins a journey that goes through three stages: separation, initiation and return. Rodriguez is the perfect example of this, as he separates from the mainstream of American culture only to return to its stratospheric heights. He enters the culture; he quickly vanishes from it and more than forty years later returns as a musical star. It is also an enduring tale of triumph over adversity.

WHY THE RODRIGUEZ STORY ENDURES:
THE HEROES

Searching For Sugar Man provides introspective analysis of a forgotten singer-songwriter, as well as his trials and tribulations. There are many heroes who assist Sixto Rodriguez' rise to commercial prominence. They are equally responsible for his acclaim.

The people who rediscovered him and promoted his legend were good guys. They wanted nothing for themselves. Stephen "Sugar" Segerman, who began the search for Rodriguez, wanted him to receive acclaim. The journalist, Craig Bartholomew-Strydom, wanted the facts right. He also hoped for some royalties for Rodriguez. The filmmaker, Malik Bendjelloul, wanted nothing more than to tell a riveting story. Simon Chinn and Sony Legacy bankrolled the project with no guarantees of success. When these heroes graced the stage at the Sundance Film Festival, they were as astonished as Rodriguez. The acclaim was overwhelming.

The other heroes are the producers for his two albums. Dennis Coffey, Mike Theodore and Steve Rowland. They combined to produce two marvelous LPs showcasing Rodriquez' original talent. This allowed **Searching for Sugar Man** to succeed, as the music is integral to the story.

When Malik Bendjelloul was asked what his film was about, he remarked: "It's about a man who didn't know he was famous." This is a reference to Rodriguez' platinum selling South African albums.

In **Searching For Sugar Man**, Rodriguez' portrayal is that of a Christ like poet. He is a symbol of defined personal lyrics and brilliant criticism of the social-economic morass that is American society. He reminds us that we have forgotten how to look deeply into our national soul. He provides a window into that consciousness. The documentary provides a creative magic to his transcendent live performances.

After his appearance at the 2012 Tribeca Film Festival, Rodriguez performed in a New York show and in attendance were a bevy of South Africans. The Tribeca Festival awarded the documentary a second place in the Audience Award category. One former South African military man, Adrian Johnson, was asked if he was influenced by Rodriguez' music. He replied: "We knew apartheid was wrong, it took Rodriguez' music to remind us that it was immoral to enforce apartheid." The soldier paused and looked forlorn. He concluded: "But I enforced apartheid."

Rodriguez walked away from his musical career to raise his daughters. He wanted to make sure that they didn't endure the indignities of an orphanage. He demonstrated that character and integrity are one and the same.

At times after work he would have drinks with his friends and play his guitar. Not once did he mention that he recorded two albums. He wanted to lead a private life. There wasn't much to dig around for in his life. It is this lack of information that created the spurious myths that were without fact.

The myths concerning his personal life created an aura that brought record collectors, journalists, moviemakers and writers into the fold. Rodriguez is the only person who isn't nervous about the story. He is quiet and unassuming. The rise of fame and fortune hasn't changed him.

As an exceptionally gifted singer and songwriter, Rodriguez brought his poetic flair to a larger audience through **Searching For Sugar Man**. There is a mythical appearance to Rodriguez with his long, flowing black hair, shimmering sunglasses and cool clothes.

It is the quality of his lyrics that range from a romantic ballad, "I Think of You," to a politically subversive song "The Establishment Blues" that caught the critic's attention. The theme of working class struggle in "Cause" was an indication that his music fits the protest idiom. His unique brand of songwriting, coupled with the myths of his personal life, spurred his reemergence as a commercial artist.

LIGHT IN THE ATTIC: THE LABEL THAT BROUGHT RODRIGUEZ BACK

Searching For Sugar Man's success, the re-release of Rodriguez' albums and their merchandising would have been impossible without a boutique record label, Light In The Attic. It was Matt Sullivan who was the driving force behind the 2008 **Cold Fact** release. In 2009, Sullivan's release of Rodriguez' **Coming From Reality** completed the project.

When did Sullivan find the Rodriguez material? It was in 2002 that he heard David Holmes,' "Come Get It, I Got It," maxi single, which sampled "Sugar Man." This began the search for a Rodriguez album. "I first heard about Rodriguez in the early 2000s," Sullivan told Joe Williams. Then he stumbled upon a Rodriguez album on the Sussex label in a Seattle record store. He discovered the Great Rodriguez Hunt website. He found Stephen "Sugar" Segerman. Sullivan was put in touch with Rodriguez. His hunt continued.

He found producer Mike Theodore and Rodriguez' daughter, Regan, and he negotiated a deal to re-release the long out of print Rodriguez albums. What was Sullivan's interest? It was more than the music.

He loved the lyrical poetry. When Sullivan heard the royalty story, he was determined to lease the Rodriguez product and pay a royalty that is more than fair.

Matt Sullivan was important in publicizing the material. Long before Malik Bendjelloul completed **Searching For Sugar Man**, Sullivan established credibility with the music press. Soon the London based rock magazines **Mojo** and **Q** were extolling Rodriguez' musical genus. Eventually, **Rolling Stone**, the **New Musical Express** and **Melody Maker** praised Rodriguez. Along the way, myths were still a part of the story, but reality set in, and Rodriguez' musical genius was recognized.

Matt Sullivan: "I found out about the movie, I don't know, maybe somewhere in '07 or '08, but we had already been working on the reissues for a couple years." Then Malik Bendjelloul got in touch with Sullivan and the label put its weight behind the project.

When asked about Rodriguez, Sullivan, said: "I'm thrilled the guy's getting his due." While attending a Rodriguez concert at the Ohio State University campus in late September 2012, Sullivan shared his thoughts on the future possibilities of Rodriguez career.

"He's an incredible, lovely human being and we just heard something in those records, something in our soul, that said we had to find a way to find Rodriguez, get these records out and do it the right way, and get him paid...." Sullivan told **The Seattle Weekly**.

As everyone celebrated the return of Sixto Rodriguez in 2012, Light In The Attic celebrated its tenth anniversary. Not surprisingly, the tenth anniversary concert at Los Angeles' El Rey Theater on September 28, 2012 featured Rodriguez. This label is important but not just for Rodriguez. They have reissued long lost albums by Serge Gainsbourg and Jane Birkin, as well as material from folk cult artist Karen Dalton and the enigmatic Lee Hazlewood. The list of Light In The Attic artists is a lengthy one. The goal of presenting great music that has been overlooked remains the label's focus. They have not consciously looked at the myths surrounding rock music. LITA releases material by long neglected artists like Barbara Lynn, recent acts like Mercury Rev and some unknown, but talented singers, like Sylvie Simmons. The blueprint for LITA is one based on recognition for a wide variety of artists.

WHAT WAS LEFT OUT OF SEARCHING FOR SUGAR MAN?

There are some other aspects of Rodriguez' career that didn't find their way into **Searching For Sugar Man**. This is understandable. Malik

Bendjelloul directed a film about two music detectives who found a long forgotten singer and brought him to international stardom.

However, it is important to note what was missing in the Oscar winning film. He didn't vanish from sight in 1973-1974; Rodriguez toured Australia in 1979 and 1981. He also continued to occasionally perform in and around Detroit. He didn't record. There is some evidence that he continues to write songs. None of these songs have seen the light of day.

His domestic life isn't examined in the documentary. He and his first wife Rayma divorced. She presently lives near the Detroit airport. His second wife, Konny, lives near her work in a Detroit suburb. Why were the wives left out of the story? The answer is a simple one. He is happy and friendly with his ex-wives. There is no scandal. There is no discord. They are still on a friendly basis with the Sugar Man. His marriages are not a part of the larger story. He is an existential philosopher who is a musician. That is the story.

WHAT RODRIGUEZ THE EXISTENTIAL PHILOSOPHER TELLS US

Rodriguez the philosopher tells us what is right and what is wrong with American society in songs that are almost a half-century-old. How strange is that? The U. S. congratulates itself on progress, but "The Establishment Blues" suddenly doesn't sound dated. "The Mayor hides the crime rate, the council woman hesitates. Public gets irate, but forgets the vote date. The system's gonna fall soon, to an angry young tune," Rodriguez wrote.

"Forget It," reminds us of the need for manners, love and compassion. The existential philosopher is one whose thinking begins with acting, feeling and living peacefully in a complex world. The key to understanding Sixto Rodriguez is to analyze his lyrics. They tell the story of his life. They also exhibit understanding, empathy and an existential view of life. This defines the Sugar Man's daily life.

What is an existential rock and roll philosopher? That question is at the heart of Rodriguez the man. The tragedy to Rodriguez' story is that he was demolishing and repairing houses in Detroit when he should have been playing stadiums and hanging out with Bob Dylan.

Existential rock and roll harks back to the Beatles. When they performed as an unknown group in Hamburg Germany, the Fab Four hung out with the exis. This was a youth movement influenced by the writings of Jean Paul Sartre and Albert Camus. In Hamburg's St. Pauli district the Star Club, where the Beatles played, was a natural gravitational point for the exis.' They combined rock music with philosophy.

Rodriguez had his Detroit exis. They were the college students, the perennial barroom intellectuals, the artists, the writers and the hangers on who are influential in the college-music scene. When Rodriguez wrote "A Most Disgusting Song," he paid tribute to the exis. When Rodriguez sings: "the local diddy bop pimp comes in. Acting limp he sits down with a grin. Next to a girl that has never been chased," he describes the barroom pimp. When the song was transcribed the lyrics ended with "chased." What Rodriguez meant was that the young lady was not "chaste." This lyrical pun was ignored in transferring the lyrics. "And everyone's drinking the detergents that cannot remove their hurts" suggests the hardcore drinkers. Then Rodriguez comments about the Mafia and the drug trade, he observes: "Getting high, getting drunk, getting horny" is the mantra of the locals.

THERE IS A DUALITY TO RODRIGUEZ' CHARACTER

There is a duality to Sixto Rodriguez' character. He is a public person. He runs for political office. He appears in concert. He is an advocate for the legalization of marijuana. He supports continued civil rights reforms. He is a staunch supporter of women's rights. That said, he is also a private person. He remains shy and unassuming. He is a public figure with a private persona. The question of finances is another important aspect of the Rodriguez tale. He is a free spirit with a penchant for helping others. Fame and fortune resulted from **Searching For Sugar Man**. The only person it didn't impact is Sixto Rodriguez. He remains true to himself. The money. He could care less.

What is essential is that Sixto Rodriguez' art knows no boundaries. He can write a cutting edge political song, a romantic ballad or an up-tempo rocker. He continues to find meaning in his daily life. That is he transcends fame to fit into a society that needs a blue-collar work ethic.

Sixto Rodriguez' imagination and career is the stuff of legend. His life, however, remains a remote island in the midst of his newfound celebrity. This is the key to the story of his life. The man, the influences and the myths coalesce to make the Sugar Man's tale enduring. Unlike many rock and roll stars, he never pursued greatness. The mantle fell on him with **Searching For Sugar Man**. It was a mantle that he didn't want. But he took it with a vengeance and went out on the road to highlight a talent that had been ignored for more than forty years. It was sweet.

THE YOUNG SIXTO RODRIGUEZ

chapter

TWO

SIXTO DIAZ RODRIGUEZ:
THE MAN, THE INFLUENCES AND THE MYTHS

"THERE WERE NO CONCRETE COLD FACTS
ABOUT THE ARTIST KNOWN AS RODRIGUEZ."
STEPHEN "SUGAR" SEGERMAN

"THE DIFFERENCE BETWEEN ME AND, SAY, SARTRE,
IS THAT I DON'T LET IT SNOW ON MY FIESTA."
TOM ROBBINS

"I THINK MY METIER IS PROTESTING AGAINST
SOMETHING." LANGSTON HUGHES OCTOBER 1934

There is an air of mystery surrounding Rodriguez. The mystery is a shroud that protects his privacy. We have his work. The question remains: "Who is the real Sixto Diaz Rodriguez?" The intrinsic genius he demonstrates in songwriting and performing is an example of his human spirit. He is private. He is modest. His incredible mental powers suggest a philosopher or a Shaman. He is a wise man, an enlightened writer. Yet, the heart of his work is rooted in the American experience. It took South Africa and Stephen "Sugar" Segerman to bring his lyrical magic to America. Along the way the real Sixto Diaz Rodriguez was lost in media myth making.

WHO IS THE REAL SIXTO DIAZ RODRIGUEZ?

Sixto Diaz Rodriguez still lives in Detroit where he was born on July 10, 1942 to a Mexican American family who immigrated to the Motor City. His family endured hardships, they valued education, they possessed a blue-collar work ethic, and they ascended to a middle class status.

The Rodriguez family came to Detroit from San Luis Potosi, Mexico. This is one of Mexico's thirty-two states or Federal Entities. San Luis Potosi is the capital city. It is a mining area with backbreaking work for small wages. Rodriguez' father's family left there to find work in Detroit's auto industry. The auto industry, the rise of unions, the increase in wages, the availability of jobs, fair priced housing and a bustling city, that seemed to get better every day, made Detroit a paradise. At least on the surface, it appeared to be the land of milk and honey. That paradise soon turned into a nightmare. But the paradise came with music.

When Berry Gordy Jr., the founder of Motown, worked on the automobile assembly line in 1955 the rock music revolution was beginning. As Gordy made up songs to escape the boredom of the assembly plant, Rodriguez' father was experiencing the American Dream.

The Rodriguez family is described as middle class. Employment records suggest that he worked on union jobs. He was also employed in demolition, and he was a handy man. His wide-ranging choice of jobs may simply be a reflection of Detroit's declining economy. The persistent urban decay that sucked the lifeblood out of the Motor City was beginning as Rodriguez matured.

When the Rodriguez family moved to Detroit, the economy was booming. The flimsy one-story houses, thrown up during World War II, were fine for the young families. The first migration to Detroit from 1910 to 1930 resulted in the population rising from 465,766 to 1.5 million. The migration of African Americans to Detroit's automobile industry led to the African American population growing from 7,741 in 1910 to 149,119 in 1940. By 1950 there were more than 300,000

African Americans. There was plenty of work until the 1960s. Then the decline in automobile production and a stagnant economy created urban blight.

SIXTO RODRIGUEZ: THE YOUNG MAN

He is an elegantly dressed articulate young man. His manners are impeccable. He is the most interesting student in a local club or coffee shop. This is how Konny Rodriguez described her future husband. She wanted to meet him. She didn't have to wait long. They met, married and began a family. There is an inner peace that people feel when they meet Rodriguez. He has dignity and a sense of privacy that draws the ladies to him. He was never without female companionship.

"I'm working class for sure, but I do make that distinction of hard working class," Rodriguez told Kevin "Sipreano" Howes. That description tells one a great deal about the Sugar Man. He is proud of his roots and he has never rebelled from them. There was from day one a boyish idealism to Rodriguez' personality. He had little concern with money, social status or middle class values. He was his own person intellectually, economically and politically. In his teens he loved going out late at night. "Street Boy" is a reflection of this part of his life. He delighted in writing songs about his early wanderings. He loved the ambiance of Cadillac Square where he might see B. B. King or John Lee Hooker walking around this tranquil downtown spot.

Poetry, music, spiritual longing and sex collided to influence young Rodriguez. It was the 1960s, and he had a sense that America was changing. It was. The power and beauty of poetry influenced the lyrical magic that Rodriguez wrote about prior to recording for Harry Balk's Impact label.

Rodriguez began writing songs earnestly throughout the 1960s. When he was not in school, which was often, he read, wrote and talked about a music future. After he dropped out of high school the streets around Wayne State University became his training ground. The coffee shops were bursting with ideas, suggestions for reading and so many political ideas it was hard to keep up with the intellectual flow. He learned to use language with precision. His writing had no constraints.

There were themes Rodriguez developed in the early years that characterized his writing. He saw and described sadness or pathos. The maturity and authenticity of Rodriguez' lyrics was obvious to everyone. As a singer-songwriter his themes were timeless. When **Cold Fact** became a chart hit, forty plus years after its release, the songs were as fresh in 2012 as they had been in 1970. The lyrics owed a great deal to Detroit's Mexicantown.

MEXICANTOWN, CIVIL RIGHTS AND THE
RODRIGUEZ FAMILY

By the 1940s, Detroit had a Mexicantown. On Vernor Street the Mexican population built homes, attended the Holy Redeemer Catholic church and sent their children to school. By the time Rodriguez was in high school, the Lithuanian Hall became the Hispanos Unidos Hall.

As Sixto wandered up and down Vernor and Bagley streets, he developed a strong sense of and identification with the Mexican American community. The Detroit Public Library Bowen Branch was a home for Sixto. In 1955, a Spanish radio station, WPAG, broadcast community news and music. Rodriguez was an avid listener. In 1961, the first Spanish movie emporium, the Alamo Theater, opened impacting Rodriguez. The Sugar Man had a strong sense of his heritage and its cultural implications.

Sixto Rodriguez has a civil rights side. Where did it come from and why? The answer is a simple one. The African American civil rights movement influenced him. He came of age in 1963 when Martin Luther King's "I Have A Dream" speech impacted his youthful songwriting. "Inner City Blues" is a tribute to King's path breaking speech and the burgeoning civil rights movement. Rodriguez wrote: "King died, drinking from a Judah's cup, looking down but seeing up." He also reflects lyrically on the curfew the Detroit Mayor instituted after the riots: "the curfews set for eight, will it ever all be straight. I doubt it." That says it all as the Sugar Man reflects on the tumultuous Motor City riots of 1967.

As the auto industry became increasingly less profitable, Sixto's father competed with illegal Mexican immigrants for the same jobs. He was a union man. He was also a foreman. When he came home, he told his son about the labor struggles. Sixto never forgot these lessons. It made an indelible impression. There were many lessons that Sixto learned from his father. These include the notion that unions are needed to protect minority labor rights.

In the decade before Sixto was born almost 60,000 workers came into Detroit from Mexico. They found jobs in the steel mills; the auto industry and as casual laborers. Poor wages, inadequate working conditions and political indifference to the worker were the norm. These forces shaped Rodriguez' consciousness. He took on a radial-liberal persona.

Rodriguez came to believe that "labor rights are civil rights." He would not work for a repressive employer. "The Establishment Blues" reflects this viewpoint. After World War II ended, Sixto's dad complained that they were not enjoying the fruits of the peacetime economy. That image stuck with Sixto. He remained a staunch supporter for worker's rights. He also realized that Detroit was two cities.

DETROIT: THE TALE OF TWO CITIES

There is a sense of loss in Detroit. It is the poster child for urban blight. Some areas in downtown Detroit are so vast and barren that they could be farms. They are. Detroit has the largest percentage of urban farms of any American city. The violence, civic corruption and persistent unemployment provided a declining future. It is images of crack houses, burned out buildings, short sales, foreclosures, senseless killings, high unemployment, civic corruption and municipal bankruptcy that provides the road map for Sixto Rodriguez' songs. Yet, Detroit wasn't always this way.

In 1950, the eight-year-old Rodriguez lived in an economically thriving city of 1.8 million. A decade later, Motown Records brought entertainment gold to the Motor City. The local neighborhoods were clean and well painted. The auto industry still provided jobs. The middle class was prosperous. The future looked bright.

Then the auto industry went downhill. The rush to the suburbs ensued. Racial strife led to the 1967 riots. Urban blight took over Detroit. It persisted into civic bankruptcy. As Rodriguez wrote in "Inner City Blues" "Met a girl from Dearborn, early six o'clock this morn, a cold fact. Asked about her bag, suburbia's such a drag, won't get back, Cos Papa don't allow no new ideas here." His lyrics poignantly point to the suburban flight that made Detroit resemble a ghost town.

The problem was more than declining wages; other factors included the outsourcing of manufacturing, intensified urban unrest, the lack of visible prosperity and the precipitous decline of the middle class. This prompted politicians to promise more than they could deliver. The Sugar Man dissented in person and in songwriting. Rodriguez' songs emphasize the property foreclosures and blighted neighborhoods.

There was, however, a silver lining. There are areas of Detroit, like Woodbridge, where Rodriguez lives, that are now revitalized. The city is also younger, racial strife has declined, and there are new investors attempting to rebuild Detroit. One statistic states the major problem was declining wages.

As Rodriguez raised his family, Detroit was one of the five most blighted American cities. Detroit's issues were unemployment, poverty, police brutality and infant mortality. These themes not only influenced his songwriting, they prompted him to work jobs that others wouldn't consider.

Some recent critics have described Detroit as festering with "death, disease, dysfunction and disorder." The poverty, racism and political corruption provide the perfect landscape for Rodriguez' songs. The persistent criticism of the police and government officials is a continual theme in his songwriting.

When a movie location scout went into the Woodbridge neighborhood to find locations for the movie **Little Murder**, a pair of bandanna wearing teenagers robbed him with sawed off shotguns. It was noon when this crime took place.

Despite these incidents, Detroit is making a comeback. The sons and daughters who left home for better jobs are returning to become part of an artistic renaissance that is causing a civic rebirth. The artists, musicians, authors and filmmakers are everywhere. In the midst of this renaissance a seventy-three-year-old Sixto Rodriguez is smiling and enjoying the cultural awakening. The cultural revolution is one where the ruins of the past are the accomplishments of the future.

DETROIT: THE VIEW FROM SIXTY MINUTES

The television show **Sixty Minutes** reported on Detroit's demise. The bankruptcy that Detroit experienced was fifty years in the making. Race riots, the decline of the auto industry and corrupt politics led to this industrial capital hitting rock bottom. They also profiled Rodriguez as a symbol of the Motor City's comeback.

What does an American city look like when it has gone bankrupt? It looks like Beirut. That is it has been through a war. As it turns dark the streetlights don't work. The police don't show up to respond to a crime. There is no money for the key components of government. The Detroit Fire Department has clean new equipment, experienced fire fighters, but they didn't have the money to connect to water.

Dan Gilbert, the owner of Quicken loans, is investing to revitalize downtown Detroit. He is attempting to do what is good for Detroit. When 60 Minutes asked him if he was doing it for Detroit or himself, he was understandably uncomfortable. Gilbert is Detroit's second largest landowner. While he has received property at a discount price, he is still gambling Quicken's corporate future on Detroit's comeback. He doesn't have a specific timetable for Detroit's recovery, but Gilbert is working on revitalizing the economy.

The decline in population prompted one million to flee Detroit for the suburbs. After Gilbert relocated Quicken Loan offices to downtown, he lured more than ninety companies to the Motor City. There are more than twenty Internet startups that Gilbert provided seed money to relocate their businesses.

While Detroit's downtown business community is making a comeback, the problem is the crime-ridden neighborhoods. It took fifty years for Detroit to run itself into a ruined metropolis. There have been so many homes torn down that there are urban farms popping up in the Motor City. It is bizarre to see a farm in the middle of a major city. The 18.5 billion dollar Detroit debt is another problem. Predatory lenders and fiscal mismanagement ruined the Motor City. Declining tax revenues, the corruption in city government, and the end of manufacturing make Detroit a bankruptcy disaster.

The bankruptcy crisis forced Detroit to cut city wages, suspend pensions, and reduce health care. Other essential government services were terminated. There is a movement to sell a portion of the major art pieces in the Detroit Museum of Art. There is so much valuable art that could be sold that it would help to pay down the city debt. That movement appears destined for failure.

After fifty years of incompetent government, excessive city employment benefits, willful disregard for financial problems and an inability to solve social problems, Detroit is bankrupt.

THE MOTOR CITY AND ITS INFLUENCE

It is the evolution of Detroit, as well as the changes in American culture, values, jobs and politics that shaped Rodriguez' character. He also came of age at a time when political-social values were erupting to influence the rise of blue-collar workers, the poor, college students and those with a limited income. These are the themes that impact Rodriguez' songwriting. He is fond of pointing out that the comparison to Bob Dylan is unfair, as Dylan has written more than five hundred songs, and Rodriguez has composed thirty. What Rodriguez doesn't mention is the power of his thirty songs, the lyrical imagery and the beautiful music. The truth is there are no thirty songs that better describe the changes in American life in the 1960s, as America eased into the 1970s.

It is the contrast of the rich and the poor that alerted him to social issues. Just eight miles from the center of Detroit the elite suburb Palmer Woods is filled with multi-million dollar mansions. They are a tribute to the Motor City's former wealth. Frank Lloyd Wright, Minoru Yamasaki and Albert Kahn designed the stately five thousand plus square foot homes with Tudor opulence.

THE CONTRAST IN PALMER WOODS AND ON TO THE CLUBS

Palmer Woods is just a few miles from Rodriguez house on Avery Street. The two areas are worlds apart. The Palmer Woods homes are a reminder of the aristocratic status, the ostentatious wealth of a bygone era, and how the common person's rights eroded.

Some residents label Palmer Woods, the Paris of the Middle West. The homes feature elevators, grand ballrooms and mahogany interiors from another time. These homes are in sharp contrast to the poverty, and the general woes of the Motor City. Rodriguez' vision in song is imparted with these stark contrasts. If you walk from Rodriguez' house on Avery Street, he is only a little more than two miles from Woodward Avenue. This is the entrance point for Palmer Woods. Detroit is a walking town; it is only a short distance from Palmer Woods to the jazz clubs.

As a young kid, Rodriguez walked down Woodward Avenue. He would look up in awe at the billing on the Paradise Theater, where the top jazz artists played. The weekly amateur contests at the Paradise led to Little Willie John emerging as a national recording artist. When Rodriguez covers "Fever," it is with the intensity of Little Willie John. One wonders if Rodriguez was in the Paradise Theater audience on the night that Detroit's amateur singers prepared for their professional careers?

Matt Lucas: "The Paradise Theater, where I often played, is next to Verner's which bottled pop and I stood outside drinking scotch and water waiting to go on stage. I remember talking to Little Willie John outside Verner's. That cat was dynamite."

When Little Willie John appeared at Detroit's Graystone Ballroom on Woodward in the "Jazz v. Rock 'n' Roll Show," Clarence Avant, the future owner of Sussex Records and Harry Balk, Rodriguez' first producer, were in the crowd just a few blocks from Rodriguez' house. It was ironic, as Little Willie John came of age as Sixto Rodriguez was learning to play the guitar. Rodriguez, like many Detroit kids, went to the local concert and dance emporiums to listen to the sounds of the Motor City.

The Warfield and Fox Theaters were big name entertainment venues close to the nightclubs on Woodward. The Warfield would show a movie like Randolph Scott's "Last of the Mohicans" and then a local rhythm and blues group, the Dynamics, would perform live. This was 1955 as the just out of high school Dynamics played to the burgeoning rock and roll scene as they performed a cover of the Danleers' "Chop Chop Boom."

Other nightspots included the Club Three Sixes and Sportees. By the 1950s, these jazz venues were bringing in rock and roll acts. When the Grande Ballroom opened in 1928, it featured the big bands, then jazz and finally rock and roll music. When it closed its doors in 1972, the Grande Ballroom provided every fledgling Motor City rock, pop or soul band with a place to play. What Rodriguez saw at the Grande was jazz legend John Coltrane, and it was later in the 1960s that Led Zeppelin, Pink Floyd, Janis Joplin and the Grateful Dead graced the stage. The Grande Ballroom stands as an urban ghost that shaped the Sugar Man.

ART FROM THE GRANDE BALLROOM

What impact did these clubs have upon Rodriguez? The answer is obvious. Musical themes, audience reaction and the variety of local and national acts helped to formulate the Rodriguez persona.

When Rodriguez appears in concert, his fans often are baffled when he covers a Frank Sinatra song or remarks that Cole Porter is his favorite songsmith. In the old days, Rodriguez was also a record store aficionado. It is probable that he hung out at Joe's Record Shop.

Joe's Record Shop at 3530 Hastings Street offered the best in recent music. The musical fervor in Detroit created the backdrop for Devora Brown's Fortune Record label and groups like Nolan Strong and the Diablos. It was in this musical stew that Rodriguez came of age. When Joe's was relocated to 12ᵗʰ Street on Detroit's West Side, Rodriguez may have been a customer. The record stores, the clubs, the street corner musicians and the large number of small record labels, like Fortune or Battle, made for influences that inspired the Sugar Man.

Matt Lucas: "I used to hang out at the D. I. Record shop which was owned by Frantic Ernie Durham. He had a radio show, and he played my records constantly. He was the number one Black disc jockey."

As Lucas reminisced about Detroit, he believed that it provided Rodriguez with artistic inspiration, as well as themes.

Matt Lucas: "I can't imagine when I hear Rodriguez' 'Inner City Blues' that Rodriguez wasn't hip to the club scene. I used to see him walking down the Cass Corridor. He is a great cat finally getting his due."

As he roamed the Cass Corridor, Rodriguez was a familiar sight. The hunched over walk while carrying a guitar was a personal trademark. As he quickly sauntered down the Cass Corridor, the Sugar Man said hello to everyone. The guitar strapped on his back made Rodriguez ready to sing at the drop of a hat. He did.

THE CASS CORRIDOR NEIGHBORHOOD AND RODRIGUEZ

The Cass Corridor is an alternative neighborhood celebrating Detroit's diversity. It is also a street that runs from Wayne State University to downtown Detroit. The Cass Café and the Old Miami bar are on the corridor.

The neighborhood cultural center provides educational programs, food services for the poor, employment training and housing information. The cultural center also plans and implements the Dally In The Alley street festival held each year to celebrate Detroit's civic pride. This festival in the late 1980s and early 1990s was when Rodriguez was a prominent cultural figure in the Cass Corridor. He often performed at the festival.

Wayne State University is the epicenter of the Cass Corridor. Musicians who come to Detroit often play downtown at venues near Cadillac Square, as well as in the dive bars, the coffee shops and the student hangouts around the college. In 1963, Matt Lucas had a hit with "I'm Movin' On." He regularly played in clubs around Detroit. He headlined at the Grande Ballroom. Lucas, who lived in Canada, used Detroit as his U. S.

base of operation. That is when he could pay the rent. John Rhys found him out on the street one day when Matt was kicked out of his apartment for not paying the rent. They have been friends since that day.

Matt Lucas: "When I came into the Grande Ballroom, the door guard asked me if I had any drugs, when I said I didn't, he gave me some. I loved Detroit. Cheap living, great women, lots of booze and the best musicians nobody every heard of made it a joy to play there. I had to leave my hotel in Cadillac Square and rent an apartment. The hookers made too much noise."

What Lucas and other musicians remembered is the cross-fertilization of jazz, pop, rock and blues music. There was one club that ruled the city, the Flame Bar. The club scene at the Flame Bar, and the rise of blues and rock clubs made Detroit a vibrant ground for musical talent.

Matt Lucas: "I spent a lot of time in the Cass Corridor. It is near Cadillac Square where the Sheridan Cadillac Hotel housed the big acts. It was close to Wayne State, and the Masonic Temple. The Cass Corridor was filled with Mexican workers, hillbillies and struggling musicians. The drugs were great, the women plentiful and the prices low. It was my kind of place."

There's a whole section of the Cass Corridor that has an identity crisis. It is now home to blue-collar workers and hordes of yuppies descending upon low priced housing. Some of the houses are pleasant, others are in foreclosure, disrepair and some blocks need total rehab.

Scott Martelle's **Detroit: A Biography** describes the Cass Corridor as a notorious drug zone with robbery, rape and murder dominating daily life. (p. 216) That seems dated as gentrification is on the rise. There is a revitalized stability and a renewed rebirth in the Cass Corridor.

When **Searching For Sugar Man** was nominated for an Oscar, Rodriguez was in Los Angeles in the Beverly Hills Hotel. He had just ordered room service when local television announced the nomination. He may have thought about his old neighborhood, as he prepared to face the media. He met with the press and remarked: "It's pretty amazing. It started at Sundance, and it's carried through to this." He must have thought long and hard about the Cass Corridor. He still lives a few blocks from Cass Street. He has fond memories of the unity, the brotherhood and the community celebrations.

There is an annual Halloween Party in the Cass Corridor. This goes a long way to explain the neighborhoods sense of community. In the 1960s, America's first rock and roll magazine, **Creem** had its headquarters in the Cass Corridor.

In early September, the Dally In the Alley Arts Festival is the event that defines the Cass Corridor's artistic bent. The first festival held in 1977 was a combination of music, poetry, art, literature and community activism. Although it wasn't called Dally In The Alley until 1982, the community spirit and artistic consciousness drew Rodriguez there each year.

DALLY IN THE ALLEY AND ANOTHER SIDE OF RODRIGUEZ

For more than two decades people in the Cass Corridor remember Rodriguez walking around at the various celebrations. In 2012, Rodriguez was still walking down Forest, between Trumbull and Third. He wears heavy clothing. He has a guitar. Rodriguez is a walker in an automobile town.

Rodriguez recalls how in the old days **Cold Fact** was played daily on Detroit's alternative FM station WABX. In 1970, the alternative Detroit magazine**, Big Fat**, had an ad that read: "Rodriguez For Common Council." Rodriguez looked around at the changes. Detroit was a different city. He still loved it. It didn't matter. One thing is constant about Rodriguez. He loves Detroit.

THE CASS CORRIDOR'S REQUISITES

The Cass Corridor has the requisite stimuli for an artist. There are art galleries, bookstores, records stores, coffee shops, small clubs, and most of all there is a sense of community. As Rodriguez wandered around the Cass Corridor with a guitar, he was anonymous.

When he is hungry Rodriguez wanders into the Cass Café. The café, located at 4620 Cass Avenue, is a few blocks from the Wayne State University campus. The Cass Café is a short walk from his house. The bartender has known Rodriguez for seventeen years. She said: "He is the same guy today that he was when I met him." She also worked on his most recent political campaign.

Why does Rodriguez frequent the Cass Café? The answer is a simple one. It is near Wayne State's College of Creative Studies and the Detroit Institute of Art. Its legendary bar is filled daily to capacity. Rodriguez has good friends at the Cass Café. When he comes into the Cass Café, Rodriguez has a twenty-dollar bill for everyone working. "He has been where we are now with no money," John the waiter said. "He takes care of us."

RODRIGUEZ FOR MAYOR, 2013

In 2013, Rodriguez contemplated running once again to be Detroit's Mayor. He had signs made, he collected money, and he had a campaign staff. A poster in the corner of the Old Miami Bar is a reminder of his aborted campaign. Conversation at the café bar invariably turns to Rodriguez' life long commitment to equality. He is considered a spiritual, as well as a political force, in the Cass Corridor. The irony is everyone listens to Rodriguez' music. They love it. They have heard it for decades.

The bartender, Sandy, was his temporary 2013 campaign manager. She collected money for his campaign. She helped to prepare campaign literature. She hired a staff. She did most of this while sitting in the bar at the Cass Café. The abortive 2013 mayoralty campaign never got off the ground. Rodriguez' newfound fame and touring schedule prevented it.

The March 2013 Rodriguez candidacy for Mayor had Bridgette Volpe organizing the campaign. She did a good job. The problem was that the Mayoralty campaign came shortly after **Searching For Sugar Man** won an academy award. The difficulty with Rodriguez' 2013 Mayoralty candidacy was that he was touring Australia and New Zealand. The petitions in the Cass Café and the Old Miami Bar were signed. There wasn't really time to finalize his campaign. He did receive the one thousand approved voter signatures to run for office. He still cared about Detroit. He kept up with the issues. He spoke up when he was at home on Avery Street.

"The Establishment Blues" and "Inner City Blues" explained everything. He had previously campaigned for Detroit Mayor twice with mixed success. He didn't want to use his celebrity for political purposes.

The Detroit mayoralty election is non-partisan. Candidates do not declare a party. They concentrate upon issues. Like most of Detroit's elections, this one was a mess. There were fourteen nominees and two write in candidates. Rodriguez was one of six candidates who were declined on the ballot, because he didn't finish the paper work. There were allegations of campaign finance irregularities against three candidates and the winner, Mike Duggan, withdrew for a time and then re-entered the race. It was a comedy show that revealed the tragic nature of Detroit politics.

LIFE AT THE CASS CAFÉ AND IN THE CORRIDOR

When he is in the Cass Café, Rodriguez likes to drink at the eight-seat bar. It is a home away from home. He has the waiters keep the people away, as fame and fortune impact his privacy.

There is a tribute to Sixto Rodriguez at the Cass Café. Since his fame and fortune a mural is painted on the concrete wall on the side of the entrance. It shows a younger Sugar Man smiling as you enter the bar. Very cool! The Cass Café is filled with art on the walls and Rodriguez' picture is a reminder of his exalted place in the community.

The Motor City Brewing Company is located just around the corner from the Cass Café. It has a horseshoe shaped bar, and there is an open-air patio. When the weather is warm they barbecue. The menu specializes in pizza and there are five local beers on tap. Scott, the bar tender, said that Rodriguez doesn't care about money. One day he came in and asked how many people were working. Scott said: "Five." Rodriguez went into his pocket. He pulled out five twenty-dollar bills. Rodriguez said: "Here's twenty dollars for each person for lunch." Scott said: "Cool."

When John Linardo established the Motor City Brewing Company, he was making beer in a small room in the back. He would go out on the street and ask people to come in and help him bottle his product. Rodriguez was one of those who helped to bottle Motor City Brewing Company beer. At times when work was slow, Rodriguez drank there gratis. Linardo, a musician, opened the Motor City Brewing Company as much to give bands a place to play as well as to brew his own beer. The great food and fine beer make the Motor City Brewing Company an iconic spot.

Rodriguez loves to come in and sample the various beers. Linardo sat drinking beer with the Sugar Man for years when fame resulted from the documentary. It also interrupted his beer drinking.

When Malik Bendjelloul was working on **Searching For Sugar Man**, Rodriguez would come into the Motor City Brewing Company and ask the bartender, Scott, if he could call Malik in Sweden. Scott said: "Sure." He did. "We never worried about the phone bill," Scott continued. "Rodriguez was too genuine a guy." The Motor City Brewing Company remains a second home to Rodriguez.

Scott: "After the **Searching For Sugar Man** documentary won the Academy Award, Rodriguez came in and he had to go to the second floor office. Everyone wanted to congratulate him. Fame took away his anonymity. He was the same old guy. He wanted to drink beer and talk music."

The Sugar Man loved to come down and talk to the owner, John Linardo, then he would move to the Cass Café for a drink at the long bar with the spacious adjacent dining tables. Then he would walk over to the Old Miami. Fame and blindness have curtailed his nights on the Cass Corridor. He has a difficult time with celebrity. He is after all just Sixto Rodriguez, the son of immigrant Mexican workers who came to Detroit for a better life.

For years, Scott watched Rodriguez walk the Cass Corridor. He liked to talk to him. He never realized that he was a musician. He was just another guy connected to the Wayne State University community. The man in black, as Rodriguez is known, always had his guitar with him. He loved to jam with other musicians.

The Cass Corridor remains unchanged. It is not uncommon to see Rodriguez walking around the community garden at 2nd and Willis. Rodriguez is comfortable there. He will never leave. The Cass Corridor is his intellectual and spiritual home.

DETROIT'S MUSIC AND DANCE SCENE

As Rodriguez grew up, he was an integral part of the local music scene. The Grande Ballroom was the place to see new acts. In 1967, as Rodriguez recorded for Harry Balk, the Motor City was a hotbed of recording and touring acts. John Lee Hooker, B. B. King, Chuck Berry, Slim Harpo, Iggy and the Stooges, Matt Lucas, Jimmy McCracklin and the MC5 among others appeared at the Grande Ballroom. One wonders when Janis Joplin played the Grande Ballroom with Big Brother and the Holding Company if Rodriguez was in the audience?

John Sinclair, the leader of the MC5, said: "I've known Rodriguez since the 60s, before and after he made his records. I knew him more as the neighborhood character who used to run for political office all the time." Sinclair and others recall that Rodriguez was always around the music scene. After he recorded two albums, the industry gave up on Rodriguez.

There were other bars that were influential on Rodriguez' singer-songwriter talent. The Red Dog Saloon on Second and Sheldon was a place where criminals, hoodlums, junkies and musicians hung out. Rodriguez played this rough venue, experimenting with his new songs. These dive bars soon closed. The Old Miami took on the mantle of Detroit's premier dive bar.

When he was bored, Rodriguez walked with his guitar down to the Trumbullplex Anarchist Collective. For twenty years this communal living group has grown a community garden. In the summer, Rodriguez would walk down to the garden where he played "Sugar Man." No one knew that this long lost recording was about to be revived.

One day, Raymond D., a commune member, found Rodriguez sleeping under a tree in the garden. He nudged Rodriguez. The Sugar Man smiled and woke up. He said to the girl with Raymond: "And who is this beautiful young girl?" He started to play her a version of "Sugar Man." She ran into the house and came back with a ukulele. She began to sing with Rodriguez. Then they all walked over to the Old Miami for a few drinks.

HOW DETROIT IMPACTED THE RODRIGUEZ FAMILY

There were cultural changes important to Rodriguez. He watched as the Motown musical revolution ran its course and Berry Gordy, Jr. took Motown to Los Angeles. Rodriguez listened to Iggy Pop and the Stooges, Rare Earth, Marvin Gaye, Smokey Robinson and the Miracles the MC5, the Four Tops or the Supremes with a young Diana Ross. Although he never recorded it, Rodriguez wrote a song, "Advice To Smokey Robinson," which contained the lyrics: "Early Sunday morning I met Smokey Robinson at an inner scene. He really looked awful. I asked him what was wrong....He said my woman she is gone." This is a rare insight into how the Motor City impacted Rodriguez' songwriting. Not only did Rodriguez observe, but also he translated what he saw with lyrical brilliance.

Steve Rowland's group, the Family Dogg, covered "Advice to Smokey Robinson," and it remains the quintessential version. The album, **The View From Rowland's Head**, is an excellent example of Steve's strong, but sensitive, lead vocals. Rowland is the mastermind behind the album, and his use of guitarist Chris Spedding suggests how he wove the Sugar Man's tune into a strong chart song. The backup singers included such English solo artists as P. P. Arnold, Doris Troy and Madeleine Bell. For Northern Soul aficionados, this is enough to make the record a continual club hit. **The View From Rowland's Head** contains the best covers to date of a half a dozen Rodriguez tunes.

Sixto's father, Ramon, was musical, well read, a talented musician and hard working. Ramon rose to become a supervisor at Great Lakes Steel. He embodied the blue collar, hard working underdog in the Motor City. His work ethic translated to his son. Then in the aftermath of World War II, the family went through financial struggles. This led young Sixto into a series of foster homes and sharpened his view of the vagaries of life. It also focused his intellect on the importance of family.

"My father, I think, would be called a laborer, but he made rank so to speak, making foreman," Rodriguez said. Ramon was Rodriguez' earliest musical influence. He also played a masterful guitar. He passed on many musical secrets to his son.

It is not clear what happened to Rodriguez when his mother, Maria, passed away. At the time Sixto was three. While his father attempted to raise six children, there were money problems. Rodriguez' father diligently raised the family. Sixto followed the same path. There is no mention of religion. One suspects that they were Catholics. There is no doubt that the family was working class and they were very close. The bond is still evident.

Rodriguez dropped out of high school to join the Army. He failed the medical. He went to work. He completed his high school equivalency. Then it was off to college while continuing to work in a wide variety of dead end jobs.

In this period, he married his first wife, Rayma, and they had two daughters Eva and Sandra. They divorced sometime in the late 1960s and then Rodriguez began dating Rainy M. Moore. This relationship was a brief one. She was his manager as well as a girl friend. When Rodriguez met her, she called herself Margaret. She decided that Rainy had a show business ring. She adopted the name.

The burden of fame came in 2012 with the success of **Searching For Sugar Man**. He shrugged off the honors. He couldn't shake the hangers on. When he played two concerts in New York in 2013 Steve Rowland, who was the mc, had trouble talking to the Sugar Man. He was deluged with backstage well-wishers.

Rodriguez does have one bit of solace. He is happy with his family and a quiet private life. That is why he schedules time off between tours.

Does he harbor misgivings about his late in life fame and fortune? He has never said.

What did school do for Rodriguez' songwriting? Plenty! The Detroit public schools, despite their undeserved reputation for mediocrity, did have rich musical programs. There were also musical instruments in the Rodriguez' household.

The other factor in Rodriguez' musical development came from the streets. He listened to Martha And The Vandellas' "Dancing In The Streets." He stood in awe as he listened in to street corner groups harmonizing. When the five girls who made up the Del-Fi's sang across the street from their high school, he watched them morph into Martha And The Vandellas. These influences helped to shape Rodriguez' music long before he recorded **Cold Fact**.

THE BRILLIANCE OF EVA RODRIGUEZ

When Rodriguez went to South Africa, after his rediscovery in 1998, his daughter, Eva Alice, met one of the bodyguards and they fell in love. She became Eva Alice Koller living for a time on South Africa's Garden Route. Then she divorced her South African husband. Eva is a brilliant person with a lengthy list of accomplishments. Her life is in many ways a sharp contract to her father. In other respects, she is much the same as the Sugar Man.

Eva Alice Rodriguez was born in February 4, 1963. She is the perfect Aquarius with wide ranging intellectual interests and a non-traditional approach to life. Early on, she displayed an interest in and understanding of science and technology. Like her father, she spent a great deal of time reading, viewing art and discussing Diego Rivera.

When Stephen "Sugar" Segerman corresponded with Eva, he published a small segment of their e-mail interchanges. Eva said: "Sandrevan Lullaby-Lifestyles' touches my heart." She also said that "I Think of You" is her favorite song. Eva's life is a complex, exciting and productive one.

After high school, Eva enlisted in the U. S. Army. This may have been strange to her father, who was an anti-Vietnam protester. Rodriguez was so unhappy that Eva's mother signed the consent form. While Eva was serving in the Army, she trained as a combat medic. She was interested in flying and began training for a new career. She was selected for flight training. In 1987, she was certified to fly a number of helicopters including Hueys and Black Hawks. She also served in the Gulf War.

Eva Rodriguez: "I loved my life of adventure as a US military helicopter pilot."

During the first phase of her military career, Eva was a combat nurse. She witnessed the brutal effects of war. She administered medicine to patients in Korea, and she also trained as a liaison to foreign governments. In other words, she was a military adviser helping other nations with their economy, their medical needs and their infrastructure. This was only the beginning. She trained as a Blackhawk helicopter pilot. Then she was sent to Columbia and Barbados where she was a military adviser to the locals. As a safety program manager, she worked in Honduras, Guatemala, Belize and El Salvador. The success and intensity of her military career, and the hard work prompted her to retire after two decades. She is not only a highly decorated military officer; she displayed extraordinary medical and flight skills. She is also a writer and a humanitarian. Eva decided that it was time to expand her life. She is, like her dad, a serious writer and her personality has a philosophical bent. She is currently writing a book, **Unloaded**, about her military career.

Eva Rodriguez: "I gained a vast amount of experience and training in many areas of government, the military, medicine, aviation and safety." But it was time to look after her son.

During the summer of 1987, while Eva was in flight training, her father Sixto Rodriguez was nattily dressed and engaging in political protests. He showed up at Detroit's Hart Plaza in 1987 wearing a brown suit with a spiffy tie and flowing long hair as he argued with the police. Rodriguez supported a local African American, Sam Riddle, who was a prominent Detroit civil rights activist. This was going on while Rodriguez' daughter, Eva, was in the middle of her military career.

Deborah G. Douglas and Lucy B. Young's **American Women And Flight Since 1940** pays tribute to Eva's military career. She flew support missions in the Gulf War. Eva was one of the first women to pass the stringent test for pilot training. She often lived on the edge as she transported patients and medical supplies in the dangerous war zones of Iraq and Kuwait during the Gulf War.

While in the military, Eva had a son, Ethan, and she ended her military career shortly after 9-11. Eva was a Chief Warrant Officer III, when she retired from the Army. She moved to South Africa's Wilderness Heights and home schooled her son. Eva also became a traditional healer. She is one of the first white women to undergo a sangoma ritual at Mdantsane near East London.

Traditional South African healers, who employ the wisdom of their ancestors to heal all aspects of a village, practice the sangoma ritual. Traditional healers are abundant in South Africa. This influence intrigued Eva who studied the sangoma ritual in depth. Traditional healers are generally not white and African culture is complex. For outsiders, it is difficult to be licensed in the sangoma ritual. Eva has no trouble understanding and practicing traditional healing. She is already trained in western medicine. By combining the two influences, she is a brilliant medical hybrid.

Eva's Mexican-Cherokee heritage prompted her to study healing and tribal customs. She learned of the mystical aspects of diverse religions and their medicinal mysteries. She completed a training course at Xhosa Mvunakufa on the Eastern Cape of South Africa.

Eva is an accomplished writer. Her first book, **The Circle of Love**, suggests how important it is for young people to achieve a spiritual awareness of nature. Her book was adapted for an arts intervention project for children at the Good Hope Seminary Junior School in Cape Town. This is a program where the children participate in forms of drama, drumming, singing, puppetry, poetry, dance, wardrobe, design and art. The George Society of the Arts in May 2009 performed Eva's program. It was nominated for a South African performance award.

In a South African newspaper interview, Eva is described as "thoroughly unconventional." When she retired as a Chief Warrant Officer, the South African newspaper pointed out that this was equivalent to a Major in the South African military.

Eva is also completing a book on her father, **The Man, The Legend Rodriguez**. It will be a welcome addition to his life. It is an insider's view of a humble man who rose to international acclaim.

HE HAS NEVER TALKED ABOUT DETROIT MUSICAL INFLUENCES OR BOB DYLAN

Detroit was a city awash in music as Rodriguez grew up. He was interested in the blues, jazz, doo-wop and classic rock and roll. He recalls listening to and playing Jimmy Reed songs. The other influences included Carl Perkins, Big Maybelle, Little Richard, Elvis Presley, Nina Simone, Bill Haley and the Comets and Frank Sinatra. These artists had little in common, and that is the beauty of Sixto Rodriguez' musical roots. His myriad influences created a unique sound. Of course, he listened intently to Bob Dylan. Rodriguez has never discussed Dylan's influence. It may have been substantial. It may have been inconsequential.

After he left high school, he worked various day jobs while practicing his guitar. It was the late 1950s and he spent a decade reading and learning how to write songs. His interest in philosophy, his serious and exhaustive reading, and his facility with the pen led in 1966 to a record contract with Harry Balk. He was twenty-four. He began to play in various Detroit venues. The majority of them were the Motor City's worst dive bars. After he met Harry Balk, Del Shannon's producer, he cut a 45 as Rod Rodriguez "I'll Slip Away" backed with "You'd Like To Admit It." It was released on Balk's Impact label. Rodriguez was smitten with the show business bug.

Balk produced "I'll Slip Away" with Mike Theodore and Dennis Coffey hovering in the background. It is not one of Harry's best-produced songs. Somewhere along the line Rodriguez' voice was lost in the lush instrumentation. Theo-Coff corrected this injustice on **Cold Fact**.

Rodriguez signed a contract with Balk that gave Gomba Music, Balk's songwriting and publishing company, a five-year exclusive on all future compositions. He was in the music business that was all that mattered. That attitude came back to haunt Rodriguez.

Harry Balk: "Rodriguez wouldn't do sox hops or promotional activity, so I couldn't promote him. He was one hell of a talent. I needed a media type guy, Rodriguez wasn't it."

When the South African record collector, Stephen "Sugar" Segerman, and his journalist colleague, Craig Bartholomew-Strydom, discovered Rodriguez, he was raising his daughters as a single parent. He continued to work construction and demolition to support his family. When he was told that he was more popular than Elvis Presley in South Africa, he was skeptical. He is an existential philosopher and a humanist. When he was asked in the documentary, if he was upset with not collecting his royalties. He smiled and said: "It's the record business."

WOODBRIDGE AND RODRIGUEZ:
FORMING THE INTELLECTUAL BOND

Detroit's Woodbridge neighborhood is culturally diverse. It has been home to Ty Cobb, James Scripps and Meg White. The area replete with Victorian homes, as well as a recognized cultural center, is located near Wayne State University.

What sets Woodbridge apart are its public art and the gentrification that since 2002 has led to a renewed sense of community? Woodbridge is home to the current renaissance that is bringing Detroit back to cultural, social and economic prominence.

At the moment, its most famous denizen is Sixto Diaz Rodriguez. For the forty plus years that Rodriguez has lived in the area, he has established a reputation as the resident intellectual, a talented musician and a community activist. The mix of residents includes college professors, blue-collar workers, professionals, musicians, college students, union workers, writers and artists. It is the perfect place for Rodriguez. He has access to Wayne State University, music venues, the Detroit art museums and the library.

One wonders did Sixto Rodriguez stand in front of the Detroit Institute of Art gazing at the Diego Rivera series of murals that showed the juxtaposition of capitalism and Marxism? Did his time reading in the local library and gazing at art form his stringent intellectual outlook? Only Rodriguez can tell us. Yet, there is no doubt that the Cass Corridor, Wayne State University and Woodbridge influenced his brilliant writing.

The college professors, who restore homes, the architects, who preserve the old mansions, and the students, who move from one home to another, give the area a feeling of excitement and resurgence. Like Rodriguez' musical career, Woodbridge is an urban fairy tale. Rodriguez came back from neglect, and lack of recognition. He has triumphed due to his songwriting, performing and people skills. Woodbridge has gone through the same transition.

JIM GEARY IS THE RODRIGUEZ OF REBUILDING

Jim Geary is the type of hero that is attracted to Detroit. He arrived in the Woodbridge neighborhood to bring change to the blighted area. "I got in my car and drove around and I stumbled upon Woodbridge," Geary continued. "Oh my God. This is awesome." He purchased a lot with a decrepit former liquor store. He describes his business venture as one of "persistence and patience." The store had been vacant for twenty years. It took Geary two years to complete a building that houses a marvelous pub with excellent food. It is also only a few blocks from Rodriguez' home on Avery Street.

Geary watched as people established home gardens to produce fruits and vegetables. He decided to purchase local produce for his kitchen. He is also proud of his local beer. Rodriguez is adamant that Michigan brewed micro beer turned Woodbridge into a comfortable community of college students, artists and young people. As he told friends: "The best beer in the world is made in the Cass Corridor."

The establishment of the Woodbridge Pub at 5169 Trumbell suggests the character and rebirth of Woodbridge. In 2006, the lot where the pub stands was just another blighted and bleak corner with broken whiskey bottles, trash and more graffiti than the eye could take in. The building was abandoned for twenty-five years. Then Jim Geary opened the Woodbridge Pub. He brought in 1890s Oak from a church in Saginaw Michigan. He completely restored the interior. Geary offers an extensive menu of food using local ingredients grown within five miles of his bar-restaurant. Woodbridge's story is one of rebirth and hope. It is much like Rodriguez' story.

Rodriguez often leaves his house and walks down Avery Street, turns right onto Warren Avenue and walks into the Woodbridge Pub. It is ironic that the Woodbridge Pub's re-emergence and Rodriguez' comeback emerged at the same time. The Cass Corridor and the Woodbridge area are typical of Detroit. They came back from a lost past.

Rodriguez is at home in the Woodbridge area. Shawn Kelly, the Woodbridge Pub bartender, pointed out that when he comes in with Bonnie, they have some drinks, they order some food, he greets and talks to everyone. He is open with the locals and happy to see them. He has a table in the corner.

Shawn Kelly: "Rodriguez sits in one booth, the same one each time, he is with his friend, Bonnie, and he is quiet, reserved, yet friendly. He is a gentle person. If someone wants to talk to him, he will do it."

Everyone interviewed in the Woodbridge area had the same story. Rodriguez is a quiet, humble person. He is also open and friendly.

WOODBRIDGE'S INTELLECTUAL SIDE

Woodbridge's intellectual and cultural achievements are helped by a large number of artists in residence. They include Connie Shea and Jeremy Wilson. They work in a wide variety of artistic endeavors. Other artists include Yvette Rock, Melissa Sherwood, Erika Fulk and the photographer Martin Vecchio.

There is the Mack Avenue Dance Company. This well-known dance company is led by Chris Masters who has been a faculty member at the University of Michigan and Wayne State University. He also taught at various leading dance and ballet schools.

A quirky Indie band, Hymn For Her, lives in the area. It is the brainchild of Lucy Tight and Wayne Waxing. Hymn For Her is a band that lives, tours and records in a sixteen foot 1961 Airstream. They also live at 1521 Hancock. There is a strong sense of musical anarchy in their product. One would suspect the Rodriguez approves of a band whose official video is highlighted by a song with the ubiquitous title: "Fiddlestix."

Hymn For Her is probably the only band to make and sell its own brand of hot sauce. The musical duo also features a cigar body guitar with three strings, two pickups and a broomstick handle. They are addicted to homemade and they are quirky. They also live in Rodriguez' neighborhood when they aren't touring in the shiny Airstream. That said, the music is pretty good.

The most colorful part of Woodbridge is the Trumbullplex, which is an anarchist housing collective at 4210 Trumbell. The anarchists often can be seen walking to the Woodbridge Pub, drinking at the Motor City Brewing Company and a number of them work at the Cass Café.

The intellectual centerpiece in Woodbridge is Detroit's Contemporary Art Institute. This Institute was established on Valentine's Day 1979, and it was a second home to Rodriguez' daughter, Eva, during her teen years. It was at times her day care.

The Woodbridge area is also home to a number of college professors who dabble in music, art, poetry and literature. The best example is Professor Tom Laverty of Mott Community College in nearby Flint Michigan. Laverty describes himself as "a disgruntled, underemployed English professor." He has an MFA from Leslie University. He is a productive scholar. He edits the online literary magazine **Pigeon Town**, and he is the Detroit Tigers number one fan. He is also a musician with a version of "Amazing Grace" on You Tube. He is a talented poet whose work has appeared in the **Cortland Review**, **Passage North** and **Unsaid**. He is also a pissed off intellectual. This makes him a perfect resident of Woodbridge. The point is that Laverty is the kind of character that makes Woodbridge fun.

Rodriguez loves Woodbridge and its residents. In turn, they praise his enormous talent. He has lived on Avery Street since 1976. The large two-story home has a new fence but the eight cement steps leading to the front door are still creaky. Rodriguez wouldn't have it any other way.

RODRIGUEZ' POLITICAL ACTIVISM

There are many examples of Rodriguez' political activism. It is well known that he ran for a number of Detroit political positions. He was prominent in the race for the Mayor's office twice, as well as the city council in 1989. These campaigns highlighted Rodriguez' intense political activism. When he ran for the Detroit City Council, Rodriguez emphasized what was wrong with the Motor City. There were too many unearned city pensions. There was unchecked spending. City services declined dramatically. The Motor City had serious fiscal inequities. Rodriguez was much like a CPA pointing out these fiscal inequities to voters.

The 1989 Detroit elections outraged Rodriguez. He watched as Mayor Coleman Young won his last election and the press roasted him for an illegitimate child, as well as a give away administration that awarded excessive pensions. Bumper stickers around town read: "Honk If You're Mayor Young's Son." There were horns going off all over Detroit.

What bothered Rodriguez, according to close friends, was that the media interest surrounding Young's personal failings took attention away from the issues. Rodriguez was lost in the electoral process. He was a voice in the wilderness crying for change. He didn't come close to winning an election. He did influence the issues.

What is ironic is that the songs Rodriguez wrote in 1969-1970, "The Establishment Blues," "Rich Folks Hoax," "Heikki's Suburbia Bus Tour" and "Inner City Blues" had their genesis in the Detroit riots of 1967 and its aftermath. What is even stranger is that these tunes were a road map to the Motor City and its political problems into the 1990s. Rodriguez, according to close friends, couldn't help but look back on the songs, as he reflected on the Motor City and its political turmoil. He had been around a long time as a political dissenter.

RODRIGUEZ SINCE 1970 CAMPAIGNING
FOR POLITICAL CHANGE

Since the 1970s, Rodriguez has been a familiar face on the Wayne State campus. Much of his political activism centered on the campus newspaper. He showed up daily in the WSU student newspaper office to ask them to cover key issues. This is one reason that he took a decade to receive a philosophy honors degree. He actually finished the WSU degree in Colorado, as the WSU honors college was phased out due to a lack of finances. During the time that he showed up at the student newspaper to convince its editor to expand their coverage of local politics, he concentrated his attention on civic corruption. At the time Detroit was undergoing dramatic change. The auto industry was crumbling, the unions were under attack, the inner city was in disarray and unemployment was rampant. But civic corruption was Rodriguez' primary issue.

The tenure of Mayor Coleman Young from 1974 to 1994 spurred Rodriguez' political activism. Young, an African American, was determined to bring Detroit back to its former glory. He failed. He ruined Detroit with his fiscal policies. By the time that Young left office, Detroit was twenty billion dollars in debt. Predatory loans destroyed the Motor City. Rodriguez was a constant critic of local government's fiscal policies.

Rodriguez criticized Mayor Young's preferential treatment of government employees. He was outraged. He saw the double standard as city workers collected huge pensions, while the police ignored key neighborhoods and reacted violently to ethnic protesters. Rodriguez was in the forefront of the call for a new city government.

When Mayor Young's police chief was sentenced to jail and convicted of embezzling funds, it recalled Rodriguez' song, "The Establishment Blues." His songs reflected the degree of police brutality and the inane activity of corrupt politicians.Rodriguez also witnessed the rise of Mexican American politics. When he went to Los Angeles in 1970 to promote **Cold Fact**, Rodriguez hung out with Mexican American political activists. He was a strong supporter of brown power. He also attended house parties for political reform movements ranging from the Green Party to the National Organization for Women. He continually played his songs for liberal political causes. He connected with his Native American roots. He frequently helped organize Pow-Wow's. He also performed at some of these events.

When Rodriguez arrived in Los Angeles the political scene was dominated by the Latino struggle. The Brown Beret's, as Latino activists were dubbed, not only demanded that the major universities institute Mexican American studies, they began the Chicano consciousness, which impacted the Sugar Man.

During the trip to Los Angeles, Rodriguez brought the leader of the Brown Beret's, David Sanchez, on stage to talk about Chicano political concerns. The Sugar Man's politician commitment did not sit well with music industry insiders. They didn't get it.

As Bob Dylan said: "You don't need a weatherman to know which way the wind blows." Rodriguez reflected on these lyrics, as he watched the Woodstock Nation create a freedom that was embraced by the rock and roll world.

As Rodriguez promoted his record in Los Angeles, he recalled that it was the anniversary of the Detroit riots. Now he was in Los Angeles feeling guilty about leaving home.

When Rodriguez heard the one off single by Smokey Robinson and the Miracles "I Care About Detroit," he felt better. He thought back upon the inane Los Angeles interviews. He returned home to intensify his efforts to rebuild the Motor City.

There was so little known about Rodriguez that when **Searching For Sugar Man** became a box office smash, **Time** magazine came looking for information. They weren't alone. **Rolling Stone** and the **New York Times** featured Rodriguez. No one had a clue.

TIME MAGAZINE ASKS TEN QUESTIONS

Time magazine on January 28, 2013 asked Rodriguez ten questions. He explained the false rumors that circulated around his life. He had no idea how the suicide rumors began. He was well and alive in Detroit. He pointed out that his first album didn't sell due to changing musical trends. He said that South Africa had "conscription there, and here in the United States the young bloods were burning draft cards." Rodriguez advocated immediate political change. This suggests why he ran for public office numerous times.

On his lack of royalties, Rodriguez commented: "It's kind of involved you know." This was his only hint of frustration, as song copyrights and publishing royalties were still in limbo. He did regularly receive royalties from Light In The Attic and Sony Legacy. The checks came from Clarence Avant's publishing company, Avant Garde. On the subject of fame, while in New York, he talked with Alec Baldwin who told him that it was a double-edged sword. Rodriguez agreed. As he concluded an interview with Belinda Luscombe, Rodriguez remarked: "I was doing demolition yesterday. I'm renovating my home." Nothing has changed. Rodriguez is still talented and humble.

Time magazine's Belinda Luscombe asked Rodriguez a number of questions; he extended the interview with timely observations. One of Rodriguez' curious character traits is to limit or extend an interview. He has a Shamanistic sense of what is and what is not important. If the interviewer is on his intellectual path the story goes on forever. If the interviewer is a dolt, the Sugar Man is polite to a fault and the interview ends prematurely.

The Sugar Man made his story even more appealing when he pointed out forty years of neglect was due to a lack of promotion. When **Time** revealed he was an artist who prefers to remain at home, there was a great deal of positive press.

RODRIGUEZ AT HOME IN 2015

Rodriguez' fame and fortune prompted many to question whether he would change his life style. He won't. He continues to live on Avery Street in a home that he purchased in the mid-1970s during a federal government land auction. It is not a fifty-dollar home as his wife, Konny stated; he paid seven hundred and fifty dollars for it in the mid-1970s.

The Avery Street home is in a historic neighborhood with a smattering of Victorian residences. The irregular-shaped district homes celebrate Detroit's rich architectural past. It is not the poor, downtrodden area portrayed in **Searching For Sugar Man**. Rodriguez is proud that he lives in a neighborhood where he can walk down Rosa Parks Boulevard. When Rodriguez strolls Woodbridge, he can run into Academy Award nominated filmmaker, Gary Schwartz, or Rose Mary Robinson, the first woman elected to the Michigan legislature. The area has been home to musicians who have moved on to other cities. Meg White, the Grammy winning drummer for the White Stripes, lived for a time in Woodbridge. Jack White and Eminem also lived in Detroit, before they relocated. Rodriguez loves the musical-literary past.

He shares the home with his partner, Bonnie, who takes care of him, as he is nearly blind from glaucoma. His second wife, Konny, lives close by in a Detroit suburb. The Sugar Man actively pursues his intellectual interests. Existential literature is at the top of his reading list. "Knowledge is nothing," Rodriguez said. "It's what you do with that knowledge. You have to make yourself heard."

That statement tells us a great deal about Rodriguez. He is a creature of habit. He refuses to leave the old neighborhood. His home in 2015 is much the same as it was in the mid-1970s. The fame and money has taken away his privacy. One wonders if Rodriguez has second thoughts on fame and fortune. Word is that he loves it!

WHY IS RODRIGUEZ UNIQUE?

What is there about Sixto Rodriguez that is unique? Plenty! His story is one of an obscure musician thundering to commercial prominence. He entered the charts forty years after he recorded two seminal albums. He is a brilliant artist who never received a dime in royalties prior to 2008. When **Searching For Sugar Man** opened to universal acclaim, the royalty question dominated the press. How could this be in the computer age? Here is a meek man whose life deserves clarity. When Vladimir Nabokov in his memoir, **Speak Memory**, wrote: "The cradle rocks above an abyss, and common sense tells us that our existence is but a brief crack of light between two eternities of darkness," he describes Sixto Rodriguez. He also suggests why Rodriguez represented Detroit's values and history.

Many songwriters look to different parts of their life for inspiration. No one does this more than Rodriguez. He launched his career writing about street boys, the establishment's power and romance. There is a special quality to lyrics that bring out the essence of a subject be it police brutality or love themes.

BIOGRAPHY AND THE SUGAR MAN

How does one approach Sixto Rodriguez? Perhaps as one of Charlotte Bronte's biographers suggests: "Get as many anecdotes as possible." What the reader wants from biography is a vivid sense of the person. Readers of biography are greedy. They want every little fact.

Rodriguez is a simple person. He is also a real person with an integrity that few possess. There is no need to praise him extensively or criticize his shortcomings. His life speaks for itself. Biographies are full of verifiable facts. Rodriguez raised a family as a single parent. He made two beautiful albums that sank from sight. He continued to write, completed a college degree, and he had a full life. Then fame and fortune intruded. That is the story.

There is a back-story. The people around the Sugar Man, the music business, college and friends, as well as his family, are in the mix. Because of the wealth of material and the myths surrounding Rodriguez, verifiable facts are at a premium.

What are biographers to do with mythical tales? Rodriguez didn't kill himself. This is only one of many stories that clouded the Sugar Man's life. Fortunately, he was alive to refute these tall tales. The myth making around Rodriguez remains. He is nervous about the various stories of his life. This makes him reclusive.

Those close to Rodriguez point out that he is conspiracy minded. He has good reason to feel paranoid. The record business did a number on him. The political establishment ignored his message and ideas for reform.

When **Rolling Stone** interviewed Rodriguez, he told close friends that he was unhappy with their reporting. He particularly disliked the personal references. He is doing his best to maintain his privacy. It is not an easy task. He almost welcomes the myths, as they hide the reality.

Much of the literature surrounding Rodriguez is self-serving. Some of it is gossip. No one seems interested in those around the Sugar Man. To understand him, it is necessary to look at the previously unknown aspects of his life. Hagiography does not make for good biography. The reverence accorded a subject prevents interpretation and objectivity.

There is a danger in romanticizing Rodriguez' story. Malik Bendjelloul fails to discuss the wives, or his early girl friend-manager, Rainy M. Moore. His present companion, Bonnie, is thanked in the credits to

Searching For Sugar Man. These facts don't alter the story, they simply add to it. The Sixto Rodriguez story is compelling. In some respects, the biographer has to be an archaeologist digging up hidden information.

What does matter is that he is a deep thinking person. As Eva Koller Rodriguez commented early on in the story perhaps intruding on his life was not the right thing. It is too late. That intrusion has taken place. But Rodriguez' sense of respect, dignity and talent shines through the story.

THE DAILY SIXTO DIAZ RODRIGUEZ

Rodriguez' Detroit friends describe him as a "man of ritual." He has ingrained habits. He needs a woman at his side. He has had two wives and two serious live-ins. He has raised three daughters. When his daughter, Eva, described her father as "eccentric," she unwittingly hit on his key character trait.

He abhors money. He challenges authority. He is shy. He has no use for the media. When he announced that he might run to become Detroit's Mayor, someone asked if he was qualified? A supporter pointed out that Martha Reeves of Martha And The Vandellas was on the Detroit City Council. That was the end of the argument. When Rodriguez ran for the Detroit City Council they misspelled his name on the ballot. He smiled. He never complained.

Sixto Rodriguez: "Nothing beats reality, so I decided to go back to work, though I never really left music. I don't have the political pull of the big guys. So you just do what you can do."

THE CASE OF THE MISSING SUGAR MAN

When Stephen "Sugar" Segerman and Craig Bartholomew-Strydom found Sixto Rodriguez they were overjoyed. One wonders what Rodriguez thought. He said that he is thankful to Segerman. He also appreciates Bartholomew-Strydom, Brian Currin and Andy Harrod. The life that the Sugar Man leads is not a complicated one.

It is a quiet life feeding logs into a wood-burning stove, a walk to the Motor City Brewing Company, across the street and around the corner from the Cass Café or he will briskly walk the few blocks to the Old Miami for a drink. Then it is back to the Cass Café for a bite to eat. This is the ritual that makes Rodriguez' life normal. None of this was portrayed in **Searching For Sugar Man**.

Sixto Rodriguez: "It's been a mystical odyssey, it's educational and it's also enlightenment."

No one is more appreciative of the Sixto Rodriguez myths more than Malik Bendjelloul. "Myths are beautiful-you can speculate and fantasize and illuminate these myths," Bendjelloul observed. He admitted that myths shaped **Searching For Sugar Man's** content and direction. The mysteries surrounding the Motor City that is so much a part of the Rodriguez mystique gives the film a noir feel with the dank Detroit backdrop.

Bendjelloul envisioned his film as a portrait of America, as well as the Sugar Man's story of redemption. "America is very much about changing the world and promoting and exporting ideas to other places without even knowing it," Malik Bendjelloul continued. "How could the U. S. be so powerful while everyone missed Sixto Rodriguez?" He would find out. He was on a mission of discovery that consumed his every waking minute.

RODRIGUEZ EXPLAINS HIS EARLY YEARS
TO THE HOLLYWOOD REPORTER

In February 2013, Rodriguez sat down with the **Hollywood Reporter** to discuss his early career. In the wake of **Searching For Sugar Man's** success, he reminisced about his early years. "I feel that the music scene is a small world, a small group of people run it," Rodriguez said.

He talked about the comparison to Bob Dylan. He remarked that he worked on an individual vocal style. "The vocal signature, I think when you have achieved that you have reached your market," Rodriguez said.

When asked about his template for writing, he reflected: "I used the protest songs of the folk music, so to speak, to address issues." He has a sense of purpose and commitment to his music that has never ended.

Rodriguez said he knew about apartheid and repressive government. He concentrated upon learning about South African governmental repression. When asked about his political views, Rodriguez remarked: "I'm a musical-political. If it's broken fix it." This was a reference to national politics.

Before he traveled to South Africa, Rodriguez wasn't sure about his popularity. When he arrived in Cape Town, he was astonished at the reception. He was a superstar. He couldn't believe it. "To see the audiences and the young bloods," Rodriguez reflected, made him overjoyed.

"I was skeptical," Rodriguez said of the idea for **Searching For Sugar Man**. He said that he met Malik Bendjelloul in 2008 when Light In The Attic released **Cold Fact**. "Some call it a fairy tale," Rodriguez continued. "Music is a living art."

Rodriguez said that he didn't have a favorite song. "I like surprises in music, you don't want to have the same cuisine in music." He ended the interview with a reflection on success. He likes his present life but pointed out that business, social, political and family life were all separate. "I think my privacy might have been eroded a bit," Rodriguez continued. "I'm a fortunate man, I'm a solid seventy."

RODRIGUEZ AS A BOHEMIAN

The Bohemian lifestyle is associated with the beatniks, coffee shops, art, angst and strong coffee. The Cass Corridor is the apex of Detroit's bohemian community. It is an area where poverty, art, music and cheap living co-exist in the shadow of Wayne State University. The Old Miami Bar remains the watering hole for the bohemian subculture. A Bohemian lifestyle is one that needs inexpensive housing, cheap eats and plenty of music. Detroit is the city where the Bohemian can still exist. Local residents describe the Motor City as "good for the imagination." That says it all.

Detroit Bohemia emphasizes that there is a long tradition of artistic, musical and literary achievement. This is combined with a living standard that is easy to get by with as Rodriguez worked rehabbing houses. He visits the garden at the Trumbellplex Anarchist Center for summer food, and he knows everyone in the Cass Corridor. It is an easy and satisfying Bohemian life. Did fame and fortune destroy the Bohemian life? That is what this book is about. The second volume looks deeper in the Sugar Man's Bohemian psyche. How the Sugar Man emerged as an international rock star is an important tale to be told in **Rodriguez: Coming From Reality**.

The definition of a Bohemian is one who spends his or her life with the arts while embracing poverty. The California poet, George Sterling, rued the day that the Bohemian lifestyle became a mass movement. Sterling urged true Bohemians to maintain their lifestyle, even if they found fame and fortune. Rodriguez listened and followed this mantra. That is the sign of a true Bohemian.

The constraints of American society and history never impacted Sixto Rodriguez. When Goethe said: "Youth is a disease that time cures," he might have referred to Rodriguez' notion that talent continues for a lifetime. The Sugar Man has demonstrated a unique Bohemian creativity since the 1960s. Fame and fortune was unintended. He welcomes it.

As a neighbor told Rodriguez: "If we knew you were going to be famous, we would have invited you to dinner." He would have declined the invitation; he had to feed his stove firewood.

chapter

THREE

SIXTO RODRIGUEZ: THE SUGAR MAN RESPECT, DIGNITY AND TALENT, STEPHEN "SUGAR" SEGERMAN'S KEY ROLE AND CLARENCE AVANT'S SHADOW

"BUT THANKS FOR YOUR TIME, THEN YOU CAN THANK ME FOR MINE, AND AFTER THAT'S SAID, FORGET IT," SIXTO RODRIGUEZ FROM THE SONG "FORGET IT"

"A HERO IS ONE WHO WANTS TO BE HIMSELF." ORTEGA Y GASSETT

In July 2012, Swedish filmmaker, Malik Bendjelloul, released a documentary **Searching For Sugar Man**. It is the story of Sixto Diaz Rodriguez, an obscure Detroit musician with two well-received but poor selling 1970-1971 albums, **Cold Fact** and **Coming From Reality**.

In 1970-1971, Rodriguez' future looked bright. He had three major producers, a record label, Sussex, with financial and artistic clout, and he also had major distribution through Buddah Records. Everything was in place to make him a star. It didn't happen. His two well-written and beautifully produced records made no impact.

There were other factors working against Rodriguez. He had a Hispanic name. There was no action on the pop charts for ethnic music. Harry Balk mentioned he changed Rodriguez name to Rod Riguez to make him more attractive to record buyers. The point is that no one was in charge of promotion for **Cold Fact** and **Coming From Reality**. Sussex had no idea how to publicize his music.

There were a number of booking agents who were interested in promoting Rodriguez. He had the looks, the talent and the drive of a rock star. The story is that he didn't like to perform. This is of course a myth. He loved to perform but not for the teenybopper audiences or the brain dead disc jockeys controlling the airwaves. He vanished from the musical limelight with no royalties, little acclaim and no interest in his work. Rodriguez' 1970 album **Cold Fact** is brilliant lyrically and musically. It is rivaled only by Bob Dylan's work. It was Rodriguez' second producer, Steve Rowland, who encapsulated his talent in a prophetic phrase.

Steve Rowland: "I've produced a lot of big-name artists with mega hits, like Peter Frampton and Jerry Lee Lewis, but I've never worked with anyone as talented as Rodriguez."

After filmmaker Malik Bendjelloul traced the real life tale of a musician whose song "Sugar Man" told the story of a drug dealer and his clients, he became a superstar. That song, the first track on the **Cold Fact** album developed a cult following that matured into international acclaim.

Bendjelloul's documentary won the Special Jury Prize and the Audience Award for the best international documentary at the 2012 Sundance Film Festival. This was the beginning of the journey that led **Searching For Sugar Man** to an Oscar. The question remained: Who is Sixto Rodriguez? He is the Zen master, as the documentary demonstrates. The legend of Sixto "Jesus" Rodriguez is compelling.

His belated success is even more astonishing. There is nothing flashy about Sixto Rodriguez. What is solid is his songwriting. What is memorable is that he is a magnificent performer. The understated style and easygoing persona that is Sixto Rodriguez has grown to mythical proportions. The clarity of his intelligence is constantly displayed. There is passion. His continual concern over civil rights, police brutality and government malfeasance is a hallmark of his personality. There is a stubborn integrity to Rodriguez. He also has a willful indifference to the music business. The quality of his musical execution, and the originality of his vision highlight Rodriguez as an American phenomenon. His superior craftsmanship finally has an audience.

RODRIGUEZ DIDN'T KNOW HE WAS RODRIGUEZ

When people describe Sixto Rodriguez, they speak of humility and humanity. One person remarked: "Rodriguez doesn't know he is Rodriguez." I wasn't sure what that meant until I read his interview with Andy Markowitz in June 2012. He was on the verge of stardom and very open about his life. The interview was typical Rodriguez. He is gracious about everyone and everything. He is humble concerning the public acclaim. He didn't think that Malik Bendjelloul needed him for the project. Rodriguez pointed out, they had interviewed Dennis Coffey, Mike Theodore, Steve Rowland, Clarence Avant, Stephen "Sugar" Segerman and every music label head and journalist in South Africa. Segerman, in Rodriguez' opinion, was a better front man for the movie, as he told the story with ease, confidence and a sense of drama. For decades Rodriguez didn't know that he was a cult hero. The thought made him uncomfortable.

Perhaps the best insight into Rodriguez' humility took place in Australia in 1979 in the midst of a sold out five date concert tour. He looked out at 15,000 adoring Sydney fans and said: "Eight years later... and this happens. I don't believe it." He was referring to his last album **Coming From Reality**. The Australian reception was so positive that he toured again in 1981 and a live album was released to adoring fans. The strange thing is that when Rodriguez was back home in Detroit, he hardly mentioned his triumphs down under.

When he returned to Detroit from the two Australian tours, Rodriguez remarked: "I thought it was the highlight of my career. I had achieved that epic mission. Not much happened after that. No calls or anything." That is until Stephen "Sugar" Segerman and his gang of record collectors contacted him. Then Malik Bendjelloul came on board to provide international acclaim.

On **Searching For Sugar Man**, Rodriguez said: "I was skeptical about it. I thought he had enough footage by just the people in the film." He said that he resisted the documentary "because I'm not visual, I'm audio. I'm guitar, I'm voice."

Rodriguez talked about his future. He reflected on music festivals. He looked forward to meeting filmmaker Michael Moore. He also discussed his love for singing. "Music is something that-it's a curse. It follows you around. If you want it, it's there. It's not something you abandon. At least I didn't, and I wouldn't. I'm in for the duration. I'm long term for this music thing."

STEPHEN "SUGAR" SEGERMAN EXPLAINS HIS SEARCH

Stephen "Sugar" Segerman is responsible for the Great Rodriguez Hunt. In an article on the Sugarman.org website, he explains his search for the Sugar Man. In 1972, Segerman was in the army serving his mandatory one-year military service at an Air Force base in Valhalla, Pretoria. In the barracks, he heard the words and music from a tape of **Cold Fact**.

Segerman was intrigued by the crude, homemade tape that blasted Rodriguez' lyrics. He had never heard such beautiful, critical and sensitive lyrics. He found the music even more intriguing. He realized that this was a Bob Dylan type singer-songwriter. Who was he? Segerman had no clue.

Then in 1977, Segerman moved into a commune in the area known as Parktown in Johannesburg. It was here that he was nicknamed "Sugar." He continued to listen to music, and Segerman became a walking jukebox. He would soon morph into a walking encyclopedia concerning Sixto Rodriguez. As Segerman's wide musical interests and deep knowledge grew, he couldn't get Rodriguez out of his mind.

For the next twenty years, young Segerman listened to all types of music, but he couldn't escape the haunting lyrics and beautiful melodies in Rodriguez's two albums. By the early 1990s, after a career in the jewelry business, he became involved in the computer industry, and then he purchased an interest in a Cape Town record store. It was from Mabu Vinyl that the Great Rodriguez Hunt took on epic proportions.

He realized that it was time to get serious in the hunt for Sixto Rodriguez. He did. The quest that was twenty years in the making was about to take another turn. After rediscovering Rodriguez, Segerman was instrumental in bringing him to South Africa for a series of triumphant concerts. But before Rodriguez appeared in South Africa, some important changes came over Segerman's life. He was about to become famous. In the end, Sugar was as nervous about fame as Rodriguez.

THE CHANGES IN STEPHEN "SUGAR" SEGERMAN'S LIFE, SOUTH AFRICAN INDEPENDENCE AND RODRIGUEZ

Like many South Africans, Segerman was overjoyed when the shackles of apartheid lifted. He also grew up, got married and started a family. The he had an epiphany. In December 1994, Segerman was on vacation at Camps Bay beach in Cape Town when he met an American girl who asked where she could purchase a copy of **Cold Fact**. He pointed to a record shop across the street from the beach. Then he suggested that she simply wait until returning to Los Angeles and purchase it there. She informed Segerman that no one knew of Rodriguez or the album. He was shocked. It got him thinking. Was it possible that Americans had not heard of Rodriguez? He would find out. The hunt was on. It became an obsessive-compulsive search for a lost hero.

There were other cataclysmic events in South Africa. In 1994, the newly elected National Assembly selected Nelson Mandela as South Africa's first black chief executive. His calm, reasoned and compromising voice slowly brought South Africa out of the dark ages and into the international community. Suddenly rock and roll was an integral part of the nation's mainstream culture. The Voelvry Movement, which had spent five years protesting apartheid, was a big part of the commercialization of rock music.

While Rodriguez influenced anti-apartheid musicians, he didn't bring an end to apartheid. Some insensitive and unassuming critics have attacked **Searching For Sugar Man** suggesting that the documentary has taken too much credit. Stephen "Sugar" Segerman has the most intelligent comment on Rodriguez' influence. "We've been accused of claiming in the movie that Rodriguez's music brought down apartheid. We didn't, and it didn't," Segerman concluded. What Segerman and others have pointed out is that those who opposed apartheid listened intently to **Cold Fact**. No one was more influenced by the Sugar Man than Johannes Kerkorrel the legendary founder of the Voelvry Movement.

JOHANNES KERKORREL AND THE VOELVRY MOVEMENT

Johannes Kerkorrel is a South African journalist turned musician who was a major influence among the white South African musicians who opposed P. W. Botha and his repressive Nazi type South African government.

In 1986, Kerkorrel, whose real name was Ralph John Rabie, began performing politically dissident music on the cabaret circuit. He employed quotes from President Botha's speeches to criticize apartheid. His group Johannes Kerkorrel and the Reformed Blues Band made reference to the Reformed Church. This was sacrilegious.

When Kerkorrel released the album **Eat Crayfish (Eet Kreef)** in 1989, it signaled the birth of the Voelvry Movement. It was also his debut

LP. His music was banned from radio airplay in South Africa. He left for Amsterdam and Belgium where he became a major cabaret performer. It didn't matter, Kerkorrel used Rodriguez' inspiration to attack apartheid. The guitarist on this LP, Willem Moller, would back Rodriguez during his triumphant 1998 South African tour.

The Voelvry Movement gave birth to a mainstream South African rock and roll. What does this have to do with Rodriguez? Plenty! The Voelvry Movement toured college campuses. It was there that white South African's realized that since 1971 Rodriguez' songs were part of the national landscape. What the Voelvry Movement did was to publicize a rock and roll culture while creating the rock concert industry. When Rodriguez played South Africa in 1998, it was partially due to Kerkorrel's influence upon the local culture.

Rock and roll was part of the South African landscape since the 1950s. Brian Currin's website lists the various rock legends that defined the nation. There were other bands that helped to popularize a local brand of rock and roll. Just Jinger is one of South Africa's premier rock groups. Their debut album sold a quarter of a million in South Africa. They toured with U2, the Counting Crows and Def Leppard. Then they relocated to Los Angeles and changed their name in 2006 to Just Jinjer. Rodriguez' influence was dominant.

When Just Jinger appeared in New York in March 1998, they covered Rodriguez' "Sugar Man." "When we recorded the song we honestly thought Rodriguez was dead," Ard Matthews, lead vocalist, remarked. Later in the year, when Rodriguez was in South Africa, he thanked the band for its support.

The Voelvry artists built their protests on South African music, which was music performed to elicit pride, a sense of history and to publicize the intellectual contributions of native South Africans.

When Voelvry artists went on tour, Rodriguez' tunes were invariably played, thereby fueling his legend. Media critics called the Voelvry Movement one filled with "naïve" lyrics. Johannes Kerkorrel responded: "They obviously didn't realize that our whole idea was to write naïve lyrics. We are liberating the language. We are making a language into rock and roll, it can't be an oppressive language anymore."

THE STEPEHN "SUGAR" SEGERMAN-CRAIG BARTHOLOMEW-STRYDOM FORCE BEHIND RODRIGUEZ

It was his Dylanesque anti-establishment lyrics that made Rodriguez popular in South Africa. After Segerman set up a website to find the Sugar

Man, there was a lull. The new facts simply added to the myth. When myth and legend clashed the story was convoluted. The truth was lost in a fog of false tales. Ultimately, this began the hunt that rediscovered Rodriguez.

The story is that a college student came to visit her boyfriend in South Africa. It was the early 1970s. She brought a copy of Rodriguez' **Cold Fact**, and someone made a copy of it. Segerman heard the LP and loved it. Segerman and his friends played it continually. They wore the tape out. **Cold Fact** was passed around all over South Africa. The record collector's and the new fans, like Segerman, went all over South Africa looking for the album. It didn't exist. Finally, South African labels contacted Clarence Avant to release Rodriguez' two albums. Everyone thought that he was dead. It didn't matter. They had the music.

Sussex went bankrupt but Clarence Avant continued to license the material in South Africa, New Zealand, Zimbabwe and Australia. There has never been any evidence of royalties paid to anyone. Steve Rowland didn't get royalties. Dennis Coffey and Mike Theodore never mentioned whether or not they were paid. The irony is that it appears that Avant didn't receive royalties. Everyone was paid once Matt Sullivan and Light In The Attic reissued the albums. The checks come from Clarence Avant's songwriting and publishing company, Avant Garde.

THE CONTINUED MYSTERY BEHIND COLD FACT

There were a number of questions that Segerman and others asked. Why didn't Sussex sell the rights to the two albums? Avant pointed out that no one was interested. The questions surrounding **Cold Fact** nagged at Segerman and his record collector friends. Why was there so much secrecy about Rodriguez? Why was it so difficult to trace the money? These questions prompted Segerman and Bartholomew-Strydom to fanatically search for the Sugar Man. They realized that Clarence Avant was an important albeit mysterious figure. He was also the key to the mystery. The answer to why Rodriguez wasn't promoted is a simple one. Clarence Avant had other business interests. He was moving into television, feature films and new record labels.

CLARENCE AVANT'S SHADOW AND SOUL TRAIN

When Motown moved to Los Angeles in the early 1970's, so did Clarence Avant. When Berry Gordy, Jr set up his offices on Sunset Boulevard, so did Avant. Then writers, performers and industry types descended upon the new Motown, as well as the smaller Sussex offices. Avant had access to the best music acts in the business. This was another reason to ignore Rodriguez' music.

Clarence Avant realized that black capitalism was on the rise. He became one of the most successful African American entertainment moguls. As blaxploitation movies led to best selling soundtracks by Isaac Hayes, Marvin Gaye and James Brown, Avant was in the forefront of this business. He became involved as Don Cornelius moved Soul Train to Los Angeles.

When Don Cornelius put together Soul Train for national television, he searched for investors. Cornelius flew to Los Angeles and Clarence Avant became the program's financial godfather. "My relationship with Clarence started almost the day I hit Los Angeles," Cornelius continued. "Avant was so enthusiastic for what we were doing that he started calling people at networks, saying: 'This Soul Train show should be on a network.'" Avant's support for African American music, television and movies was a part of his business plan since the early 1960s.

Due to Avant's influence and hard work, he secured Cornelius a spot on national television. The William Morris Agency and Dick Clark Productions threatened Avant, they told him to say out of their business. He was so outraged that he bought a radio station in Los Angeles, KAGB. It became Los Angeles' first African American owned radio outlet.

By 1971, Soul Train was broadcasting from a studio, Maverick Flats, on Crenshaw Avenue in the heart of Los Angeles' African American community. **Searching For Sugar Man** did a disservice to Clarence Avant when it failed to detail his business brilliance. There is no excusing Avant's decision not to promote Rodriguez' music. But that was his business decision. When he calls Rodriguez "my man" in **Searching For Sugar Man** it is an interesting interlude.

There was another problem. Dick Clark was attempting to prevent Soul Train from national television exposure. Avant wouldn't stand for Clark's monopoly on teen dance shows. He vowed to save Cornelius and Soul Train. He did. In the process, Avant dropped Rodriguez from the Sussex label.

HOW CLARENCE AVANT SAVED SOUL TRAIN
AND STOOD UP TO DICK CLARK

Dick Clark and American Bandstand did not appreciate Soul Train. For all of Clark's statements about liberalism, his support for African American music and his sense of equality, he was determined to destroy Soul Train. To accomplish this goal, Clark produced a Soul Train look and sound alike show **Soul Unlimited**. He hired Buster Jones, a smooth talking African American Los Angeles announcer, to preview the intended television show on a special edition of American Bandstand. It failed miserably.

Clarence Avant single handedly kept Soul Train on national television. It wasn't easy to go up against Clark and his juggernaut of lawyers. As Los Angeles' emerging African American music dealmaker, Avant became an industry giant. In the process, he also evolved into a multi-millionaire. He convinced ABC and other television networks to open up the airwaves to African Americans. Later, when the Jefferson's became a major television hit, Avant deserved as much of the credit as anyone. He was a civil rights pioneer in the black community. As Avant said: "I don't make speeches, I make deals." He just didn't have time to make deals for Sixto Rodriguez.

BOOTLEGS IMPACTED RODRIGUEZ' SOUTH AFRICAN CAREER AND SEGERMAN TO THE RESCUE

After the **Cold Fact** LP was bootlegged in South Africa, it sold so well, it led to contracts with three separate South African record labels. It appears that all of these releases were licensed from Clarence Avant. No one had an answer on the royalties. Where the royalties were paid remains a mystery.

After the legitimate South African albums were released, Segerman not only wrote the liner notes to one of the re-releases, he was a one man Rodriguez publicity machine. The intriguing portion of Segerman's liner notes dealt with the legend. Segerman is not only a marvelous writer, he has a knack for describing the arcane, the supernatural and the mysterious. There were many stories on why or how Rodriguez died. He had burned himself up on stage, he died of a drug overdose or he shot himself in a club. These urban legends bore no resemblance to reality. Segerman realized that there was more to the mystery.

Segerman was determined to find Rodriguez. After he set up the website: "The Great Rodriguez Hunt," things got interesting. It took about two years to find Rodriguez. For Stephen "Sugar" Segerman, it was a journey that began when he listened to a bootleg copy of **Cold Fact**. It was a twenty plus year journey. Then his friend, Craig Bartholomew-Strydom, wrote a literary article that became the final piece in the puzzle to finding Rodriguez.

After **Searching For Sugar Man** debuted, Locke Peterseim remarked: "At first the documentary **Searching For Sugar Man** feels like a music-industry murder mystery but it turns out to be much more interesting and uplifting...."

THE BARTHOLOMEW-STRYDOM ARTICLE AND
THE RECORD COLLECTORS

The Craig Bartholomew-Strydom article in the October 1997 **Directions** was a major turning point. This article detailed the search for what Bartholomew-Strydom called a "mystical guru, musician, poet, prophet...in other words I was looking for Jesus Rodriguez."

Like a private detective, he initiated a nine month odyssey that led to Rodriguez' rediscovery. The first thing he did was to analyze the lyrics. Bartholomew-Strydom continued with calls to PolyGram Records. Then he made inquiries to an early distributor, RPM. They treated him like he was nuts. But the serious record collector-journalist never gives up. The next step was to secure a company biography from PolyGram. He was their best selling South African artist, but there wasn't any information on the singer known as Rodriguez.

Rather than give up, Bartholomew-Strydom recalled the lyrics "climb up on my music and it will set you free." He didn't give up and after three phone calls to PolyGram, someone gave him a telephone number for a lawyer, Michael S. Traylor at 3660 Wilshire Boulevard in Los Angeles, California. Bartholomew-Strydom sent a letter, then a fax, and he also called Traylor. The result was that he was once again stonewalled. It didn't take long for Bartholomew-Strydom to realize that something was amiss.

At the time Michael Traylor was a high profile Los Angeles lawyer. His specialty was in the entertainment and digital media industry. His long and successful career as an entertainment lawyer prompted Avant to employ his firm to deal with litigation. He also worked with the Walt Disney Company. It was working with Disney's Hollywood Records that made Traylor perfect for Avant's business needs. Traylor had no interest in talking with Bartholomew-Strydom or in discussing Sixto Rodriguez. He may be the person who knows where the money went. Then again!

Like a good detective, Bartholomew-Strydom began following the money. PolyGram didn't have a clue. RPM didn't have a clue. All they knew was that the former head of Sussex Records, Clarence Avant, collected the money. When Bartholomew-Strydom met the ultimate fanatic, Stephen "Sugar" Segerman, he found a person dedicated to finding Rodriguez. They became a smooth running investigative team, it was only a matter of time before they found the Sugar Man.

THE RECORD COLLECTORS DESCEND UPON POLYGRAM

Segerman, Bartholomew-Strydom, along with Brian Currin, Andres Bakkes and Andy Harrod, descended upon the PolyGram office to inquire about releasing the lost Rodriguez albums. PolyGram realized that they were not going away and listened to the Rodriguez fans. Nothing appeals to a record label more than greed. They talked at length about **Coming From Reality**, and PolyGram released it after changing the LP's name to **After The Fact**. The Rodriguez phenomenon continued. The only person who didn't know about it was Sixto Rodriguez.

There was another important person in the mix. His name is Roger Armstrong. He is the founder-president of the London-based Ace Records. A serious record collector, as well as a label mogul, Armstrong had the contact information for Dennis Coffey, Mike Theodore, Harry Balk, Clarence Avant, Steve Rowland, as well as the various world labels that dealt with Rodriguez. Although he is a behind the scenes type of guy, Armstrong was as interested as anyone else to find Rodriguez.

Then the search came to an end. Mike Theodore told the South African's that Rodriguez was alive and living in Detroit. It was a simple phone call to Theodore that led to Rodriguez' rediscovery. As Segerman observed, it was only the beginning. The second phase of the Rodriguez tale led to the 1998 South African concerts. Then came **Searching For Sugar Man**. The Great Rodriguez Hunt website made a historical connection. The story was just beginning. The results made Rodriguez an international star.

In 1997, Segerman's website included a faux milk carton with Rodriguez' picture on it. The milk carton read: "Have you seen this person?" There was more interest in Rodriguez than Segerman realized. Soon there was a tribute website. It took less than a year for the Segerman-Bartholomew-Strydom duo to connect with Rodriguez. Along the way another South African music aficionado, Brian Currin, established a website that tore myth from reality. Then the Great Rodriguez Hunt website heard from Rodriguez' eldest daughter Eva Alice Rodriguez.

Eva wrote: "Rodriguez is my father! I'm serious. He recently received an article from a journalist there who told him of the following. I went on line to try to find out more info and was shocked to see he has his own site. Truly amazing! Do you really want to know about my father? Sometimes the fantasy is better left alive. It is as unbelievable to me as it is to you." –Eva Rodriguez Friday, September 12, 1997.

As the breakthrough brought word that Rodriguez was alive, Segerman was elated. He had found Rodriguez. The story, Segerman thought, was over, but he had a mission. He would bring Rodriguez to South Africa and place him in the proper concert venue to display his talent. A series of Rodriguez appearances would be the end of the story. It wasn't. Unbeknownst to Segerman, the Sugar Man's tale roared on. The fame and fortune that eluded Rodriguez was just around the corner. No one was ready for the whirlwind success that was coming like a runaway locomotive.

Stephen "Sugar" Segerman: "On Sunday 14th September 1997, I called up my email and found a message from Eva Rodriguez Koller, who said she was Rodriguez' daughter and asked me to phone her at her home in Junction City, Kansas. We spoke for quite a while as I told her the whole story and she told me all about her father. She also told me that Rodriguez was somewhat of a recluse and she did not want to give out his phone number. I told her I respected that but would be very grateful if she could ask him to please give me a call sometime. She mentioned that Rodriguez would be willing to discuss the possibility of a tour to South Africa and we agreed that we would liaison with each other over the following few weeks."

The problem was that Rodriguez didn't have a telephone. He walked up to the Motor City Brewing Company, used the telephone and called Segerman in South Africa in the middle of the night. Although it was one A. M. in Cape Town, Rodriguez was calling from the Cass Corridor where it was only four P. M. It didn't matter. Segerman was delighted. He was also ready to talk Rodriguez into appearing in South Africa. The stage was set for another part of Rodriguez' improbable journey.

It was that Internet message, a phone call from Rodriguez, and Segerman's hard work to secure bookings that brought the story to what many saw as its conclusion. He would come to South Africa and perform a few concerts and go home. The problem is that not everyone believed that he was the real Rodriguez. By 1997, there was a Rodriguez impersonator working steadily in South Africa. A segment of South African journalists and record executives thought it was an American scam. It took a year to prove that they were wrong. Among the fans that believed in Rodriguez was web marketer Brian Currin. He added to and supplemented Segerman's work.

THE BRIAN CURRIN WEBSITE AS A TRIBUTE

In 1997, Brian Currin set up a website, Climb Up On My Music, as a tribute to Rodriguez. Who is Brian Currin? He is a web marketer and music consultant in the Cape Town area. He works as a free lance Web Marketer, while maintaining a strong interest in Sixto Rodriguez' career. Since the early 1980s, he was involved in the sales and marketing of technological products. He was the perfect Internet guru to publicize the Sugar Man.

Brian Currin describes himself as "the web guy who knows a bit about music." He designed the Sugar Man.org website. This is the official Rodriguez website. At http://sugarman.org you can find out everything you need to know about Sixto Rodriguez. His presence on Facebook indicates the degree of his interest in a wide range of music. He is one of those who helped find Rodriguez, and he loved the process.

The Rodriguez hunt was over. A message from Rodriguez' oldest daughter, Eva, read: "My father is in great health, physically and mentally. In my eyes, he is ageless, creative, strong, intellectual and different. He has kept his hand and mind on music, living a surprisingly average and somewhat alternative life. He has raised three daughters, labored, got an education, ran for political office and pays dues and debts like the rest of us." That said it all.

Brian Currin has musical interests that go beyond Rodriguez. In October 2012, at age fifty-three, he began a radio show dedicated to the blues on a South African Internet radio station. The special focus on blues by South African performers gives Currin another vehicle to discover the lost local Rodriguez types. He calls the show "Vagabond Blues," because of his penchant for the esoteric and arcane. He is still a major player in maintaining Rodriguez' legacy.

The joy when Currin found Rodriguez was well and alive was readily apparent. Rodriquez was living in Detroit. While the journalist, Craig Bartholomew-Strydom, was a key figure with his writing, the leg work of Segerman and Currin set the stage for Rodriguez' rediscovery.

HOW MUSIC SAVED RODRIGUEZ' LIFE

When you examine Sixto Rodriguez' life you learn that he takes music seriously. He uses music to obliterate the lines between everyday life and art. He views songwriting as a vehicle to highlight social-political problems. Life without music is impossible for Rodriguez. His wives share his passion for music. They haven't shared his alternative life style.

He spent years working dead end jobs. He survived emotionally due to music. The reading, writing and performing life is the one that Rodriguez has chosen. He revels in it.

The short poetic lines in Rodriguez' songs define his life. They also speak to his mortality and his frame of mind. He provides a form of lyrical autobiography. It is works of art, people and ideas that intrigue Rodriguez. He is a rock star so unlike others that he is refreshing.

While his criticism is autobiographical, he has an ability to highlight social-political problems. Since his rise to fame, there is an increasing secrecy and silence from his management. Rodriguez continues to be open and opinionated. His management is doing its best to keep the myths alive. That direction has led to fewer interviews. This in itself is smart. The money train is rolling. Rodriguez deserves to get paid.

Rodriguez' continuing appeal, as a writer and performer, makes him a fascinating biographical subject. The political, musical and psychological questions surrounding his life will alternately fascinate and haunt biographers. He performs a service to our culture by analyzing what is right and what is wrong with it.

Like many artists, Rodriguez must come to terms with the practical side of the music business. Most artists have a five-year window. These were words of wisdom from Harry Balk that Rodriguez never forgot.

Harry Balk: "I told Del Shannon he had five years. I said the same thing to Rodriguez." Since he had to wait forty years for recognition, that five-year window looks inviting. Commercial success is a blessing and a burden. Rodriguez handles it with aplomb.

THE CREATIVE MUSE AT WORK

The creative muse differs for each artist. For Rodriguez his muse is determined by life in and around Detroit. The rhythms of the Motor City drive his music. No one has a better look at Detroit's government problems, its social deterioration, its civic unrest and the recent rebirth of its community spirit than Rodriguez. His creative muse takes in all aspects of the Motor City. It continually drives his art.

What is it that makes Rodriguez creative? It is a combination of philosophy, politics, family values, ethnicity and surprisingly religion. There is a moralistic tone to Rodriguez' writing that the pompous and imperious critics miss. Rodriguez has an urban wisdom, which comes through in "Street Boy." He also follows a path of conventional wisdom, as shown when he raised a family as a single father. No one has offered an explanation for why he was a single father. When fame and fortune came his way, the first two wives acted like nothing had happened. They were onboard for the fame. This is a personal story still untold. Has it fueled his creativity since **Cold Fact** and **Coming From Reality** were released? Only Rodriguez can tell us how his creative muse works.

Rodriguez is an existentialist. He is also a certified member of the counterculture. What is an existential philosopher? It is a way of approaching life by suggesting that the human subject, the person, is the starting point to wisdom. In this mantra each individual is responsible for giving meaning to his or her life. Rodriguez has followed this path. As he has made large sums of money since 2012, he has given most of it away. That is the true existentialist.

The **Paris Review** noted the link between existentialism and Rodriguez' life when Anna Hartford wrote: "Rodriguez never needed any of us, or any of this, and he still doesn't." What Hartford described was a 2013 Rodriguez Cape Town concert. As the South African audience worshipped their idol, she reminded us that he is the same person who worked in construction.

What is unique about Rodriguez is that he doesn't romanticize his musical story. Everyone praises his march to commercial stardom; Rodriguez remains humble and self-effacing.

Rodriguez' fluid sense of thinking is expressed in one brilliant song after another. The extraordinary depth of the Sugar Man's songs amazes even the skeptical critic.

As he eases into his early seventies, he appears to be humored and humbled by his success. There is nothing that will change the Sugar Man. He remains a liberal civil rights advocate with a penchant for activism. His innate intelligence and integrity are reflected in his music. As Rodriguez writes: "Come along for the ride."

JOHANNES KERKORREL & STEF BOS
featuring Tandie Klaasen

AWUWA
(Zij Wil Dansen)

RARE PICTURE DISC OF JOHANNES KERKORREL

chapter

FOUR

WHO IS MALIK BENDJELLOUL AND HOW DID HE CAME TO RODRIGUEZ?

"THE FIRST WHITE ANTI-APARTHEID MOVEMENT DE-
RIVED [INSPIRATION] FROM A FEW ROCK BANDS, RO-
DRIGUEZ WAS THE FIRST ARTIST THAT ACTUALLY HAD
POLITICAL CONTENT THAT WAS ANTI-ESTABLISHMENT
THAT GOT HEARD.... BY REMOTE CONTROL, RODRIGUEZ
WAS ACTUALLY CHANGING A SOCIETY." MALIK BENDJEL-
LOUL

"WHEREAS THERE WAS DISCOURAGEMENT, THERE WAS
NEVER SURRENDER." SEYMOUR EPSTEIN, AUTHOR OF
LEAH

Malik Bendjelloul is the hero in the Rodriguez story. He is a
Swedish filmmaker who took a sabbatical from a television newsmaga-

zine to tour the world searching for documentary material. "I went backpacking in 2006 looking for stories with a camera," Bendjelloul said. While wandering around Cape Town, South Africa, he walked into Stephen "Sugar" Segerman's record store Mabu Vinyl. Bendjelloul said it was "the best story I ever heard in my life." It was the tale of an elusive Detroit street poet Sixto Rodriguez. When Stephen "Sugar" Segerman told the Rodriguez story, Bendjelloul was hooked. He thought about the story for some time after he went back to work for Swedish television.

He was completing small music mini-documentaries for Swedish television. As Bendjelloul told Rachel Does: "There was no way I could tell it in seven minutes." This began a six-year documentary project on Sixto Rodriguez. There were some problems. Bendjelloul didn't have any money. He was not known as a documentary filmmaker. He was in his late twenties. His early years, however, offer a clue to his artistic talent.

BENDJELLOUL'S EARLY YEARS

Malik Bendjelloul grew up in a small Swedish town. He is the son of an Algerian born doctor, Hacene, and a Swedish translator-painter, Veronica Schildt. His parents were liberal and intellectual. They also had a distinct feel for visual imagery. Malik adopted their sense of vision. As a young child he talked of films. At seven, he had a notebook in which he sketched scenes. He was already a filmmaker.

His brother, Johar, became a journalist. His nephews, Peter and Johan Schildt, are well known actors. The family atmosphere was intellectual with books, movies and social-political discussions prevalent. Malik's early college education was in the social sciences. Then he returned to school to study journalism and media production. His education was broad and diverse. He was fascinated from an early age with the documentary.

Before he was a documentary filmmaker, Malik Bendjelloul had a multi-dimensional show business and journalism career. He grew up in a small town in central and southern Sweden. He was featured in the Swedish TV series Ebba and Didrik. Later, he studied journalism and media production at Linnaeus University of Kaalmar in southern Sweden. He soon abandoned acting for a media career. For a brief time, he worked as a reporter for the Swedish public broadcaster SVT. As he developed his skills as a rock filmmaker, he produced short TV documentaries on Elton John, Rod Stewart, Bjork and Kraftwerk. This was a training ground for feature documentaries.

TAKING TIME TO WANDER THE GLOBE AND
FINDING THE RODRIGUEZ STORY

While taking six months to wander the world in search of a commercial film project, Bendjelloul met Stephen "Sugar" Segerman in Cape Town. As Segerman wove the story of Rodriguez' fame, his vanishing myth and his rediscovery, it was a classic tale of failure and redemption. He realized that the Rodriguez tale had multiple focal points. He couldn't address all of them. He decided to concentrate upon the uplifting South African story.

It wasn't just the music that interested Bendjelloul. It was the contrast between sunny Cape Town and dreary Detroit that made the story appealing. It had the potential to be a visual masterpiece. But first Bendjelloul needed a script. He picked Stephen "Sugar" Segerman's brain and the South African record store owner shared his vast knowledge of Rodriguez. As Segerman filled in the story, Bendjelloul worried about concert footage. There didn't appear to be any concert footage for Rodriguez' 1998 shows. Then a local, who filmed parts of the 1998 Rodriguez concerts, sold the eight-millimeter film to Segerman who lent the footage to Bendjelloul for inclusion in **Searching For Sugar Man**.

To Bendjelloul's surprise, Rodriguez' daughters also had home movies of the 1998 South African shows. Segerman and his detective buddies had the ideas, the facts and the intensity. Malik Bendjelloul had the filmmaking genius. Suddenly **Searching For Sugar Man** was born in Mabu Vinyl.

Bendjelloul said: "I had never heard Rodriguez' music when Stephen Segerman first told me about him. I fell so totally in love with his story that I was almost afraid to listen to his work. I thought the chances were very slim that the music would be as good as the story; that I'd be disappointed and lose momentum." He wasn't.

What kept him interested in the project? Bendjelloul sums it up: 'This is the best story I've ever heard! It was kind of a fairy tale." Bendjelloul explains that he realized that he had a winning subject. He repeatedly told the story to his friends, who were a sounding board for **Searching For Sugar Man**.

MEETING STEVE ROWLAND: THE IMPETUS TO
SEARCHING FOR SUGAR MAN

Steve Rowland wound down his production career in September 2006. He had made his mark as a lead singer with the Family Dogg, a group he founded and nurtured to multi-hit status in the U. K and

Europe. He also produced numerous hits with other artists including a string of thirteen hits with Dave Dee, Dozy, Beaky, Mick and Tich. Their single, "The Legend of Xanadu," went number one in the U. K. Then Rowland discovered Peter Frampton and the Herd. He was the producer who convinced Frampton to sing. By 1971, when Rowland accidentally picked up and listened to **Cold Fact**, he was already an acclaimed producer with more work than he could handle.

From the time that he arrived to live in London in 1967, Rowland had a multi- dimensional career as a performer, a producer, and he was also a songwriter. His work in the London recording studios made him a much sought after producer. There were a number of early productions that created Rowland's studio legend. When he produced P. J. Proby's album **Three Week Hero**, he brought Robert Plant, Jimmy Page, John Paul Jones and John Bonham in to back up Proby's psychedelic infused "Jim's Blues." It was the initial studio recording for the members of the future heavy metal band Led Zeppelin. For almost four decades, Rowland produced, performed and wrote non-stop.

By late 2006, he was worn out. The London lifestyle no longer appealed to him. He was financially secure. Steve returned to his first love writing.

Steve was finishing his book **Hollywood Heat**. His book contract specified a Fall 2008 publication date. He was ready for a new phase in his life. He was pondering retirement. After forty years in London, he decided to move back to America. He considered Florida. He decided to move to Palm Springs California. It was a two-hour automobile ride to Los Angeles, where he still had friends and contacts in the movie-music business. While he was in London pondering the move to Palm Springs, he received a phone call from Malik Bendjelloul.

In September 2006, Rowland was enjoying a cup of tea in his townhouse in Chiswick. This is an upscale area on the Thames filled with natural beauty. It is also close to all of the action in and around London. It was perfect for Rowland. He could retreat to write his book, **Hollywood Heat: Untold Stories of 1950s Hollywood**, which prompted him to return to London in September 2008 for the book launch. Rowland was contemplating a slower pace of life. As he reflected on the changes that he was about to make in his life, the phone rang.

Steve Rowland: "I answered the phone. The voice asked if I was the producer of Rodriguez' **Coming From Reality** album? I said: 'Yes.' The person introduced himself as Malik Bendjelloul. We talked briefly about a Rodriguez documentary. I told him how much I respected Rodriguez. I said he is the most talented artist I produced. There was a long silence. Malik said: 'Wow.' I told him that I would be happy to do an interview. He asked me for my opinion on his proposed documentary."

For almost an hour, Bendjelloul described the film that he was contemplating. He remarked that he was organizing the material and working on storyboards. Bendjelloul said he loved the albums. He talked at length about the music's power. He proudly told Steve that he had copies of Rodriguez two albums, and they came from Sergerman's Mabu Vinyl shop. Bendjelloul confessed that he was having trouble deciding what numbers to feature in the film. Rowland listened and gave his opinions.

Steve Rowland: "Malik asked me: 'You produced 'Cause?' I said: 'It is one of the greatest songs I have ever heard in the world. I told him that it broke me up when I recorded it."

They talked about "Cause," the last song Rodriguez recorded for Sussex. "Cause' is the saddest song I have ever heard," Rowland recalled. Then Rowland went into detail about the opening line of "Cause" "lost my job two weeks before Christmas." It caused Steve to wipe away a tear. For five and a half minutes and two hundred and thirty nine words, Rodriguez traced a part of his life. In the process, he reflected on the music business.

For a moment there was silence. "Are you there Malik?" Steve said. "I am! What a powerful story," Bendjelloul remarked. They were both silent for a moment. Then the conversation returned to the proposed documentary. They vowed to talk again.

ROWLAND'S CONVERSATIONS INFLUENCING BENDJELLOUL ON SEARCHING FOR SUGAR MAN

At this point, Bendjelloul was unsure exactly what was the best way to get the story line across. He knew that Rowland had appeared in dozens of television shows, and he also acted in mainstream movies. Malik wondered what the best approach was to introduce the mysterious Rodriguez. He also knew that Steve's father, Roy, was a top Hollywood film director. His mother, Ruth, was a writer. They were a Hollywood power couple. Bendjelloul was aware of Rowland's lineage, and he tapped into Steve's expertise.

Bendjelloul was at a crossroads. He was planning a Sixto Rodriguez documentary. The problem was that he knew very little about the Detroit music scene. The area where Rodriguez grew up was foreign to

Malik. He decided to ask Rowland for a history lesson. Steve provided the information on the Detroit music landscape, the industry and the reasons for Rodriguez' descent into obscurity. As he did, he shook his head with disbelief. He told Malik that Rodriguez was the most talented songwriter that he recorded. He just couldn't imagine why he didn't become a superstar. For the next year, Bendjelloul and Rowland were in touch weekly. They exchanged e-mails about Rodriguez' music, life and career.

Steve Rowland: "Malik said that he wasn't ready to film an interview with me, he had a concept for the movie and he was proceeding in that direction. We talked at length about what he might do with the project."

When Steve told Malik that he was moving to America, the fledgling filmmaker told him not to worry they would keep in touch. As they did by e-mail for the next year, the **Searching For Sugar Man** script took shape.

Steve Rowland: "He called in the early part of 2007 and asked me if I knew when I was moving. I told him that I wasn't sure where I would be but I would stay in touch by e-mail. When I got to Palm Springs in September 2007, I contacted him via e-mail. He e-mailed me back. He wasn't ready to do an interview. I was going back to London for a book launch in July 2008."

Bendjelloul came to Palm Springs to film Steve on two separate occasions for **Searching For Sugar Man**. When he arrived the first time, Malik had cinematographer Camilla Skagerstrom in tow. She is an award winning filmmaker who set the lighting, the mood, and the interior shots for the first of two Steve Rowland interviews.

Steve Rowland: "When Malik and Camilla came into my house I said: 'The invasion of the giant people.' He was 6-3 and she was 6 foot. It broke the ice."

After the first interview, Bendjelloul began the editing process. He loved the shots with Rowland. But Bendjelloul needed comment on the music. They had talked about Rodriguez at length. There was one song that Bendjelloul felt was haunting. That tune was "Cause." Malik called Steve and said: "Your interview turned out great, I would like to add some more to it." Steve agreed. But Malik was running out of money. He had worked on the project virtually non-stop, and he couldn't afford to bring Skagerstrom back. Bendjelloul decided to film another interview himself. He was out of money, but he had the same enthusiasm since the day he began **Searching For Sugar Man**.

They filmed the segment where Steve walked through his beautiful and artistic iron front gate leading into his comfortable Palm Springs home. Bendjelloul told Steve to play the record "Cause" and comment on it. As it turned out, the second visit was crucial to the documentary. Steve's emotions got the best of him. It was heart breaking when Steve commented that Rodriguez was fired two weeks before Christmas.

Steve Rowland: "How can it be that nobody, nobody recognized his talent? How can that be?"

During both visits to Palm Springs, Bendjelloul talked at length with Rowland about the direction of the documentary. He questioned Steve at length about the film business. Steve was an actor, his father was a director and Rowland grew up around the business. The mood oriented shots of Detroit and Cape Town resulted from Bendjelloul's conversations with Rowland. "Keep the mystery alive," Rowland continued, "but never forget Rodriguez' songwriting wizardry."

Bendjelloul hoped that Rowland's music career, as the Family Dogg lead singer, as well as a multi-gold and platinum producer, would help him frame the songs. It did. He had no idea how to script the film. Once he introduced Rodriguez, Malik believed that he could tell the story. He worried that no one would watch a documentary about someone so obscure. Rowland disagreed. He pointed to the Sugar Man's intellect, his humility, his recognized talent among industry types and the mystery surrounding the Sugar Man. These factors made the story compelling.

Steve Rowland: "I told Malik, he had a winning project. It was Oscar material."

What would Rowland suggest? Steve spent a great deal of time writing an opening for the documentary. His idea was to have a black screen for an introduction that explained the mysteries, the rumors, the myths and the drama associated with Rodriguez. In this way the viewer would have some idea about the elusive Sugar Man. One of Rowland's main points was to limit Rodriguez' appearances in the movie to keep the mystery alive. Bendjelloul embraced this idea. The story needed continual suspense to work.

They talked about possibly using the black screen as an opening. Steve wrote it out. He sent it to him. However, when producer Simon Chinn joined the production, the idea was scrapped.

Steve Rowland: "When Malik showed up with Camilla Skagerstrom, we did the first part of the interview. They left. Then about three weeks or a month later he wanted to come and did some more stuff. That's when he did the thing with the gate and taking the photographs out. That is when I did the thing about 'Cause.' I told him that if he wanted anymore I would be happy to do it. I told him that I was going back from London after my book launch. I didn't hear from him for a long time. I e-mailed him in October 2008 that I was back from the book launch. I asked if there was anything he wanted, I was here to help. He got back to me and told me he would stay in touch."

There were other complications in Rowland's life. He was about to get married. Then things went awry.

Steve Rowland: "I was busy preparing to marry Judy Lewis who was Clark Gabel's illegitimate daughter with Loretta Young. Judy and I became boyfriend-girlfriend in high school. We reconnected after more than forty years. We prepared to marry in 2011. We sent out the invitations, we booked the wedding, we booked an Alaskan cruise. I was in love and ready for a new life."

Then in November 2011 Judy Lewis passed away. Rowland was devastated. The **Searching For Sugar Man** documentary was in its final stages of production. Rowland threw himself into the project with daily e-mails to Bendjelloul.

Steve Rowland: "Bendjelloul sent me the footage for **Searching For Sugar Man**. Judy was still alive. She looked at it and said one word. 'Oscar.' I thought that it was really great. He constantly e-mailed me. Finally, he said that he had completed it. "

He told Steve that he was worried about the possible reception. There was an obsessive-compulsive drive that made Bendjelloul want to redo parts of the documentary. Steve told him it was perfect. Simon Chinn agreed. He said that it was ready for the prestigious Sundance festival. Malik couldn't believe it.

Steve Rowland: "Malik and Simon Chinn did the right thing opening the film with Stephen "Sugar" Segerman driving down the stunning Chapman's Peak. It was a visual masterpiece setting the tone for the documentary."

Shortly after **Searching For Sugar Man** opened, Rowland's London friends began calling with accolades for his brief appearance. His ex-girlfriend Sally Farmiloe wrote: "Your film has won the BAFTA." Rowland corrected her. He told her it was Bendjelloul's documentary, and none of this would have happened without Sixto Rodriguez.

From September 2006 until early 2012 Rowland and Bendjelloul talked weekly. They discussed the music, the scenes that would highlight the Sugar Man's career and how the documentary fit into the South African and American experiences. Bendjelloul was proud of the stark contrasts between Cape Town and Detroit as it impacted **Searching For Sugar Man**.

BENDJELLOUL'S LACK OF MONEY AND HIS STRANGE ROAD TO CALIFORNIA AND LONDON

Due to his lack of money, his inexperience in feature documentaries and no one to guide him, Bendjelloul purchased a $150 Logic Express computer program to create a musical score. He also developed animation techniques that allowed for a recreation of the gritty and often depressing Detroit urban landscape that inspired Rodriguez' life and music. By 2011, Bendjelloul spent $80,000 of his savings. He was not only out of money, his inspiration faded. He was momentarily depressed.

The strangest aspect of Bendjelloul's journey occurred when he ran out of money. He was forced to improvise. He discovered a Super 8 app for his Iphone. "It was a $1," Bendjelloul reflected. "I tried it and it looked the same. I did quite a few shots with that Iphone." His friends told him that no one made a documentary using an Iphone. Bendjelloul ignored them.

To make ends meet, Bendjelloul took a job with a Swedish fashion blogging company who sold their material to Stockholm television stations. It was while working this job that Bendjelloul came to California. He traveled to Palm Springs to work on a segment on tanning. While in the sun baked Palm Springs environment, Bendjelloul called and met with Steve Rowland, who produced Rodriguez' second album **Coming From Reality**. They talked about the singer's career.

Rowland, in long discussions with Bendjelloul, convinced the Swedish filmmaker that the story was as much, if not more, about the songwriting. Rowland pointed out the lyrical brilliance behind Rodriguez. He urged the filmmaker to feature key songs in separate segments. This suggestion led Bendjelloul to use the app that made it possible to play Rodriguez' songs with surrealistic drawings of the Sugar Man walking down dank Detroit streets in brilliant animation.

Steve Rowland: "I originally thought that the myths should open the film, what Malik did was to run them through the documentary. This was a perfect approach. He also used the songs beautifully throughout **Searching For Sugar Man**."

Rowland's architecturally unique Palm Springs home is also a Rodriguez picture museum. He invited Bendjelloul into his home and graciously showed him an album of the Sugar Man's pictures. Then Rowland spun his magical tales of Rodriguez' songwriting. In the midst of this a frustrated Rowland stopped and said: "He was the best artist I ever produced, I just can't figure out why he isn't a superstar." Bendjelloul thought a lot about Rowland's' comments. But the story of "Cause" stuck with the director.

Steve Rowland produced some of the major U. K. acts from the 1960s to the 1990s. Bendjelloul speculated on Rowland's recommendations. He realized that he was getting deep insights into the Sugar Man's persona. After he thought about it, he was determined to complete **Searching For Sugar Man**. Steve Rowland was the final inspiration. He urged a deeply depressed Bendjelloul to finish the documentary. There was too much in the can not to complete the project. It was a story that deserved a documentary.

This was a pivotal moment in the process. Rowland is an acclaimed producer, as well as an accomplished movie and television actor. He earned nineteen gold records producing a wide variety of artists. Rowland was not only well known in the music industry, he has a reputation for integrity and credibility. This is not an easy thing to do in the music business. Bendjelloul told Rowland he was ready for a distribution deal. He received one thanks to Simon Chinn's persistence and financial support.

A CHANCE MEETING WITH SIMON CHINN
LEADS TO SONY LEGACY

The meetings with Steve Rowland were one of many steps in Bendjelloul's good luck. On the way home to Stockholm, he had an unexpected layover in London. His flight got canceled. He had a day to waste. He took a cab to Piccadilly Circus. This London tourist infested area provided inspiration. Bendjelloul called the office of Simon Chinn. He was a well-regarded documentary film producer. They talked for fifteen minutes. Bendjelloul opened the conversation: "I have a story just as good as **Man On A Wire**." Suddenly Bendjelloul had Chinn's attention. This reference to Chinn's cult documentary on Philippe Petit intrigued the London filmmaker.

Bendjelloul told Chinn that when he struggled to organize **Searching For Sugar Man**, he went to the theater to see the 2008 British documentary **Man On A Wire**. He was inspired by the story of high wire aerialist, Philippe Petit's, 1974 walk between New York's Twin Towers and the World Trade Center. He also read Petit's book. To Bendjelloul this was a story similar to Rodriguez.' It smelled of box office gold. Simon Chinn was one of the producers of **Man On A Wire**. He was the logical person for Bendjelloul to approach for funding. As he shot his footage, Bendjelloul never forgot the stunning visual shots in **Man On A Wire**. He told Chinn that he had similar visual shots of Detroit and Cape Town.

It was after viewing early **Searching For Sugar Man** footage that Chinn came aboard as a producer. His reputation and ability to raise money prompted the Swedish Film Institute to grant Bendjelloul $400,000. He finished the movie.

When Bendjelloul informed Chinn that the cinematography in **Man On A Wire** inspired **Searching For Sugar Man**, Chinn listened. He realized that the Oscar he won for his documentary was possible with Bendjelloul's project. Throughout the final phases of production, Chinn was with the filmmaker at every step. By the time that **Searching For Sugar Man** arrived at the Sundance Film Festival, it had professional backing. More significantly, it was a documentary like none other in the rock music realm.

Bendjelloul had a private showing for the Swedish Film Institute when **Searching For Sugar Man** was 90% finished. After the screening, Bendjelloul looked at the film board. He was nervous.

They concluded that it was not a commercial documentary. They withdrew future financing. He had spent only $150,000 of the original $400,000 grant. In desperation, Bendjelloul appealed to Simon Chinn who continued the funding. Chinn sent the finished product to the Sundance Festival and Chinn eventually convinced Sony Legacy to come aboard as a financial angel. They signed on as the distributor after watching the audience at Sundance give the film three standing ovations.

What is intriguing is that Sony Legacy was slow and deliberate in their decision to distribute the documentary. The continual applause at the Sundance premier swung the pendulum to a distribution deal. The soundtrack to **Searching For Sugar Man** quickly went gold and eventually platinum.

After **Searching For Sugar Man** became a box office sensation, there were a number of key interviews. One with Jonathan Crow in late January 2013 was particularly revealing. The journalist wondered how he had come upon such an obscure story?

Malik Bendjelloul: "I really stumbled on it…I wasn't looking for a story to make a film about. I'd never done a film." This comment suggests that Stephen "Sugar" Segerman's role was pivotal. He convinced a reluctant Bendjelloul to begin the project. Then he abandoned it. He went to Palm Springs to work on a fashion shoot. It was here that he contacted Steve Rowland, the producer for **Coming From Reality**. It was Rowland who persuaded Bendjelloul to get back on the project. He did.

When the Sundance Festival selected the documentary for inclusion in the 2012 program, Bendjelloul wanted to withdraw it. He didn't believe the film was ready. He was going to send an e-mail to withdraw **Searching For Sugar Man**. He received word that it would open the festival. He couldn't withdraw it.

At the Sundance Festival, Sixto Rodriguez sat with Bendjelloul. He was his usual cool self. He endured rejection, outright deception, an up and down career and promises that no one kept. Unlike the Sugar Man, Malik was a nervous wreck. The perfectionist nature that inspired his work was also a detriment. He wasn't sure he had made a commercial film.

Bendjelloul remarked that the film wasn't finished. "They say that a work of art is never finished, just abandoned, which is basically true," Bendjelloul concluded. This is a rare insight into his obsessive-compulsive personality.

A You Tube video of Bendjelloul, along with Stephen "Sugar" Segerman, as well as Rodriguez, appeared at the Sundance ASCAP Music Café. It was an in-depth interview. The tale of Rodriguez' re-emergence was told to a rapt audience. Segerman is the straight man, as Bendjelloul asks a number of key questions. When Segerman is asked about Rodriguez' fame, he points out that he was more famous in South Africa than the Rolling Stones. In this clip, Rodriguez performs "Sugar Man." Then he talks about his life and career. It is a marvelous insight into Rodriguez' and Bendjelloul's creativity, as well as Segerman's pivotal role in bringing the story to the general public. Bendjelloul never dreamed that his film would be included in the Sundance Film Festival. He appeared shocked by the thunderous applause.

Sony Legacy didn't have distribution rights until the night of the Sundance premiere. When **Searching For Sugar Man** rolled onto the screen, Sony quickly made the deal and they were out the door before the documentary ended. Everyone smelled an Oscar. Sony began the publicity blitz and the money train started rolling. It was unexpected but sweet.

Bendjelloul remarked to friends that he was surprised that the Sundance committee selected the film to open the festival. The Swedish filmmaker was as humble as Rodriguez.

As the movie opens with Stephen "Sugar" Segerman driving his car down a scenic peak into downtown Cape Town, there is a sense that something special is afoot. The story gets better with every frame, and the mystery and myths associated with Sixto Rodriguez dominate the story.

MALIK BENDJELLOUL SITS DOWN FOR SOME QUESTIONS

After the success of **Searching For Sugar Man**, Bendjelloul sat down for an interview with **Filmmaker** magazine. Bendjelloul pointed out that he found the story after he quit his job with Swedish television. He met Stephen "Sugar" Segerman and the documentary slowly unfolded. "I worked for four years straight to make it happen…I was 75 percent finished after six months, and then the last three years were basically working on the last 25 percent."

What is incredible is that Bendjelloul worried that he didn't have enough professionals behind him. Thank goodness, he didn't. It might have spoiled the film. The story of redemption, discovery and fame is one that everyone embraces. That is everyone except Sixto Rodriguez. He seems more amused than awe struck. He is the same person who puts coal in his stove at his Avery Street home. Then he wanders the Detroit streets in search of new songs. The artistic brilliance that is Rodriguez is reflected in the box office success of **Searching For Sugar Man**.

By 2013, the box office receipts for **Searching For Sugar Man** exceeded expectations. In Sweden there was more than a million dollar box office. As Rodriguez tours and enjoys the benefits of the film's popularity, the story has other implications. By early 2015 the U.S. box office figures totaled $3,696,196. In nineteen foreign countries **Searching For Sugar Man** was also a massive hit. The problem is that there are not accurate figures for these areas but a preliminary total is in excess of four million dollars in theater revenue.

SEARCHING FOR THE SUGAR MAN
RECEIVES AN OSCAR NOMINATION

When **Searching For Sugar Man** was nominated for an Oscar, there was universal acclaim. The Detroit folk-protest singer and the Swedish director were an unlikely pair for fame and fortune. True to his personality, Rodriguez commented: "I was in the movie for eight minutes." He gave Bendjelloul credit for the planning, hard work and the film's success.

On the nomination, Bendjelloul observed: "It feels surrealistic, crazy. It never occurred to me that it was something anyone ever achieved." There is no doubt that Bendjelloul's humility is not far behind Rodriguez.'

As Rodriguez received word of the Oscar, his wife Konny remarked: "We got rid of a lot of debt....So it's a good thing you know...." When director, Malik Bendjelloul, was reached for comment, he gave Rodriguez credit for the film's success. When he met Rodriguez, he had to convince him to become a part of the documentary. "Rodriguez is Detroit, in a way," Bendjelloul continued. "He is the son of Mexican immigrants who stayed true to his unique, somewhat eccentric style...." What that means is that Rodriguez has never forgotten his humble origins. He doesn't care about the money. He doesn't care about the fame. When he returned from one of his overseas concert tours with $700,000, he gave much of it away. His daughter, Regan, remarked: "He lives' a very Spartan life. I almost want to call it Amish. He once told me there are three basic needs-food, clothing and shelter. Once you get down to that level, everything else is icing." Regan also told **Rolling Stone** that she wished her father would spend some of the money on himself or the house. To this date, he has refused to use the money for his own purposes. One would expect no less from Sixto Rodriguez.

Those close to Bendjelloul credit his friendship with Regan Rodriguez as the turning point in finalizing **Searching For Sugar Man**. The two were inseparable during the planning, filming and final production. It was Regan who unearthed the cultural artifacts of Rodriguez' life. On camera, looking beautiful and sounding sweet, she delves into a fascinating box of Rodriguez memorabilia. It is a poignant and heart warming aspect of **Searching For Sugar Man**.

There were one hundred thirty films that qualified for selection for the Academy Award. Then the list for the 85th Academy Award was narrowed to five. **Searching For Sugar Man** was in the hunt. It was the eventual winner.

THE CRITICAL RESPONSE

Roger Ebert, the **Chicago Sun Times** critic, called the documentary a 4 Star success. "It exists because we need it to," Ebert wrote. He wasn't alone. The **New York Times** critic, Manohla Dargis, called the film: "...a hugely appealing documentary about fans, faith and an enigmatic Age of Aquarius musician who burned bright and hopeful before disappearing." When it won the Special Jury Prize and the Audience Award at the Sundance Festival, this guaranteed major distribution. As Sony stepped in and provided the clout to make **Searching For Sugar Man** a hit at the art theater box office, the academy took note. Rodriguez finally had the promotion he lacked in 1970-1971 when **Cold Fact** and **Coming From Reality** languished in Woolworth's cut out bin or gathered dust in a New York warehouse. The Academy Award nomination brought the documentary into mainstream theaters.

There were awards other than Sundance. The Los Angeles Film Festival presented the documentary with the Audience Award, as did the Durban International Film Festival and the Melbourne Film Festival. It was a second place winner in the Audience Award category at the Tribeca Film Festival. The Moscow International Film Festival presented the Grand Jury Prize.

Malik Bendjelloul, Sixto Rodriguez and Steve Rowland at the Los Angeles Film Festival: Photo Courtesy Steve Rowland

Steve Rowland: "Sony didn't have a final distribution deal when the Rodriguez documentary was screened at Sundance. To their credit, they saw the commercial gold and found Malik and Simon Chinn to get the deal done."

The audience reaction was three standing ovations, and this made it clear to the corporate suits at Sundance that Rodriguez was commercial gold. At the end of the screening, Rodriguez walked on stage to a standing ovation. He smiled. He looked perplexed. He couldn't understand the excitement. This is the charm and character of Sixto Rodriguez.

While the Sundance Festival and New York's Tribeca are important venues, there are other equally important festivals. It was in Austin's elegant Paramount Theater at the SXSW Showcase that music and documentary history was made for **Searching For Sugar Man**. This venue is so important that Sony Picture Classics-Co-President and Co-Founder, Michael Barker, attended the showing. He couldn't believe the thunderous applause.

The millions of dollars spent refurbishing the Austin movie palace make it a hot spot for top-level Texas entertainment previews. The Paramount draws a music and movie crowd that is America's toughest audience. Not surprisingly, there were raucous cheers, as Rodriguez looked on with a quizzical expression. The tale of a forgotten artist with as much talent as Bob Dylan is one that the Texas audience embraced. **Billboard's** Phil Gallo covered the event. He followed Rodriguez to a local venue, the Mohawk, where he delivered a standing room only show.

There was a problem. Rodriguez refused to say no to the fans who wanted autographs. In Austin, one of the strangest sights was the fan with the South African record store t-shirt that read Mabu Vinyl. This fan talked at length to Rodriguez and let him know that South Africans were with him musically since the early 1970s. Rodriguez smiled. He was polite. He was amused. He was also thankful to South Africa.

It was minutes after midnight when Rodriguez appeared on stage at the Mohawk. There was thunderous applause. Austin is a tough audience, but for Rodriguez it was a piece of cake.

When Rodriguez walked on stage at the Mohawk, he felt mellow. He opened with a cover of Frank Sinatra's "Nice And Easy." The eight songs that followed were from his albums with the exception of the crowd pleasing Cole Porter standard "Just One of Those Things." Matt Sullivan, of Light In The Attic Records, was at the show. He is a person that Rodriguez is comfortable with in his newfound fame. When Rodriguez worried that he had misplaced his guitar, Sullivan assured him that it hadn't vanished. It was safe. As Rodriguez left Austin, Sony's distribution deal gained steam as the publicity machine worked overtime. The media avalanche helped Sony distribute the documentary in the U. S. and abroad with lightning speed. The five and a half months after **Searching For Sugar Man's** release was a time of constant awards.

The awards kept coming. On January 2013 **Searching For Sugar Man** was awarded the 24th annual Producers Guild trophy. The Critics' Choice Movie Award was received in Canada. The Vancouver Film Critics Circle and the National Board of Review named **Searching For Sugar Man** the best documentary. The acclaim continued with an Outstanding Achievement in Graphic Design, as well as the Animation Award from Cinema Eye Honors and two prizes from the Dutch Film Festival IDFA. Bendjelloul was awarded a cash prize of 2,500 Euros.

LOCKE PETERSEIM COMES CLOSEST TO UNRAVELING BENDJELLOUL AND RODRIGUEZ

The whirlwind interviews, as **Searching For Sugar Man** became a phenomenon, were difficult for Malik Bendjelloul and Sixto Rodriguez. Most of the interviews were perfunctory. One stands out. Locke Peterseim asked the right questions and listened.

When Peterseim sat down with Bendjelloul and Rodriguez in Chicago in August 2012, they were in the midst of a media circus. For some reason, the Sugar Man and Malik were comfortable with Peterseim.

The interview began with Rodriguez remarking that his success was one of "these kinds of cycles." He also thanks Segerman, Bartholomew-Strydom and Currin for their fanatical and continual support. The Rodrigologists were the key to excavating the Sugar Man's mystery. Then Malik cuts in pointing out that as a sort of "street drifter" he was "almost surreal." Those feelings defined the documentary.

When Peterseim asked Malik about meeting Rodriguez, the director responded: "I heard so much about him, so I was nervous and eager."

Searching For Sugar Man's success took everyone by surprise. No one was more intrigued by the documentaries acclaim than Bendjelloul. He was asked time and time again to reflect on the awards. He did so reluctantly.

BENDJELLOUL: REFLECTING ON SUCCESS

On the eve of winning an Oscar at the 85th Annual Academy Awards, Malik Bendjelloul sat down with the **Los Angeles Times'** Irene Lacher. He talked at length about **Searching For Sugar Man's** success. As he reminisced about the thirty plus awards, Bendjelloul said: "It's pretty surreal. The idea that this was my first film before I only had shot short stuff for Swedish television."

The Irene Lacher interview clarified another hidden detail of how Bendjelloul arrived at the Sixto Rodriguez story. He met the Sugar Man's daughter, Eva, who was married to a South African. She spun out the stories of how her father arrived in Cape Town in 1998, and in the process charmed the locals. She spoke of the debt that the family owed Segerman. It was Eva who asked Bendjelloul: "Don't you think this could be something more? A documentary?" Bendjelloul thought about that for a long time. He told Lacher: "It took me a while to start thinking that a documentary was a possibility. Then I started and I couldn't stop." Thank goodness for Bendjelloul's obsessive-compulsive nature.

Bendjelloul said: "A man living in a house without a telephone, Rodriguez wasn't normal." In this stilted description, Bendjelloul discovered what he called "the uncompromising" nature of the Sugar Man. It also took Bendjelloul three visits to Detroit to Rodriguez' Avery Street house to get him to participate in the film. Each time that Bendjelloul climbed the concrete steps to Rodriguez' wooden porch, he had a sense of foreboding. Finally, the Sugar Man came aboard. There were four subsequent visits to Rodriguez home and a fifteen-minute interview. "In the end that was enough," Bendjelloul concluded.

Regan Rodriguez deserves as much credit as Bendjelloul or Rodriguez. She continually reinforced her father's talent, she talked at length about his politics, and she was adamant that he still had a commercial future. Without Regan, **Searching For Sugar Man** would not have been completed.

Rodriguez stayed in touch with Bendjelloul. He would go into the Motor City Brewing Company and have Scott, the bar tender, call Bendjelloul. It didn't matter where the filmmaker was in the world, the Motor City Brewing Company footed the bill for the phone calls. That tells one the love that Detroit has for Rodriguez.

EXPLAINING BENDJELLOUL'S SUICIDE

In May 2014, there was no explanation for Malik Bendjelloul's suicide. When he jumped in front of a metro train at the Solna Century subway stop in a busy downtown Stockholm station, the world was shocked. His friends point out that for some time he was depressed. He also was acting erratic. He was traveling non-stop. In the six months before his tragic death there were some clues.

Bendjelloul ate the same breakfast each morning. He walked around his apartment once before he left, and then once again when he returned home. How did such an accomplished person fall into the clutches of despair?

In the months before his death, Bendjelloul was lonely and isolated. He struggled with personal problems, due to his inability to fund a feature film project. While living in New York, Bendjelloul developed insomnia. He missed his Stockholm friends and family.

His suicide was just over a year after his Oscar triumph. It was a shock. When the Stockholm police described the incident as "one of an indeterminate cause," this was a puzzling statement. Mats Eriksson, the press officer for Stockholm's western police district, spun the story for the press. No one believed it.

Then Malik's brother, Johar Bendjelloul, who is a radio journalist, clarified what had happened prior to and during the suicide. "It was recent," Johar, continued: "the onset of a...mental illness." Johar had trouble putting his thoughts in order. He couldn't understand it. "My brother had been struggling with depression for a short period of time and depression is something you can die from," Johar concluded. Everyone was shocked by his death. Karin af Klintberg, a producer for a Swedish arts and cultural program, Orba, said: "He was the happiest person I knew." Simon Chinn, who co-produced **Searching For Sugar Man**, observed that the notion of suicide was preposterous and out of character.

The fear of failure was evident as Bendjelloul reached the top with **Searching For Sugar Man.** He had doubts about a proposed feature film project that he was circulating among the major studios. Those close to Bendjelloul remarked that he feared being typecast as a documentary filmmaker. He had ambitions beyond that genre.

When he went home, it was to see his mother, Veronica Schildt Bendjelloul. She was turning seventy. A family reunion was planned. She was still working as a painter and translator. Malik was looking forward to the family gathering.

What killed Malik Bendjelloul? It was fame. The onset of fame and fortune takes away ones privacy, ones friends and creates a new world. Malik couldn't fit into a place where the media, fans, hangers on and the industry co-opted his life. The emotional energy expended in **Searching For Sugar Man** took its toll.

Those who were close to Bendjelloul commented on the persistence of the hangers on, and the industry types who wanted to get on the Bendjelloul and Rodriguez' quick buck train. There were also investors for a number of flim flam projects. The Sugar Man and Malik had to hide out from the vast army of potential economic suitors. It wasn't fun. Fame and fortune had its downside.

Stephen "Sugar" Segerman, perhaps Bendjelloul's closest friend outside of Stockholm, recalled a dinner at the Sundance Film Festival, where Bendjelloul was unusually gracious. Segerman remains puzzled by Bendjelloul's suicide. Segerman watched as Malik thanked everyone who helped him on the long journey to a 2013 Oscar. He appeared to be the best adjusted person in the room.

Steven "Sugar" Segerman: "When he took the stage to accept his Oscar, the drive that had gotten him there was replaced in an instant by the characteristic charm and innocence that endeared him to so many."

Like everyone else, Segerman was at a loss for words. There was no one with an explanation for Bendjelloul's suicide.

Bendjelloul's personality traits offer some clues. He was obsessive about his projects. He could be rigid, unbending and he had some unexplainable personality quirks. He told a radio interviewer that he would only listen to songs that began with the letter I. He ate only one type of tomato sauce on his pasta. When that company went out of business, he called every shop in Stockholm and purchased their remaining stock. One of his friends described these obsessions as "quirky but normal."

There were also signs of harmless fantasy in Bendjelloul's life. He told his mentor, Per Sinding Larsen, that he descended from nobility and his family fortune was lost to unsavory influences. Larsen thought these tales charming. He had no idea that Malik was clinically depressed. When Larsen recalled Bendjelloul's work, he found only words of praise.

Per Sinding Larsen: "I couldn't figure out how he did it. He didn't have the money or the means to do the things he was doing at the time."

The praise from his Swedish colleagues was genuine and overwhelming. They commented that he knew the media in a way that few Swedish journalists did, and this impacted his documentary genius. But he was ultra sensitive. This went a long way toward explaining a behavior pattern that led to his untimely suicide.

Stephen "Sugar" Segerman recalled that at the Vanity Fair Oscar Party, Bendjelloul sat in the corner talking to his friends. He wasn't interested in celebrity. He also didn't enjoy socializing with strangers, even famous personalities. At Swedish television there is a small shrine to Bendjelloul. The shrine is composed of two small pictures, three candles and a black condolence book that is empty. When a reporter inquired: "Why has no one signed the condolence book?" A Kobra TV employee said: "We think he is coming back."

The mystery of Malik Bendjelloul's suicide hangs over the Rodriguez story. The Sugar Man loved Malik. He couldn't believe he was dead. It was a strange twist in a feel good story. No one can explain what happened. Perhaps it is better that way. Bendjelloul will be remembered not only for his creativity, but also for his infectious enthusiasm about Sixto Rodriguez' music and career.

There is no mystery to **Searching For Sugar Man's** success. Bendjelloul tells the Rodriguez story in a stylized, streamlined manner. One critic used "electrifying, inspiring, spiritual and reaffirming" to describe the documentary. As Rodriguez observed about his friend: "I didn't have anything to do with the film…I didn't pick any of the shots or choose any of the music. It was entirely a work of art made by Malik-rest in peace." No one was more upset by Bendjelloul's premature suicide than Sixto Rodriguez.

WHAT HAPPENED TO BENDJELLOUL?

No one knows the answer to Bendjelloul's tragic suicide. There are some hints. He had trouble living and sleeping in New York. Insomnia played havoc on his life. But it is in Stockholm that there are clues to why he committed suicide. He was working on a project for Swedish television. Whether or not he had begun this task is unclear. What is obvious is that Bendjelloul told Karin Af Klintberg, the producer for a Swedish arts and culture program, Korba, that he couldn't commit to anything because Hollywood would soon be calling. They didn't. His dream of a feature film faded. Then Bendjelloul took his life. His death was particularly hard on Stephen "Sugar" Segerman who commented: "It's been a wonderful journey, but this is just too sad. It's absolutely shocking." No one could disagree.

At Swedish Korba television there is now a "Studio Malik." No tribute could be more fitting.

ONE OF RODRIGUEZ' FAVORITE CAFES

chapter

FIVE

HARRY BALK: DISCOVERING RODRIGUEZ

"I RECOGNIZED THAT DEL NEEDED SOMETHING TO
MAKE 'RUNAWAY' HAVE A HIT SOUND. SO WE INCREASED
THE SPEED ON THE MASTER TAPE AND VOILA WE HAD
A HIT." HARRY BALK REMINISCING ABOUT PRODUCING
"RUNAWAY"

"I REMEBMER SEEING THIS INCREDIBLE GOOD LOOK-
ING, CHARISMATIC YOUNG MAN IN SOME DIVE DETROIT
BAR. I HEARD THESE BEAUTIFUL SONGS. I WONDER WHO
WROTE THEM? WHEN I FOUND OUT IT WAS THIS SINGER
SIXTO RODRIGUEZ, I SIGNED HIM." HARRY BALK

Harry Balk is one of Detroit's legendary music men. He discov-
ered Little Willie John, Johnny and the Hurricanes, Del Shannon and
Sixto Rodriguez among others. He helped Marvin Gaye introduce a jazz
Motown sound with the **What's Going On** album and along the way he

dominated the Detroit music scene. His connection to Rodriguez is an important one. He discovered him. He was the first person to record the Sugar Man. He introduced the **Cold Fact** producers, Dennis Coffey and Mike Theodore, to Rodriguez. He also believed that the Sugar Man's primary skill was songwriting. There is a mysterious, soap opera quality to the aftermath of the feel good **Searching For Sugar Man** documentary.

HARRY BALK'S SONGWRITING DEAL WITH
RODRIGUEZ AND LAW SUITS

On April 20, 1966 Harry Balk copyrighted five Sixto Rodriguez songs for his Gomba Publishing Company. The Sugar Man signed a five-year songwriting deal with Gomba Music. He received a one-dollar advance. Of the songs Balk copyrighted, one was from the **Searching For Sugar Man** soundtrack, "I'll Slip Away." That tune forty-five years later became the basis of Balk's lawsuit against Clarence Avant. What Balk's company, Gomba Music, alleged was that Rodriguez and Avant conspired to ignore his 1966 contract with Rodriguez. Avant denies any wrongdoing, and he countersued Rodriguez. It is a mess.

The other songs "You'd Like To Admit It," "Forget It" and "To Whom It May Concern" were well known album cuts. The only non-released song, "That Discotheque," is an unknown Rodriguez composition. Mike Theodore and others speculate that Balk may have copyrighted a tune that didn't exist. There is no record of Rodriguez writing "That Discotheque."

When Balk copyrighted these songs, he had exclusive rights to Rodriguez' songwriting for five years. The contract also contained a clause where Balk could extend the agreement year by year. In 1969, Rodriguez signed with Clarence Avant and Sussex Records. No one knew of the Gomba Music agreement. The Sugar Man changed some copyrights using Sixth Prince and Jesus Rodriguez as the songwriter for Clarence Avant's Interior Music.

In late May 2014, when Balk sued Clarence Avant, he alleged that Rodriguez and Avant knowingly and willingly conspired to practice fraud. Avant took exception to the lawsuit. He sued Rodriguez alleging fraud. Avant said that he had no idea there was a prior claim to the songs when he copyrighted them under his Interior logo.

Rodriguez' position was no one promoted his material, no one licensed it, he never received a royalty statement, and his songs were out of print. Rodriguez concluded that two years after the Gomba Publishing deal, he had a contract that was virtually servitude He reasoned that signing with Avant's Interior Music was within his legal rights. In a press release, Interior Music said that Rodriguez concealed his contract with Balk's Gomba Music. Rodriguez denied the allegation. The courts will decide the issue.

BALK'S INITIAL THOUGHTS ON RODRIGUEZ
AND A TRIAL 45 THAT FAILED

Balk wasn't sure what to make of the young singer-songwriter. He had an independent mind. He had firm ideas about how his songs should be recorded. He wasn't malleable like other artists. Rodriguez was his own man. This bothered Balk. Rodriguez talked in the studio about his sound, and how he hoped to achieve it. Balk had never worked with an artist who demanded that his songs, his sound and his musical direction follow a script. Harry wondered: Who in the hell is this kid? Rodriguez wasn't typical of artists that Balk recorded. Balk loved Rodriguez' songwriting. He liked his lilting vocals. But Harry was concerned that Rodriguez was too counterculture. He was also too independent minded. The music business had parameters that Rodriguez refused to meet.

He wasn't convinced that the young man would fit into the teen dance and disc jockey interviews dominating the rock marketplace. Harry met with his partner, Irving Micahnik. He praised the kid's talent. He had the looks. He had the songwriting. He had the voice. However, the kid was too damned smart. He asked too many questions. Irv said he would sell the records despite Sixto Rodriguez. Harry decided to release a 45 on his Impact label. If it went well, he would get the kid a contract with a larger label.

The 1967 single "I'll Slip Away" backed with "You Got To Admit It" (Impact 1031) was released with little fanfare. It was a muddled production with the music drowning out Rodriguez' fragile vocals. That single set the stage for Rodriguez to sign with Clarence Avant's Sussex label.

MIKE THEODORE REFLECTS ON RODRIGUEZ:
THE BALK CONNECTION

In **Searching For Sugar Man**, Mike Theodore remarks that everything was in place to make Sixto Rodriguez a major recording star. He recorded and worked with the legendary Detroit producer, Harry Balk, and then the Sugar Man signed a contract with Clarence Avant's Sussex label. As Theodore observed, the planets weren't aligned to make Rodriguez a star. Why didn't Rodriguez break out? That is a question that remains unanswered. He did become an international star in 2012. Why the wait? The answer lies in Harry Balk's career, as well as the strange trajectory of the music business.

By examining Harry Balk's career, his thinking, his recording techniques and his life, it is apparent why Rodriguez had to wait forty years for stardom. It is a look into the vagaries and realities of the music business. Balk's journey to being a legendary producer began when he discovered the Detroit sound.

HARRY BALK: DISCOVERING THE DETROIT SOUND

Balk's first step into the music business was to find a singer to manage. It didn't take long for Harry to discover Little Willie John. He found him at a Detroit talent contest in one of the movie emporiums Harry owned. As his movie theater chain fell into decline in the mid 1950s, Balk entered the music business.

At this stage in his career, Balk knew little, if anything, about producing records. He watched King Record producer Henry Glover with great interest. "I didn't know the first thing about cutting a session...I couldn't read music, but I had ideas for songs," Balk recalled. He became one of the legendary rock music producers of the 1960s.

Balk's strength was in identifying hit records. When Del Shannon recorded "Runaway," Balk sped up the master tape to make it a faster song. It was a number one hit. When the Shades of Blue hit in the Detroit area, it was Balk who took them national. He booked them on the Dick Clark Show and a major tour. It didn't matter if he was producing or managing, Balk had the magic touch. He was the heart and soul of the white Detroit sound.

When Balk and his larger than life partner, Irving Micahnik, signed Del Shannon to Embee Production's, they found gold. As they managed Shannon's early career, Balk was the organizational genius behind Embee. His experience helped Del Shannon reach national stardom. Irving was the moneyman, and this contributed to Balk's constant need for funds. Irv never met a racehorse that he didn't like to place a bet on.

Matt Lucas: "Some people called Micahnik the bag man. Not me. I had respect for Irv." There was a twinkle in Lucas' eye.

The disc jockey's, the club owners, the record labels and the dance promoters found Michanik unreliable. He was not always on the job. Irving gambled, he was the ultimate womanizer, and he spent more time than necessary promoting Bobbi Smith and the Dreamgirls. Irving relocated to New York after one of Embee's female singers turned up pregnant. Things were better for Harry after that took place. Micahnik paid very little attention to business. When he did work, he was a great promoter. He was also not missed on the Detroit record scene.

BALK'S ROAD TO FAME AND FORTUNE
WITH LITTLE WILLIE JOHN

When Balk's musical career began in the teeming nightclubs, after hour's spots and small theaters, which graced Detroit in the 1950s, he realized that there was big money in the music scene. The tall, distinguished, nattily dressed, handsome, cigar smoking Balk was seen eyeing the amateur acts, talking to the new musical groups and drinking with the fledgling entertainers. The Detroit nightlife was filled with aspiring singers, comedy performers and would be actors. Balk decided to take advantage of the talent. He organized a series of amateur shows in his movie theaters.

He also haunted the local music clubs. The Flame Bar was a favorite hangout. Balk had his own table at the Flame Bar. It didn't take long for him to realize that he witnessed amateur acts as good as the professionals.

Soon Balk's small movie theaters were presenting amateurs who had big time careers in their future. These acts included Little Willie John and the Four Tops. After signing Little Willie John, he negotiated a contract for the diminutive singer with King Records. They began a long musical association. Little Willie John's hits included "Fever," "All Around The World," "Sleep" and "Talk To Me." "Little Willie John was simply too hard to handle," Balk remembered. "I was always getting him out of jail or out of some jam." Although Little Willie John tested Balk's patience, there was much for Harry to learn in the raucous world of rhythm and blues music.

In 1955-1956, Balk watched as small independent labels, like King, produced a highly profitable product. The labels usually paid the artist next to nothing. Syd Nathan, King's founder, often paid the big hit acts with a Cadillac. He did this with James Brown writing off the Cadillac as a business expense, while refusing to pay Brown his royalties. Despite the rumors about Balk not paying some of his acts, the truth is that he negotiated a fair contract and paid an adequate royalty. The small independent labels and managers had a difficult time surviving in the 1950s. Harry Balk was determined not to be a casualty in the rock and roll marketplace. His contracts were tough, but fair, and the artist could count on good management and careful supervision.

Harry Balk: "The number of records that didn't make money doesn't interest anyone. We paid those artists that had hits. Those who didn't we ate the costs."

The earliest sign of Balk's expertise came when Little Willie John refused to record "Fever." He called it "a cracker song." Harry pointed out that mainstream, pop ballads were hits and Little Willie John would be playing the Copacabana if he cut it. Little Willie was in the studio the next night.

Balk observed Henry Glover diligently when he produced Little Willie John's King hits. Syd Nathan referred to Balk as: "tough, but honest, by the standards of the 1950s. I never wanted to cross Harry." Henry Glover preferred to have Balk in the studio when the diminutive and tempestuous Little Willie John recorded. Little Willie John was a drunken prankster. Only Balk could control him.

There was a place where Harry Balk could test his product. It was at Joe's Records on Hastings Street It was in the black Detroit ghetto, where Balk cut demos for Little Willie John. The irony is that Rodriguez knew of and probably frequented this record shop.

The 12ᵗʰ and Philadelphia location that housed Joe's Record Shop was a gathering spot for performers and would be producers. Joe Von Battle operated a record store where the fledgling musicians, producers and songwriters met to talk. He also had two local record labels, J. V. B. Records and Battle, which he founded in 1948. You learned from Joe, as he recorded John Lee Hooker, the Rev. C. L. Franklin with his daughter Aretha, Memphis Slim, Willie Dixon and Mongo Santamaria among others. He continued to release records until 1967. It was here that Harry Balk received his musical education. At Joe's Record Shop, Harry met Berry Gordy Jr. who he hired to play piano on some early demos. They talked about the music business for years. They became good friends. In time, Balk went to work for Motown. Their friendship was beneficial to both men as Balk learned about African American music and Gordy was taught lessons about local white performers.

AN EARLY JOHN LEE HOOKER 45 FROM JOE'S RECORD SHOP

Finally, in 1957, Balk released Little Willie John from his contract with two years remaining. "I decided that I was never going to fly to another small Southern town to bail Little Willie John out of jail," Balk remembered. "I just cut him loose and looked for a new place in show business."

Among black entertainers and management types, Balk's legendary reputation prompted Berry Gordy Jr to remark: "Balk was one of the few white guys in Detroit who knew something about black music." Balk had an eye for the developing teen-age market. He realized that white acts sold more records, played in better venues and made more money than their black counterparts. He began to pay close attention to the teen market. He searched for a white group or a young singer with the Fabian, Frankie Avalon or Bobby Rydell look. Harry found that singer in Del Shannon.

"It was song writing and publishing that brought in the money," Balk recalled. "I always took care of business." When Harry formed Vicki Music Publishing, named after his daughter, he registered it with BMI. The Vicki Music imprint earned Balk a sizable income. It was common practice for managers to place their name on songs and Balk was no exception. He used the name Tom King when he wanted to own a piece of a song. Micahnik used Ira Mack. Together they copyrighted most of Johnny and the Hurricanes' songs, as well as many other artists. To find new talent and record it, Harry and Irv formed Embee Productions. Harry Balk: "Irv and I founded Embee productions because no one would distribute Twirl Records, so we became both the record company and the distributor."

Balk had an uncanny perception listening to new songs, auditioning groups and singers. Like most record executives, Harry spent hundreds of hours producing demo 45s and leasing them to major labels. His ear for talent led him to sign Don and Juan, as well as the mega-hit instrumental act Johnny and the Hurricanes. These acts helped to reinforce his management skills and business knowledge.

The initial foray into rock and roll took place when Balk signed a local Detroit band, the Royaltones. The group hit the **Billboard** Top Forty in 1958 with "Poor Boy."

Other Detroit acts that Balk brought into his management company were Jamie Coe and the Gigolos, Mickey Denton and Johnny Gibson who had minor hits with "Beachcomber" and "Midnight."

Harry Balk: "I realized early in my career, that I had to stay ahead of the crowd and look for an original sound. I went down the dumper if I tried to copy someone else."

Not only were Harry's words apocryphal, he quickly discovered the instrumental group with a unique and commercial sound, Johnny and the Hurricanes. The road that Johnny and the Hurricanes took to Harry Balk was a long and involved one.

Johnny Paris was a young musician in Toledo, Ohio who organized the Orbits. After playing for high school dances, Paris and the Orbits recorded with local rockabilly legend Mack Vickery. The recordings with Vickery were completed in a small Detroit studio, and after he returned to Toledo; Johnny Paris decided to move the band to Detroit. He loved the Motor City.

In 1959, Detroit was a hotbed of musical talent, and Paris's Orbits had a unique instrumental sound. When Fred Kelly and the Parliaments signed a recording contract with Balk and Micahnik's Talent Artists, Inc., Paris's Orbits were hired as the back up band. After Balk listened to the Parliaments, he fired them and signed Johnny Paris and the Orbits. He quickly changed their name.

Johnny and the Hurricanes' first hit in June 1959, "Crossfire" quickly rose to number 23 on **Billboard**. It remained there for fourteen weeks. Johnny Paris was impressed with Balk's ability to take their honking saxophone-organ sound onto the national charts. "I had a plan with Johnny and the Hurricanes," Balk remembered. "I knew Johnny's sound was unique and hence commercial." From 1959 to 1961, this commercial path was a successful one, as Johnny and the Hurricanes charted nine songs on the Billboard Hot 100.

"I had a new partner, Irving Micahnik," Balk recalled. Micahnik was a mixed blessing. Not only was Micahnik unreliable, when royalties were paid it was due to Balk. Irving allegedly didn't pay anyone. Every person interviewed for this book labeled Micahnik one of the unsavory characters in the music industry. But Irving did have the ability to sell the product. He was a public relations genius. That is when he wasn't drinking, gambling or womanizing. Which wasn't often.

After recording "Crossfire," Balk and Micahnik took the demo to New York to shop it to the major labels. Mitch Miller, at Columbia Records, listened and declined. None of the other majors were interested. "They thought Johnny and the Hurricanes music was kids stuff," Balk recalled. But Harry knew better, because he watched the reaction to the Hurricanes at local Detroit sock hops. As Irv and Harry drove their old Chevrolet from New York back to Detroit they were frustrated.

"How much does it cost to put out a record?" Harry asked Irv.

"I don't know, but it can't be that much," Irv replied.

When they returned home Harry went to a local one stop record distributor, Irv Snider. Over a long lunch, Balk talked about Johnny and the Hurricanes' commercial potential. Snider was interested. He pointed out to Harry that for $250 to $300 a thousand records could be pressed and a local hit was possible. Balk founded Twirl Records releasing "Crossfire." The record hit the charts in and around Detroit, and then it received national airplay. Johnny and the Hurricanes were so hot that every major label wanted to lease the master. Balk was a careful businessman. He wanted to deal with someone he could trust.

Balk contacted his old friend Morty Craft at Seven Arts Craft who was President of Warwick. A deal was cut and Johnny and the Hurricanes' "Crossfire" was released nationally reaching the Top 40. There were three other Warwick releases, which charted in the Top 40. These tunes included "Red River Rock" at number 5, "Beatnik Fly" at number 15 and "Reveille Rock" at number 25 on the **Billboard** Hot 100.

Once Johnny and the Hurricanes hit the charts, Balk recorded their material at New York's Bell Studio. At this state of the art recording facility, Balk hired the best session musicians. There were problems finding new material. Harry Balk's expertise rescued Johnny and the Hurricanes' career.

One night while they were in Bell Studio, Johnny and the Hurricanes were having trouble cutting "Red River Rock." Harry found a hit by accident. "We took a break," Harry continued. "Then the kid on the organ made a crazy sound. That's it." What Balk recalled was the special organ sound that made "Red River Rock" a popular record. Harry had a constant ear for hit records.

Another example of Balk's nose for a hit occurred when Johnny Paris went to the bathroom one day during a recording session, wet his sax reed and then to clean it, Johnny blew through it. Harry, who was passing by the bathroom, hollered: "Stop that's a hit sound." Johnny Paris thought Balk had lost his mind. But the strange sound that came from Paris's wet reed turned into the hit "Honkin' Goose." Johnny and the Hurricanes were an important part of Balk's early success. He preferred black music, but the white acts easily crossed over into the mainstream. The profits were Harry's mantra. Unfortunately, much of it went to cover Irving Micahnik's gambling debts.

While he was managing and producing Johnny and the Hurricanes, Balk met two housepainters. One day a talent agent, Peter Paul, brought Roland Trone and Claude Johnson, who were using the professional name Don and Juan, to see Balk. After listening to their demo of "What's Your Name," Balk quickly signed Don and Juan to a recording contract.

One of Balk's indicators of an artist's or group's talent was their past ability to sell records and perform in concert. Don and Juan hung around the fringes of the music business for a decade before Balk brought them into the studio. Claude "Juan" Johnson was a member of the Genies who had a minor doo wop hit in 1959 "Who's That Knockin." Then Roland Trone and Claude Johnson became housepainters. They were discovered when a record agent heard them singing while they were painting a building frequented by music people. This is what led them to cut their demo "What's Your Name."

But Balk wanted to recut "What's Your Name." His ear for a hit record prompted him to inform Don and Juan that production changes were needed. They drove to New York to Bell Studios where they cut "What's Your Name" backed with "Chicken Necks" (Big Top 3106).

How did Balk's production genius alter "What's Your Name?" It was simple. Harry said: "You blend pop and doo-wop." He changed the arrangement and used a softer instrumental background. The smooth ballad style made it the duo's only hit. In February 1962, it rose to number 7 on the **Billboard** Top 40. Don and Juan's hit came at the time that Balk was working with Del Shannon, and it demonstrates his diverse hit making abilities. Balk concentrated on Shannon's career to keep the fiscal ship afloat.

THE TOXIC PARTNERSHIP WITH IRVING MICAHNIK ENDS

The partnership with Irving Micahnik was a stormy one. When it ended, Balk was ecstatic. Not surprisingly, Irving owed Harry money. Irving quickly relocated to New York. It took Harry some time to track him down. But Micahnik rebounded in the music business.

Micahnik went on to manage Chubby Checker. It was the second or, as Irving told Harry, "the budget phase" of Checker's career. Micahnik brought the Twist King back with commercials, re-recordings of his old hits and concerts on the oldies circuit. Irving was once again in the money. Chubby Checker didn't see much of the money. After Balk left the partnership, he didn't think much about Micahnik. Then he found out that his old partner was collecting royalties that he should be sharing. Balk took legal action.

Micahnik was typical of the 1960s shady rock and roll promoter. When Chubby Checker complained about a lack of royalties, Irving told him to increase his concert fees. Balk also lost a lot of money due to Micahnik's poor business decisions. Finally, a frustrated Harry sent Irving a bill for $20,000.

Finally, Harry tracked Irv down as Micahnik agreed to pay Balk the past royalties. They made an appointment to meet the next day. When Harry arrived at Irv's New York apartment, his wife was crying. Micahnik died a few hours after agreeing to pay Harry. It was a fitting way for Irv to go, as he avoided paying most people during his lifetime.

It was September 1978 when Micahnik passed away in New York leaving behind a host of bad debts. It was Micahnik who wrote the contracts that give him and Harry 6.5% of the royalties leaving 1.5% for the artist. Johnny Paris fought this contract for years and won some concessions prior to his untimely death in May 2006.

DEL SHANNON IS THE MONEY FORCE

"Del Shannon was the first or second artist we signed after Johnny and the Hurricanes," Balk remembered. "We recorded Del right away without Max Crook. It didn't work out. Then I brought in Crook and the musitron." It was after the October 1961 session that Balk realized that Crook's eerie musitron sound was an integral part of Shannon's sound. The result was a number one hit record "Runaway."

When he recalled the background to "Runaway," Balk had a sly smile on his face. "I thought that Del was a great songwriter. We took one of his tunes 'Mr. Lonely,' and gave it to Johnny and the Hurricanes. They did a good job with it."

"Runaway" was an immediate chart buster. The musicians in the Bell Studio realized that it was a potential number one hit. Al Caiola offered Shannon and Balk $15,000 for a piece of the songwriting. He also made an offer to Balk to take over Shannon's management. Harry responded: "I don't need any partners, thank you." As Balk recorded Del Shannon, he realized that his newfound star often sounded uneven. "He used to sing songs to me he had written while on the road or in his hotel room. These new songs would sound great," Harry continued. "Then the same songs would sound flat in the studio. Del was a guy who was up emotionally or was down, never in the middle." Shannon's early songs benefitted from Balk's careful production.

After Del cut the final version of "Runaway," Balk, unbeknownst to Shannon, altered the speed of the master tape. "When I played it for Del, he cried and said it didn't sound like him," Harry recalled. "Hell, I said, no one knows what you sound like." Then Balk sent out promotional copies of "Runaway." Before the song was released there were large orders from New York distributors. "At one point," Balk recalled, 'Runaway' was selling 80,000 copies a day." Not even Shannon could believe his good fortune. He had Balk to thank.

When "Runaway" appeared on the Billboard Top 40 on March 27, 1961, Del was still working for Peter Vice at a carpet store in Battle Creek, Michigan. He also appeared four nights a week at the Hi Lo Club. The story of how Shannon was able to record "Runaway" and change his name from Charles Westover to Charlie Johnson to Del Shannon tells us a great deal about rock and roll music. It also tells us about Balk's studio and promotional genius.

On July 29, 1961, Del Shannon appeared on the cover of **Cash Box**. The story predicted a bright future for Shannon. Everyone in Detroit realized that Harry Balk was the reason for Shannon's stardom. Balk concentrated upon Del Shannon and soon "Hats Off To Larry," "Little Town Flirt," "So Long Baby" and "Hey! Little Girl" were 1961 Top 40 hits.

THE MYTH OF THE EARLY 1960s BOBBY BOYS

The myth that the early 1960s was a time of non-talented singers, poor production and a rehashing of old pop tunes is exploded by the Del Shannon story. The Frankie Avalon's, the Bobby Rydell's and the Fabian's did have stage presence. They couldn't sing very well. That didn't matter to Balk, he could sell any good-looking young kid, and he could produce a great sounding record. Talent! Balk laughed. He would handle that parameter.

When Balk looks back upon the early 1960s, he has fond memories. "I always thought Del was a better songwriter than singer," Harry continued. "Another thing about Del is that he always loved country and western music."

The relationship between Balk and Shannon was a rocky one. Del signed a contract with a small royalty. That decision bothered him. He continually asked Balk to renegotiate the deal. Harry said no. They reached an impasse that eventually led to a nasty and prolonged lawsuit.

Harry Balk: "The stories about me not being fair with Del or not paying him are bullshit. Del signed the contract. I told him live up to it. Be a man."

Despite their differences, Harry Balk was an integral part of Shannon's commercial success. From "Runaway" through the mid-1960s, when Balk and Shannon parted company, they had numerous hits. Del never again had this level of success. Their differences were over royalties. They were on the same page creatively. Del said that his royalties were below the industry standard.

Harry Balk: "I never forced Del Shannon to sign a contract. He did it. He regretted it. In later years, he told me that he was sorry that we parted company. That's the music business."

When Del Shannon sued Balk, the case took on a life of its own. In l963, Shannon sued Embee Productions for back royalties. At the time Del's royalty was two per cent. The case went through the court system for almost a decade. Shannon formed his own record label, Berlee, and then he went on to record for Amy before moving to a series of major labels. The music business is a cutthroat jungle and the copyright questions are constant ones. The court's dealt with so many of these cases that eventually federal laws were passed attempting to straight out the copyright problems.

HARRY BALK'S CAREER AFTER DEL SHANNON: THE SOUL YEARS AND SHADES OF BLUE

Harry Balk continued to be a mover in the music business. In 1966, while hanging out with soul singer Edwin Starr, whose hit "Agent Double O-Soul" had established him as a major soul act; Balk heard a dynamite new Detroit musical act. Starr took Balk to see the Shades of Blue in a local club. He couldn't believe their talent. Harry told Starr that they were a hit group waiting to happen.

Harry Balk: "The Shades of Blue had a gospel sound that made them hit bound. They also had the look, the dress and the stage mannerisms. I worked on nursing them from one big hit to a number of chart songs."

This was a shrewd judgment, as Balk nurtured the group with a drop dead good looking female vocalist, Linda Allen, and a songwriter, Edwin Starr, to produce a bevy of hits. John Rhys was brought in to clean up their vocal styling and create hit oriented arrangements. Harry hired a choreographer and the concerts featured a slick dance style, as the group combined a gospel-soul sound with a doo-wop vocal style. In the U. K. the group was on Sue Records, and the English believed that they were a black act.

The original Detroit based group consisted of three men and a female vocalist. They were photogenic, they had extensive experience performing in Detroit clubs, and they wrote their songs. It was the perfect combination. They had performed together since the ninth grade and Linda Allen as the second tenor gave them a unique sound.

John Rhys began working with them long before they cut a demo or a hit record. He was instrumental in smoothing out their sound. In January 1966, Rhys spent an inordinate amount of time in Ed Wingate's Golden World Studio remixing their future hit.

They made a demo of a gospel tune, "Oh How Happy," and Balk's Impact records released it in May 1966. Harry Balk was in charge of the publicity, and he did his job creating a buzz for their first release. "Oh How Happy" was featured on Detroit radio stations WKNR and WXYZ and in Canada on Ontario's CKLW. The Canadian station was beamed into Detroit, and it was the top rated Motor City rock and roll outlet. The result was huge sales and another feather in Balk's creative cap.

The song rose to number 12 on the **Billboard** Top 40. Although most major record labels turned down the Shades of Blue, Balk had a hit on his Impact label. His reputation as a talent scout, producer and manager was a strong one. Eventually, Balk's talent brought him a major position as a talent coordinator with Detroit's most prestigious black label, Motown.

In the late 1960s, he went to work for Motown. Berry Gordy, Jr hired Balk as a Vice President. For two years, he advised Gordy and then one day in early 1971 he heard a marvelous demo by Marvin Gaye, "What's Going On." Gordy was in Europe. The other producers at Motown didn't like it. Then at a board meeting, Balk suggested that they press extra copies of the Gaye song. He was ignored. Then Balk wrote his prediction on the blackboard in Motown's office. It was going to be number one and introduce Motown's jazz-soul sound. Most Motown producers laughed. Harry had the last laugh, as it became Gaye's biggest selling cross over hit. Balk said: "Gaye has introduced a new type of soul music, I embraced it."

When Gaye's "What's Going On" hit the Billboard Top 40 in March 1971 the songs blended a jazz blues sound into soul music. "It had that jazz feel that I just love," Balk remembered. So did the general public as Gaye took Motown into a new commercial direction. "I worked at Motown for a few years, in the late 60s and early 70s," Balk recalled. "One of my jobs was to develop white acts." This never sat well with Balk. He could produce any type of music.

While the promotional activity for Gaye's "What's Going On" was in full swing, Balk told the Motown pressing plant to print 250,000 45s. They reported that Mr. Gordy wanted 20,000. Harry responded: "To hell with Berry, get me 250,000 now." Gordy was in Europe on business. When the Motown founder returned, he fired Balk. Harry had the last laugh. The Gaye hit went platinum. Gordy immediately rehired Balk.

Balk discovered Motown's biggest white act, Rare Earth. They were still known as the Sunliners when Balk and Mike Theodore began working with them. In 1969, Harry listened to a demo from the Sunliners. He knew that he had another hit group. What Balk had most other Motown producers lacked was a knowledge of the club circuit. Rare Earth performed around Detroit in other incarnations in the top clubs. They were already a seasoned, veteran band with good knowledge of the industry.

When Rare Earth arrived for an interview, Balk was impressed. In person they were articulate, knowledgeable about the music industry, and they had a hunger for commercial success. In concert, the band had a soul quality, as well as a strong stage presence.

After interviewing the group, Balk talked at length with three of the founding members Gil Bridges, John Persh and Pete Rivera. He realized that as the Sunliners they were not only one of Detroit's top club bands, but they understood the industry. Balk wondered could they make the transition to headlining rock shows? He listened carefully to their demos. They had brilliant covers of black music. They had a stage presence, and they were young, good-looking guys. Harry asked Mike Theodore to rename the group. There was a Texas group the Sunliners. "I looked at the periodic chemistry elements chart and we renamed them Rare Earth," Theodore said.

When the Sunliners became Rare Earth in 1968 they signed with Verve for the **Dream/Answers** album. Then Balk helped secure a deal with Motown and Berry Gordy founded a new label, Rare Earth, to release their gold records. Balk and the band were ready for mega stardom in 1970-1971, when they had six **Billboard** Hot 100 hits. Rodriguez was lost in the shuffle.

After Rare Earth was signed to Motown, their second album **Get Ready** (Rare Earth RS 507) was released to platinum sales. Harry's magic hand was behind the hit "Get Ready," which became the college drinking song of the early 1970s. Smokey Robinson's "Get Ready" was taken into a new and energetic musical direction. The Rolling Stones listened to Rare Earth and a guitar riff borrowed from Rare Earth was the foundation point for the Stones' "Bitch," which appeared on their 1971 **Sticky Fingers** LP.

John Small, a disc jockey at WKNR-FM in Detroit, wrote the liner notes to Rare Earth's second LP predicting stardom. The single, "Get Ready," rose to number 4 on the Billboard Top 40 and led to five other hits. Harry Balk's eye for talent continued with other artists.

In September 1970, R. Dean Taylor, a white singer from Toronto, Canada, showed up at Motown with a demo he believed was a hit.

Harry Balk: "Every kid who showed up thought he had a hit. This guy was different, he wrote, recorded and produced. He also had the good looks. I knew I had a one hit artist."

Taylor was a thirty one year old songwriter who had never recorded with commercial success. In 1960, he made a record for the Parry label that went nowhere. He continued to release 45s without success. When Taylor co-wrote the Supremes "Love Child" in 1968, he came to the attention of Motown's production staff.

Balk listened to Taylor's demo of "Indiana Wants Me." He went to Berry Gordy, Jr., predicting it would be a hit. Gordy wasn't sure. He trusted Balk's instincts. When Taylor's "Indiana Wants Me" was released it went to number 5 in September 1970 on the Billboard Top 40. "R. Dean Taylor was a lot like Del Shannon," Harry Balk recalled, "but he didn't have the staying power of Shannon."

HARRY BALK AND SIXTO RODRIGUEZ: THE 1966 CONTRACT AND ITS AFTERMATH

On the morning of July 25, 1966 Sixto Rodriguez got up at eight in the morning. The Sugar Man was not a morning person. This was a special morning. He had a meeting later that morning with producer Harry Balk at his 1711 Third Avenue office. Sixto looked around his humble living space at 558 W. Grand Avenue. He was about to make some money writing songs. The living conditions would improve.

As was the case with Rodriguez, he dressed in a stylish suit, a French cut shirt, an elegant tie and specialty boots. The cool sunglasses finished off the Sugar Man's stylized persona. He had an elegant air. He was ready for Rainy M. Moore to pick him up.

As Moore drove Rodriguez downtown, she talked at length about why his music was commercial. She told the Sugar Man that Balk had one thing and only one thing in mind and that was profit. Rodriguez listened. It didn't sound like a promising interview.

When he arrived, he found Harry sitting behind his desk smoking a cigar. There was no sign of a secretary. There was no phone. There were a lot of papers on Balk's desk. Harry smiled. The phone rang in the hallway. Harry answered it. He had a long conversation. Rodriguez sat uncomfortably on a chair. Harry walked back in the room.

Harry Balk: "See that phone in the hallway kid. It is good business not to have to pay a phone bill. Keep that in mind. Take care of your money. In this business they will steal from you." Harry lit another cigar.

He went into his desk drawer and took out a five-year contract. It commenced that day, July 25, 1966 and ended the same day in 1971. The advance was one dollar. Harry pulled out a dollar bill. He smiled handing it to Rodriguez.

It was a standard industry contact. It paid four cents for sales of domestic copies and five cents for foreign sales. Balk's Gomba Productions received fifty per cent of all songwriting and publishing royalties, as well as licensing rights. The contract also contained a provision granting Balk's Gomba Music the right to all future songs, even the co-written ones, for the duration of the contract. Perhaps the most curious aspect of the agreement is that Gomba Music had the right to extend the contract for a year at a time. It was like perpetual servitude.

In May 2014, Harry Balk sued Clarence Avant alleging that the former Sussex chief "concocted a scheme to fraudulently conceal the writings and compositions by Sixto Rodriguez." The legal document named a fictional brother, Jesus Rodriguez, as the purported vehicle for copyrighting his songs. Avant discovered there was no brother named Jesus. There was a brother, Jesse, but the position that Avant's attorneys took was that Rodriguez practiced fraud. This is a puzzling indictment as Rodriguez was simply attempting to take his music into the commercial marketplace. Everyone agrees that royalties were not paid. No one knows where the money went. The courts will decide the issues.

Clarence Avant's third party complaint filed in Los Angeles was served to Rodriguez at the time he was playing a sold out concert in Los Angeles' Greek Theater. It was a strange time. The Sugar Man had sold out shows, he has a steady source of income and now he was in the middle of a legal action from two industry heavyweights, who allegedly had not paid royalties. It didn't make sense.

The legal maneuvers were already underway when Rodriguez' attorney claimed rescission. This is a legal term to demand separation from management for non-performance. In other words, Rodriguez' attorney abrogated the deal because his career was not advanced by Harry Balk. Gomba had a stranglehold on Rodriguez' songwriting, his lawyer alleged. That was, according to Rodriguez' attorney, "perpetual servitude."

The craziest part of the various legal actions is Avant pointing the finger at Rodriguez alleging fraud. Rodriguez' attorney countered that he had delivered his songs free of third party rights.

Avant's lawyers quoted a provision in the original contract that included a provision for Rodriguez to cooperate in any future litigation. There was also a provision to withhold royalties in the event of third part concerns. That stipulation was aimed at preventing Rodriguez from signing binding contracts with other labels. He had such an agreement with Balk. That contract didn't expire until July 1971.

There is an irony to Avant suing Rodriguez. Avant lives on Maytor Place in Beverly Hills, California in a 4017 square foot home that has three bedrooms and four baths. It is valued at just over seven million dollars. Rodriguez lives on Avery Street in Detroit in a two story four bedroom, one bath home worth in excess of fifty thousand dollars. Everyone interviewed pointed out that Avant didn't need the Sugar Man's money.

The pundits on the street claim that Avant is angry over his interview in **Searching For Sugar Man**. According to close friends, he loves Rodriguez. He also quietly funded Rodriguez' comeback album with producer Mike Theodore in 1997-1998. That contract ended when Craig Bartholomew-Strydom located Rodriguez and then Stephen "Sugar" Segerman came into the picture with a series of lucrative South African concerts. Because of Avant's support for Rodriguez' third album, many observers believed that Avant acted to clarify the royalty and contract controversy. He may be guilty of arrogance but not of avoiding royalties.

The lawsuit is not about the Sugar Man. It is a response to Harry Balk's suit. Every indication is that Avant paid Rodriguez when he received royalties.

Some conspiracy theorists suggest that Avant's lawsuit is driven by his desire to get even with the filmmaker for the **Searching For Sugar Man** interview. This is nonsense. Before the documentary was released, Sony screened it for Avant. They were willing to edit out the interview. He said put it in. He had done nothing wrong. Avant is a businessman. The lawsuit was about business. Revenge was never a motive.

Harry Balk saw no future in Rodriguez as a performing and recording artist. He did envision a bright career as a songwriter. The problem is that Harry moved on to Motown. His work with Berry Gordy Jr. and a bevy of Motown artists turned his attention from Rodriguez. The Sugar Man was lost in the mix.

IN CONCERT IN SEATTLE

chapter

SIX

WHO IS STEPHEN "SUGAR" SEGERMAN?

**"I READ A QUOTE THIS MORNING, WHICH SAID SOME-
THING LIKE: 'SOMEHOW, EVEN IF YOU'RE ON YOUR OWN,
IF YOU HAVE MUSIC, YOU'RE NEVER ALONE." STEPHEN
"SUGAR" SEGERMAN**

Stephen "Sugar" Segerman is a South African jeweler turned record storeowner. He co-owns Mabu Vinyl. Jacques Vosloo opened the
shop in 2001. Then Segerman came on as a partner. Mabu Vinyl is the
best record store in Cape Town, if not in South Africa. This eclectic shop
maintains the most comprehensive Internet site on Sixto Rodriguez
while presenting museum quality rock and roll. The store is a shrine
to all forms of rock music, vinyl, eight tracks, CDs and 45s. If they don't
have it, they will get it for you.

SUGAR'S UNIQUE BACKGROUND:
THE ROAD TO RODRIGUEZ BEGINS

Segerman was born in Johannesburg then moved on to settle in Oranjezicht, which is a tony Cape Town suburb. He lives with his wife, Ronit, their children, a dog, two cats and the "blue trommel basement." The later reference is to his vast and eclectic collection of records, tapes, CDs, books and rock paraphernalia that occupies a special place in Segerman's home.

Segerman is exceedingly normal and conventional. His children are grown. Natalia, now in her late twenties, works with her boyfriend sculptor, Danny Popper. She is a recognized artist. Raphael is part of a band known as the John Wizards. The remaining sibling, Daniell, is studying psychology. Now that the children have busy lives, Sugar is at home tending to the "blue trommel" collection when he is not stocking Mabu Vinyl. His vinyl collection is the stuff of legend among South Africans.

Segerman's parents provided a nurturing environment. His mother, Joyce, a teacher, emphasized reading and his father, a jeweler, also operated a bookstore. "As a child, I would go into the shop and look at all the books and records." A childhood reading books, listening to the radio and developing a record collection defined young Segerman. He started collecting early, and he has never stopped. When he wants something, he finds it. That explains the success in finding Sixto Rodriguez.

"What is most important to me is that I have a happy marriage and a happy home," Segerman told Sue Segar. That sums it up. Sugar is much like Rodriguez. He is humble, ethical, happy and hard working. He wonders what all the fuss is about over **Searching For Sugar Man**.

UNDERSTANDING STEPHEN "SUGAR" SEGERMAN

Ironically, it is from the vast CD, book, vinyl and memorabilia museum that is his collection that the search for Rodriguez began and concluded. To understand Stephen "Sugar" Segerman's seminal role in the Rodriguez story, it is necessary to mix South African history into Sugar's life. He grew up at a time when apartheid was the rule, and, as he matured, there was a gradual change in the national consciousness. South Africa became more liberal, democratic and slowly opposed to apartheid, which didn't end until 1994.

The influence of Rodriguez' music, as Segerman points out in a number of interviews, impacted South African attitudes. He was an icon to the native population, as well as to the white settlers. Rodriguez' music began influencing South Africa in the early 1970s. Songs like "The Establishment Blues" became a prominent force upon developing democratic attitudes. But had it not been for the obsessive-compulsive record collectors, like Segerman, Craig Bartholomew-Strydom, Andy Harrod and Brian Currin, the Sugar Man might have languished in obscurity.

In a South African interview, Segerman pointed out that the American trailer for **Searching For Sugar Man** did him a disservice by suggesting that the Sugar Man was not political. He was aware of the early South African protests, and the role of artists like Miriam Makeba and Hugh Masekela in publicizing the oppressive apartheid atmosphere. As Segerman remarked in the documentary, a person went to jail for criticizing the government.

INSIDE THE MIND OF THE RECORD COLLECTOR

When **Searching For Sugar Man** won an Oscar at the 85th Academy Award's, everyone praised Malik Bendjelloul and Sixto Rodriguez. This was fitting. There was a silent hero. He was in a tuxedo smiling at the Oscar ceremony. He was low key. He simply enjoyed the privilege of being in Los Angeles and attending the Academy Award ceremony. His name was Stephen "Sugar" Segerman.

The smiling, handsome man from Cape Town, South Africa is modest and self-effacing. He should have talked about himself and his accomplishments. He didn't. He appeared more interested in going through the vinyl at Amoeba Records on Sunset Boulevard than he did hanging out with the celebrities. Stephen "Sugar" Segerman is first and foremost important as a record collector. Segerman would take issue with this description. He is also a businessman, a writer and a cultural historian. Those traits would not have mattered had he not been a serious record collector.

When Segerman is interviewed, he describes Mabu Vinyl as a museum. There is almost a look of hurt on his face when he talks of selling his stock. He describes himself as a serious collector. There is an obsessive-compulsive drive to find certain records, key performers and information on obscure subjects. It is this fanatical drive to find new information that led to the Sixto Rodriguez story. Segerman was so persuasive that he single handedly convinced Malik Bendjelloul to begin and finish **Searching For Sugar Man**.

There is a garage/pop tone to Segerman's collection with a paean to punk. He lights up when he reads the liner notes to an album. The photographs and sales history also intrigues him. The strange and fascinating subculture of the record collector stretched to Craig Bartholomew-Strydom, Andy Harrod and Brian Currin, who became partners in the fanatical Rodriguez search.

The serious record collector is an eclectic one. In Segerman's case, he became a partner in Mabu Vinyl to increase his own collection, while providing people in Cape Town a serious record shop. "I wanted a shop that you could just load up with stuff," Segerman commented. There is more to Mabu Vinyl than just the shop. The neighborhood is filled with artists, writers and musicians. It is a cultural mecca for those in and around Cape Town.

As Segerman reflects on his collection, he acts as though he has reduced it. To told the **Union Kloof**: "I've still got a private collection of around 5000 CDs, 4000 cassettes, and 3000 records and then I've got the 15,000 songs that I've collected on iTunes since I started using it five years ago." Case closed. What does his record collection do for Segerman? He summed it up: "If you have music, you're never alone."

In a South African television interview, Segerman remarked: "When you sell records you need to look at the vinyl." That says it all, Stephen "Sugar" Segerman is a committed record collector who believes in pristine vinyl.

WHY AND HOW MABU VINYL PAVED THE WAY FOR RODRIGUEZ

Stephen "Sugar" Segerman: "I like to think that it's because there's no other shop quite like it in the city-it's intentionally unique in it's look and feel." This is an understatement, as the cultural artifacts within Mabu Vinyl rival that of any major American or English record store.

In Cape Town, it is the store for the serious record collector. Segerman is also a normal guy. Sort of. He remains committed to making sure that Rodriguez' music is not forgotten. He is also a prime mover in Rodriguez' South African touring schedule, as well as a close friend. When Rodriguez is in London, Segerman is often by his side. He is the Sugar Man's number one fan.

Since **Searching For Sugar Man** opened, Mabu Vinyl has been besieged with tourists. It is now one of Cape Town's major attractions. He appears as bewildered as Rodriguez with the buzz over the documentary. In 2013, at fifty-eight years of age, Segerman enjoyed Rodriguez' rise to fame and fortune. Although personally uncomfortable with it, Segerman is now a celebrity. His road to Rodriguez' music began when he entered the South African military.

THE SOUTH AFRICAN JOURNEY BEGAN IN 1972

In 1972, while he served his one year in the South African military, he became enamored with **Cold Fact**. He was a young man who collected all forms of music. Like many South Africans, Segerman realized that Rodriguez was as he said: "The soundtrack to our lives."

Stephen "Sugar" Segerman: "I was born in Johannesburg in 1954. The same year that Elvis Presley recorded in the Sun Studio. I'm a true baby boomer."

No one said it better of **Cold Fact** than Segerman: "To us, it was one of the most famous records of all time." The anti-establishment message in **Cold Fact** intrigued Segerman. Rodriguez influenced South Africans, as his music became the national anthem to a segment of the anti-apartheid movement. It helped to end South Africa's repressive governmental policies. The Voelvry movement of white South African musicians protested the brutal repression in their homeland, and they marched to Rodriguez' songs. There were also Americans who protested apartheid.

AMERICAN ROCKERS AGAINST APARTHEID, 1985

In 1985, American rock performers began a movement to affect a musical boycott of South Africa. Steven Van Zandt of Bruce Springsteen's E Street band, organized a boycott of Sun City. This was the major South African venue that international entertainers appeared. The release of a record, Artists United Against Apartheid, placed American and British musicians squarely against apartheid.

Van Zandt put together an All Star cast of thirty musicians who recorded the 1985 song, "I Ain't Gonna Play Sun City." The album's participants included Bob Dylan, Ruben Blades, Pat Benatar, Herbie Hancock, Miles Davis, Lou Reed, Jackson Browne, Peter Gabriel and Keith Richards among others. Although "Sun City" charted no higher than thirty-eight in the U. S. on **Billboard's** Hot 100 in December 1985, it was an indication that the South African policy of apartheid was on its last legs. In the U. K. the song charted at twenty-one and number four in Australia. It was a top ten single in Canada, and in the Netherlands it reached the Top 40.

Steven Van Zandt and Danny Schecter produced a documentary comparing the treatment of black South Africans to that of Native Americans. The film, **The Making of Sun City**, had difficulty gaining distribution. The Public Broadcasting Service turned down the non-profit documentary. Finally, in 1987 New York's WNYC-TV aired the documentary.

Despite these obstacles the album and documentary raised more than a million U. S. dollars for anti-apartheid projects. South Africans embraced **The Making of Sun City**, and Johnny Clegg created a South African organization to fight apartheid. The South Africa Now TV series was a byproduct of the album and documentary. Clegg is an important figure in South African politics. He is a British born musician and anthropologist whose bands, the racially mixed, Juluka, and Savuka, blended African sounds with European influences. He is significant to South African popular music history for incorporating Zulu with English lyrics and African influences with a number of western music styles. Clegg's music is political and it attacks any system of government based on racial separation. He was a strong influence upon Paul Simon and Clegg appeared on stage with Nelson Mandela when he turned ninety-five.

ORGANIZING THE VOELVRY MOVEMENT

In 1989, the Voelvry Movement dominated the white middle class music listening public. Voelvry musicians built their protest songs on forty-one years of black African songs and discontent. It was as much a part of the social and musical revolution in the South African university system as it was about the music. The rapidly developing white counterculture employed Rodriguez' music and lyrics in opposition to the racist atmosphere and government collusion with those who would continue apartheid. As is the case in many countries, university students would not let apartheid continue.

When Stephen "Sugar" Segerman in **Searching For Sugar Man** talks of the Voelvry Movement and the musicians who helped end apartheid, he doesn't mention the earlier native South African protest music. The black South African majority provided the soundtrack for revolution.

The earliest protest tunes came from Vuyisile Mini's "Watch Out, Verwoerd." This was a song directed to the prime minister. After a decade of political activism, Mini was arrested, tried and sentenced to death. His crime! He was critical of the South African white supremacist government. He was also a labor union activist, a talented actor, a dancer, a poet and a singer. South Africa's apartheid government in 1964 executed him.

As repression worsened, the South African government forcibly removed native Africans from their homes. The government created new white suburbs. A protest song, "Meadowlands," was critical of the government forcing natives to leave Sophiatown for lesser housing. The famed singer, Miriam Makeba, popularized Benedict Wallet Vilakazi's, "Meadowlands." She also sang lead vocals on Hugh Masekela's "Soweto Blues." This song reflected on the 1976 Soweto riots.

Miriam Makeba was a major force for the South African fight against apartheid. In 1957, she recorded "Pata Pata," which charted on **Billboard** at twelve a decade later. She was, from day one, a strong critic of apartheid. The brutal repression from the South African government was demonstrated when her passport was revoked.

She toured the United States in the early and mid-1960s opposing apartheid. In 1965, Makeba recorded a Grammy Award wining album with Harry Belafonte, **An Evening With Belafonte/Makeba**. It is not a concert LP but a studio album featuring twelve South African songs. There are two duets and Makeba wrote five songs and Belafonte the remainder. Belafonte was active in promoting South African artists and speaking out against apartheid.

There were also American songs in the movement to end apartheid. In the late 1980s, pro-apartheid supporters violently attacked protesters to maintain the repressive system. This hastened the end of apartheid. The records protesting apartheid helped to liberalize South Africa. The American producer, Lee Hirsch, recorded Chicco's "Papa Stop The War." This song featured the voice and poetry of Mzwake Mbull. He was a trade unionist who wrote poetry. South African police repeatedly detained him. He was unjustly sent to prison for armed robbery. He was released from South African prison in November 2003, and he continued to work for social reform.

Once anti-apartheid leader, Nelson Mandela, left prison after serving twenty-seven years, he united South Africa. How much did protest music have to do with Mandela's release? Plenty! A great many performers from all over the world opposed apartheid. Mariam Makeba was only one of many South African artists who lobbied the world for an end to apartheid.

As Mandela served a life sentence, music became a weapon of the anti-apartheid struggle. One song, "We Will Leave Our Parents," became a protest favorite. This song talked of leaving to make one's future in another country. This song led to large numbers of future native South African students being educated abroad and returning to fight and end apartheid.

For musicians, artists and writers, censorship made creativity impossible. At least any form of creativity in the mainstream entertainment industry. The degree of censorship and degradation was enormous. A

London producer, Mickie Most, who was known as the Elvis of South Africa, controlled the early 1960s rock scene in South Africa. He made a fortune with a brand of rock and roll that was acceptable to the South African government. His dreadful pop tunes led him to record and perform for South African audiences where he had thirty-five hit records. He moved on to become one of London's legendary producers. When he signed the Animals in 1963, Most was off and running in the U. K. production business. His importance to early South African rock and roll is introducing the mainstream, pop hit record. The point is that when **Cold Fact** emerged in South Africa in 1970 it was a breath of fresh air. Most's eleven consecutive number one South African hits established the template for white, pop, minimally talented performers.

In 1961 Most's last South African release "D In Love" began a record revolution where young kids looking for fame and fortune wrote, produced and recorded on their own. One of these kids, Syd Kitchen, went to University in the late 1970s, he recorded hundreds of songs and he became a one man South African record industry. Like Rodriguez, he had a documentary filmed on his life. Joshua Sternlicht made a feature film on Kitchen, **Fool In A Bubble**. When the film premiered in 2010 at the Durban Film Festival, it was a Rodriguez story without commercial acclaim. All this would not have been possible without Mickie Most's records and later his Hall of Fame U. K. producing career. But from the 1960s to the late 1980s, there was little freedom for South African musicians. Rodriguez filled the void with his contentious lyrics screaming out for equality and personal freedom.

Three is another interesting early South African rock and roll release. It is a ten-inch LP featuring Janis Martin and Elvis Presley. It was issued in 1958 by RCA and RCA's Teal label. Since Martin was billed in the U. S. as "the female Elvis," RCA reasoned that it would be a best seller. Col. Tom Parker, Presley's manager, stepped in and stopped the printings are a few thousand were placed on sale. "Nobody shares a record with Elvis," Parker said. The record added to Presley's South African mystique and it is important to early collectors. Most and the Elvis-Janis Martin release intrigued SA musicians for a decade, then along came Sixto Rodriguez.

South African musicians had to leave the country to tour and record. When Miriam Makeba, Hugh Masakela, Abdullah Ibrahim and Vusi Mahlasela found fame, it was abroad. South Africa treated its artists shamefully. These native musicians were forced into substandard living, inadequate performing venues and miserable financial conditions. They were also threatened over their lyrics.

Abdullah Ibrahim: "Apartheid created an environment of denial and lies. You had to live it from day to day." This statement suggests the bone crushing repression that the native South African's faced. When the Voelvry Movement began in 1989, it benefitted from more than forty years of protest songs from black South Africans.

SEGERMAN AND THE OTHER RECORD COLLECTORS BEGIN THEIR OWN PROTEST AS THE VOELVRY MOVEMENT ARISES

Once the white anti-apartheid movement took shape it flourished. It took some time for white South Africans to join forces with those who opposed apartheid. It was Sixto Rodriguez' **Cold Fact** which introduced words that white South Africans hadn't considered.

Segerman observed: "We didn't know the word anti-establishment until Rodriguez." This may seem like a strange statement considering the amount of protest music from the black majority. But, as Segerman said, it was a divided society.

The songs in **Cold Fact** continued to educate the college students who made up the initial liberal thrust. For five years the Voelvry Movement faced police hostility, bureaucratic concert delays and disinterest from South African record companies. Then white South African musicians began employing the term "rebel music." The result was constant criticism of the political process. The role of music in freeing South Africans from political repression is a major one.

As Segerman mentioned in **Searching For Sugar Man**, white South African's had no idea what anti-establishment meant. The repressive government controlled speech and assembly. There was little interest in black protest music. Voelvry performers defined their songs. This was due to Rodriguez songs like "The Establishment Blues" and "I Wonder."

VOELVRY MOVEMENT AND RODRIGUEZ

In 1989, the Voelvry Movement led by Johannes Kerkorrel, Koos Kombuis, James Phillips and Bernoldus Niemand, among others, continued the development of white anti-apartheid rock and roll. To a man, Rodriguez' songs provided the inspiration for their anti-government criticism. The Voelvry musicians redefined the political role of white South Africans via music. It was accomplished with Rodriguez' lyrical brilliance. His songs provided the template to latent liberalism. The Voelvry musicians were the mainstay of music on college campuses. This helped to give birth to the South African rock concert industry. Segerman was there to praise, support and help this movement.

There is a great deal in Segerman's background that made his hunt for Rodriguez a successful one. He is an accomplished business-man. He is more significantly a musical detective. He also didn't be-lieve the Rodriguez myths. It was from the time of his compulsory military service that Segerman blossomed into an original Rodriguez music detective.

COMPULSORY SERVICE AND JEWELRY INFLUENCES

In the early 1970s, Segerman served his compulsory time in the South African Air Force. He discovered Rodriguez' music. He was en-thralled by it. South Africa's changing political-social culture was broad-cast through Rodriguez' lyrics.

The poetic images intrigued Segerman. "His lyrics offered a drug-fueled escape from the harsh realities of life and a raw look at the sexual politics of the time," Segerman observed. It was while living under South Africa's stringent apartheid government that Segerman questioned his country. Censorship bothered him.

After his compulsory military service, Segerman received a law de-gree. The legal career didn't work out. He entered the family jewelry business. Then he had an illness that forced him to relocate to Cape Town. For a time, he was an Internet entrepreneur. He also worked in the cell phone business. There were also personal-political issues that made Segerman search for Rodriguez.

Growing up as a practicing Orthodox Jew, Segerman was unhappy with South Africa's lack of personal freedom. He saw in Rodriguez a road map to the future. He also envisioned intellectual liberation. He strongly opposed apartheid. "As one of the Jewish baby boomers, born soon after the Second World War and the Shoah, I feel we had even more reason, and responsibility, to be aware and sensitive to prejudice of any kind, and that is why there were many South African Jews to be found among the ranks of the anti-apartheid movement in South Africa and across the world," Segerman concluded.

As he came of age in his twenties, Segerman lived in a South Afri-can society isolated from international influences. There were very few touring rock music acts. When anyone purchased Rodriguez records, they were told he was dead. It was this lack of knowledge that drove Segerman. He found a mystery. He was determined to solve it.

THE ROAD TO MABU VINYL AND EVENTUALLY RODRIGUEZ

Stephen "Sugar" Segerman's road to Mabu Vinyl, and the rediscovery of Rodriguez took a sharp turn in the mid-1990s. He moved from Johannesburg in 1996, and he settled in Oranjezicht. This Cape Town suburb is beautiful and picturesque. It was once primarily agricultural but over time it developed into an artistically pleasant community. Segerman set down roots. He became adept on the Internet. In 1996, the website founded to locate Rodriguez began drawing attention. A few years later, he changed professions. He decided to purchase a share in Mabu Vinyl.

When he is not operating Mabu Vinyl, Segerman lives in Cape Town's City Bowl with its spectacular mountain view. He also hangs out on nearby Long Street with its fashionable restaurants and two music clubs. He is seen regularly dining at Toni's and the Café Paradiso. As Segerman remarked in an interview about Oranjezicht: "This area is the land of the lotus-eaters – everyone just sits on the slopes, gets on with their lives and keeps to themselves. And if you want to do that, this is the best place in the world. It's also great living on the side of the mountain and having a nice view."

It's an arty neighborhood. Segerman fits right in with his extensive record collection, books, CDs, DVDs and assorted rock and roll paraphernalia. He is the ultimate collector.

SUGAR THE RECORD COLLECTOR

The record collector side to Segerman drove him to find Rodriguez. It all began in 1964 when his father gave him the first Beatles album. He was ten years old. In the next half century, he became a serious collector.

While growing up, Segerman spent a lot of town reading the London based **New Musical Express**, as well as **Melody Maker**. He was hooked on the music. He soon was drawn to English Punk. The Sex Pistols, Joy Division and Pitchfork dominated his collection. By 2012, he graduated to M83, Metronomy, P. J. Harvey and Bon Iver. He loves anything new in the music field. His collection continues to expand. Like most music collectors, he is now an I Tunes user.

He also promotes such Indie bands as Yo La Tengo, Luna and the Brian Jonestown Massacre. He admits to collecting albums and not singles. The American author, Joseph Heller, is one of his heroes. Segerman said: "You must read chapter 15 of **Catch-22**, it's brilliant! But you'll actually need to read the whole book in order to understand and appreciate it, and it should be the same with an album. Don't just pick a few of its songs; listen to the whole thing."

In South Africa, Syd Kitchen and the Utensils are among his favorite bands. Syd Kitchen is one of South Africa's most political and unpredictable musicians. Kitchen was hostile to the record business. He spent forty-five years performing and releasing material before he passed away at sixty. If Rodriguez has a musical brother, it is Syd Kitchen.

Segerman talked about his other favorite albums. They include Van Morrison's **Astral Weeks**, Bob Dylan's **Blood On The Tracks, Led Zeppelin II** and naturally Rodriguez' **Cold Fact**.

As Segerman reminisces about rock and roll, he observed: "I would've liked to be on the stage at Woodstock." So would ninety-nine percent of Americans who missed this epic event. On the wall of Mabu Vinyl there is a cover of the Sex Pistols **Never Mind The Bollocks**. That tells it all about Segerman.

WHAT SOUTH AFRICANS KNEW ABOUT RODRIGUEZ

Like many South Africans, Segerman assumed that Rodriguez was a well-known American musician. After all he was a platinum selling artist. To quote one South African record label executive: "Rodriguez was much bigger than the Rolling Stones."

Since there was no biographical data on Rodriguez, Segerman looked extensively at the lyrics. There were references to London, troubled American cities and Amsterdam. He searched these clues for information. He found nothing. He also looked for an American city with problems and the tallest building. He ruled out New York's Empire State Building. It seemed to Segerman that all U. S. cities had problems. After he wrote the liner notes to a South African reissue of **Coming From Reality**, he believed that he was through with his search for Rodriguez. Ironically, he was just beginning.

It was Segerman and Craig Bartholomew-Strydom who discovered, the word "Dearborn." This is when the search for Rodriguez took a turn toward the Detroit suburb of the same name. An American Atlas told Segerman and Bartholomew-Strydom that Dearborn was near Detroit. That was the clue that led to the eventual discovery of the Sugar Man.

SEARCHING FOR THE SUGAR MAN AND ON TO AN OSCAR

The road to finding Rodriguez was a long and circuitous one. Segerman spent more than twenty years listening to and thinking about Rodriguez. Along the way, he researched the elusive singer and found nothing. This piqued his curiosity. Segerman wrote: "From the 70s to the late 90s Rodriguez was mostly invisible, apart from two successful tours to Oz." The reference of "Oz" was to the 1979 and 1981 Australian appearances.

When the Academy Award nomination was announced for Malik Bendjelloul's documentary, Segerman was too nervous to watch the news on South African television.

Segerman said of the Academy Award nomination: "No, this is too much for me, I switched it off." After he received a phone call from his brother in Australia, the importance of the Oscar nomination was evident. He also had some good news for Rodriguez. Segerman told the Sugar Man the people who viewed **Searching For Sugar Man** refused to download the music. They were purchasing it as a protest against Rodriguez' lack of royalties.

Segerman received over a thousand e-mails from expatriate South African's after the Oscar announcement. "Just this morning I got an e-mail from someone saying (after watching the documentary) it's the first time ever they're proud to be South African," Segerman concluded.

SUGAR AND CRAIG BARTHOLOMEW-STRYDOM
AT THE 85TH OSCAR'S

As Stephen "Sugar" Segerman flew from Cape Town to Los Angeles for the 85th Oscar Awards, he was elated. He felt like he was living in a dream world. He had started out to find what had happened to Sixto Rodriguez. He wrote the liner notes to a reissue Rodriguez CD. He met Craig Bartholomew-Strydom. Together they brought Rodriguez into a mainstream commercial career.

Then it was 2013, Segerman and Craig Bartholomew-Strydom were flying into Los Angeles to attend the 85th Academy Award ceremony. When Bartholomew-Strydom got off the plane, he hoped that his father-in-law's tuxedo would fit. Segerman didn't have a tuxedo. He did have some love beads. They couldn't believe their good fortune. They had brought the Sugar Man back.

The press asked Bartholomew-Strydom about his article on the search for Sixto Rodriguez. He replied: "I knew I had an incredible story on my hands when I wrote my first piece on the subject, but it took a sensitive director to turn the story into a film."

Segerman wandered around West Hollywood. He was interviewed wearing a t-shirt and love beads from the 1960s. He also went to all the sights. One wonders did he go into Amoeba Music? My guess is yes. He was living a dream. It is a dream that he created. He was now experiencing it.

Then it was time for the 85th Oscar awards. Sugar and Craig showed up in tuxedos looking spiffy. By the end of the evening, they were holding the **Searching For Sugar Man** Oscar. It was as improbable journey.

When Malik Bendjelloul and Simon Chinn accepted the Oscar for best documentary, Segerman and Bartholomew-Strydom beamed. They had been on their quest for two decades. It had paid off. They were the first Rodrigologists and they had found the Sugar Man.

ADVENTURES IN THE LAND OF RODRIGUEZ:
THE RODRIGOLOGISTS

The Rodrigologists began with Stephen "Sugar" Segerman and quickly expanded into a group of true believers. It started with one song, "Sugar Man." It continued into a litany of tunes. Then the carping critics came out of the woodwork with inane ideas that Rodriguez was peripheral to anti-apartheid. This criticism didn't square with the facts.

The bitter criticism toward Sixto Rodriguez that he was not truly an anti-apartheid supporter is the work of people with either too little knowledge of the Sugar Man or too little knowledge of South African history. There is no doubt that Rodriguez influenced racisms decline in South Africa. In numerous interviews, Rodriguez recounted his long interest in South African politics. The end of apartheid wasn't due to his music, but the lyrics changed attitudes and accentuated a democratic impulse. Those who listened to Rodriguez,' "The Establishment Blues," received a message that began the slow march to making apartheid obsolete.

The Rodrigologists were most important in trumpeting the importance of his music. It wasn't just publicizing the lyrics that set Rodrigologists apart from those who simply listen to the music; they also make pilgrimages to Detroit. The gritty streets of the Motor City were what made **Searching For Sugar Man** a documentary filled with pathos. The Rodrigologists understood pathos, patience and perseverance.

The fandom that has grown up around Rodriguez, since the success of **Searching For Sugar Man** forced him into seclusion. When he performed at the Luckman Hall at the California State University, Los Angeles in late May 2014, the back stage demand to visit Rodriguez began at two in the afternoon. The security guards kept everyone out as Rodriguez calmly sat in a small room. He could no longer roam free. There were too many obsessive fans. Fame has its downside.

Backstage at the Luckman Center, Steve Rowland talked to Rodriguez about a third album. The Sugar Man was tired. He discussed visiting Rowland at his Palm Spring's home. Rowland has the best jazz musicians ready to go into the studio with Rodriguez. Rowland's recording studio is private and quiet.

Rodriguez remains polite, happy, and he is enjoying every minute of his well-earned fame. After they discussed a third album, Rodriguez hopped on the tour bus and it was off to Los Angeles' downtown Ace Hotel for a well deserved rest.

It was as if Rodriguez cast a spell. His calm life was now chaotic. He had arrived as one of the most important artists of his generation. His arrival came more than forty years after his initial splash. It was due to the Rodrigologists. Thank you Stephen "Sugar" Segerman, Brian Currin, Andy Harrod and Craig Bartholomew-Strydom. The Rodriguez story is much like a multi-layered mystery.

HOW TO BECOME A RODRIGOLOGIST

For the Rodrigologist, Detroit is the first step. The area near Wayne State University, a walk down the Cass Corridor and a visit to Rodriguez' hangouts is a must. Then it is off to Dearborn, a Detroit suburb, to view the imagery that burns in his songs.

One wonders if the Rodrigologist's believe that they are preserving history? Perhaps they are also looking after an artist, Sixto Rodriguez, who has amongst the most loyal followers in the annals of music history. The Rodrigologist's are territorial. They don't like other people writing about the Sugar Man. They feel that only they can tell the story. This is understandable. They are like archaeologists preserving a part of history. They start in Detroit, they move on to South Africa, Australia and England before circling back to the U. S. and South Africa. The Sugar Man remains the fountainhead.

When Stephen "Sugar" Segerman talks about the first time that he held **Cold Fact**, there is a feeling that he had found the Holy Grail. The bulk of Segerman's record collection is varied, and it is Rodriguez who occupies the most important place in his musical hierarchy. That is a good thing. Without Segerman, Rodriguez wouldn't have been found and thrust into international acclaim.

To Rodrigologist's, most of the clubs in Detroit are gone, but the neighborhoods remain intact. The Detroit Public Library and Art Museum contain hints of his past. The pilgrimage to Detroit is not always a pleasant one. But the true Rodrigologist can still catch Dennis Coffey playing in a local club, meet someone who has hung out with Rodriguez or find a person who watched an early show in the Sewer By The Sea or a later show at the Old Miami. The Avery Street house is easy to find, as is the Cass Café, the Old Miami Bar and the Motor City Brewing Company.

The Hall of Fame Rodrigologist believes it is necessary to find out about some of the fabulous ruins. The Anderson Garden Temple, located near the Cass Corridor, was a notorious hooker bar. Rodriguez performed there and talks about it in song. The Anderson Garden Temple was located on the second floor of the Hotel Fort Wayne. The hookers simply walked downstairs for a room. The place was so popular that two bartenders and four bar maids showed up at nine thirty in the morning. Rodriguez played there many times.

At times Rodriguez watched jazz acts at Cobbs. He also wandered into the Sweetheart Lounge, which was another hooker bar. Whether or not he played these venues is unknown.

As Rodriguez looked back he commented: "Now I think I'm more grounded than I would have probably been then."

Now it is up to the Rodrigologists to get grounded. There is still a great deal of research for Rodrigologists.

SOME THOUGHTS ON SEGERMAN'S IMPORTANCE

There are so many important points connected to Stephen "Sugar" Segerman's role in the making of **Searching For Sugar Man**. He almost single handedly made it a reality. He helped Rodriguez appear in concert in South Africa. He continued to publicize Rodriguez in the U. K. Due to Segerman; the major London rock publications began covering his music.

On October 5, 2014 the **Cape Town Sunday Argus** headlined: "The Man Who Found Sugar Man." The Sue Segar piece recounted Segerman's epic search and eventually rediscovery of Sixto Rodriguez. Segerman said: "We have tourists arriving in the shop every day. People just love coming in. And it's so nice that our little record shop in Cape Town has survived." The story centered on Segerman's love for and happiness with Rodriguez' entry into the music world mainstream. Sugar went on to describe the possibility of a book contract, a feature film and a Broadway musical based on Rodriguez' story. He is as obsessed about the Sugar Man, as he is about promoting the music.

At the present time, Segerman and Craig Bartholomew-Strydom have completed a Rodriguez biography. This will be the insiders view that solves the Rodriguez' mysteries and provides the final word on the Sugar Man. It will be a great book.

There is no doubt that without Stephen "Sugar" Segerman, there would not have been **Searching For Sugar Man**. But Segerman is also thankful to Malik Bendjelloul and Sixto Rodriguez. "Mabu Vinyl is my shop, my livelihood, my passion, which, after eleven years, has reaped the benefit of the resurgence of vinyl, plus the wonderful public the Rodriguez movie brought us," Segerman continued. "I can't tell you how happy it makes me to know that Rodriguez is now touring the world with his family and having the best time."

MATT SULLIVAN IN PALM SPRINGS

chapter

SEVEN

MATT SULLIVAN AND LIGHT IN THE ATTIC: HEROES ARRIVE UNEXPECTEDLY

"THE GOAL SINCE I WAS SIXTEEN WAS TO START A RECORD LABEL," MATT SULLIVAN

When Light In The Attic was founded in Seattle in 2002, it was just another independent record label. It soon built a cult following as a reissue label. The master plan for LITA was to re-release soul, funk, hip-hop and reggae artists. The notion of re-mastering, beautifully packaging and providing copious liner notes to long ignored gems was Matt Sullivan and Josh Wright's dream. It became reality as they established LITA.

They were not only the co-founders of LITA; they had been friends since grade school. They quickly became Rodriguez' reissue label. When LITA formed in 2002, it was a decade of prior experiences in the music business, a collector's mania, and an attitude that they would pay the artists a fair royalty that shaped the business model. When Matt Sullivan showed up at Sixto Rodriguez' Avery Street home, to offer an eighteen per cent royalty, the Sugar Man was on board. But to get to Rodriguez the label already had spent five years in business.

THE LONG ROAD TO RE-RELEASING RODRIGUEZ

The road to re-releasing **Cold Fact** and **Coming From Reality** was a long and convoluted one. It began for Matt Sullivan in grade school, continued on to high school, then on to University of Arizona, eventually to Spain and then back to Seattle. What did Sullivan have in common in all these places? Record collecting. The vinyl disease was well and alive in the LITA co-founder since his Bellevue, Washington grade school days. It is in Sullivan's formative years that the path to a record label began. He would be a record label honcho. It took some time. At the ripe old age of twenty-six, he began to achieve his dream founding Light In the Attic.

Along the way, Sullivan's goal was to discover, to re-release, to publicize and to bring to the record buying mainstream long ignored artists and their albums. This is how he found Sixto Rodriguez. Light In The Attic released the Sugar Man's two LPs long before fame resulted from **Searching For Sugar Man**.

The formula for releasing the obscure and the arcane worked. By 2014, more than one hundred fifty CDs and vinyl LPs, as well as a litany of the other products, graced the Light In The Attic catalogue. The label was so successful that they opened a distribution arm. Sixto Rodriguez couldn't have found a better label. They understood Rodriguez. He also received firewood every winter from LITA. For the Sugar Man this is as important as the royalties. LITA was the first music business company to treat him equitably.

SULLIVAN'S FORMATIVE YEARS

The dye was cast for Matt Sullivan to become a vinyl collector, a record label owner and one of the Rodrigologists who brought the Sugar Man back from obscurity. He was in the fourth grade and although he was only nine years old young Matt already had musical interests. He looked around his Bellevue Washington grade school. He couldn't possible imagine that there was anyone else like him. Surprise! There was. He met Light In The Attic co-founder, Josh Wright, in the fourth grade. Then it was on to Bellevue High School where they were DJ's on a ten-watt FM station. Although they were sixteen years old, they talked about forming a record label. Their record collections grew as Sub Pop and other Seattle Indie labels sent out copious amounts of free records.

Matt Sullivan: "Because it was the 90s and we were in Seattle, labels would send us all kinds of good stuff. "

Then Sullivan enrolled at the University of Arizona. Tucson is as close to a counterculture city as there is in Arizona. Sullivan continued to make plans to found a record label. He majored in an academic area with media education. The music scene in and around the University was a vibrant one. It was the mid-1990s and Tucson was in the midst of catching up musically. This fact was not lost on Sullivan.

In the 1990s, the Tucson alternative music scene centered around the Club Congress and a host of small clubs with a wide variety of bands playing in and around Fourth Street. The Indie bands included Digital Leather, Rainer Packet, Doo Rag, Bog Log III, the Sidewinders and the Phantom Limbs among others.

It was at the University of Arizona that Matt carefully formulated his plans for a record label. He realized that he needed more of a practical education. Not a book education. He began to research the business side of the music industry. He received this education almost by accident on a European trip.

For a time, Matt traveled around Spain. He was a typical young kid seeing the world. He had a backpack. He had a notebook. He had some ideas about his musical-business future. But how was he to accomplish his goals? The answer came accidentally.

Sullivan was driving a Fiat in Spain when he crashed into another car. The other driver, Inigo Pastor, had a car filled with records. He was also the owner of two Spanish re-issue labels Vamp Soul and Munster Records. They quickly forgot about the damaged autos, as they talked music. Pastor had records by Iggy Pop and The Stooges, Love, Suicide and the MC5 among others. Sullivan knew all about the music, and this intrigued Pastor.

Munster Records became Matt Sullivan's new university. As an independent Spanish record label, founded in the 1980s, the thrust was to merchandise obscure CDs and limited edition vinyl. The idea of meeting the demands of the record collector was foremost in Inigo Pastor's business plan. The Munster releases are an eclectic mix. None of this was lost on Sullivan, as he learned from working with and observing what went on at Munster.

The remainder of Sullivan's European tour was put on hold as he hung out every day at the label. It was while in Madrid that the joy of finding an obscure record and re-releasing it took hold. Matt had a plan.

He would become the head of a reissue label. But he was a smart kid. He realized how few people made money in the record business. He needed a further education. It was time to return to Seattle. He also needed some money. He had to get a day job.

Once Sullivan returned to Seattle, he went to work for a wide variety of local labels including Sub Pop, and Loosegroove. He confessed to Susie Tennant, Sub Pop's radio promotion director that he was thinking of forming a label. She encouraged him.

Then it was time to contact his old friend, Josh Wright, who he wanted as a partner. Since Bellevue High School, Wright had bounced around from Ithaca College to Washington State University before settling in Hawaii. For all practical purposes, Wright forgot about the record business.

He called Wright who came home to work on the project. They needed to raise some money to found Light In The Attic. The initial thrust behind LITA took place when they promoted live shows by cutting edge acts Saul Williams, Clinic and Kid Koala. These shows provided seed money for LITA. Their first album came out in 2002, when they released the Last Poet's, **This Is Madness**. This was a brilliant reissue. When the LP was originally released in 1971, the reviews were ecstatic. The idea of bringing one of the hip-hop pioneer sounds back created great publicity. It also led to strong sales.

The label is now thirteen years old and stronger than ever. The key to LITA's success is the excavation of forgotten or long ignored vintage nuggets. From time to time LITA signs a new artist and releases their material. The forte of LITA, however, is the reissue. They do this with quality re-mastering, beautiful cover art; visually attractive packaging and in-depth liner notes. The vinyl releases cost double the amount to produce compared to other vinyl labels. They still sell for a fair price. The care, the quality, the tenacity and the physical appearance of LITA's various products introduced a new template to the record business. LITA quickly became the Cadillac reissue label.

LITA'S TEMPLATE FOR SUCCESS: REINVENT THE GENRE

What is it that sets Light In The Attic apart from other Indie labels? LITA employs the care, the quality and the selection of the right material in their reissues. This is only a small part of the equation. The goldmine of undiscovered gems is the real key. There is no template for success in the Indie music business. If is there one LITA broke the rules. They asked porn star Ron Jeremy to write the liner notes for a reissue of the **Deep Throat** soundtrack. Jeremy said no. Then LITA went into action.

They are tenacious. When they approached Ron Jeremy about writing the liner notes, his agent said to go away. They wanted to pay him $750 to compose the liner notes. Jeremy's agent said that he got twenty thousand dollars for standing on a street corner. When Sullivan told the manager that Public Enemy endorsed their first release, The Last Poet's album, **This Is Madness**, LITA had his attention or at least someone close to the porn legend. Jeremy agreed to write the liner notes.

Eventually, LITA released Sixto Rodriguez' two albums. It wasn't an easy task. The albums were hard to find. Clarence Avant who licensed the material initially wouldn't talk to Sullivan or answer his letters. Once again tenacity took over. Matt Sullivan cornered Clarence Avant at a Seattle wedding to secure the rights to release Rodriguez' material. Not all the LITA releases were tough sells. By 2014, the label not only had a cult following, it was making money and the artists who were approached readily agreed to the reissues. LITA did something most labels wouldn't consider; they actually paid royalties in a fair and timely fashion. But it was the obscure artists that intrigued Sullivan.

A case in point is the great female soul guitar-vocalist Barbara Lynn whose debut record on Atlantic in 1968 **Here Is Barbara Lynn** led to positive reviews and a top ten **Billboard** hit, "If You Lose Me, You Lose A Good Thing." It was also number one on the **Billboard** R & B chart. She bumped Ray Charles' "I Can't Stop Loving You" from the number one slot on the **Billboard** R & B listing. The club appearances, the concerts and the beginning of a successful mainstream career soon took a back seat to a normal life. She was off the radar, happily married, raising three children and semi-retired in Beaumont Texas. In late November 2014, LITA re-released Lynn's debut Atlantic LP. Times had changed. There was no need for a hard sell. She was on board with the project.

When Sullivan tracked down Barbara Lynn in her Beaumont Texas home, she was pleased with LITA's eighteen per cent royalty, their attention to detail and the superb packaging that brought her debut LP back into the limelight. The result was a scheduled 2014 CD **Here Is Barbara Lynn**. Like Rodriguez, Lynn descended into cult status and obscurity. Then along came LITA to bring her back onto the road.

How did Sullivan find Barbara Lynn? He caught one of her shows in Los Angeles. Then he listened to her vast and carefully recorded catalogue. The Atlantic **Here Is Barbara Lynn**, LP released in 1968, remained a blues masterpiece. It was also a classic that no one heard again after success in the late 1960s. Sullivan found black and white videos of Lynn performing in the 1960s. Discovering Lynn's wonderful album was the easy part, now it was on the Warner Bros to secure a contract for the re-release.

He went to Warner Bros where LITA has a distribution relationship. They owned the rights to Lynn's material, and they readily agreed to the project. LITA sent a writer to her home in Beaumont to interview Lynn; she provided pictures and information for the liner notes.

This Is Barbara Lynn is a template for LITA's success. She received the same treatment that every LITA re-issue artist is accorded. The copious liner notes, by Jessica Hundley, include an artist interview and rare pictures. The album is re-mastered from the original tapes. The vinyl LP cover is beautiful with a deluxe Stoughton gatefold "Tip On" jacket. That means it is a beautifully designed and visually appealing vinyl re-issue. This is the trademark of Light In the Attic. The Matt Sullivan label is a first class operation with continual growth to meet the ever-changing marketplace.

Sullivan prefers to have the artist fully cooperate before releasing their material. Not everyone was as enthusiastic as Barbara Lynn. "For the LITA team, patience isn't just a virtue," Matt Sullivan continued. "It's a job requirement."

SULLIVAN'S TENACITY: RELEASING KRIS KRISTOFFERSON

By the time that LITA put out its fiftieth release, Kris Kristofferson's **Please Don't Tell Me How The Story Ends: The Publishing Demos 1969-1972** in May 2010, the label was profitable. The Kristofferson tapes were a major coup. Once again Sullivan's tenacity and ability to cajole, while finding obscure material, led to the tapes. It also took six years for Sullivan to make the Kristofferson deal. The story of how LITA was able to release the CD is a testimony to Sullivan's business skills. Not surprisingly, the Kristofferson release has a defunct record store and its owner as the source for the project.

The Kristofferson tapes came about when Mark Linn was going through EMI's publishing vault in Nashville. He found the tapes, and Linn gave them to a former employee, Al Milman, who owned the Seattle University District record store, Bedazzled Discs. Milman give the tapes to Sullivan. Then tenacity set in as the LITA founder began the laborious process of negotiating a deal.

The dealings with Kristofferson took only a year. He readily agreed to the project. Then the fun began. "The next four years were trying to figure out who owned the damned thing," Sullivan said. There was a problem. LITA released long forgotten LPs, Kristofferson's tape contained demos. This was new territory. But Sullivan didn't want the material lost to the wastebasket of forgotten history.

Matt Sullivan: "What we try to do is give something a new life and help it reach a wider audience."

The Kristofferson release contained sixteen groundbreaking demos from the established outlaw country icon. This wasn't LITA's usual release. Josh Wright was instrumental as the LITA distributor. He has close ties with record storeowners, and they said that the Kristofferson material would fly off the shelves. It did. The sixty-page booklet that came with the CD was another indication of the in-depth information and seriousness that LITA took completing the project. The two 180 gram LPs sold out quickly to collectors. Even more fascinating are the liner notes, which reveal that Merle Haggard and Dennis Hopper were around to help Kristofferson with the demos.

Josh Wright: "Whether it's Rodriguez or Karen Dalton or Betty Davis, we always approach these projects as if they were a new artist."

The person who appreciates this comment is Kris Kristofferson. He has said that the stripped down demos of "Me And Bobby McGee," "The Lady's Not For Sale" and "Billy Dee" provide a rare window into his songwriting talent. Kristofferson loves the CD.

DISTRIBUTING AND ON TO SIXTO RODRIGUEZ

LITA also distributes its product. They have broken all the rules for an Indie label. They have not only survived, they are profitable. In 2012, the two Rodriguez albums became international best sellers. Thanks to the fame and acclaim from **Searching For Sugar Man**, there is an explosion in Rodriguez sales. While reissues are the key to the label, there is a contemporary side.

There is more to Light In The Attic than reissues. They also release material by contemporary bands like the Black Angels and Nicole Willis and the Soul Avengers. The reissues include such diverse artists as the Monks, Karen Dalton, the Louvin Brothers, Serge Gainsbourg, Jim Sullivan, Betty Davis, Jane Birkin, and the Free Design as well as a host of other acts.

In 2008, after LITA released **Cold Fact** and the following year **Coming From Reality**, they spent a great deal of money publicizing the material, thereby increasing the Sugar Man's cult following. The sales for the Rodriguez material were steady and there was foreign interest. In London, Rodriguez was an icon. He performed there after his triumphant 1998 South African shows. There are a large number of South Africans living in and around London, and they provide a ready market for the Sugar Man. He played a variety of small London clubs, but the Roundhouse in Camden Town is his favorite venue.

The obsessive-compulsive record collectors and the vinyl lovers who sought out the albums wanted more information. Matt Sullivan and Light In The Attic came to their rescue with not only great packaging, but in depth liner notes. When Light In The Attic re-released **Coming From Reality**, there was suddenly a Rodriguez cottage industry. The Sugar Man had exquisite CDs, vinyl albums, a 45, T-shirts, and a cassette. He was back for a small genre of record collectors. The vinyl loving young crowd couldn't get enough of his music. The general public was still three years away from falling in love with the Sugar Man. How did Sullivan come upon **Cold Fact** and Sixto Rodriguez?

It was when Sullivan heard David Holmes' version of "Sugar Man" that he became a Rodrigolgist. This 2002 release by David Holmes is in an album that includes selections from 1960s and 1970s rock, blues and pop classics. Sullivan was intrigued. David Holmes' album **Come Get It, I Got It Introducing The Free Association** is a collection that includes not only Rodriguez' "Sugar Man" but brief clips of Johnny Otis, Muddy Waters, Cyril Neville and Ray Bryant among others. It is an eclectic mix that showcases Holmes' producing talent. He also completed the soundtrack for the George Clooney movie **Ocean's 11**. Holmes mix album was a U. K. sensation. It went a long way toward establishing Rodriguez as a London cult artist. This was a decade before **Searching For Sugar Man**.

As a remix producer, Holmes reworked tracks by U2, the Doves, the Manic Street Preachers, Primal Scream, Saint Etienne and Ice Cube among others. He has also completed soundtracks for seventeen films.

When Holmes mix collection was introduced in London on March 25th 2002 the dye was cast. The record collectors, the vinyl geeks, the obscure concert promoters, the record aficionados living in their parent's basement and the trendy London music press discovered Rodriguez. Long before **Searching For Sugar Man** made him an international superstar, the Sugar Man played London venues. He was back in small concert venues after his triumphant 1998 South African appearances.

The London based **New Musical Express** listed every track on Holmes compilation. They favored one-"Sugar Man." **Face**, a London based magazine, gave "Sugar Man" a special reference with a comparison to Bob Dylan. Londoner's suddenly began looking for used **Cold Fact** albums. It wasn't an easy task. The only available **Cold Fact** LP that wasn't a bootleg was the Australian import on the Blue Goose imprint. It sold out in London's Camden Town in weeks.

Sullivan wondered what the original version of "Sugar Man" sounded like? He searched around Seattle record stores until he found the **Cold Fact** album. He walked into the now defunct JAM Records and there was a copy of the Rodriguez album. This small Seattle store in the Wallingford district, pitched their product to the record geeks. Not surprisingly, JAM Records soon went bankrupt. This was shortly after Sullivan established Light In the Attic.

Not only was Sullivan obsessed with Rodriguez' music, he began collecting bootlegs, purchasing Australian and South African records, looking around for recorded shows, and finding out everything he could about the Sugar Man. The next logical step was to fly to Detroit and see if Rodriguez was on board with the two reissues. But first he had to get Clarence Avant to agree to license the product. This turned into a major endurance test. He wondered if he could complete the deal? He did. Now it was off to Detroit and the Woodbridge district. Sullivan wondered if Rodriguez was onboard with the project? He was.

It was 2006 and Rodriguez welcomed Sullivan to his Avery Street home. He was ecstatic about the reissues. The Sugar Man was even happier that LITA commissioned new liner notes and spared no expense in completing the two reissues. The care with which LITA operates led to an intensive two year production schedule. It was worth it.

EVEN IF THEY'RE DEAD WE TREAT THEM WELL

The reissues are generally ones for living artists. When you release material from the stoner artists of the 1960s and 1970s, there is a good chance many are dead. No problem.

Matt Sullivan: "We work these artists like they are current contemporary artists. Even if they're dead."

Lee Hazlewood is a good example of a cult artist no longer on the scene. Light In The Attic has a virtual Hazlewood cottage industry. While Hazlewood is best known for his collaboration with Nancy Sinatra on "These Boots Are Made For Walking," "Jackson" and "Some Velvet Morning," he has a lengthy, if often obscure, solo career. When Hazlewood left Coolidge, Arizona and moved on to Los Angeles, he began a peripatetic life. Light In The Attic began releasing Hazlewood's solo material. It is massive, interesting and formidable.

Light In The Attic released **Lee Hazlewood-The LHI Years: Singles, Nudes & Backsides (1969-1971)** as a tribute to his late genius. There is much more in the LITA catalogue, and the point is made that when Sullivan likes an artist he releases whatever he can negotiate. Is this a way to run a record label? It is! I had everything Lee released until LITA came along. This is the void that they fill. The collector mania is the key to their success.

What is the importance of LITA's release of the material from Hazlewood's label, Lee Hazlewood Industries? In his quirky, generally obscure, solo career, Hazlewood's short lived label released three hundred and five songs from 1966 to 1971. LITA rescued this material, which is as historically important for its country psychedelia, as well as for the obscure artists that Hazlewood recorded.

By recounting the story of Hazlewood's label, LITA tells the tale of a singer-songwriter and producer who had a nose for undiscovered and non-commercial talent. Hazlewood did have some commercial acts producing Gram Parsons and Nancy Sinatra for Reprise, but he was generally a quirky producer with limited success for his vast catalogue.

There is a Detroit connection to Rodriguez. When a Motor City girl group, the Mama Cats, showed up at his 900 Sunset Boulevard office, Hazlewood signed them and renamed them Honey Ltd. They had two songs, written by Bob Seger, that became their initial single as the Mama Cats, "Miss You" backed with "My Boy." (Hideout 1225). Hazlewood released a 1968 album **Honey Ltd**. That didn't; sell but quickly emerged as a cult classic.

Light In The Attic released **Honey Ltd: The Complete LHI Recordings** (LITA 102) in 2013. As the liner notes indicate, their album was long out of print, and it sold for $2000 at the Austin Record Show and or on E-Bay. The Honey Ltd. CD is a blend of girl group influences including an attempt to perform a folk oriented Ronettes' style set as well as influences from the Shangri Las and strangely the Pentangle. One of the differences between Honey Ltd. and the girl groups is that they also recorded an anti-war song, "Warrior," which described their attitude toward Vietnam. Jessica Hundley's literary liner notes suggest that even without hits, Honey Ltd. had a presence in the late 1960s counter-culture.

STEVE ROWLAND ON SULLIVAN

When Matt Sullivan had a vision to bring back long forgotten albums, Steve Rowland couldn't have been happier. He never imagined that a young kid would re-master **Coming From Reality**, provide copious and accurate liner notes, and package Rowland's forgotten production in a grand style. He was ecstatic.

Steve Rowland: "I had recently arrived in Palm Springs in September 2007, Matt called and told me that he was going to release Rodriguez' album, **Cold Fact**, and that my album would follow a year later. At that point he started talking about the film, **Searching For Sugar Man**."

Then all hell broke loose. **Searching For Sugar Man** became the sensation of the Sundance Film Festival and Steve Rowland's phone began ringing off the hook. "I couldn't believe the number of phone calls and e-mails I received," Rowland continued. "I told everyone that Rodriguez was the greatest artist that I produced. Finally, someone was listening."

Steve Rowland began appearing at movie theaters, answering questions about the documentary, as well as fielding a slew of radio and television interviews. He had trouble answering the many e-mail requests and newspaper interviews. He was continually discussing his career and connection to Rodriguez. Until the documentary slowed down, Steve was spending much of his time telling anyone who would listen: "Rodriguez is the greatest singer-songwriter that I have produced."

Rodriguez was back on the road. He had more offers to perform than he could handle. Steve Rowland heard from him, and when he came to the West Coast the Sugar Man was on the phone to Steve requesting that he show up at the El Rey Theater on Wilshire Boulevard in Los Angeles. Rodriguez has great respect for Rowland's producing talent. He counts him as a close friend more than forty years after the release of **Coming From Reality**.

Steve Rowland: "The first Rodriguez concert I went to was at the El Rey Theater. It was there that I met Matt. I thought that Matt was a great guy. I loved his attitude about neglected artists. Light In The Attic is a Godsend for obscure and forgotten artists. Without LITA, Rodriguez' music would have had only a cult audience."

When Steve listened to Light In The Attic's release of some previously unavailable Sly Stone material, he realized that Sullivan had the right attitude about re-releases. They were moving into uncharted territory.

Sly Stone's **I'm Just Like You: Sly's Stone Flower, 1969-1970** (LITA 121) is a brilliant example of what LITA does in unearthing hidden nuggets. This reissue is licensed from Stone's small label Stone Flower. It contains an electro-funk sound, which demonstrated that he was moving beyond his group.

Steve Rowland: "There is a sense about what is historically important in Sullivan's reissues. I love that. All the big wigs in the record industry don't seem to get it. You have to please the record collectors."

Steve reminisced about Sullivan. He considers him a person who has the mentality to help the guys who are completely neglected. Rowland pointed out that Light In The Attic is an artist-based label. The record business has changed and Matt Sullivan is in the forefront of that revolution. There are no longer big advances, an artist can't take a year or two to record an album, and much of the promotion has to be on the artist's nickel.

What LITA does is to secure the recording rights properly, obtain the artist's full cooperation, pay an eighteen per cent royalty, and then turn out a quality product. It is what the vinyl and CD collector's want. It is also expensive to produce. No problem. Matt Sullivan and the crew at LITA are not as interested in profit as they are in quality.

Steve Rowland: "Matt is very important. He went to Clarence Avant to properly obtain the rights to re-release those albums. No one had come out of the woodwork to re-release **Cold Fact** and **Coming From Reality**. Matt listened to a remix that David Holmes had made on the Rodriguez tracks 'Sugar Man.' He heard the talent that had been hidden for more than thirty-five years. Sullivan searched out the masters. The rest is history."

COLD FACT AND COMING FROM REALITY:
BEFORE SEARCHING FOR SUGAR MAN

When the special edition of the **SA Digest** came out to celebrate Rodriguez' 60th birthday, Nils Van der Linden wrote an affectionate tribute to the Sugar Man: "The Rodriguez Story...So Far." It was poignant and well written. "Rodriguez is an unlikely icon," Van der Linden continued. "He is sixty years old and has only recorded twenty songs and has not released any new material in the past thirty years." Van der Linden went on to emphasize the timeless nature of the Sugar Man's music. He concluded: "The legend lives on."

What the South African, Australian and English aficionados appreciated was the return of vinyl. For a time, it looked like vinyl was on its way out. Then LITA and other small Indie labels brought a vinyl resurgence, and Rodriguez was an artist that benefitted.

Matt Sullivan makes sure that Light In The Attic's vinyl is visually stunning. The inclusion of rare archive photos, re-mastering from the original tapes and in the case of Rodriguez reissues the liner notes by Kevin "Sipreano" Howes are a valuable addition. In Vancouver British Columbia, Howes has spent almost twenty years searching out records from the 1960s and 1970s. "A lot of eyes are on Light In The Attic since the Rodriguez work and the success of **Searching For Sugar Man**," Howes remarked. He concluded that Rodriguez is a cultural and spiritual artist.

Howes describes himself as a collector who seeks "off the grid" garage rock. He began working with Light In The Attic in 2003. His initial contribution to LITA was a Jamaica-Toronto series of six albums that traced the musicians who immigrated to Canada in the 1960s and 1970s from Jamaica. This was a music scene that went virtually unnoticed in Toronto, and then the LITA releases popularized the artists and the genre. In other words a group of Jamaican Rodriguez.' There is no one better suited to write the liner notes to **Cold Fact**. His graceful writing and insider knowledge helped to defuse many of the Rodriguez' myths.

THE GOAL IS QUALITY AT LITA:
IT IS OVER THE TOP ON THE WAY TO PROFITS

Light In the Attic is a reissue label that has had success with a wide variety of artists including the Lost Poet's first two LPs, several reissues of The Free Design, Betty Davis, the wife of Miles Davis, had two soul funk LPs, the rights to reissue Serge Gainsbourg's **Histoire de Melody Nelson**, Kris Kristofferson's early 1968 to 1972 demos and a host of Lee Hazlewood albums. What do these releases have in common? Quality! Cultural interest! The re-mastering makes the sound like a newly recorded album.

The hundreds of hours spent on re-release's makes the profit level enough to prosper. The Indie record market is an unforgiving one. The cost of an Indie release is about two dollars a unit. LITA spends three to five dollars. The licensing, ornate packaging, sophisticated liner notes and an eighteen per cent artist royalty drive the cost upward. Even with this cost factor, LITA's first eighteen releases broke even by September 2006. They were posed to make money, and they needed a best seller.

`That best seller happened unexpectedly when a CD **Wheedle's Groove: Seattle's Finest In Funk And Soul: 1965-1975** sold very well. This 2004 release highlights the music in Seattle's African American Central

District. This is the first quality collection of Seattle based funk music. The record collectors went out and found some pretty unusual material. The Overton Berry Trio covering the Beatles' "Hey Jude" is a masterpiece as is "Deep Soul, Part One" by Ron Buford with vocals by Ural Thomas originally on the Camelot label. The obscure and the arcane are brought to the listener by LITA. It is a brilliant collection.

The first volume of **Wheedle's Groove** developed a cottage industry for LITA as a second volume and an award winning feature documentary on disco and modern soul continued the project. The second volume of **Wheedle's Groove** tells the story of Seattle soul from 1972 to 1987 and it was developed and documented by DJ Supreme La Rock as an eighteen track compilation with the inclusion of the blue eyed soul song by Don Brown "Don't Lose Your Love" as well as Robbie Hill's Family Affair's soul-jazz masterpiece "Don't Give Up."

Where did the name **Wheedle's Groove** originate? It was the brainchild of KEXP DJ Johnny Horn. He had a Seattle radio show "Preachin' The Blues" on Sunday mornings and he played in a number of Seattle bands. Horn is also good friends with Matt Sullivan. Once again the obsessive-compulsive (that is a good thing) musician-collector comes to the forefront. The musicians included the legendary Seattle jazz artist Overton Berry, as well as Patrinell Staten, Ron Buford, and Kearney Barton was brought in to record the sound. The resulting albums collected serious funk songs from a wide variety of Seattle musicians. Each track was designed to be an untold history lesson. There were nine new songs recorded by legendary soundman Kearney Barton who cut the Wailers and Sonics 1960s classic Pacific Northwest songs. The inclusion of Overton Berry was a coup. The sales were extraordinary, and Light In the Attic was now an established label.

What is the importance of **Wheedle's Groove**? It is an example of the archeology of the record collector. The forgotten records in thrift shops, oddball record stores and garage sales were lovingly uncovered and brought to a small, but eager, audience. The liner notes explain everything for those who are not familiar with the artists. There is a sense of many Sixto Rodriguez's in these two CDs. The award-winning **Wheedle's Groove** documentary tells one all that you need to know about the soul-funk scene in and around Seattle. My only complaint is there should have been some live tracks from Birdland or the Black and Tan. But that was from my days living in Seattle. There are other LITA artists who could have been Rodriguez.

THE LIGHT IN THE ATTIC ARTISTS
WHO COULD HAVE BEEN RODRIGUEZ

The obscure artist is a Light In The Attic favorite. Karen Dalton's two re-releases **In My Own Time**, which came out in 1971 on the Just Sunshine label, and her mainstream Capitol record **It's So Hard to Tell Who's Going To Love You** are legendary reissues. Who is Karen Dalton? Why did LITA release her material? She was an early 1960s Greenwich Village folkie who performed with Bob Dylan. She eventually became homeless and died on the New York streets. She is a folk legend. She is Sixto Rodriguez without **Searching For Sugar Man**.

Another band that is reminiscent of Rodriguez is the Monks. They were an avant-garde rock group formed in Germany by U. S. servicemen. They were a classic American garage band that played Hamburg's Top Ten Club. This is where the Beatles plied their music on the notorious Reeperbahn. Their cult album, **Black Monk Time**, came out in 1966 on Polydor. The LITA reissue in 2008 presented another Rodriguez type group that continued to have a legendary status.

When Charles "Packy" Axton's **Late Late Party, 1965-1967** was released in 2009, LITA brought out the guitar brilliance of a former member of the Mar-Keys, who was the son of Everett and Estelle Axton. He developed his rhythm and blues guitar skills playing with Steve Cropper and Donald "Duck" Dunn. Why release Packy Axton's material? The answer is an obvious one. His guitar work ranks with that of Steve Cropper and James Burton. He drank and drugged himself to death before achieving solo fame and fortune.

THE BIRTH OF MODERN CLASSIC RECORDINGS

In 2011, LITA debuted their Modern Classic Records. These releases are from the classic collections of people in and around the label. It is actually music recorded recently and not found in the cut out bin of your local thrift store. "I was born in 1976 and we've never reissued much past that," Matt Sullivan remarked. When pressed for the details of how records are selected, Sullivan said the selections come from "our personal stash." When LITA released a Mercury Rev CD, Sullivan observed: "It's a bit surreal to be reissuing an album that we bought upon its original release. I remember sitting on the floor at Tower Records in the U-District and flipping through the British weeklies and monthlies, as they shelled out a 5 Star review for **Deserter's Songs**."

There is no sign of LITA slowing down. In November 2014 there were seventy-five reissue projects in various states of completion. The labels Modern Classic Recording series concentrates on vinyl pressings from the 1980s to the early 2000s. The albums slated for release include Morphine's **Cure For Pain**, Mercury Rev's **Deserter's Songs** and D'Angelo's **Voodoo**. When Matt Sullivan was asked if he made any money for the re-releases, he observed: "Not to be too negative, but there's a lot of crap in the world. I want to be able to put something more positive back out there." Sullivan also confesses he loves releasing the vinyl. He is still the consummate record collector.

On Friday November 14th 2013 Sixto Rodriguez headlined the tenth anniversary celebration at Seattle's Showbox Theater on First Avenue across from the Pike Place Market. When Rodriguez is asked about the concert he smiles and says: "I love the label, they send me firewood every winter for my stove." That is Sixto Rodriguez. He is thankful for the little things.

The lavish attention and detail that Sullivan and Wright go to at Light In The Attic is a tribute to their skills. Not to mention their love for the music. By uncovering previously obscure history, LITA is a path breaking enterprise. Not bad for two guys who met in the fourth grade.

chapter

EIGHT

CLARENCE AVANT AND THE RODRIGUEZ STORY: IS HE THE DEVIL OR IS THERE ANOTHER SIDE TO THE STORY?

"AS FAR AS I'M CONCERNED YOUNG MAN RODRIGUEZ NEVER HAPPENED." CLARENCE AVANT IN SEARCHING FOR SUGAR MAN

"I CAN'T MAKE SPEECHES, I MAKE DEALS." CLARENCE AVANT SPEAKING AT THE 2013 BET AWARDS

"CLARENCE WAS TOTALLY A BELIEVER. EVERY TIME I TALKED TO HIM ABOUT RODRIGUEZ, HE WOULD GET REALLY CHOKED UP." MATT SULLIVAN

"CLARENCE AVANT IS AN HONEST BUSINESSMAN. HE NEVER CHEATED ANYONE." MIKE THEODORE

In **Searching For Sugar Man**, Clarence Avant does not come off well. He takes the director, Malik Bendjelloul, to lunch. After a pleasant meal, they sit down in what looks to be Avant's sumptuous Beverly Hills mansion. It is. They are in a home Avant purchased in the 1970s. Avant smiles into the camera. He is at ease. Avant remarks that he was emotional at lunch when he thought about Rodriguez. He appears to genuinely care for and have the Sugar Man's best interests at heart.

He is asked about Rodriguez. Avant laughs. Then sheds some tears, as he recalls how much he loves Rodriguez. Out of the blue, the filmmaker asks: "What happened to the royalties?" Suddenly, the cackling, seemingly happy Avant turns into an angry businessman. He isn't used to being ambushed on camera.

He suggests to Bendjelloul that he doesn't appreciate the question. He pauses and looks at the camera. There is abject anger. It is a telling moment. His body language radiates the question is unfair. He is visibly displeased. But Avant has survived in the music business and prospered due to his knowledge, his ability to answer tough questions and his fifty years of dealing with questions concerning royalties. He is no stranger to controversy. He is also capable of defending himself. He is also pissed.

"You think somebody's getting to worry about a 1970 contract? If you do, you're out of your fucking mind," Avant angrily remarks to Bendjelloul. That comment went viral. What people miss is what Avant thought about the documentary. He did a number of post-**Searching For Sugar Man** interviews in which he explained his comment in the documentary. No one listened. Avant realized that he had made a mistake. He didn't care. He hadn't cheated Rodriguez out of a dime. Others had. But Clarence Avant is pure and simply innocent. Rodriguez didn't receive his royalties. The reasons are convoluted and often unclear. The bottom line is that Avant controlled a corporate empire where his distributor, Neil Bogart, his partnering record labels, A & M, perhaps the various South African and Australian labels and his label, Sussex, which went bankrupt in 1975, clouded the royalty question. He continues to license Sixto Rodriguez' material. Royalties are now paid timely.

In **Searching For Sugar Man** the South African record executives remarked that they sent the royalties to Avant's production company. The story ends there. It appears that he may not have paid royalties from these statements. Perhaps he did. Perhaps he didn't. No one has clarified the issue. The amount of royalties paid and the expenses of recording and producing the two albums were deducted from the royalties.

A former Avant employee remarked: "There were heavy expenses, they were deducted and nothing was left. In fact, Clarence lost money." What is known is that when Matt Sullivan's Light In The Attic licensed the Rodriguez' albums, Avant's company, Avant Garde, paid royalties promptly twice a year. The issue of past royalties is still clouded and unclear. But Clarence Avant is not the devil.

When Brian McCollum of the **Detroit Free Press** called Avant, he thoughtfully remarked: "I wish him the best. The fame will be over within a year. I'm happy for Rodriguez. I'm glad this thing came about. It just pisses me off that all of a sudden (people are saying), We're owed this we're owed that."

A kid ambushed Clarence Avant. Bendjelloul is in his early thirties, and he has the demeanor of a choirboy. Avant is a show business veteran in his eighties. He realized that the Bendjelloul interview was a mistake. It was too late.

SUSSEX RECORDS: A MINI-HISTORY

When Clarence Avant established Sussex Records in December 1969, he benefitted from working with MGM. The money for production and distribution was in place. Success seemed guaranteed. Sussex was also an artistically broad based label appealing to a wide variety of consumers. After Avant hired Dennis Coffey and Mike Theodore to produce, he worked to expand the label roster into the pop and soul realm. He did with hits by Bill Withers, Dennis Coffey and the Gallery.

The origin of Sussex Records had its roots in past Clarence Avant labels. He worked for a time with Neil Bogart and Buddah Records and for that reason Buddah became Sussex's distributor.

The Sussex artist roster included performers who were considered to have unlimited hit record prospects. A case in point is Priscilla Coolidge-Jones. She was Rita's sister and married to Booker T. of Booker T. and the MGs. Jones produced her album, and he convinced everyone that she was the next big female vocalist. Her 1970 album, **Gypsy Queen,** contained dynamic and unique vocals much like Janis Joplin or Genya Ravan. Did her cover of Leon Russell's "Hummingbird," have top 40 hit airplay written all over it? Clarence Avant thought that it did. The hits didn't happen. There were other Sussex acts that had hit potential. Chuck Brown played a musical style known as Beat: Go Go Music. This sound was redefined as funk. It was a type of sound that celebrated the pride of African American males. It was a decade too early. Avant's interest in jazz was shown with the signing of Willie Bobo. There was an eclectic side to Sussex. Avant signed an Amish band from Canada and early heavy metal rocker Mutzie. **Bill Cosby Presents Badfoot Brown & The Bunions Bradford Funeral Marching Band** was a very strange 1973 release of jazz funk. No one purchased it. It wasn't a Cosby comedy album. Cosby produced it, which turned out to be a gigantic mistake.

There were some one-hit wonders that made Sussex money. They included the Wadsworth Mansion's "What's On Tonight," which peaked at seven on the **Billboard** Hot 100 in 1971. One of the members of the Fifth Dimension, Ron Townson, brought Sussex Records a group, Creative Source, who had a number of hits and four albums in three years. Their 1973 R & B hit "You Can't Hide Love," peaked at forty eight, and it was followed in 1974 by a cover of Bill Withers' "You're Too Good To Be True," which charted at twenty one on the **Billboard's** R & B listing.

The ability to recognize talented producers was one of Avant's strengths. He brought Van McCoy in to produce a Washington D. C. band, the Presidents, who had a number eleven pop hit with their funk-soul song: "5-10-15-20 (25-30) Years of Love."

Just before Sussex faded into history in 1975 Faith, Hope and Charity had a number one **Billboard** R & B hit, "To Each His Own." It wasn't enough to save the label. When the IRS padlocked the doors, took the typewriters, froze the bank accounts and seized the office materials. Avant was on his way to new enterprises. He quickly founded another label, Tabu. But Sussex remains a confusing saga.

WAS BILL WITHERS LIKE SIXTO RODRIGUEZ?

When Bill Withers hit the top ten on **Billboard**, it was at the time that Rodriguez was cutting his albums. In Withers' Hollywood Hills home two Grammys sit side by side for the 1971 "Ain't No Sunshine" and the 1972 "Lean on Me" hits. In his eight-year career, Withers recorded some of the best pop-soul music and his 1980s award for the best R & B song for "Just The Two of Us" capped his legendary career. Then he simply walked away from the music business. The bullshit was too much, and he had a rich life outside the business.

. In 2015 Withers was surprised that he had been inducted into the Rock And Roll Hall of Fame. He celebrated by driving down to Le Petit Four for dinner. As his Lexus SUV pulled into the parking lot locals waved to Withers.

Like Rodriguez, Withers is humble, self-effacing and he doesn't think that he has done anything special. "What few songs I wrote during my brief career there ain't a genre that somebody didn't record them in," Withers told **Rolling Stone's** Andy Greene.

When Clarence Avant heard Withers' songs he immediately signed him to Sussex. "You just had to listen to his lyrics," Clarence Avant continued. "I set him up with Booker T. Jones to produce his album." At Sussex, Withers had total control over his music and he was paid. When Sussex went bankrupt in 1975, Withers moved on to Columbia Records where he had no control and fewer hits.

Clarence Avant treated Withers fairly. He helped him set up a publishing company, which his wife operates from a tiny office on Hollywood's Sunset Boulevard. Avant showed him how to copyright his songs, control his publishing, understand his mechanical rights and keep track of the finances. Withers' wife, Marcia, has an MBA and the money flows in to provide a nice lifestyle.

The Withers' have invested wisely in Los Angeles real estate and they live in a 5000 square foot house that is a million miles from his poor rural birthplace Slab Fork, West Virginia. What is missing in the Bill Withers story is that Clarence Avant found him, signed him, paid him and helped him to a brief but lucrative career. Clarence did pay him. End of story. Bill Withers took the money and made the most of it. He was through with the music business in the 1980s and the attempts to have Withers record or perform have gone for naught. Thanks to Clarence Avant's training and business fairness, Bill Withers did just fine. He didn't need the music business. The business needed him as his songs continue to generate a substantial income.

THE CONFUSING SUSSEX RECORDS SAGA AND AVANT'S GENIUS

What happened to Rodriguez' royalties? That is the nagging question that persists in the Sugar Man's story. It is a tale that surrounds the Sussex Record saga. There is a currency known as rands in South Africa that Rodriguez is owed. There are dollars in the U. S. There are pounds in the U. K. In Australia who knows what he is owed in royalties? The point is that there is a lot of money out there. No one seems to know where it went. Or for that matter how to find it.

The South African record executives interviewed in **Searching For Sugar Man** claim that royalties were sent to Sussex Records. Robbie Mann, the head of RPM, said that the label sold half a million copies of Rodriguez' albums. In the aftermath of the documentary, each album sold in excess of 200,000 copies and Rodriguez received royalties.

Neil Bogart, at Buddah Records, distributed Sussex and collected royalties. In **Searching For Sugar Man**, Craig Bartholomew-Strydom remarked that he found a London address to which royalties were sent. There was also a phone number. He called it. They told him to call back. He did the next day. The London phone was disconnected. This raised the conspiracy hackles of the Bartholomew-Strydom and Segerman team. They persisted in the hunt for the Sugar Man. Suddenly, the Sussex Record saga presented the Rodriguez hunters with another question. Who had the royalties? They met with filmmaker Malik Bendjelloul. They convinced him to ask Avant the royalty question. The end result is that they concluded that Avant had not paid royalties. They were wrong! It wasn't that simple. Avant licensed the material. Others collected the money. Neil Bogart was in charge for a time.

When Craig Bartholomew-Strydom was interviewed in **Searching For Sugar Man**, he had the best explanation of the royalty mystery. He found Avant's Los Angeles attorney, he contacted the various labels, he discovered a London post office box where royalties were sent, and he had some phone numbers. But people stopped talking to Bartholomew-Strydom. As Bartholomew-Strydom said, the question remains unclear and unsolved.

Although **Searching For Sugar Man** didn't portray Avant very well, few people questioned this depiction. He may be guilty of not paying royalties, and, then again, he may have a contractual reason for not paying royalties. A number of record company executives told me that Avant paid when there were royalties. He has paid Rodriguez since Light In The Attic re-released his two albums. The court cases will clarify Avant's malfeasance or lack of it. The reality is that Avant is an African American musical-business pioneer of skill and success.

Clarence Avant is one of the smartest and most accomplished individuals in the music business. He is also a pioneering African American entrepreneur, as well as an established force in Democratic Party politics. He remains a leader and innovator in music and the movie industry. Who is Clarence Avant? What did he do to further Rodriguez' career?

WHO IS CLARENCE AVANT?

Clarence Avant is a major music executive. He was born on February 25 1931 in North Carolina. He grew up in a hardscrabble Southern environment. He displayed a strong work ethic from his teen years.

He entered the music business in the 1950s working as the manager of Teddy P's Lounge in Newark, New Jersey. This nightclub, owned by a well-known promoter, Teddy Powell, provided the bright and inquisitive Avant with his earliest business-musical education. He learned to operate as a music manager while running a club on the East Coast. He dealt with record label owners, he learned production, he was a booking agent, he was a road manager, and he handled personal and legal problems. There wasn't much that Clarence Avant didn't do or know about the business. Along the way he decided to find an artist to manage.

That artist turned out to be Little Willie John. For a time, Avant was one of the guiding lights to John's career after Harry Balk parted ways with the diminutive singer. Avant helped Little Willie cross over into the pop market. Little Willie John made a lucrative living on the nightclub circuit. Then Clarence Avant got rid of the troubled singer. Like Harry, he got tired of bailing him out of jail.

Jazz was Avant's first love. For a time, he managed Sarah Vaughan and Jimmy Smith. When he was in Detroit, Avant was a regular at the Flame Bar. His knowledge of music in different cities, their labels, their nightclubs, their concert venues and their habits made him successful as a label owner and deal maker.

During his formative years in the music business, Avant lived for a time in New York. He developed a reputation as a jazz innovator. When Jimmy Smith and Lalo Schifrin produced the classic album, the **Cat**, Verve released it in 1964. Avant was the brains behind this break out jazz piece.

While working on the East Coast, Avant learned a great deal about the record business and bookings from Joe Glaser, who managed Louis Armstrong. Glaser was a major agent who booked one thousand African American acts into a wide variety of venues.

WHAT DID AVANT LEARN FROM JOE GLASER?

What did Clarence Avant learn from Joe Glaser? Plenty! Glaser emphasized the necessity of making tough business deals. From day one, Avant was known as a dealmaker. He didn't like the media. He preferred to be a lone wolf. That is the path Avant pursued.

He quickly developed not only a contract expertise; he also navigated the music businesses murky waters. He continued to learn from Joe Glaser who had precise business goals.

Glaser also believed in managing and booking as many artists as possible. The bottom line, according to Glaser, was profit. Avant has done this throughout his career. Although Glaser was a jazz aficionado, he believed in promoting all types of music. It was a good lesson for

Avant. Glaser schooled him not only in the subtle nature of contracts, bookings and business dealings, he also pointed out the importance of public relations.

Glaser lectured Avant on the need for a strong, somewhat vocal, personality. But Clarence was his own man. He listened. The reality was that Avant was a sharp contrast to Glaser. He is subtle. He is quiet. Like Glaser, he is a fierce dealmaker. The lasting lesson from Glaser, who was white, was not to bend to racial concerns. Clarence Avant always has had a sense of fair play. That is a trait ingrained in his upbringing, as well as his influence from Glaser.

AVANT LEARNS NEW LESSONS ABOUT
THE BUSINESS IN LOS ANGELES

When Avant founded Venture Records in 1967, prior to the Sussex label, he partnered with Motown A & R director William "Mickey" Stevenson. He also partnered with MGM Records. The idea was to create a bridge between African American entrepreneurs and a major record label.

Venture Records' biggest hit was The Ballads "God Bless Our Love," which peaked at eight on **Billboard's** R & B listing in 1968. Once he settled in Los Angeles, Avant signed Larry Williams and Vernon Garrett. They didn't have hits. The reason was a simple one. Larry Williams was well known for "Bony Maronie," "Short Fat Fannie" and "Dizzy Miss Lizzie." His hit window was over. Vernon Garrett is a marvelous blues-soul singer who was on the fringe of hit records.

What Avant learned is that his label needed young, contemporary performers. The number of acts recorded by Venture is amazing. For some reason virtually none of this excellent material is on compilation CDs. This is the price one pays for going into business with MGM. The label just didn't get it. Avant did. He quickly dissolved the partnership.

MGM was the worst Los Angeles record label to begin a business relationship. They had no idea how to promote their records. They single handedly killed Conway Twitty's rock and roll career. They gave Roy Orbison a million dollar signing bonus, and he never had the same level of hits on MGM. There were internal problems at the label. MGM had no direction, inadequate A & R people, a corporate structure that didn't like or understand rock and roll and a publicity department that seldom worked. It was a mess.

When he partnered with MGM in the late 1960s, Avant was a globetrotting entrepreneur. He moved to Los Angeles, but he remained a presence in Detroit, New York, Philadelphia, Chicago and Memphis. This was the first time that an African American businessman and a major record label did extensive business. As Avant partnered with MGM Records from 1967 to 1969, It was an important business lesson.

Venture Records was the blueprint for Sussex. He didn't want just a soul label. Avant developed a diverse artist roster. As Avant left MGM, they signed Petula Clark, the Osmonds and Sammy Davis Jr. Always the gentleman, Avant didn't point out that MGM Records was headed toward financial insolvency under executive Mike Curb. Not surprisingly, the label was sold to PolyGram/Phonogram.

Avant moved into ABC Management where he represented Duke Ellington, Lionel Hampton, Woody Herman, Dave Brubeck, B. B. King, the Allman Brothers and Barbra Streisand among others. He was a quiet adviser to the Stax's label. This turned out to be one of Avant's key strengths. He was a deal maker behind the scenes.

AVANT'S EARLY BUSINESS SUCCESSES

In 1968, Avant was involved in the business side of Memphis' Stax label. Al Bell, the president/owner of Stax had a distribution deal with Clive Davis and CBS Records. He called his good friend, Clarence Avant, for advise on the label's business problems. Davis was indicted for payola. He was out of the picture. The new group of CBS executives refused to honor the Stax distribution deal. They said that it cost too much money. They refused to distribute Stax's product and treated Bell's company like a competitor. That was the end of Stax.

When Stax closed its doors on December 17,1975 Bell's label had $304.59 in the company bank account. The irony is that Clarence Avant was having the same problems at Sussex. He did his best to advise Al Bell but Stax never recovered. Sussex quickly went bankrupt.

Avant was well thought of in the industry for his behind the scenes attempts to save Stax from bankruptcy. He failed. He did strike up a partnership with Stax's writers and artists. He began directing his creative energies toward legitimate theater. It took some time to find the right theater project.

Prior to the bankruptcy, Avant had business successes working with Bell. In August 1969, Avant, along with Stax's Al Bell, produced "The Reckoning," a well publicized African American play featuring the Negro Ensemble from New York's St. Mark's Playhouse. "The Reckoning" was a successful off-Broadway production. It starred Jeannette Dubois who later went on to stardom, in the television show, Good Times. Avant didn't make much money from this theater production. He did enhance his already stellar show business reputation as a producer and consummate dealmaker.

WHAT SUSSEX RECORDS MEANT TO THE RODRIGUEZ STORY

As 1970 broke in the music business, Avant had a solid reputation. He also had the idea for another record label. This is when he founded Sussex. The label's office at 6430 W. Sunset Blvd was located in the midst of Hollywood's record row. Avant believed that he had made a mistake at Venture Records by concentrating upon black music. He wanted a diverse roster at Sussex.

His biggest business mistake was to partner with Buddah's Neil Bogart The problem with Bogart's business practices is that the money arrived slowly. That is if it arrived at all. By 1974, Avant ended the agreement with Buddah. Then he went bankrupt. There were some best selling artists despite Neil Bogart's alleged business malfeasance.

Bill Wither's was Sussex's biggest selling artist with a number of pop and r and b hits. Withers' three million selling singles "Ain't No Sunshine," number 3 pop, 6 R and B in 1972, "Lean On Me," number 1 pop in 1972 and "Use Me," number 2 pop also in 1972 brought in enough money to keep the label afloat.

After Avant signed a distribution agreement with Bogart, it looked like a smart move. It wasn't. Bogart invented bubble gum music, and he had an interest in the Monkees. He was a hard sell guy. He convinced Avant that he could profit from Bogart distributing Sussex's product. But an alleged drug problem, poor business practices, a heavy ego and a lack of organization doomed Buddah.

As Avant continued to live in Beverly Hills, he directed Sussex Records through the dangerous corporate waters that made owning a record label perilous. Sussex benefitted from Dennis Coffey and Mike Theodore's skilled production. Avant moved them to Los Angeles to take over studio and production duties. It worked for a while, and then Coffey relocated back to Detroit. Theodore moved to New York, where he founded a recording studio with Bob Babbitt. He also became one of the most sought after producers in a wide variety of musical styles. Theodore and Coffey had one group, the Gallery, which saved Sussex for a time.

The Gallery was a soft rock group formed in Detroit in the early 1970s. Their 1972 hit, "Nice To Be With You," peaked at four on **Bill-**

board's Hot 100. They had two other minor hits thanks to Coffey and Theodore's productions, as well as John Rhys' guiding hand.

The Gallery's two albums and six singles sold well. In 1972, the Gallery's "Nice To Be With You" spent twenty-two weeks on the **Billboard** pop chart tying with War's "Slippin' Into Darkness" for most consecutive weeks on the pop chart that year. By 1974, the hits dried up and the band moved on to day jobs.

Clarence Avant ignored Sixto Rodriguez. Why? In **Searching For Sugar Man** Avant gave a clue to his thinking. He said that Spanish music wasn't happening. The soft, pop rock sound emanating from other Sussex artists was the opposite of the Sugar Man's music. He simply had no supporters at Sussex. Steve Rowland, an independent producer, wasn't consulted on how to market Rodriguez or for that matter how to record the Sugar Man. That turned out to be a mistake. Rowland knew how to produce a Rodriguez LP. He also had specific marketing ideas. Sussex ignored him.

Steve Rowland: "I simply said leave him alone, prepare the studio and make him comfortable. He will do the rest."

Rowland made the point that with proper publicity, Rodriguez would sell a large cache of records. No matter what Rowland said about how to promote the Sugar Man, no one listened. The one positive aspect of Sussex Records is that Clarence Avant spared no expense in recording **Cold Fact** and **Coming From Reality**. More than forty years later, the productions hold up beautifully.

There was another reason for ignoring the Rodriguez material. In the 1970s, Avant had his fingers in so many fiscal pies it was hard to keep track of his frenetic activity. He was the consummate businessman.

AVANT THE ENTREPRENEUR'S SUCCESSES: FROM THE 1970s TO THE 1990s

He was always an entrepreneur looking for new investments. In 1971, he founded Avant Garde Broadcasting becoming the first African American to own an FM radio station in the greater Los Angeles area.

His specialty was investing in businesses that served the minority community. He became a part of the Urban National Company, which was a private venture capital fund that financed high-risk minority businesses. Avant's objective was to level the playing field for African Americans. He convinced Harvard and Yale, as well as such heavyweight businesses as John Hancock, Atena Insurance, Mobil Oil, Gulf Oil and J. P. Morgan, to finance a ten million dollar fund to aid minority businesses.

The Urban National Company was short lived. On November 20, 1975 Urban National declared bankruptcy. The IRS seized company records, equipment and froze its assets. Avant lost over half a million dollars. The intertwining of Avant's businesses allowed him to escape total bankruptcy. He had a defined, stable and legally organized group of businesses. When Sussex Records went bankrupt, it was a minor blip in his financial empire.

He ventured into film. Paramount Pictures released **Save The Children** in September 1973. This feature film highlighted some of the best African American musical acts. Almost unnoticed in the film credits was Clarence Avant, executive producer. Others received most of the credit but without Avant the documentary wouldn't have been financed or released.

He single handedly convinced Paramount to release the film. He also sat in the background, while the Rev. Jesse Jackson, took more credit than he deserved. That was fine with Avant. He likes to remain in the background and make the deals.

This was one of the earliest African American civil rights protests on film. The Watts Riots of the 1960s; the decline in jobs, educational change and business opportunities prompted Avant to work for increased African American rights. In the process, he became one of Los Angeles' most respected and savviest entrepreneurs.

Avant, as executive producer, was responsible for securing the major acts for **Save The Children**. The film was shot at the Operation Push Black Expo in Chicago. When the film premiered at New York's Apollo Theater, Avant was recognized as a force in bringing black music into the broader commercial mainstream.

Clarence Avant is a shrewd businessman. His forte is contracts. This is why it is difficult for the Sugar Man to collect royalties. The agreement that Rodriguez signed with Avant's publishing company, Interior Music, set up safeguards against earlier contracts. There was a third party clause that stated royalties would not be paid until any third party claims, suspected or otherwise, were settled. There was nothing illegal in Avant's contracts. He knew show business inside and out, and he was successful.

CLARENCE AVANT'S SECOND MUSICAL ACT

Shortly after Rodriguez was dropped from Sussex Records, the label declared bankruptcy. In 1975, Avant founded Tabu Records signing the SOS Band, the soul singer Cherrelle, Alexander O'Neal, as well as Kool and the Gang. Avant had a change of heart about his new record label. He no longer wanted pop acts or a diverse roster. Tabu was a funk, rhythm and blues label. He had a brief distribution deal with RCA. He increasingly concentrated upon disco. He made a quick fortune.

By 1982, Avant began working with Jimmy Jam and Terry Lewis who produced for Solar Records. The result was a flood of hits and another fortune. By 1987, Avant had deals with Sony and CBS. The money flooded into Tabu's coffers.

In 1987, Avant promoted Michael Jackson's first world tour netting one hundred and twenty five million dollars. When he was named Chairman of the Board at Motown in 1993, it had as much to do with his successes with Jackson's tour as anything else. Avant was considered the major dealmaker in the African American music-business community.

PAVING THE WAY FOR SUCCESS AT MOTOWN

The upshot of Avant's business activity paved the way for other African American entrepreneurs. If there is one deal that Avant made that saved a company, it was his business plan for Motown. When he became Motown's Chairman, in 1993, the finances, planning, production and business direction indicated that bankruptcy was a possibility. Avant had experienced every con act, every jive explanation, and every shady deal in the music business. He was able to work with Jherly Busby, the CEO at Motown, to turn the label's finances around. By 1992, Motown sales dropped to twenty million dollars a year down from one hundred million in Motown's heyday. Most of Motown's revenue came from its back catalogue.

Avant convinced Busby to concentrate on a young, talented, newly emerging artist roster. He did. The results were extraordinary. By 1993, the profits returned and PolyGram purchased Motown for three hundred and one million dollars. Busby was named president. Avant quietly went on to other ventures. He saved the label. How did he do it? He learned from his previous business failures.

AVANT AND SOUTH AFRICA

In 1993, Avant began investing in South Africa, where he partnered with the World African Network for a twenty-four hour pay TV cable network. Avant supplied musical acts to the network. This venture was not a profitable one. The irony is that he was in the midst of South African business. He never mentioned whether or not he knew of Rodriguez' enormous record sales.

By 1997, Avant was the first African American to serve on the International Management Board for PolyGram. Ironically, in the late 1990s, as Rodriguez emerged in the flesh for South African concerts, Avant was part of an investment group that created a twenty million dollar partnership with Pepsi Cola to build a bottling plant in South Africa. As Rodriguez performed before adoring crowds, Avant was selling Pepsi Cola to the locals. No one realized that Avant and Rodriguez had careers that flourished side by side. It was Avant who urged Pepsi Cola to take a socially responsible position in matters of race.

He must have been aware of Rodriguez' record sales. If not, he had to have some idea about the stunning 1998 South African tour. It was the media event of the year. It was billed as "Dead Man Walking" in the Cape Town media.

This was Pepsi Cola's first business venture in South Africa since 1985. It turned out to be a commercial disaster. After apartheid ended, Avant talked Pepsi into returning by pointing to the new and increasingly liberal fiscal climate. Avant's South African bottling venture lost money when sales declined. Local investors complained of mismanagement. In May 1998, Pepsi Cola agreed to pay stock shares to investors who lost money in the South African bottling company. Pepsi Cola stated that it stood by its policy of partnering with minority businesses.

Avant then took his minority business plan to Florida. During the late 1990s, he was a principal investor in the Royal Palm Crowne Plaza Hotel in Miami. It was the first major African American owned hotel in the U. S.

In February 1999, Avant departed Motown to join PolyGram, which was purchased by Seagram's. He had worked with PolyGram on a film distribution project. Why did PolyGram hire the sixty-eight year old Avant? The answer is a simple one. He had worked for the labels and corporations that PolyGram acquired including Motown. He was also a fierce and respected dealmaker with a sterling reputation. Some saw him as a contract fixer.

HOW AVANT BECAME THE FIXER FOR SEAGRAMS AND WHAT DID THIS HAVE TO DO WITH RODRIGUEZ?

When Seagram's purchased PolyGram, they acquired a complicated and multI- layered corporation. In 1995, PolyGram acquired ITC Entertainment for $156 million, now they had a first class television and film library that needed packaging. Avant was a major force in the lucrative repackaging. Seagram's also decided to merge PolyGram into the Universal Music Group. When Seagram's bought PolyGram they realized that a knowledgeable music man had to come in and straighten out their business affairs. That music man was Clarence Avant. He was paid a CEO's salary. His net worth continued to expand. He cleaned up the fiscal and management problems at PolyGram and the Universal Music Group.

Avant's most ambitious business plan in 1998 was as the chairman of the Urban Box Office Network, Inc. This was a media outlet aimed at a minority audience. It wasn't properly funded. UBO declared bankruptcy in 1999. Without missing a beat, Avant joined the advisory board of Mjuice.com, the Web's largest secure digital music retailer. That company continues to be profitable. By 2000, Avant approaching seventy was one of the most powerful and richest executives in the music industry.

AVANT MENTORED SOME OF THE BEST IN THE MUSIC BUSINESS AND HIS POSITIVE FEELINGS FOR RODRIGUEZ

Clarence Avant has mentored giants in the music industry including Quincy Jones, Miles Davis, Kenneth "Babyface" Edmonds, Antion "L. A." Reid, Sean "Puffy" Combs and Stevie Wonder among others.

While Avant has licensed Rodriguez' material over the years, there were few deals for the Sugar Man's music. In August 2008, Matt Sullivan concluded an agreement with Avant to release **Cold Fact**. In 2014 Sullivan pointed out that his dealings with Avant were excellent ones. Sullivan says that Avant has a personal fondness for Rodriguez. He believes in his music. Sullivan implies that Avant is not the ogre portrayed in **Searching For Sugar Man**.

The licensing agreement with Light In The Attic guarantees Sixto Rodriguez royalties, as well as payments for Steve Rowland, Dennis Coffey and Mike Theodore. They are now receiving twice yearly checks from Clarence Avant's company, Avant Garde.

AVANT'S POLITICAL AND PHILANTHROPIC SIDE AND HIS DAUGHTER NICOLE

Avant is also a recognized philanthropist. His daughter, Nicole Avant, is a music executive and, like her father, she is active in Democratic politics. She was nominated by President Barack Obama to become the American Ambassador to the Bahamas. Secretary of State Hillary Rodham Clinton swore her into office on September 9, 2009. She served in that position with distinction until returning to private life on November 21, 2011.

In 2008, Nicole, raised more than twenty-one million dollars for Barack Obama's presidential campaign. She also talks politics regularly with California Governor Jerry Brown. She has business connections with Magic Johnson.

Nicole Avant was an excellent ambassador. She concentrated upon a five-point program emphasizing education, alternative energy, economic growth combined with small business development and women's rights. She introduced extensive programs for people with disabilities. The level of business between the U. S. and the Bahama's increased. Perhaps her most notably achievement was in the field of education, where the Bahamas literacy rate improved dramatically. She personally visited more schools than any previous ambassador.

Ambassador Avant received the Sue M. Cobb Award for Exemplary Diplomatic Service in 2011. The following year, she was honored at the 20th Annual Trumpet Awards for her dedication to public service. The **Bahama Tribune** headlined: "Ambassador Avant-A Job Well Done." She was one of the most popular U. S. Ambassadors to serve in the Nassau Embassy.

Since leaving her position as Ambassador to the Bahamas, Nicole has become an activist for Obamacare. She continues to be a force in Democratic politics, as well as an accomplished businesswoman.

Like her father, Nicole made a name for herself in the music business. She began her career doing promotional work for A and M Records. She is also a Vice President with Interior Music Publishing. Her work in the music industry is combined with charity events. Her mentorship program for high school students through the University of Southern California is a catalyst to minority students attending college. The American Cancer Society and a wide variety of other organizations have recognized her contributions to public service and philanthropy.

When he turned seventy-five in February 2006, Avant was featured on the cover of **Billboard**. He remains one of the most respected and influential figures in the music industry. **Billboard** noted: "He's the perennial godfather of our business." Quincy Jones pointed out that if an artist hoped for a career, they should consult Avant.

RODRIGUEZ ON CLARENCE AVANT

When **Searching For Sugar Man** was released, there was an intensified interest in Avant's relationship with Rodriguez. There are many opinions and even more ideas on where the money went over the years. There are still no concrete answers. At least not publicly.

Rodriguez weighed in on Avant during one interview. He said that he hadn't talked to Clarence for thirty-five years. He also pointed out that there were numerous bootlegs of his material. "It's not like there's not a trail there," Rodriguez said of the South Africa and Australia releases. He continued: "I think that that will be resolved. I really think it will be because it's so public now."

It is typical of Sixto Rodriguez that he apparently has no ill will toward Avant. The problem is that there are no concrete cold facts that prove that Avant knowingly or willingly didn't pay Rodriguez. But there is royalty money. Where? That is the question.

CLARENCE AVANT AS THE VILLIAN OR IS HE?

An industry insider told me that the image of Clarence Avant in **Searching For Sugar Man** is akin to Milton's sexy Satan, Balzac's scheming driven master criminal Vautrin or Shakespeare's Iago. This seems an extreme judgment. Most people said that Avant was being forthright. Avant is none of these fictional characters. He represents the typical music business insider who has contracts favorable to his companies.

In **Searching For Sugar Man**, Clarence Avant is cast as the villain. He is remembered for his comment in the documentary on whether or not Rodriguez was paid royalties: "You think it's something I'm going to worry about, a 1970 contract?" Avant continued: "If you do, you're out of your God damned mind."

When he watched the film, Avant had second thoughts about his participation. He also speculated that he had nothing to do with where the money went. He regrets appearing flippant.

Those who know Avant claim that he didn't get the money from either Australia or South Africa. They have said that he is innocent of not paying royalties. "I don't know who the South Africans were paying and I don't know who had my foreign rights," Avant remarked. No one has shown that this is not true.

In the next breath, Avant admitted to controlling Rodriguez' music. This doesn't seem to make sense. He claims that he didn't receive royalties, but he controls song publishing and licensing agreements. In a 2012 interview with **New York Times'** journalist, Larry Rohter, Avant remarked that he made a deal with Universal Music, the largest music publishing company in the world, to license Rodriguez' songs. The mystery remains. Where is the money? No one seems to know.

When Light In The Attic issued **Cold Fact** in August 2008 and **Coming From Reality** in May 2009, Matt Sullivan was a key force in getting Rodriguez back into the clubs. He brought him into Seattle to appear at the Triple Door. He also booked him into New York's prestigious Joe's Pub. A booking in Los Angeles' Echo Club turned up further interest in Rodriguez. In 2009, he headlined in London at the

Barbican. Long before **Searching For Sugar Man** made him famous, he was back on the road. This was due to Matt Sullivan. These venues are small but high-end clubs. They attract a great deal of media attention. Had Avant not licensed the material, none of this would have been possible. So maybe he is not the villain.

THE POLITICAL SIDE OF CLARENCE AVANT

Clarence Avant is not only a multi-millionaire, he is a liberal Democrat who hangs out with President Barack Obama, Congresswoman Barbara Boxer, New York Representative Charles Rangel and former Secretary of State Hillary Clinton. He is a major figure in California Democratic politics. He is a formidable person in the entertainment and political arena.

His ability to hold fundraisers and to support key Democratic Party candidates provides him with access to the governor's office, as well as the White House.

Democratic National Committee
   23 contributions • $176000 ('89→'12)
Barack Obama 44th President of the United States
   12 contributions • $117900 ('04→'12)
Democratic Congressional Campaign Committee
   15 contributions • $51000 ('93→'12)
Barbara Boxer US Senator and Representative from California
   15 contributions • $38100 ('91→'10)
DNC-Non-Federal Individual
   3 contributions • $30000 ('93→'99)
Democratic Senatorial Campaign Committee The Democratic Senatorial Campaign...
   14 contributions • $27600 ('92→'11)
Charles Rangel US Representative from New York
   12 contributions • $16500 ('94→'12)
Hillary Clinton Former Secretary of State
   8 contributions • $14500 ('03→'08)
John Conyers Jr US Representative from Michigan
   14 contributions • $12150 ('94→'11)
Howard Lawrence Berman US Representative from California
   8 contributions • $11500 ('01→'11)

How politically connected is Clarence Avant? The answer is a simple one. He is extremely connected. The Avant home hosted fundraisers for Governor Jerry Brown, President Jimmy Carter and a new candidate for the presidency in 2008, Barack Obama. Former Los Angeles Mayor Tom Bradley is a friend and frequent guest in the Avant household. Gray Davis, before he became California's governor, had an office in Interior Music and Avant Garde Music.

For more than two decades Bill and Hillary Clinton attended Democratic Party fundraisers at Avant's home. But it was Barack Obama that Avant supported with a concerted set of campaign fundraisers. Avant was known as a "bundler." This is a person who raises a half million dollars or more for a political candidate. A bundler delivers campaign cash in a large sum from a number of donors. The Federal Election Commission doesn't require that bundled funds be reported unless the money comes from a lobbyist. Avant is not a lobbyist. He sent the money to the Obama campaign as a bundler. Avant was one of 769 bundlers who raised more than one hundred and eighty six million for Obama's 2012 re-election campaign. This was almost twenty percent of Obama's campaign war chest.

A few days after Thanksgiving, 2013, Clarence Avant attended a fundraiser at Magic Johnson's Beverly Hills mansion is support of the Affordable Care Act, otherwise known as Obamacare. The President, Magic Johnson and Avant had a friendly, spirited discussion. Avant is politically connected, and he enjoys it.

Clarence Avant, the Godfather of Black Music, remains a business-political figure on the Los Angeles music scene and the liberal Democratic political scene. He shows no signs of slowing down.

Clarence Avant has only good thoughts about Sixto Rodriguez. He quietly funded an abortive 1997-1998 attempt at a third album. He has paid Rodriguez royalties since 2008. There is no one happier than Avant about Rodriguez' late in life success.

HITSVILLE U. S. A. THE HOME OF MOTOWN

chapter

NINE

MIKE THEODORE: THE QUIET GENIUS BEHIND COLD FACT

"GENIUS IS NOTHING MORE NOR LESS THAN CHILD-HOOD RECAPTURED AT WILL." CHARLES BAUDELAIRE

Mike Theodore is the quiet genius behind **Cold Fact**. Why? The answer is a simple one. It is his arrangements and sophisticated production techniques that define his brilliance and that of the album. Theodore is quiet and unassuming. He has that in common with Rodriguez. They are content to simply work, produce and hone their craft in a timeless manner. Theodore seldom mentions that he has engineered, arranged or produced almost eight hundred albums.

There was a drive in Theodore to become an integral part of the music industry while he was in high school. He pursued the mastery of record production. After a successful high school music and academic career, as well as four years of studying college biology with good grades, he pursued music with a frenetic zeal. Theodore's desire was to wear all the musical hats. As a result, he learned production, arranging, songwriting, mixing and performing. He has done it all over a fifty plus year career. But biology was never far from his mind.

Mike Theodore: "I wanted a backup career in case the music business didn't work out."

THE MIKE THEODORE CONNECTION
TO SIXTO RODRIGUEZ

It is common knowledge that Mike Theodore co-produced **Cold Fact**. What is his connection to Sixto Rodriguez and why is it important? The answer is not a simple one. Theodore, like Rodriguez, grew up in Detroit, and the local musical scene influenced him. That helped him understand the Sugar Man when they recorded **Cold Fact**.

Theodore's insider knowledge of the record business is one reason that he was important to the Sugar Man. Theodore, along with Dennis Coffey, crafted pop songs that were headed for the charts. They also had the lyrical content that the critics loved. After watching Rodriguez perform in clubs, Theodore, along with Coffey, was able to coax an album out of him. It is in Theodore's extensive and diverse background that **Cold Fact's** foundation was laid. The obvious conclusion is that Theodore understood Rodriguez. He also knew how to get the best of out him in the studio.

THEODORE'S FORMATIVE YEARS: BIOLOGY AND MUSIC

It is Theodore's early years that set the stage for his emergence as one of the music industries premier arrangers and noted producers. Along the way, he became proficient on three instruments. He also developed as a prolific songwriter. He learned the subtle nuances of production. He was an experienced engineer. He built a recording studio. He was an in demand arranger. He worked in most of the recording studios in and around Detroit. He managed three studios in New York. He hawked records around the Motor City. He also played in various bands, and, for a time, he had his own record label. His Detroit based label, Sound Score Records, was Theodore's initial venture into the music world. He founded a publishing company appropriately named High Hopes. He did much of this while still in high school, and he continued his studio wizardry for more than forty years.

It is Theodore's early years in the music business that made him a natural to co-produce **Cold Fact**. He was twenty-five years old when he began production on Rodriguez '**Cold Fact**. Despite his youth, he had a decade of experience in the record business.

IT ALL BEGAN AT ST. BENEDICT

When Theodore was born in 1944 the Detroit economy boomed. He lived near Highland Park and attended St. Benedict. This was the premier Catholic high school.

Mike Theodore was fourteen years old when he decided to pursue a music career. Then he thought long and hard about it. He was also a terrific science student. He loved school. So he committed his school days to biology and by night he was a music fanatic.

When he heard Henry Mancini, he found a sound that shaped his early musical development. The soundtrack to **Peter Gunn** was a constant inspiration. The ABC TV show from 1958 to 1961 provided a musical theme that brought a heavy duty brass influence to Theodore's future musical productions. It was listening to Mancini's sophisticated music with the light orchestra style and the scintillating string arrangements that provided his earliest role model. The crisp and clean Mancini sound caught Theodore's attention, and he began figuring out ways to replicate it.

As a young kid, he also listened intently to RCA's **Victory At Sea** soundtrack. This music peaked his interest in orchestration. The semi-classical soundtrack was another influence on a fledgling musician. "As I got older, I really appreciated the classics," Theodore remarked. The irony is that years later he would mix hit records in New York's RCA studio. There was of course rock and roll music in which he developed a major interest.

THE STARLIGHTERS AND THE EARLY MUSIC BUSINESS

Theodore organized his first music group, the Starlighters, even before he attended St. Benedict. He was in grade school and doo-wop was the style. They performed covers and Mike wrote original songs.

He graduated from St. Benedict in 1963 and spent the next three years with his label running around Detroit radio stations promoting his 45s. He had some local success and learned a great deal about the business.

Although he was just a kid, Mike Theodore's Sound Score Records, operated from 273 W. Montana which was his home. He arranged, wrote and produced a 45 for Nickey, Lorraine and Lucy, "The Way It Goes" backed with "All Over But The Crying." Theodore recalled that he printed about 300 copies. The girls attended Mumford High, and their manager Ian Gaum was a student at St. Benedict whose mother drove him everywhere. It was a strange sight as Gaum had music aspirations, but he wasn't old enough to drive a car.

The Starlighters were hired eventually by George Golson to perform at teen clubs and to sing back up for the Four Imperials on their 1958 record "Lazy Susan," backed with "Let's Make A Scene." This 45 was eventually picked up by Dot.

They were an instant hit. Golson took the group to meet Harvey Fuqua at Motown. Nothing came of this meeting. But Theodore, who never worked for Motown, was in the mix, and he took note of Motown's style.

In 1960 the Starlighters recorded "Zoom" backed with "Big Feet" (HI-Q 5016) for the Hi-Q label. The 45 received extensive Detroit area airplay. This single was an early experience in the woeful problems of the record business. Theodore didn't have a distributor. He was a one-man show determined to succeed. He went to every Detroit radio station with his product and a strong pitch. His records were carefully written and beautifully produced. Nothing happened. It was a great learning experience.

THE D TOWN RECORD EXPERIENCE

D Town Records was one of many Detroit labels that Theodore worked at briefly. It was a rhythm and blues and soul label, and in the present day many U. K. Northern Soul classics emanate from D Town. Mike Theodore had a limited experience with D Town. He did two pop records for the R and B label.

Theodore wrote and produced for the Dimensions "Little Lotta Lou" (DT 1038) in 1964. He also produced and arranged "My, My Love" for Armand Kay in 1963. Theodore remarked that he learned a great deal from D Town founder Mike Hanks. What Theodore didn't say is that Hanks often took producing credit. That was the music business in the 1960s.

Rodriguez faced many of the same obstacles as the predatory nature of the record business defeated most artists. Even those with mega hit records, like Del Shannon, had continual complaints about collecting their royalties. It wasn't just a problem that Rodriguez faced. It was the face of the industry.

Although he was still a teenager, Mike Theodore got behind D Town Records. He helped to promoter Armand Kay's solo career. Kay is an interesting figure in the Motor City. He went on to a local career releasing "Always Be True" backed with "The Bigger They Are" (DT 1714-1715) on the D-Town label in 1963. The nineteen-year-old Theodore was the creative brain behind some of D Town's best 45 releases. By 1966, D Town Records faded into obscurity.

Mike Theodore: "We had another group, the Castaways, they were from Highland Park College. They weren't the same group who had the hit 'Liar Liar.' They were local kids who were popular playing at the sox hops. I did some recording with them."

When Theodore met the Castaways at Palmer Park, he booked them into the teen clubs and did a demo record that received some airplay on local radio. At the time, Theodore was a drummer. He soon tired of this instrument. He began playing the sax. "I didn't want to lug around a saxophone, so I learned to play the piano," Theodore recalled.

GOLDEN WORLD'S IMPACT ON THEODORE AND COFFEY

Mike Theodore met Dennis Coffey in 1966. Theodore was playing guitar on the Holidays' "I'll Love You Forever," and they talked at length. They had common musical interests. After the producer asked Theodore to come into the studio to arrange some violins and horns, he worked with Coffey. They split the fee. The experience with the Holiday's was an important one. Theodore not only witnessed the inner workings of Ed Wingate's Golden World studio, he quickly learned the production process.

Theodore recalled his meeting with Coffey at Golden World. They had the same musical ideas, and they clicked working as a team. They started hanging out together and eventually this led to Theo-Coff Productions.

Mike and Dennis got together the next night at Theodore's Montana Street home near Highland Park to work on arranging Jack Montgomery's Scepter single "Dearly Beloved" backed with "Do You Believe It" (SCE12152). Montgomery's 45 eventually became a Northern Soul favorite. That 45 record release led to the formation of the company known as Theo-Coff Productions, and it began Coffey and Theodore's legendary partnership.

The number of major record labels, like Scepter, that sought Theodore's help to fix, arrange or produce suggests the level of his talent.

MIKE THEODORE ON MEETING DENNIS COFFEY

After Theodore met Coffey, he said: "We were on the same journey. So why not double our power?" That began a friendship, a working relationship and a company, Theo-Coff, which helped to define the Detroit sound from 1966 to the present day. The Theo-Coff Production team also worked on commercials or any project that brought in a paycheck.

There were many things that Theodore and Coffey had in common. They worked with and knew the important session musicians. They could write charts, they could arrange the sessions, they were songwriters, and they could produce. They were aware of every subtle nuance in the record business. This helped Theo-Coff to achieve an extraordinary level of success.

The Theo-Coff Production team worked for a number of local labels. There were more than four hundred small record labels in and around Detroit in the 1960s. These obscure labels were a training ground for Theodore. He worked with a wide variety of acts, including soul singer Spyder Turner, Irene and the Scotts, Jack Montgomery, Nabay and Tommy Frontera among others.

It was Theodore's ability to arrange and write charts that made him an in-demand producer. Eventually, Theodore and Coffey found a studio where they could produce day and night. Once they entered the Golden World Studio and then Tera Shirma, the road to a Northern Soul legendary production career was in place.

ENTERING GOLDEN WORLD AND FINDING A
CAREER AND EARLY NORTHERN SOUL ARTISTS

In 1963, eighteen-year-old Mike Theodore went to Golden World Studio looking for a job. He was attending Highland Park College. He had a music career in mind. He met John Rhys at Golden World. They talked. Theodore told him that he had arranging talent. Rhys listened. He wanted a job. Why not, Rhys thought. "The kid had chutzpah coming in the door looking to arrange hit records," Rhys said.

By 1966, Theodore was a Golden World mainstay. He was at times a fixer. The Fantastic Four's "Girl Have Pity" (RIC Tic 119) was a single that he was brought in to clean up the arrangements. "I went home after Ed Wingate asked me to write the string section and I completed the arrangement. Gene Redd produced it," Theodore said. George Clinton was involved in the songwriting, as he hung around the studio learning what he could about production. They also had a hit record, as the single was a monster Detroit hit. It was featured daily on 50,000 watt CKLW and the Fantastic Four moved on to a degree of national exposure.

The Fantastic Four was Ric Tic's biggest selling artist. Wingate, who owned Golden World, used Theodore extensively in the studio and while he didn't always receive label credit, he helped to fix the production on many early hit records. The Fantastic Four had five **Billboard** R & B chart hits and surprisingly they outsold Edwin Starr and J. J. Barnes.

MIKE THEODORE'S BACKGROUND INDICATING
A SOUL FUNK PRODUCER

Mike Theodore is a producer with a pop touch. He has a soul, funk and disco background. He also likes the sound of a big band. For a time, he led the Mike Theodore Orchestra. If there is a Hall of Fame for disco producers, Theodore is a candidate for immediate induction. As a multi-instrumental musician, a skilled songwriter with innovative production skills, he had many ideas for **Cold Fact**. When he combined with Dennis Coffey to bring Rodriguez' visionary folk lyrics into the pop musical realm the hits didn't come instantly, but the dye was cast for future greatness. No one believed that it would take forty plus years to recognize **Cold Fact's** genius. It did.

Their production company, Theo-Coff, laid the foundation for Rodriguez' **Cold Fact**. What Coffey and Theodore saw in Rodriguez was a humble, honest, shy and simple songwriter. They also discovered a unique talent. He wrote lyrics and music that no one surpassed.

They compared him to Bob Dylan. But Rodriguez didn't like talking. He had a manger. Her name was Rainy M. Moore. In this scenario, she is as elusive as Rodriguez. But she was the key to producing the Sugar Man. She arranged the recording sessions, she brought him to the studio, and she took care of the Sugar Man's business needs. Mike Theodore appreciated Moore, as she made it easier to record Rodriguez.

FINDING GOLD IN DETROIT: NO PUN INTENDED

The fertile Motor City musical stew provided Theodore some surprises. One night he and Dennis Coffey wandered into a club. They sat and listened to Jim Gold and his group. They were blown away. The group became Gallery and went on to have numerous hit records. Another night Theodore and Coffey arrived at a small club, the Poison Apple, and listened to Gold singing in a duo. He was performing with his friend, Bill Nova, who later joined Gallery. After Theodore heard them, he loved Gold's pop voice. The reason that they came into the bar is that there were so many cars out front. The ninety-seat club was filled to capacity. A sign read: "Live Music." Theodore and Coffey were intrigued. They listened to Gold for two or three more nights. The yard long beer at the Poison Apple was cheap and it came with good music. In 1971 before Rodriguez left for London to record **Coming From Reality**, the Poison Apple featured John Hammond, Jonathon Edwards, Leo Kottke, Kate Taylor and Kris Kristofferson among others.

Mike Theodore had a number of live musical training experiences. He conducted the house band for the Tom Shannon Show. It was September 30, 1969 when this teen television show hit the airwaves.

This Detroit teen show was broadcast on CKLW Channel 9, a Canadian station. Theodore's band for the Shannon program included Bob Babbitt on bass, Johnny Griffith on piano, Dennis Coffey on guitar and Pistol on drums. The show also had a horn section and some of the most sophisticated arrangements broadcast on television, thanks to Theodore. The band was basically the Motown rhythm section.

One of Theodore's strengths was his ability to bring diverse musicians into a cohesive band. He had the ability to organize a band for any type of music. This is what made him an in demand producer.

Kick out the jams and view the new Tom Shannon Show.

4 p. m. Monday-Friday in color

THE NINE SPOT CKLW TELEVISION 9

CKLW-TV advertisement in the March 22-28, 1969 issue of TV Guide Magazine (Detroit Edition)

Tom Shannon was an impressive local musical figure. He co-wrote the Rockin' Rebels, "Wild Weekend," before he became a well-known Detroit disc jockey. As a CKLW TV personality, he had a great deal of influence upon the Motor City music scene. He also employed Theodore to make sure the music was top notch. It was.

MIKE THEODORE'S VARIOUS PRODUCTIONS

If Dennis Coffey was a blues-rhythm and blues guy, Mike Theodore was the smooth pop producer that flushed out Rodriguez' most poetic musical images. Theodore continued to write and produce with Coffey after they signed a long-term contract with Sussex.

Mike Theodore: "The truth is that we did the same thing. As time went on Dennis would write rhythm and I would do the orchestration. We could crank out an album a month."

What Theodore is known for is producing and engineering with a bit of brilliant mixing and arranging. He is an absolute genius when it comes to getting the right sound.

When they left Sussex, Theodore and Coffey were signed by Detroit's Westbound label to produce disco hits. That led to the 1977 mega disco hit "Devil's Gun." Rather than use their own names, Coffey and Theodore formed a disco group. It was known as C. J. & Company and also as C. J. & Co. or C. .C. & Co. "Devil's Gun" peaked at thirty-six on the **Billboard Pop** chart. But it was ranked as one of the best 100 songs of the year and spent twenty-nine weeks on the chart. It also rose in 1977 to number two on the **Billboard** R & B listing. In the U. K. "Devil's Gun" was a number forty-three single. Heavy D and Doyz sampled it.

After Westbound struck gold with "Devil's Gun," they released two LPs **Devil's Gun** in 1977 and **Deadeye Dick** in 1978. In 1998, a compilation, brought the song back. When New York's Studio 54 opened "Devil's Gun" was the first song played.

In 2004, the Theodore and Coffey productions featured in an album produced by Westbound U. K and released as a CD, **U. S. A. Disco**, containing ten of their best songs. The idea was to release "Devil's Gun," as the market has never ended for this tune. The reviewers noted the other nine songs were equally commercial. No one tired of "Devil's Gun," and there have been numerous singles sampling it.

Westbound benefitted from Theodore and Coffey's production techniques. "Once disco arrived, we abandoned Theo-Coff Productions and we became guns for hire," Theodore recalled. The hits at Westbound came quickly. King Errisson's hit "Manhattan Love Song," the Detroit Emeralds "Turn On Lady" and Caesar Frazier's "Child of the Wind" all bore Theodore's distinctive production style.

THE HATS THAT THEODORE WEARS

From 1968 through 2012, Theodore worked on producing one hundred sixteen albums. It is the breadth and depth of his musical interests that defines Theodore's talent. He has worked with hard rockers Rare Earth, guitar genius Dennis Coffey, the wild Wu Tang Clan, the pop hit maker Gallery, jazz legend Bill Evans, and the one hit wonders the Shades of Blue, as well as a number of other million selling artists.

While he was under contract with Sussex Records, Theodore produced five hit albums for Dennis Coffey and the Detroit Guitar Band. Coffey's mega gold hit, "Scorpio", benefitted from Theodore's arrangements. He also produced Coffey's **Billboard** Top 20 hit "Taurus." Coffey's **Evolution** LP had Theodore's magic touch. His experiences with Sussex and Westbound went a long way toward intensifying his disco and pop productions.

THE LESSONS THEODORE LEARNED AT
WESTBOUND AND SUCCESSES

When Theodore moved over the Westbound Records, he hit his commercial peak. He became a much in demand soul, funk, blues and disco producer. The results were financially lucrative for Westbound, which had a distribution deal with Atlantic. They mined the hotbed of talent in and around Detroit. Theodore was the producer, the arranger and the brains behind much of Westbound's success.

Westbound Records was a strange label. No one seemed in charge. When Westbound put out the first Funkadelic LP in 1970, it was a hodge podge collection of singles. No one received royalties. George Clinton recalled that Westbound bought his group a van. That was it. As a record label, Westbound lacked business credibility. As a place for Mike Theodore to produce, it was a gold mine. Royalties! The producers had full run of the studio. No one cared about money. It was after all the music business.

As disco faded in 1979, Theodore moved on to new projects. He concentrated on the Mike Theodore Orchestra. After releasing two albums, Mike continued as a session arranger, producer and artist. He was still in demand. The 1988 club hit, "No Use To Borrow" by Blue Moderne found Mike as the engineer/producer. He also worked with Boz Scaggs and Lori Jacobs among others.

MIKE THEODORE IN SEARCHING FOR SUGAR MAN

When Mike Theodore was interviewed in **Searching For Sugar Man,** he reflected on why Rodriguez wasn't successful. Theodore couldn't figure it out. He had great songs, a well-produced album, major production money, as well as distribution and promotion. Rodriguez also had the persona for rock and roll stardom. It just didn't happen.

Theodore speculated that Rodriguez' songs were lost in the changes in musical trends. The two Rodriguez albums simply didn't fit into the prevailing changes in the rock and roll marketplace. This obscured what Coffey and Theodore accomplished in producing **Cold Fact**. The bewildered look on Theodore's face, as he described Rodriguez' lost opportunities, suggests that he was puzzled by **Cold Fact's** lack of commercial success.

John Rhys was also important to Theodore's early production career. During his seven years working on the Detroit music scene, Rhys discovered a great many new artists, he produced million selling records and he gave a lot of young kids their first job in the industry. One of those young kids was Mike Theodore.

JOHN RHYS ON MIKE THEODORE

While producing the Shades of Blue, Rhys needed a b-side for "Oh How Happy." Mike Theodore wrote the b-side "Little Orphan Boy." (Impact 1007) "I remember that Mike did the chord charts for "Oh How Happy," Rhys continued. "Mike's strength is that he is an experienced arranger, Harry never liked the arrangements. He thought that they were too white."

Rhys recalled Theodore was "a great arranger." He had the hit touch. The **Cold Fact** album was where Theodore's arranging talents took the Sugar Man's folk-psych songs and placed them into a commercial context. "I have never worked with anyone who was better as an arranger than Mike Theodore, he is one hell of a talent." Rhys concluded.

MIKE THEODORE ON RODRIGUEZ

When Theodore heard Rodriguez at the Sewer By The Sea, and later at Anderson's Garden, the Sugar Man's talent intrigued him. "A part of Rodriguez' magic came from the Detroit streets," Theodore continued. "Rodriguez' natural habitat is the Detroit streets." This is what makes his sound unique. Theodore understood this, and he was able to translate the Sugar Man's brilliant lyrics into commercial songs.

When they were in the studio recording **Cold Fact**, Theodore recalled: "It was more or less a job that was done fairly quickly." The liner notes to **Cold Fact** speculated on the differences between Rodriguez and his production team. Theodore points out that this isn't true. It was a smooth production process.

Mike Theodore: "I can't say we had any problems with Rodriguez. He came in to sing his songs, we wrote down the chords, he pre-recorded himself singing and he accompanied himself on his guitar. It went smoothly. It was a joy. It was the kind of production we like to have."

Much of this was due to Rainy M. Moore. She was the ballast that held everything together. It was Moore who handled Rodriguez' business affairs and kept him on time in the studio. "Rodriguez on his own was rather erratic," Theodore recalled.

MAKING AN ALBUM WITH RODRIGUEZ 1997-1998

In 1997, without warning, Rodriguez called Theodore, who was operating his New York recording studio, Mike was surprised. The Sugar Man was working on new songs, and he was considering making an album. Theodore told Rodriguez that he was on board with the project.

Theodore called Clarence Avant. They discussed a new Rodriguez album. Avant gave him the green light. He said that he would finance it. Money wasn't an object. Clarence had fond memories of the Sugar Man. He wanted to help him cut a chart busting CD. Then Mike got hold of Dennis Coffey. They were ready to record a third Rodriguez album.

For the next six months, Rodriguez called Theodore and played music over the phone. When Mike asked him the lyrics, the Sugar Man said that he was working on the words. He wasn't ready to reveal the songs that he had so carefully crafted for more than twenty years.

A series of sessions were booked in Dearborn's Pac 3 Recording Company. This is a technologically sophisticated studio that has seen the Red Hot Chili Peppers, Fleetwood Mac, David Bowie and the Beach Boys among others cut tracks. It was the perfect studio to record a third Rodriguez album. Since 1963, PAC 3 had cut some of the best records in the Motor City. Early on Stevie Wonder, Mitch Ryder, and the Ohio Players recorded in the funky house that was PAC. Rodriguez would be comfortable and the equipment was state of the art.

There were some musical tracks recorded. Rodriguez was furtively working on the lyrics. Everything was in place for a third album. Then disaster struck with the proposed South African tour and the Sugar Man lost interest. He simply walked away from the third album.

Mike Theodore: "We had the framework or the structure for half a dozen songs. He dropped out and lost interest in doing it."

In 1997-1998, Clarence Avant not only funded Rodriguez' abortive third album, he continued to champion the Sugar Man. **Searching For Sugar Man** did Avant a disservice in hammering him over royalties. If Avant has a sin, it is pride, arrogance and power, not dishonesty.

Mike Theodore: "Clarence is one of the best guys I have worked with in this business. He was always there for us. He had no interest in screwing anybody out of anything."

The comments about Avant during interviews for this book uniformly suggested he had so much money there was no need to withhold royalties.

The series of events that derailed the 1997-1998 Rodriguez album project began when Craig Bartholomew-Strydom called Theodore who put the South African's in touch with the Sugar Man. In 1998, Rodriguez traveled to Cape Town for the series of triumphant concerts that cemented his legend. In the process, a third album was lost to the South African shows. Theodore still has the master tapes.

THEODORE MOVES ON TO PLANET
SOUND STUDIO, NEW YORK

After leaving Detroit and settling in New York, Theodore and bass legend Bob Babbitt ran Planet Sound Studio. For twenty-five plus years they recorded and produced jazz, funk and rock albums.

Mike Theodore: "Jon Grossbard was the owner of Daily Planet Studio. Babbitt and I entered into a partnership with him. We all worked together on projects. We did a lot of PBS. It was a good studio in its time, you can't keep up with the equipment and we eventually moved on to other things."

When Theodore and Babbitt began working at Daily Planet, it was a rehearsal Studio on 30th Street in Manhattan. They were in the mix as the studio was upgraded to establish Planet Sound Studio. It quickly gained a reputation as one of New York's top recording facilities. It has a 24 track recording facility, a grand piano and to help out local musicians, Theodore provided the unheard price of seventy-five dollars an hour to record. He also worked for hundreds of hours with unknown, as well as commercial recording artists. Theodore is a studio guy. He simply loves to engineer and produce.

Eventually, Planet Sound Studio was located around the corner from Madison Square Garden. It was a favorite recording spot for a wide variety of musicians. The Planet Sound Studios at 244 West 54th Street, Suite 800A is a seven hundred square feet studio with a mixing room, a floating recording room, as well as a comfortable lounge with a kitchenette. The studio has long been a gathering spot for hip-hop, dance, live instrumental overdubs, vocal overdubs and narration work.

A wide variety of artists including Barbra Streisand, Peter Wolf, Jennifer Love Hewitt and the Osmond Brothers, among others, have cut records in this studio. When Bill Evans recorded his jazz masterpiece **Bill Evans: The Alternative Man,** Theodore engineered the project, featuring guitarist John McLaughlin.

There was one artist that Theodore loved working with, and his name was Copernicus. As he worked with him on his material, Copernicus became a cult artist with a worldwide reputation. He was a New York based performance poet whose name was Joseph Smalkowski. He played piano, and he emerged on the New York rock and roll scene with jazz, classical and avant-garde influences. He was an independent minded 1980s artist whose booming delivery accentuated his abstract words.

Mike Theodore: "Copernicus is a raving guy, he came from Poland and bought some New York buildings, he converted himself into Copernicus. He was kind of like a beat poet. His projects were some of the best stuff I have ever worked with. One project we did was the **Sound Of The Mind**; it was fun to run through the experimental music with him. He has been all over the world. I did three albums with him, I did some producing, mixing, arranging with him. His projects were the ones I enjoyed the most, it was unstructured, like a journey into a center of your mind. His stuff was far from crap. It was one of the better projects I did in New York."

THE MIKE THEODORE ORCHESTRA

The Mike Theodore Orchestra was another reflection of his producing genius. This group also characterized the disco craze. It was Detroit's Westbound Records that was the vehicle to bring Theodore's two decades in the music business to the disco forefront.

There are two albums associated with the Mike Theodore Orchestra that define disco. They also define Theodore. The 1977 album **Cosmic Wind** (Westbound 305) is a disco masterpiece. This is the first Mike Theodore Orchestra album. It was completed quickly, and the material simmered for some time. Theodore said that he had written a great deal of the music as "it brings a picture into my mind and I create the music around my mental picture." The Detroit studio where Theodore recorded was a catalyst to his revolutionary disco sound.

Richard Becker's Pac 3 Studio was one that Theodore was not only familiar with but he loved to record there. It was a converted garage that provided ultimate freedom. Not surprisingly, the Mike Theodore Orchestra sounded superb. The dance clubs play the albums to death to this day.

One Westbound album, distributed by Atlantic, was a club favorite into the early 2000s. In 1979, **High on Mad Mountain** (Westbound 6109) was a more sophisticated disco piece with electronic, funk and soul sounds expanding Theodore's production techniques. It has had more than three decades of club popularity. The singles that played repeatedly in dance clubs, "Disco People/On Mad Mountain" and "The Bull," were continual club favorites. The Mike Theodore Orchestra provided the sound for the major nationwide dance clubs. If you wanted a life on the dance floor, the Mike Theodore sound was as close to heaven as possible. But there was more than the albums.

There were five singles released and one twelve-inch as a promo, "Disco People/Dragons of Midnight," went disco gold. The 12" promo is also highly collectible. The critics believe that **High On Mad Mountain** is the best disco album of all time. The singles continue to thrive in the U. K. club scene.

Westbound shut down shortly after the Mike Theodore Orchestra released the two albums. Although Theodore planned a third album, the changes in public tastes and Westbound's moribund financial condition altered his plans. There is a Rodriguez tone to this story, as Theodore has a great deal of royalty money that is swirling somewhere in the wind.

MIKE THEODORE REFLECTING ON
THE OLD DAYS AND THE NEW ONES

When I asked Theodore: "What happened to Theo-Coff?" He responded: "Once the Northern Soul days began, we stopped using that name. We started using our names." That made sense as the Mike Theodore Orchestra and Dennis Coffey's solo material brought them alternate U. K. careers.

Now Theodore is back in Detroit working with Coffey. He is also putting together a series of CDs featuring Detroit artists that he has produced. So far there are ten compilation albums in the works.

Mike Theodore has a great deal in common with Rodriguez. They are people who like to remain under the radar. Theodore is happiest simply working in the studio. He did eventually promote himself as a solo act. The Mike Theodore Orchestra remains a paean to the disco generation.

When Mike Theodore and Dennis Coffey went into the Tera Shirma Studio in August and September 1969, they had no idea that they were producing a legendary album. Theodore's keyboards added a nice touch to **Cold Fact** but with his characteristic humility, he didn't list himself as a studio musician. That is Mike Theodore. He remains as humble as Rodriguez, and he is as equally talented.

THE MIKE THEODORE ORCHESTRA ON YOU TUBE

To appreciate Theodore's music one only has to go to You Tube. The Mike Theodore Orchestra has a number of songs on You Tube including "Ain't Nothing To It," "Cosmic Wind," "The Bull," "Moon Trek," "High On Mad Mountain" and "Disco People." How important was Theodore's music? It not only defined disco but in the movie "Last Vegas" the Mike Theodore Orchestra's music was an integral part of the background music. In 2013 when "Last Vegas" burst onto the big screen the Michael Douglas, Robert DeNiro Kevin Kline and Morgan Freeman movie briefly sampled "High On Mad Mountain" but it wasn't included on the soundtrack. The sampling indicated how important Theodore's music is to the disco era.

The critics pointed out that Theodore was one of the few producers to use a real orchestra rather than studio tricks to produce his disco masterpieces.

DENNIS COFFEY AND MIKE THEODORE

60 MINUTES WITH BOB SIMON SHOT A FEATURE IN THE BAR

chapter

TEN

DENNIS COFFEY GUITAR GENIUS-PRODUCER

"WE THOUGHT HE WAS LIKE THE INNER CITY POET. YOU
KNOW, PUTTING HIS POEMS TO MUSIC OF WHAT HE SAW.
AND IT WAS DEFINITELY A VERY GRITTY LOOK AT WHAT
HE SAW ON THE STREETS OF DETROIT. THE ONLY WRIT-
ER THAT I HAD HEARD OF AT THAT TIME PERIOD WAS
MAYBE BOB DYLAN, THAT WAS WRITING THAT WELL."
DENNIS COFFEY IN SEARCHING FOR SUGAR MAN

"ROCK LEAD GUITAR CHOPS. TIGHT, ECONOMICAL...AR-
RANGING SKILLS. FUNK SENSIBILITY. AND LICKS THAT
THE TOP HIP-HOP ARTISTS TURN TO AGAIN AND AGAIN.
WHAT'S THAT? DENNIS COFFEY." BILL KOPP'S MUSIC
BLOG.

Sixto Rodriguez' sound would have been impossible without
Dennis Coffey and Mike Theodore. In the studio they worked magic.

Their production on **Cold Fact** took Rodriguez' songwriting masterpieces into a defined commercial context. They were a dissimilar pair. Coffey, an instrumental funk guitarist with a penchant for the blues worked more with African American musicians. Theodore was classically inspired. He could produce and arrange all types of music. Coffey was a member of legendary Motown session artists known as the Funk Brothers. Coffey's talent as a solo act, songwriter, session musician and producer meshed into Theodore's strengths. The road to Dennis Coffey as Rodriguez' co-producer began during his formative years.

DENNIS COFFEY: THE EARLY YEARS

Coffey, born on November 11, 1940, began playing guitar while living in Michigan's Upper Peninsula. When he was thirteen, he spent some time in the little town of Copper City. His cousins, Jim and Marilyn Thompson, practiced their guitars daily. Soon Coffey was hooked on the music. Copper City is a remote town on Michigan's Upper Peninsula with little to do, so Coffey fervently practiced his guitar. Country music provided his first songbook. The family soon returned to Detroit, where Dennis attended Mackenzie High School. He graduated in 1959. Then he went into the U. S. Army for two years, spending most of his time in South Carolina.

Prior to serving in the military, he lived with his mother, Gertrude Schultz, in a frame and brick house much like the one that Rodriguez' inhabits on Avery Street. His mother listened to big bands, and this music became one of Dennis's earliest influences. He had some guitar heroes. The gold age of rock and roll was vibrating from the small family radio. When Bill Haley and the Comets' "Rock Around The Clock" hit the airwaves in 1955 Dennis Coffey saw his future. He began to listen to every guitarist to find out how they made their magical sounds.

Dennis Coffey: "Chuck Berry was playing some guitar licks so innovative, I couldn't even imagine what the hell he was doing."

After a decade practicing guitar licks, his heart was in soul, blues and instrumental music. He almost single handedly developed the funk guitar style. By his late twenties, he was America's most accomplished funk guitarist.

Dennis Coffey: "I was born and raised in a middle-class neighborhood in the city of Detroit. It was actually my mom's side of the family that was musical."

As he grew up, he listened to his aunt play Chopin and Brahms. While in high school, he played in bands on Friday nights for teen dances. Most Saturdays found Coffey playing for weddings.

From 1959 to 1961, while Coffey was in the U. S. Army, he discovered the South Carolina music scene. At the time, Maurice Williams, of "Stay" fame, was living and working in the Beach music scene. Coffey got to know him. When he was discharged, he began playing in South Carolina clubs. He recorded with Maurice Williams. Coffey cut an instrumental track "Holding Hands" (MY 104) released by the May label under the name Clark Summit. The label did list Coffey as the composer.

Dennis Coffey: "They gave me this name, Clark Summit, because they said Dennis Coffey could never have a hit."

When he returned to Detroit, he met Marcus Terry an incredibly talented musician who became Jose Feliciano's drummer. In 1961, they both joined the Royaltones, Detroit's top bar band. Coffey was working six nights a week. He was in the embryo stage of a legendary guitar career.

COFFEY AND THE GOLDEN AGE OF ROCK AND ROLL

When Coffey arrived on the music scene, it was in the first Golden Age of Rock And Roll. In 1955, while a high school student, his guitar was featured on Vic Gallon's "I'm Gone." Coffey has fond memories of the Gallon session.

Dennis Coffey: "We met Vic at a small basement studio located on the northwest side of Detroit. Vic greeted us warmly, and played his songs on guitar while he sang. We had never heard the songs until that day. There was no music, so we began to create the parts we would play on the record. Vic had a good rockabilly voice, and the desire to record and release his own record. Vic counted off the first song, an upbeat rockabilly tune named 'I'm Gone,' and began singing and strumming a rhythm guitar. I played rockabilly finger style in the verses while Larry added a strong drum beat."

This initial studio experience excited Coffey. Gallon's next recording "I'll Keep On Lovin' You" featured guitar riffs that Coffey made up on the spot. When Gallon released the 45 on his Gondola label, Coffey rushed home and played it on his Hi Fi.

Dennis Coffey: "I created a guitar riff in the introduction that Vic thought was so fantastic; he used it again in the middle of the song." This riff on "I'll Keep On Lovin' You" stuck with Coffey, as he continued to experiment with new sounds.

By the time that he turned sixteen, Coffey and a friend wrote a rockabilly-Elvis style record. He wrote with Durwood Hutto, and the resulting song, "Crazy Little Satellite," was a demo they took to Devora Brown's Fortune label. She turned it down.

When Coffey was a young kid, he didn't require much money. This appealed to the parsimonious producers who ran the Detroit music scene. By the time Coffey met Rodriguez, he had almost fifteen years of experience in the record business. Like Rodriguez, Coffey was a star that didn't know it.

In the studio, Coffey cut most records in one take. His career performing in the bars in and around Detroit, after he got out of the military, prepared him for the recording studio. He is often labeled a funk guitarist. This description is only a part of the equation. He can play any guitar style. He is also a producer, who can put together a pop hit or a blues riff. Funk was still in his future. It would define his sound and bring him fame.

By the late 1960s, Coffey was one of the Funk Brothers. This was a group of studio musicians who backed Motown acts. He played on dozens of Motown hits and producer Norman Whitefield swore by Coffey's funk guitar riffs. But it was working with the Royaltones that whetted his appetite for performing.

THE ROYALTONES WERE COFFEY'S FIRST TASTE OF SHOW BUSINESS

The Royaltones were an instrumental group who dominated the Detroit music scene. A honking saxophone and Dennis Coffey's guitar riffs from 1961 on made them a Motor City favorite. The band began as the Paragons in 1957 with guitarist Karl Kay; Mike Popoff joined him on piano and his brother Greg Popoff played drums. They partnered with George Katsakis, a legendary studio musician. He can be heard on Jack Scott's "Leroy" and "My True Love." Katsakis was a regular session musician on most of Scott's Carlton recordings.

The Royaltones' "Bad Boy" charted at number twenty in 1958 and "Flamingo Express" came in at eighty two on the **Billboard** Hot 100. Coffey didn't play on these tracks. Like most bands, the Royaltones went through numerous personnel changes. In 1961, as Coffey joined the Royaltones, the Popoff brothers and Katsakis wrote: "The Peppermint Twist." It was a different song from the Joey Dee and the Starlighters hit. It featured Dennis Coffey's guitar and Bob Babbitt's signature bass. Suddenly the Royaltones had a new sound.

As Coffey was welcomed into the Royaltones, Bob Babbitt also came on as the bass player and a second saxophonist, Dave Sandy, joined the group. Marcus Terry came in on drums and the dual sax, with Katsakis remaining, gave the Royaltones a signature sound reminiscent of Blood, Sweat And Tears or Chicago.

Harry Balk signed them to his Twirl label. They also inked a management contract with Balk and Irving Micahnik's Talent Inc. Balk hoped to make the Royaltones the next Johnny and the Hurricanes. After Coffey worked with George Katsakis on "Our Faded Love," Balk smelled a hit. It was a Detroit hit and Mala Records, a subsidiary of Bell, released it nationally. Then Bobby Rydell covered it on Cameo. It wasn't a national hit for either the Royaltones or Rydell. This success inaugurated a blistering writing pace for Coffey. His follow up tune, "Lonely World," was a beautiful slow song featuring Katsakis' clarinet. Coffey was the brains behind the flip side "El Toro." When the 45 was released in the spring of 1964, the Beatles and the British Invasion doomed this record.

The Royaltones hung out at Harry Balk's office. But despite their musical talent, the instrumental sound was no longer commercial. After listening to Del Shannon's "From Me To You," the Royaltones decided to find a singer. They had an excellent one in the band, Dave Sandy.

The Royaltones selected Coffey's "Lonely World" to inaugurate their newfound vocal style. Sandy's haunting vocals made him a popular club act, and the tune was frequently requested at the Somers Point Resort. The Royaltones had a 1964 New Jersey summer residence there, and the reception for this song inspired Coffey. While looking out at the sea one day, Coffey composed "Misty Sea." The Royaltones were due to go into the studio to back the Young Sisters on "She Took His Love Away." They decided to record some new vocal tracks.

Balk believed that the Royaltones had a national future. He brought Del Shannon out to the resort to work on their music. Dennis Coffey also recorded with Shannon on his cover of Jimmy Jones' "Handy Man."

Harry Balk: "Del needed a fresh sound with the 'Little Town Flirt" sound having run it's course, so I teamed him up with the Royaltones."

By 1965, Coffey realized that he could write and produce. He was already an accomplished session musician. It would be another six years before his solo 45, "Scorpio," became a million selling single. The dye was cast for a legendary career. The Royaltones called it quits.

Dennis Coffey moved on to fry bigger fish. He was already an in demand studio musician. He quickly evolved into a million selling solo artist. He partnered with Mike Theodore to become a respected producer.
The time with the Royaltones was a great training ground.

DENNIS COFFEY PRODUCING RODRIGUEZ

How did Coffey, along with Mike Theodore, get every song right
on **Cold Fact**? The answer is a simple one. During the late 1960s, Coffey
was at times a member of the legendary Motown session band, the Funk
Brothers. What he learned about production is obvious. On Rodriguez'
"Crucify Your Mind," he and Theodore layered the music over the poetic
lyrics. On "I Wonder" the bass line has an eerie almost surreal touch.
These sounds are completed without gimmicks. There are no synthesizers. There are no studio tricks. It is Coffey's producing talent, working
with Mike Theodore's arranging-producing genius that has prompted
the duo to be praised as legendary studio guys.

In 2012, PBS highlighted Coffey's genius during an interview on
History Detectives. He discussed the authenticity of the Ampeg B-15
amplifier. What this program demonstrated is that Coffey's production
skills belied his youth. Coffey and fellow Funk Brother, bassist James Jamerson, provided some clues into why Coffey and Theodore had success with Rodriguez. The obvious conclusion is that Theodore's arrangements and Coffey's instrumentation impacted the lyrics and song styling.

It is Coffey's lead guitar on **Cold Fact** that created a sound so
unique that it survives more than forty years later. Theodore's eerie instrumental sound and his arrangements solidified the LP. But they had
a history with the Sugar Man.

Dennis Coffey: "The first time Mike and I worked with Rodriguez was
when we arranged two songs for him to be produced by Harry Balk, the
owner of Impact & Twirl Records. Nothing happened with those two songs.
Later we went to hear Rodriguez at a club on the Detroit River called The
Sewer. When we entered the club we saw Rodriguez singing while facing
the wall with his back to the audience. We thought that was a bit strange,
but it did force you to listen to his lyrics. We liked what we heard, so we got
him a deal to record the **Cold Fact** album on Sussex Records."

The decade of experience Coffey and Theodore had in the studio,
prior to recording Rodriguez, was an asset. When **Cold Fact** failed to sell,
Coffey and Theodore moved on to other projects. Rodriguez was never
far from their thoughts. They believed that **Cold Fact** was a gold album. It
didn't work out.

COFFEY AND THEODORE ALBUMS
PRODUCED FROM TERA-SHIRMA

Although they were in the early stages of their career, Coffey and Theodore had produced a number of well thought of albums. In 1968, Coffey went into the Tera-Shirma Studio and co-produced the Sunliners **Dreams And Answers** for Verve/MGM. Then the Sunliners changed their name to Rare Earth and became a million selling white soul act. It is in the obscure LPs that Coffey and Theodore excelled.

A good example of a rare LP is the 1970 Theo-Coff' album **Light Of Your Shadow** released on Sussex. The artist, Mutzie, combined hard rock with heavy psychedelic overtones. Mutzie's sound was blues based. His single, "Cocaine Blues," was a short-lived Detroit radio hit. The sales were good enough regionally for Buddah, in partnership with Sussex, to release a four song EP in October 1970. It didn't sell.

Mutzie, a popular Detroit act, opened for Johnny Winter, Alice Cooper and the Allman Brothers among others. The guitarist, Eric "Mutzie" Levenberg, was a Detroit hard rock, psych legend. Eventually, Mutzie left the music business and purchased a bar in downtown Detroit.

MUTZIE'S LIGHT OF YOUR SHADOW ALBUM

COFFEY'S STRENGTHS IN THE DETROIT MUSIC SCENE

Coffey was a walking musical encyclopedia. By 1969, when he produced Rodriguez, he had worked with acts as diverse as Del Shannon and the Temptations. As he played clubs in and around Detroit, he discovered an enormous cache of new talent. He also developed diverse production techniques. He became a studio wizard.

When he worked with Harry Balk, Coffey extended his craft. As a Funk Brother at Motown, Coffey observed studio techniques from a wide variety of producers. What set Coffey apart from the other Funk Brothers? Berry Gordy Jr. was never able to sign him to an exclusive recording agreement. The other Funk Brothers were tied to Motown, whereas Coffey was a freelance employee. This is one reason for his diverse productions.

Coffey played on many collectible 1960s cult records produced by Harry Balk. These included the Inner Circle's, "Sally Go Round The Roses." Coffey worked with Tony Frontera an enormously talented Detroit musician. For the dedicated record collector, Frontera's "Street of Shame," written by Mike Theodore, with Dennis Coffey's guitar, remains a cult 45.

There is a marvelous You Tube version of Frontera's "(You're My) Leading Lady" which highlights his unique vocal styling. His sound was that of the up-tempo 1960s teen idol. Like Rodriguez, he was a regional legend who was a great performer. It just didn't happen nationally.

MIKE THEODORE WROTE AND
CO-PRODUCED WITH COFFEY

The combined studio brilliance of Dennis Coffey and Mike Theodore made Theo-Coff successful. They knew which Detroit studios produced the best sound, and which studio musicians to hire to augment their arranging and production skills. They also knew enough about production to be fiscally efficient. Which of the two major studios, Golden World or Tera Shirma, was most important? This is a matter of opinion. For Rodriguez it was Tera Shirma. For Dennis Coffey the combination of both studios' formed his production genius. Mike Theodore liked both studios. But office space at Tera Shirma and a carte blanche ability to record anytime of the day or night made it easier to work at Tera Shirma.

Ralph Terrana bought a recording studio in 1966 and named it Tera Shirma. The building at 15305-15341 Livernois was owned by Ernie Stratton and called Rainbow Studio. When Terrana purchased and renamed it, Tera Shirma, he brought in every independent producer in and around Detroit to make his studio profitable.

It was Terrana's vision that was important to the Motor City rock scene. He gave Coffey and Theodore an office and carte blanche use of the facilities. The result was a bevy of hit records, regional favorites and cult albums like **Cold Fact**.

COFFEY REFLECTS ON HIS EARLY RECORDING
STUDIO EXPERIENCES

Denis Coffey: "The most difficult part of recording was learning how to play guitar lines and fill ins that didn't interfere or cover up the vocals."

As Coffey observed Harry Balk produce his acts he learned valuable studio lessons. He also picked up production pointers from working at Motown. It was a lengthy learning process and Coffey was an adept student.

Dennis Coffey: "The Golden World Studios were equipped with all the latest recording gear and audio technology, even more impressive than the one at Hitsville, Motown's studio on Grand Boulevard."

When Coffey stepped into Golden World for his initial recording sessions, he played a solid body Fender Stratocaster. What Coffey learned at Golden World was to arrange, produce and complete a production within a tight budget. This was training for later successes at Tera Shirma. The lessons learned at Golden World also helped Coffey when he played on numerous Motown recordings.

When I asked Mike Theodore which Detroit studio that he liked best. He replied: "It's apples and oranges, they both have something to offer." That comment summed up the world of Detroit studios.

The Golden World Studio at 3246 West Davison was also the home of Ric Tic and Wingate Records. Ed Wingate and Joanne Bratton set up the labels to record Detroit soul acts. They were so successful that Berry Gordy Jr. paid them a million dollars for the label in 1968. Edwin Starr, the Detroit Emeralds and J. J. Barnes were Ric Tic artists who moved on to Motown.

John Rhys: "Berry Gordy paid a million dollars to shut down Golden World. He bought the artists, he bought the recording studio and he simply ended the competition from Ed Wingate. At that point I left."

THEO COFF'S EARLY PRODUCTIONS

Detroit's Golden World Studio was where the earliest Theo-Coff 45s were produced. The building at 3246 West Davison was nothing special. The studio was well equipped, and it had one major selling point-an echo chamber. The large number of Detroit artists who recorded at Golden World included the Reflections, the Sunliners, the Adorables, Barbara Mercer, Laura Lee and the Manhattans. In later years, these artists became Northern soul giants, and today their records commanded hundreds of pounds in the lucrative U.K. record market.

Wingate was a character. He loved to go to the racetrack. One day he walked into Golden World with a large paper bag filled with cash. It was his horse race winnings. He cleared out Studio B. He began shouting and throwing money around the room. Then he called the group in recording and told them to keep whatever money they could find on the floor.

Wingate drove Berry Gordy Jr. crazy by hiring the Funk Brothers to play at all hours. He ignored their exclusive contract with Motown. He paid them in cash. Not surprisingly, when Wingate died at age eighty-six in 2006 a large segment of Motown performers showed up for the funeral.

HOW DID COFFEY-THEODORE GET
TO GOLDEN WORLD STUDIO?

It was almost by accident that Dennis Coffey and Mike Theodore recorded at Golden World. "The first time I got a call from Golden World," Coffey continued. "Wingate told me to come over and save a recording session." This was a common story. Mike Theodore experienced the same request from Wingate. Someone comes into a Detroit studio that doesn't know how to write charts, set up production or work with the musicians, Dennis Coffey and Mike Theodore specialized in fixing these studio problems.

When Wingate asked Coffey if he could do the charts and the arrangements? Coffey said: "Yes." His legendary studio career was on its way. He had to take his three-year-old daughter to this session. He was on his way as a session musician, arranger and producer.

During Coffey's early studio days, he met Edwin Starr. He helped to produce Starr's "Stop Her On Sight (S.O.S.)" (Ric Tic 109) which charted in 1966 at nine on the **Billboard** R & B listing, as well as forty nine on the Pop 100. Starr's single was licensed in the U. K. to Polydor. It became a hit. Starr was so successful in England that he moved permanently to the U. K.

Coffey also helped J. J. Barnes produce "Little Humdinger" for Ric Tic in 1966. Then Barnes' covered the Beatles "Day Tripper" (Ric 115). By that time, Coffey and Theodore were off to new projects.

The studio expertise Coffey and Theodore acquired was important. They realized that Golden World wasn't the right place to record Rodriguez. This is one reason that Tera Shirma was selected to produce **Cold Fact**.

When Motown purchased Golden World, it affected everyone in and around this legendary recording studio. Coffey realized that things had changed. It wasn't the same. Motown musicians lobbied management to sign Coffey to an exclusive session contract. Gordy dispatched James Jamerson, the Funk Brothers' legendary bassist, to persuade Coffey to sign a permanent Funk Brother's contract. He had already signed with Clarence Avant due to the weekly paycheck. When Jamerson told Gordy he had failed, the Motown president instructed Hank Cosby to call Coffey. Gordy said to make a "hard sell pitch" to Coffey to become a permanent Funk Brother. Coffey politely declined. He was still available for sporadic sessions.

HOW MOTOWN SHAPED COFFEY'S
PRODUCTION TECHNIQUES

After Motown purchased Golden World Studio, the producers inaugurated a 7 to 9:30 P. M Studio B production meeting. The idea was to come up with new songs, improved production and to continue to turn out hits. There were no studio costs for talking about production. Berry Gordy Jr. made it clear that he wanted less money spent in the studio.

It was at these sessions that Coffey came into contact with the Temptations' producer Norman Whitfield. After Whitfield played a version of "Cloud Nine," Coffey took the song and added his wah wah pedal sound. Whitfield said: "That's it. That's what I'm looking for." Coffey played on the majority of the Temptations 1960s hits.

After Coffey provided the psych-funk guitar on the Temptations' "Cloud Nine," the wah wah pedal sound emerged on a host of hits. Coffey remarked that listening to Sly And The Family Stone was one reason for this innovative sound. Another key to Coffey's studio wizardry was the use of the echoplex. This was a tape delay device created by Mike Battle. Such guitar legends as Duane Allman, Chet Atkins, Steve Miller and Jimmy Page used it.

While working at Motown in 1967-1968, Coffey was aware of protest songs. Norman Whitfield had no idea how to produce a protest song. It was anathema to Motown. Then he heard Coffey's experimental guitar riffs. That led to the Temptations and Edwin Starr's brief chart incursions into protest tunes.

When Dennis Coffey reminisced about his days at Motown, he recalled the joy of working with the Jackson 5, Stevie Wonder, Diana Ross, Gladys Knight, Marvin Gaye and the Four Tops among others.

TERA SHIRMA'S EARLY YEARS

In 1966, Ralph Terrana purchased the Rainbow Studio. He spent a fortune remodeling it. The first time Coffey recorded at Tera Shirma, he was asked if he had produced a record. Coffey answered: "No." It didn't matter. He was hired as a producer.

Dennis Coffey: "The way we learned to produce was that a friend of ours owned Tera Shirma Studio, and he gave us the keys to the studio… We'd bring these bands from the clubs we knew, about 3 AM….that's how we learned to produce."

Ralph Terrana, a founding member of the Sunliners-Rare Earth, not only owned the Tera Shirma Studio, he was the studio Godfather to a part of Detroit's soul-funk sound.

When Clarence Avant offered Coffey and Theodore a five-year recording-production deal, their career blossomed. The guaranteed weekly paycheck persuaded them to sign. The first record that Coffey produced for Clarence Avant was with the Lyman Woodward Trio. Coffey played with the group in local clubs. Avant liked their demos. Theo-Coff Productions quickly became Avant's talent scouts. They were instrumental in convincing label executives that Rare Earth, as well as Jim Gold and the Gallery, had chart-topping talent. Gold's Gallery had a 1972 hit "Nice To Be With You." The Gallery had two minor hits "I Believe In Music" and "Big City Miss Ann." Avant spent his time promoting the Gallery, Rare Earth and Bill Withers. This is another reason that Rodriguez was lost in the mix.

The deal with Avant was advantageous to Theo-Coff. They had distribution, they could hire the best session musicians, they had access to some of the most powerful people in the industry, they had financial resources, and Theo-Coff had total production freedom.

They also received a regular salary. Coffey wrote in his memoir: "When you finally arrived and started making hit records…all the major labels and big artists wanted to throw money at us to work with them on projects." As Coffey acknowledged, once the hits slowed, so did the money.

JOHN RHYS AND THE DETROIT MUSIC SCENE

There were a number of people who recognized Mike Theodore and Dennis Coffey's talent. John Rhys met Theodore when he was in college. Rhys, the Sunliners engineer-producer, recalled that Theodore was attending Wayne State University. Rhys didn't know that the kid was a producer. After he talked with Theodore, he realized that the kid had a wealth of studio knowledge.

He was aware that Coffey worked with Theodore. Rhys said: "I saw the inner workings of Theo-Coff before they formed the production team." Rhys vowed to use them. He did and doing so he helped them along the way to a production career.

In Detroit, Rhys produced some of the early 1960s hits at Detroit's Golden World Studio. When Rhys arrived in Detroit in April 1964, Motown and the independent studios were in full swing. At the time, Rhys was doing promotion for a number of record labels.

Shortly after settling in the Motor City, Rhys rented an apartment, while working toward an engineering and production career. Warner Brothers paid Rhys $4500 a month to promote records. He was one of the best in breaking new songs. He left that position to work at Golden World as a $1500 a month producer. "People thought I was nuts," Rhys continued. "That is until I started turning out hits." Rhys is one of early, often unsung, production pioneers who brought the Motor City record gold. He also was a constant man on the street seeing Rodriguez and others escape the vicissitudes of the music business.

John Rhys: "One day I left my apartment. I walked down the street, it was cold as hell. I stopped. There were two people shivering at the side of a building. They were well dressed but they looked homeless. I asked them if they needed something. They said 'coffee.' We went to my apartment. The good-looking homeless guy said that he was Matt Lucas. I couldn't believe it. I broke his hit 'I'm Movin' On' in the South."

For a time, Lucas and his wife lived with Rhys. Then Matt moved on to gigs that paid the rent. He wanted to pay Rhys back for his kindness. "I never forgot John's kindness," Matt Lucas reflected. "He was a guy who saved me from a brutal Detroit winter. I did my best to repay him."

John Rhys: "Matt was something. He took me to see John Lee Hooker and when we arrived the place was sold out. Matt went to the doorman and gave him five bucks. We went inside, met John Lee and after the show Hooker came back to my apartment where we drank and smoked dope into the night. I wish I had recorded Hooker singing in my apartment."

The high point of Rhys engineering-production career came in 1966 when he convinced Ed Wingate to bring the Shades of Blue into Golden World. They cut Edwin Starr's "Oh How Happy." They were known as the Domingo's when Wingate signed them. Rhys quickly changed their name to the Shades of Blue, and he refined their sound over time in the studio.

Harry Balk released an album on his Impact label **Happiness Is The Shades of Blue**. It sold well and Harry had Rhys continue to write, engineer and produce the group. Almost single handedly, Rhys kept the Shades of Blue career alive despite only one major hit. He convinced Edwin Starr to write their follow up "Lonely Summer," which charted at seventy-two. Then Rhys wrote "Happiness" which charted at seventy-eight and the Shades of Blue were about to be history.

While in Detroit, Rhys worked for Harry Balk. Then tragedy struck. His father died. His mother had her house repossessed. She was in the street. Rhys went to Balk. He explained everything. He didn't know what to do. Harry pulled out a checkbook and handed John a $20,000 check. "Don't tell anyone," Balk said with a twinkle in his eye. "They will think I have gone soft."

Rhys never met Rodriguez, but he watched as the Sugar Man's local legend developed. Rhys had seen many local legends, like Jamie Coe, continue to work on their talent but he had never witnessed a singer-songwriter like the Sugar Man.

John Rhys: "Rodriguez is one of the most talented musicians I have ever heard. He was around Detroit gigging at small places. I heard the two albums and loved them. I always wondered why he wasn't a hit artist. He is now. He deserves it. What a great songwriter. He is also one hell of a performer."

DENNIS COFFEY: THE STAR WHO DIDN'T KNOW IT

Dennis Coffey had a lot in common with Sixto Rodriguez. He is a brilliant artist with an original touch. Coffey broke into the Detroit music scene in 1961 with the Royaltones. After a decade on the Detroit music scene, Coffey had a million selling record.

In 1971, Coffey's instrumental "Scorpio" went gold. The follow up in 1972, "Taurus" sold well and charted. Coffey was an established solo artist. His success as a solo act was as important to Coffey as what he could accomplish in the studio.

When Coffey recorded "Scorpio," not only did the instrumental earn a gold record, it enhanced his studio reputation. When "Scorpio" peaked at six on the **Billboard** Hot 100, Coffey was busy in the studio and on the road.

"Scorpio" crossed over into the African American market and Coffey became the first white artist to appear on Soul Train. The audience was predominantly African American. Don Cornelius told Coffey that his live performance of "Scorpio" was the highlight of his Soul Train experience. Coffey's Soul Train appearance to support his new album, **Evolution**, was so successful that the LP charted at thirteen.

During his lengthy career, Coffey had three **Billboard** chart albums and four on the Rhythm and Blues listing. He had his greatest chart success recording for Clarence Avant's Sussex label. The partnership was a brilliant one. Coffey's funk guitar riffs enhanced by Mike Theodore's production and Avant's knowledge of the industry made for a profitable partnership.

WHAT DID COFFEY AND THEODORE D0 FOR COLD FACT?

The Coffey-Theodore team was instrumental in **Cold Fact's** brilliant production. They provided the children's choir, they helped to write two songs to round out the album, and they arranged and produced the music to compliment Rodriguez' lyrical genius. Some critics believe that **Cold Fact** is superior to **Coming From Reality.** While this is a value judgment, it reflects the skill of their production techniques. Other critics have suggested that **Coming From Reality** is a personal album, where Rodriguez has more studio freedom and his songs are broader. Like Mike Theodore said in **Searching For Sugar Man**: "It's apples and oranges."

Mike Theodore created the brass and string arrangements that make **Cold Fact** commercial. The psychedelic funk sound combines Coffey's guitar style with Theodore's unique arrangements. "I Wonder" sounds like a Top 40 songs and "Sugar Man" with its drug infused lyrics and musical bells and whistles was perfect for the 1970 hip subculture.

Coffey and Theodore had a vision. It was a commercial one. Rodriguez was surprised by some of the changes. "I never expected to hear a marimba on the album," Rodriguez continued. "I had played these songs for the producers and when I heard what they did to them, it was quite a jump." After he listened to **Cold Fact**, Rodriguez loved it. "I knew I wasn't going to get airplay in the Bible Belt," Rodriguez continued, "but then the record company went bankrupt. It was a changing world back then...."

WHATEVER HAPPENED TO DENNIS COFFEY?

In 1972, Coffey moved to Los Angeles. He married his second wife, Kathy, and he relocated his family near Motown's West Studio on Los Angeles' Santa Monica Boulevard. He also had less work in the studio and clubs. One wonders how Rodriguez' career would have changed had he moved to Los Angeles?

After Coffey rented a house in the San Fernando Valley, his life turned into a Los Angeles nightmare. Coffey was the guy who wore the Armani suits. Clarence Avant was footing the bill. Coffey didn't appear comfortable with the star struck Los Angeles mentality. As studio opportunism declined, Avant's money slowly dried up.

Suddenly, Coffey was not as financially comfortable. The vagaries of the music business led to fewer recording dates, as it created a rapidly changing local music scene. He still performed in local clubs. Then things got weird. The Los Angeles club appearances were a continual disaster. At the Troubadour one night he wore a Dezi Arnez style Cuban shirt to back a male singer who changed into a female wedding gown for the second set. Coffey knew he was in the wrong place. It was time to go back to Detroit. He looked back fondly on portions of his Los Angeles career.

There was redemption of sorts, as Coffey worked with Barbra Streisand in concert and Ringo Starr in the studio. On Starr's 1974 **Goodnight Vienna** album, Coffey was one of eight guitarists. He was lost in the mix as a host of stars and noted session musicians including Dr. John, Steve Cropper, Harry Nilsson, John Lennon and Klaus Voormann brought Ringo commercial success. But it was getting pretty strange in the West Coast musical world. Los Angeles wore on him. He didn't particularly care for what he described as "the King Cocaine atmosphere." But he had a second act in Los Angeles.

He moved into movies, television and other areas of musical production. He made a nice living. He learned some of the tricks of the Los Angeles recording industry. He cut an album with the Osmond's. When it came out the liner notes stated the Osmonds played all the instruments. It was Dennis Coffey's guitar that made this Osmond's LP a hit. He kept that fact to himself. The weasels at the Osmond's' record company hired him as a session guitarist without credit. Welcome to Los Angeles. Suddenly Detroit looked pretty good.

Then Coffey and Theodore went to Clarence Avant, and he graciously released them from their contract. They signed with Detroit's Westbound Records. They had gigantic disco hits. Then Coffey relocated to New York in 1979. He was no longer the rock roll and roll kid, Coffey continued making a living as a studio guitarist and producer.

In the 1990s, after Coffey moved back to Detroit, he rented a house in Farmington Hills. The Detroit record industry was a disaster as was the Motor City. The local bands played cover tunes and wore ridiculous costumes. There was little recording activity. He went to work in the Detroit auto industry.

But it wasn't over for Coffey. He enrolled at the Wayne State University and he earned a bachelor's degree. He graduated with a solid A average. He completed a master's degree in instructional technology. He worked for GM, and then the Ford Motor Company hired him as a consultant.

He also became involved in the United Auto Workers. He continued to play his exquisite and original guitar solos in local clubs. By 2011, after a lengthy absence from the studio, Coffey was back as a former Motown Funk Brother touring and recording.

DENNIS COFFEY IN RETROSPECT

The breadth of Coffey's production is demonstrated in recordings with Diana Ross and the Supremes, the Temptations, Del Shannon, George Clinton and the Funkadelics. That says it all. He is diverse. In a 2002 documentary, **Standing In the Shadows of Motown**, Coffey stands out for his diverse musical talents.

When Rodriguez was asked about Coffey's production, he smiled. The Sugar Man not only approved of Coffey's production, he loved his solo guitar. Rodriguez realized that his updated, commercial sound on **Cold Face** was due to Theo-Coffey's production. Rodriguez never forgot their studio wizardry. When he could, the Sugar Man vowed to repay Dennis Coffey kindness. He did forty some years later.

In March 2014, Coffey opened for Rodriguez in London and Birmingham during a brief U. K. tour. The sold out crowds knew Coffey's signature hits "Scorpio" and "Taurus," as well as a number of his other Northern Soul staples. Rodriguez praises Coffey's innovative guitar and production to this day.

The U. K. show at the Birmingham Symphony Hall was an excellent one. The calls for Coffey's signature guitar sound filled the air. In both venues the Northern Soul favorites had the audiences on their feet. Dennis Coffey was back on the concert trail with a vengeance.

The Northern Soul market has been a continual boon to Coffey's career. He went on a whirlwind tour of the U. K. with his book **Guitars, Bars And Superstars**, and he was amazed his 45s sold for hundreds of pounds. Then he played at a British festival, he opened for the Velvettes. He found that the Brits not only coveted his instrumental 45s, they knew everything about his career. He was amazed. Like Rodriguez, Coffey is humble and he is back with new music.

COFFEY AND WHISKEY CAMBODIA

National Public Radio honored Coffey with a program on its World Café. He also produced a 2014 album, **Whiskey Cambodia**, for the Cambodian Space Project. This album, featuring Coffey's brilliant guitar strokes, is a commercial one featuring five vintage Cambodian rock songs with lilting vocals by Srey Thy. Her husband, Julien Poulson, provides amazing guitar accompaniment. The Cambodian Space Project carried Coffey into a new creative direction. No one would have expected anything less.

Whiskey Cambodia was recorded in Detroit with a host of Motown musicians. It is a psych-soul CD with a funky Detroit sound. The Cambodian Space Project is a popular live band. They have developed a large cult audience. Nick Cave summed up their concert appeal: "They're a great band, I thought it sounded great and it was a great night and the singer was beautiful and sang beautifully." This was a reference to a sold out U. K. concert.

The Cambodian Space Project provides an eclectic mix of styles and musicians. By combining a Motown sound with a psychedelic direction the band highlights Srey's magnificent vocals. The songs are surprising in their originality. "Here Comes The Rain" sounds like the Jefferson Airplane. There are five other songs that present the best of Cambodian rock and roll. On their third album one song stands out, "Whiskey Cambodia," with its eerie, infectious lyrics and Dennis Coffey's brilliant guitar.

Dennis Coffey was the perfect influence to help produce the **Whiskey Cambodia** album. In Cambodia there has been a thriving pop-cultural history that embraces the Motown and American funk scene. It was natural for the Cambodian Space Project to seek out Coffey. The band covers tunes from the lost golden age of Cambodian pop. Coffey was there to produce a masterpiece. It was 2014 and he had not lost a step. Srey and her husband, Julien Poulson, have brought back a Cambodian pop that was systematically wiped out by the Khmer Rouge. Like Rodriguez, they are political dissenters. Like Rodriguez, Dennis Coffey was there every step of the way for them.

COFFEY: STILL A STUDIO LEGEND

Coffey continues to perform in and around Detroit while working on new material. He is also back working with Mike Theodore. Coffey has fifteen studio albums. One of the supreme ironies of Coffey's career is that his second biggest 45 was a disco version of "Wings of Fire/Free Spirit." This is not surprising, as he can play any type of music.

Coffey's signature guitar riffs have been sampled by a wide variety of artists. In 1985, when Coffey realized Public Enemy sampled his guitar riffs from a 1971 song "Getting It On" to produce their mega platinum hit, "You Gonna Get Yours," he was amazed. His kids told him that his signature guitar sound was all over the rap and hip-hop landscape. He was immediately on the phone to Clarence Avant for past royalties.

The number of rap, electronic and hip hop artists who have sampled Coffey's brilliant guitar include L. L. Cool J, Young MC, Moby, the Fugees and the Jedi Knights as well as more than fifty other artists. "Scorpio" has been sampled seventy-six times.

The irony is that after he called Clarence Avant requesting royalties, the hip hop and rap labels acted like they had never heard of his guitar riffs. As Rodriguez has said repeatedly: "It's the music business." Coffey decided to figure out how to collect his royalties. He decided that his old friend, Clarence Avant, the former head of Sussex, was the person to collect his past royalties. The moment that Coffey called Avant, he began receiving royalties.

Dennis Coffey: "I started getting paid for the samples....And I guess what sampling did overall for my career was to let all the hip hoppers know who I am."

In many respects, the rap and hip-hop artists are responsible for Coffey re-entering the music mainstream. He also had more in his instrumental tank than just soul-funk sounds. In 1989, Coffey's CD **Under The Moonlight**, released by Orpheus Records, brought a smooth sound to ten tracks that highlight his jazz riffs. Or perhaps it was just the jazz that he loved for decades.

LISTENING TO DENNIS COFFEY

As a session guitarist, Coffey's wide-ranging talents were featured on LPs selling more than one hundred million records The irony is that he had very little publicity for his efforts.

The Coffey solo discography is an impressive one. His songs continue to be covered and interpreted by a wide variety of artists. From 1969 on, Coffey's studio albums define his brilliant signature guitar. His early albums, co-produced by Mike Theodore, remain as interesting and relevant today as when they were released in the 1960s and 1970s.

The turning point in Coffey's solo career came when he recorded "It's Your Thing." He sent it to Clarence Avant. Mike Theodore produced Coffey's funky guitar. It was a new and highly commercial sound. Sussex released five albums. His first demo for Sussex sealed the deal. Coffey and the Lyman Woodward Trio cut "It's Your Thing" in 1969. The 45, produced by Mike Theodore, was a perfect instrumental transition in developing a psych soul sound for Coffey's unique guitar riffs. It had the hit instrumental sound that Avant desired.

By 1970, Coffey was ready for a solo career. After the **Hair And Things** album was released, Coffey had nine LP releases and six singles on various labels. He established multiple credentials in the industry, the clubs and in the larger concert halls.

THE EARLY COFFEY ALBUM GEMS AND MIKE THEODORE'S CONTRIBUTIONS

Coffey had some gems at Sussex, three LPs, **Evolution** in 1971, **Goin' For Myself** in 1972 and **Electric Coffey** in 1973 charted. The label went bankrupt. Coffey signed with Carrere and a 1975 album **Getting' It On** failed to chart. But the LP's single, "Getting It On 75," appeared briefly on the **Billboard** Rhythm and Blues listing. Coffey was ready for the changing musical trends.

The early Coffey albums, produced by Mike Theodore, are some of the best psych-funk LPs. The three albums for Westbound were also brilliant. **Finger Lickin' Good**, features Coffey's songs, as well as a unique cover of David Bowie's "Fame." When it was released in 1975, Coffey's instrumental brilliance helped to define and popularize disco. A cover of Bill Doggett's "Honky Tonk" reminds the listener that Coffey's musical roots hark back to the 1950s.

In 1976, Coffey's **Back Home**, a soul-funk masterpiece, produced a Northern Soul hit single "Our Love Goes On Forever" backed with "Back Home." (WB5402) The opening LP track on **Back Home**, "Funk Connection," indicated Coffey's signature Detroit guitar sound was intact. The experimental, "Free Spirit," was over five minutes of exquisite jazz with a disco feel complimented by Larry Nozero's dynamic flute. The album's big surprise was the vocals by Brandy. She was featured on "Our Love Goes On Forever." You only get a few lines from Brandy, but it makes the song. In the U. K. it eventually became a Northern Soul club staple.

"High On Love" featured Coffey's jazz chops. "Boogie Magic" is Coffey at his best with Roderick Chandler's bass and a kickass horn section. Like Rodriguez, some of Coffey's best material was lost in the commercial abyss.

A twelve-inch vinyl release of "Wings of Fire" became a Studio 54 favorite, it also played in other top tier clubs. Synthesizers and horns made this song a dance club staple.

Roger Armstrong, at London's Ace Records, recognized that Coffey was a genre-crossing artist. Ace released an album that it termed "sensual break beat soul." The Ace CD **Sweet Taste of Sin** (BGP2 141) is a double disc with Coffey's "A Sweet Taste of Sin" leading off the sixteen tunes that also feature the Detroit Emeralds' "Set It Out." Another Ace reissue **Dennis Coffey, Live Wire, The Westbound Years, 1975-1978** brings fifteen of his best tracks from the Detroit label. "Wings of Fire' is the tune that made this LP a hot U. K. seller. With copious liner notes and remastered tracks the releases are another reminder of Coffey's genius.

In 1978, **The Dennis Coffey Band, A Sweet Taste of Sin**, released on Westbound, was a funk-soul LP perfect for the disco market. "Gimmie That Funk" backed with "Calling Planet Earth," was picked up by Atlantic for distribution. They released a twelve-inch single, and it was a monster U. K. club hit. "Our Love Goes On Forever" and "High On Love" are instrumentals that recall Coffey's smooth sound. The dance clubs featured these tunes nightly.

By 1980, Westbound was out of business. This is one reason that it was almost seven years before Coffey released another solo album. In 1986, **Motor City Magic** was a brilliant digital production. It was one of the first albums to employ this technology. Coffey arranged the songs and his co-producer, Kathy Coffey, was instrumental in crafting the beautifully sounding vinyl masterpiece. With Detroit legends Earl Klugh on guitar and Lyman Woodward on organ, there is a decided jazz feel. It is now one of Coffey's most difficult records to find. From this album, a cover of the Miracles' "Tracks of My Tears" became another dance club favorite. The number of Motown alumni playing on the record include drummer Uriel Jones and keyboardist Earl Van Riper. They helped to produce a retro record that didn't sound like it was from the past. Eminem's collaborator, Luis Resto, provided synthesizer sounds and worked on the arrangements. Like Rodriguez, Coffey produced a masterpiece that no one heard.

Motor City Magic was released on the TSR label. The smooth jazz sound was atypical Coffey. TSR is primarily a techno-dance label that moved on to new age and smooth jazz releases.

Another great release is the Strut 2011 CD, **Dennis Coffey**. For Rodriguez fans "Only Good For Conversation" featuring Paolo Nutini's vocals is a must. It is a cover of Wilson Pickett's "Don't Knock My Love," with Fanny Franklin's over the top vocal, that makes the album. Coffey's guitar on "Somebody's Been Sleeping" reminds the listener why he is a guitar legend.

In 2011, Fuel released **Dennis Coffey: Absolutely The Best of Dennis Coffey** with twenty signature guitar riffs, as well as Bill Dahl's copious liner notes. This CD is the best of Coffey's career for an overall view of his guitar genius. Unlike previous releases, many of them bootlegs, the sound quality on this CD is superb. The tracks are remastered with "Scorpio," "Taurus" and "Getting It On" sounding better than any previous release. There are some bonuses. The cuts on this Fuel re-release are the best of the Sussex years. It includes not only solo material but cuts from the Detroit Guitar Band.

WHAT COFFEY HAD IN COMMON WITH RODRIGUEZ

Much like Rodriguez, he was forgotten for a time by the music business. Then in 2002, he was interviewed for the documentary **Standing In The Shadow of Motown**. A high point of the documentary is when he talks about selling his Fender Stratocaster to purchase a Gibson Firebird after he heard Funk Brother Eddie Willis weave his magic with the Gibson.

In 2004, the University of Michigan Press published his memoir, **Guitars, Bars And Motown Superstars**. It is an incisive and analytical look into the Motor City music scene. It is also a window into Coffey's multi-layered life. That is a life dominated by an innovative, signature guitar sound. The Northern Soul aficionados were in touch and he appears regularly at festivals in the U. K. Again, like Rodriguez, he was rediscovered after thirty years of rappers and hip-hop artists ripping off his guitar riffs.

Now in his mid-seventies, Coffey is back touring, producing and adding to a signature sound that defined soul, pop and the blues. His appearance in **Searching For Sugar Man** brought his unique talent back to the general public. It is a welcome return for a legendary artist.

THE BEST OF DENNIS COFFEY ON YOU TUBE

The guitar wizardry that is Dennis Coffey is all over the Internet. On You Tube there are a number of key Coffey listening pleasures.

1.) "It's Your Thing" This is the 45 single on Maverick Records with the heavy psych/funk sound that defines Coffey.

2.) "It's Your Thing" This is a February 13, 2010 Coffey show from Detroit's Baker's Keyboard Lounge. The bonus here is that he is with the Lyman Woodward Trio.

3.) "Scorpio" This is the video from the January 22, 1972 Soul Train program. He was the only white performer to that time to appear on the program.

4.) "Scorpio" This is a marvelous Lincoln Center Concert outdoor live version on July 31, 2010.

5.) "All Your Goodies Are Gone" This is a live performance with Mayer Hawthorne in Detroit.

6.) "Scorpio" This is a live version from the Bonaraoo Music Festival on June 11, 2011.

7.) "Just My Imagination" This is a live television session in which Coffey covers a Motown song that he favors with his funk/psych sound.

8.) "F**k You" This is a great You Tube clip with Dennis holding a sign while promoting his Strut album. The video is priceless with a take off on Bob Dylan's signs in D. A. Pennebaker's **Don't Look Back**.

9.) "Dennis Coffey Tells The Story of His New Self-Titled Album" As the description suggests there is all you need to know about his Strut CD.

10.) "Scorpio" This is a live in New Orleans track from the Circle Bar during the jazz festival.

Dennis Coffey remains an iconic figure with a brilliant career in a new incarnation. Stay tuned. The best is yet to come. He is not only back in the studio but if you arrive in Detroit, Coffey is playing in local clubs. He is also in the studio. His website has more material on his legendary career as he continues to make new music while merchandising his past catalogue. Coffey's musical output remains varied and brilliant. Don't miss it.

ONE OF RODRIGUEZ' FAVORITE LUNCH SPOTS NEAR
HIS AVERY STREET HOME

chapter

ELEVEN

DENNIS COFFEY, MIKE THEODORE AND CLARENCE AVANT, THE MAKING OF COLD FACT

"DON'T WASTE YOUR TIME, MAKE UP YOUR MIND, AND MAKE IT HAPPEN." RODRIGUEZ

"ART TO ME IS AN ANECDOTE TO THE SPIRIT." MARK ROTHKO

At first glance Harry Balk's Twirl Records and Gomba Publishing, appear to have little, if anything, to do with **Cold Fact**. The reality is quite different. Dennis Coffey and Mike Theodore had worked with Balk who had a contract with Sixto Rodriguez that didn't expire until late July 1971.

The only mystery is Balk's relationship with Clarence Avant. He didn't appear to have one, but Harry had his fingers legally in the pie due to his contract with Rodriguez. The 1966 songwriting deal with Gomba

Music would come back to haunt Rodriguez in 2014. This is when Harry alleged that he should be paid for the songs on the **Searching For Sugar Man** soundtrack, as well as any song Rodriguez recorded until Balk's contract expired. By that time **Cold Fact** and **Coming From Reality** were released. They didn't sell so Harry ignored the LPs. This ended in the 2014 lawsuit that went after Rodriguez' royalties. This further confused the issue. The background to **Cold Fact** began with Balk and his role in Rodriguez' first album.

Harry was the catalyst to the Detroit recording community discovering music beyond Motown. He also discovered the Sugar Man. In order to place **Cold Fact's** production in perspective it is necessary to analyze Balk's pivotal role in the Motown music scene.

BALK'S PLACE IN THE SCENARIO AS
COLD FACT IS ABOUT TO BE RECORDED

Harry Balk and his partner, Irving Micahnik, are best known for bringing Del Shannon's "Runaway" into the marketplace. Balk also produced Rodriguez, mentored Dennis Coffey and Mike Theodore, and he became a Vice President and a producer at Motown. He had a vast catalogue of songs in his Gomba Music. These songs included five of Rodriguez' highlighted by a 45 release "I'll Slip Away" backed with "You'd Like To Admit It," (Impact 1031). The others songs are the familiar "Forget It" and "To Whom It May Concern." There is one lost Rodriguez song, "That Discotheque." Balk copyrighted these songs, and they are the basis of Gomba's 2014 lawsuit against Clarence Avant who then countersued Sixto Rodriguez. The resulting lawsuits further clouded the royalty question.

Not only is Harry Balk important in discovering Rodriguez, his continued interest in the Sugar Man after the documentary won the 2013 Oscar added another element in the clouded royalty picture. The lost Rodriguez song, according to Balk's copyrights, provides another mystery.

THE LOST RODRIGUEZ SONG: THAT DISCOTHEQUE

On April 20, 1967 Harry Balk's Gomba Music copyrighted a Rodriguez song "That Discotheque." There are no words, no music and no sign of the tune. It is now an urban legend. The other tunes that Balk copyrighted are well known. When Harry was asked about "That Discotheque," he remarked: "It was one of Rodriguez' early songs." No one remembers him talking about it. No one can recall lyrics or music. Perhaps Balk had the idea to release it on his Impact label. No one knows. Mike Theodore pointed out that discos were not mainstream entertainment venues. This makes the song title suspect. He doubted the veracity of the tune. He pointed out that no one was using the word. Everyone interviewed had no knowledge of the song except for Balk. It is theoretically out there somewhere.

HOW DID HARRY BALK DISCOVER RODRIGUEZ?

As Rodriguez was discovered, it was a pivotal moment in Motor City music history. His songwriting was recognized as a valuable commercial asset. Harry was never keen on the Sugar Man as a performer. Balk, like other musical moguls, received as much songwriting credit as possible. Harry realized lyrics were not only a creative goldmine; they were a constant source of royalties.

The notion of taking a portion of the songwriting credit for the manager or label head that had little, if anything, to do with the creative process. It was what went on in the industry. The industry allows the predators who control the labels to receive songwriting credit. Harry Balk is a man of integrity who didn't place his name on any of Rodriguez' songs. He did have a portion of the publishing and mechanical royalty rights.

When Balk talks to an artist or listens to a song people take note. He has a nose for hit records. After Rainy M. Moore went to Harry Balk's downtown Detroit office, he was curious about her description of the elusive singer. She described him as "shy and brilliant." Harry had heard this many times. Moore's description intrigued Balk. Moore said: "He is a mystical Shaman." This prompted Balk to ponder the artist. He also listened carefully to the demos. What Harry heard was a brilliant songwriter who needed a producer. The lyrics were powerful, the music smooth, however, the demos were unprofessional. Harry could solve that problem. He needed to watch Rodriguez in a club. The songwriting genius was there. Could he perform in public?

Moore's explanation prompted Balk to visit the Sewer By The Sea and Anderson's Garden. Harry was impressed. The sound was unique. Rodriguez was young, well dressed, charismatic, and handsome. He was magnificent on stage. He was also too shy. Balk wondered if Rodriguez' personal charisma could radiate from the stage?

Rodriguez' persona was a professional one. He had a soft, pop voice. It was perfect for the Detroit clubs. His marvelous original songs completed the package. The club patrons didn't always recognize these songs. As a result, he performed a wide variety of covers. Balk sat smoking a cigar and listened. The audiences at the various bars Rodriguez played liked his music. Even the patrons that ignored him while playing pool would occasionally stop and listen to the music. That was the sign Harry needed.

When Rainy M. Moore asked Harry if he could produce a hit record for Sixto Rodriguez. He smiled. He took out an envelope. He wrote on a piece of paper. He sealed it. He told Moore that there was a date for a hit record. He saw commercial possibilities. As Moore exited Harry's office, she left a tape with six songs. Harry liked five of them. He decided to bring Rodriguez into the studio. Moore wondered: What was in the envelope? She didn't open it. She thought it was bad luck. Harry was a mysterious, powerful and all knowing person, Moore told Rodriguez, they would be wise to listen to him.

Harry Balk: "Rainy M. Moore was a godsend. She brought Rodriguez to the studio on time. It went well thanks to her."

A month later, Moore opened the envelope. She read the answer. Harry identified, "I'll Slip Away," as Rodriguez' first hit. When Rodriguez arrived to record, Balk was ready to provide him with a five-year career.

Harry Balk: "The average artist has a five year window, I told Del Shannon that and I told Rodriguez if he had a hit, save your money kid, you got five years."

When Balk sent Coffey and Theodore to watch Rodriguez perform at the Sewer By The Sea. Theodore recalled Rodriguez was "the most original artist I have heard since Little Willie John."

When Balk produced Rodriguez' debut 45 release, he brought Coffey and Theodore into the mix. Theo-Coff helped to write the charts for the first Rodriguez single on Balk's Impact label. The single failed to chart. "It was Harry's production," Theodore observed.

When Berry Gordy Jr hired Balk as a Motown Vice President, this put Rodriguez on the back burner. Harry wasn't sure that the Sugar Man could perform in the teen circuit. Rodriguez let him know that he wouldn't go to high school dances, inane disc jockey appearances or do interviews with the insipid press. This immediately cooled Harry on Rodriguez.

The reviews for his Impact 45 were positive ones. On September 23, 1967 **Cash Box** reviewed "I'll Slip Away" released as a Rod Riguez 45. The b-side "You'd Like to Admit It" (Impact 1031) was also a strong song. Balk was listed as the producer, and the song is included in the 1997 release **The Best of Impact**. "I'll Slip Away" had a 4 Star

Review in **Cashbox**. The cruel lesson was no one promoted the Sugar Man's Impact release.

WAS RODRIGUEZ GOING TO FRONT THE DETROIT WHEELS?

The Detroit Wheels were the last group to record for Impact. There were problems with lead singer, Mitch Ryder, as Johnny "Bee" Badenjek on drums, Jim McCarty on lead guitar, Earl Elliott on bass and Joe Kubert on rhythm guitar decided to go it alone. Harry stepped in and suggested Rodriguez as the new lead singer. For whatever reason, it didn't work.

Mitch Ryder tells a different story. He went to New York to record with Bob Crewe, who told him they would make him a solo star. He didn't need the Detroit Wheels. Crewe pointed out that session musicians Michael Bloomfield and Barry Goldberg provided better backing. Ryder was held in high esteem in the music industry. Jimi Hendrix asked him to be the lead singer in his band. The Electric Flag also inquired if he was available as the lead singer. Ryder wanted to go solo.

The partnership with Crewe almost ended Ryder's career. He recorded Las Vegas lounge style songs. Only one of Ryder's solo efforts with Crewe, "What Now My Love" hit the **Billboard** pop chart coming in at thirty. When Ryder was through with Crewe, he told a friend that he had fifty dollars. It was not a pleasant experience.

Later, he left Crewe and recorded an album, **The Detroit-Memphis Experiment** with guitarist Steve Cropper before reuniting with drummer Badanjek for an album **Detroit**. That album didn't sell and Ryder continued his solo efforts in Germany with continuous U. S. bookings.

Harry Balk: "Mitch Ryder was hanging out in Detroit and he didn't get along with his former band mates. I thought Rodriguez would be great as the Detroit Wheels lead singer. He wasn't interested."

Balk believed Rodriguez' track "I'll Slip Away," was a potential hit. Coffey and Theodore were in the studio, but it was Harry's magic that made "I'll Slip Away" an early and brilliant Rodriguez tune. Balk sold the label. He was off to work for Motown.

THE DETROIT RIOTS, 1967: IMPACTING THE SUGAR MAN

When Rodriguez cut his Impact sessions for Balk at Detroit's Tera Shirma Studio, a riot broke out on July 23, 1967. This came at a time when they were working on the Rod Riguez 45 "I'll Slip Away." The riots prompted Rodriguez to sit down and write "The Establishment Blues." Then two years later he recorded it. It was 1967; Rodriguez reacted to the Detroit riots with a poignant song that put the Motor Cities continuing problems into perspective. The Sugar Man believed that he had a sure hit. Harry Balk listened and didn't agree. It was too personal. It was too honest. It was too political. It was too close to the truth. The Bob Dylan protest era, Harry argued, was on the wane. Rodriguez wasn't pop or commercial enough for Balk.

Matt Lucas: "Rodriguez is a unique talent. No one in Detroit could produce him. His songs were beyond the Motown sound. I am happy that he is finally getting his due. I watched him scribble songs in bars and cafes in the Cass Corridor. He is the best political songwriter I ever heard."

Mike Theodore recalls that the building in which they were recording Rodriguez was on fire. He had to move quickly to save the master tape. Harry Balk's Impact label was on its last legs. So many of the early Rodriguez songs would have to wait for Sussex.

What did Rodriguez think? His strong and well developed social conscience, as well as his blue collar, civil rights activism, prompted him to identify with the protesters. His mind may not have been solely on the music. When Sussex Records and Clarence Avant came into the picture, nothing went right commercially. Avant funded two Rodriguez LPs. Nothing happened. He moved on and forgot about the Sugar Man. **Cold Fact** and **Coming From Reality** cost a combined sixty plus thousand dollars. Avant points out that no one recognizes this fact.

THE ELUSIVE RAINY M. MOORE: WAS SHE THE CREATIVE DIRECTOR?

One of the intangibles in the Rodriguez mystery is the Rainy M. Moore question. She is listed as Rodriguez' manager, or his creative consultant on **Cold Fact**. According to Steve Rowland, she was five feet five inches tall with dishwater blonde hair. She was great looking. She was also smart and knew the ins and outs of the music business. She had previous dealings with Harry Balk. Rodriguez wanted her included as a part of the **Cold Fact** production. Those close to Rodriguez describe Rainy as much like his present girl friend, Bonnie, who is concerned about Rodriguez' health and career. Rainy M. Moore remained in the background, but she had a strong influence on his early career.

When Rainy and Rodriguez met in 1965, she was a student at Wayne State University. She went to Harry Balk's office in the spring of 1966. She had him listen to some demos. Balk was intrigued. In late July, Rodriguez signed a five-year songwriting contract with Balk's Gomba Music. Harry told Rodriguez his future was as a songwriter and not as a performer. From day one, Harry had no interest in publicizing or promoting Rodriguez as a performer. This didn't go down well with the Sugar Man. A few years later, Moore began searching for producers. She found Dennis Coffey and Mike Theodore. At her urging, they checked out Rodriguez. When Rainy M. Moore invited Coffey and Theodore to the Sewer By the Sea, the Rodriguez solo story unwittingly unfolded. Was she really a manager? No! She was a friend. That is Rodriguez' mantra. He has never trusted music professionals. For good reason, he has been lied to, manipulated and promised the moon before he recorded for Harry Balk. After Balk, he was in the hands of Clarence Avant. Rainy M. Moore ran the show. But quietly in the background, Rodriguez was pulling the strings. He continues to do that to the present day.

When Rodriguez played a gay club, the In-Between, Rainy was the booking agent. She was educated and spoke her mind. Rodriguez had no trouble getting gigs. It was Rainy's knowledge of local clubs that brought him more weekend gigs than he could play. Work in the week, music at night and performing in dive bars Thursday to Sunday defined Sixto Rodriguez' early life.

As Mike Theodore recalled: "He didn't really have a manager, just people who helped him and introduced him to people. He was pretty shy. I'm not sure we even knew it was the same guy when we saw him at the Sewer. It didn't really matter because he sounded so different."

Rainy M. Moore was instrumental in Rodriguez' career, not just for the meetings with Harry Balk, Dennis Coffey and Mike Theodore, she was also an important asset in convincing Clarence Avant to sign the Sugar Man to a three record deal with Sussex.

The liner notes to the second Rodriguez album, **Coming From Reality,** lists Rainy M. Moore as a creative consultant. Rainy reminded the session musicians of a press officer. She worked well with the producers and diligently kept Rodriguez comfortable.

Steve Rowland. "She never tried to interfere. Rowland appreciated her support for Rodriguez. She really helped him in the studio."

The mysterious countenance that is Rainy M. Moore is countered by Rowland's observations. He saw her as not only intelligent but committed to Rodriguez' musical journey.

Steve Rowland: "Rainy was a nice, efficient young lady. She watched over Rodriguez. She wanted to make sure that there was no bullshit. She was quiet. She acted like a manger should act. She asked the right questions."

The road to **Cold Fact** began in 1969 when Rodriguez signed with Sussex. This decision, as well as creating new songwriting and publishing entities, would surface in 2014 in a nasty series of lawsuits. Harry Balk was in forefront of the legal action.

There is another reason that Balk is important. After he cut the first Rodriguez single, he worked extensively with Coffey and Theodore. While he had nothing to do with **Cold Fact**, his earlier involvement made his imprint on the album. Balk is the most important and respected independent producer in Detroit. Berry Gordy Jr and Motown's success have overshadowed him, but his place in the Motor City Hall of Fame is secure. Few people pursued a music career without consulting Harry. If they didn't they wouldn't have a career.

IS CLARENCE AVANT THE GRINCH WHO RUINED THE PRODUCT OR IS IT NEIL BOGART?

When Avant founded Sussex Records on December 18, 1969, he spent almost six years making records. He had a distribution deal with Buddah Records. His quasi-partnership with Neil Bogart at Casablanca Records prompted bankruptcy. Over time Bogart was more interested in promoting disco than Rodriguez's literary gems.

Neil Bogart may be the grinch who ruined Rodriguez. He was the distributor who allegedly didn't keep good records; didn't pay royalties on time and more importantly Bogart's private life left little time for business. Rumor has it that he stockpiled Rodriguez' album in New York, and then he either shipped them to Australia or pulped the remainder.

When Avant closed shop in 1975, he was in debt to the IRS to the tune of $62,000. He owed the State of California back taxes; no one was able to collect. The IRS put padlocks on the offices and auctioned the assets. Somewhere in the shuffle, Rodriguez' music got lost.

As Rodriguez went gold and platinum in South Africa, as well as in Australia, the royalties somehow bypassed Clarence Avant. In the documentary, Avant claims he didn't receive any royalties. Avant may be guilty of nothing more than being in business with Neil Bogart. Or perhaps having a multi layered business structure that didn't keep track of the small royalties. Who knows! Perhaps the ongoing lawsuits will sort all this out. Until that time Clarence Avant may be innocent. Then again!

THE MAKING OF COLD FACT

When Coffey and Theodore went into the studio, they produced **Cold Fact** during thirty recording dates. Most of the recording was done at night at Tera Shirma. There were a small number of day sessions. With

Coffey on guitar and Theodore on keyboards there was an easy working relationship. Funk Brothers Bob Babbitt on bass and Andrew Smith on drums added to the jazz inflected sound. Rodriguez was comfortable. Theo-Coff productions gave him leeway to interpret his songs his way. It still took a great deal of adjustment to bring the sound to the final edit.

Mike Theodore told Kevin "Sipreano" Howes: "We were captivated by his songs. We knew he wasn't mainstream. So we tried to approach it differently."

Theodore's quote goes a long way to explaining the freedom that Theo-Coff accorded the Sugar Man in the studio.

Mike Theodore: "Rodriguez was front and center, so we tried to do things that were hip."

The production emphasized brilliant orchestral accompaniment, a fuzz guitar, a horn section and a string ensemble. On "Crucify Your Mind" Theo-Coff's dreamy accompaniment created a Bob Dylan like euphoria that Rodriguez' vocals fit into a surrealistic mold.

The philosophy degree that Rodriguez was working on was an important part of his songwriting. His illusion to philosophical ideas was no accident. The Sugar Man has specific ideas about his songs. This led to some conflict in the studio. But these difficulties turned out to be an asset. The songs were stronger as a result of these creative differences.

NOT EVERYTHING WENT SMOOTHLY: RODRIGUEZ' VISION

Not everything went smoothly. Rodriguez had a vision. He wanted his songs without multi-tracking. The bells and whistles of the psychedelic era were not to his liking. "He's a little bit too eccentric," Dennis Coffey remarked. To solve this problem Coff-Theo recorded Rodriguez alone and added the music later.

Mike Theodore: "We recorded him playing his guitar and singing. We didn't have any trouble with him. It was cut and dried."

Theodore went on to point out that the changes in cadence or meter made it difficult to record Rodriguez. They had to take a great deal of studio time overdubbing the music. They spent the extra time. Clarence Avant paid for it. **Cold Fact** evolved into a legendary album. Theo-Coff's production was ahead of its time. Subsequent reviewers have commented on the use of synthesizers. Mike Theodore simply smiles. Synthesizers were not used.

Sixto Rodriguez: "When you over produce, you lose something."

There was no overproduction. One of the urban myths surrounding **Cold Fact** is that there was a significant degree of conflict between the production team and the artist. The interviews for this book suggest that there was no more discord than was common in producing any album. Theo-Coff and Rodriguez were on the same wavelength for the entire recording process.

EXPLAINING RODRIGUEZ' LYRICAL BRILLIANCE

There are few explanations of where Rodriguez acquired his lyrical brilliance. The songs are important in elucidating Rodriguez' themes. "Sugar Man" talks of a street drug dealer, and it is a moralistic lyrical adventure through the counterculture. "Only Good For Conversation" is the Sugar Man's unhappiness with a craven female acquaintance. "Crucify Your Mind" is critical of a plastic person with little to offer. "The Establishment Blues" indicts local Motor City politics. "I Wonder" is a philosophical tome about two disparate souls. "Like Janis" carries on the theme of people who lack commitment. "Rich Folks Hoax" is a window into a part of Detroit life that the Sugar Man detested. "Jane S. Piddy" tells the tale of a devious young lady who failed to fool Rodriguez. What these songs have in common are brilliantly crafted lyrics and soulful music. Each song is a beautiful and poignant autobiographical story.

When asked about his songwriting, Rodriguez explained to **Boston Globe** reporter Saul Austerlitz in 2008: "I guess looking out that window were some of those visuals like Kent State, the assassinations of so many people in the 60s, unrest, the resistance against the war." Looking back with the hindsight of almost forty years, Rodriguez said of **Cold Fact:** "Those are probably very real, those feelings and things in the album. It was pretty chaotic, I think."

ADDING TWO SONGS TO COLD FACT

The songs Rodriguez wrote for **Cold Fact** provides the key components for a commercial debut album. Theo-Coff needed two more tunes to complete the twelve-track LP. They wrote the music and then Coffey and Theodore hired lyricist Gary Harvey as the wordsmith. The two non-Rodriguez songs have sparked a debate among Rodrigologists. Some love the songs. Others hate them. Both were written in Rodriguez' style.

"Hate Street Dialogue," took its theme from the San Francisco Haight Ashbury Summer of Love. It had been two years since the abortive hippie dream crashed into a drug hazed infusion. When Harvey sat to write the lyrics, it was 1969 and he looked back on San Francisco's Summer of Love nostalgically. The song paid tribute to love, peace and the qualities of the 1960s that made the counterculture Rodriguez' focus. The lyrics are at times heavy handed but so was the Summer of Love. "Hate Street Dialogue" is a pseudonym for Haight Street the focal point of San Francisco's Summer of Love.

The themes in "Hate Street Dialogue" are contemporary ones. The image of women set free from the drudgery of the past reflects Rodriguez' feminist concerns. There are also political lyrics. Harvey's stated: "The pig and hose have set me free." This was a reference to the clashes between Haight Street denizens and the San Francisco Police Department.

There are also key drug references: "the inner city birthed me, the local pusher nursed me...make it on the street, they marry every trick they meet." This is a wonderful description of the descent of the Summer of Love into violence and drug addiction. Yet, Harvey's lyrics also reflect the positive side of the Haight Ashbury. The birth of the counterculture with alienation from the mainstream is a part of "Hate Street Dialogue's" message.

What did Rodriguez think of the two songs? He has never said publicly. To close friends, he remarked that he is not really happy with the lyrics. The music is fine. The key is that the Sugar Man didn't write the songs. That is the basis of his criticism. It is private criticism, not public.

In a post on the Sugar Man official website, Harvey wrote: "Pig and hose to bust our game' from the song 'Hate Street Dialogue', refers to the continual harassment of the hippie-subculture by the San Francisco police department on the Haight-Ashbury youth in 1967. 'Pig' was the referral to the POLICE, and 'hose' was in reference to the length of 'garden-hose' used to beat the citizens into submission usually in the confines of the police station. The title was changed in spelling from 'Haight Street', to 'Hate Street' to further emphasize that feeling of alienation, by both sides of the establishment, at that time." Gary W Harvey, June 2002 See http://blog.sugarman.org/2012/08/11/the-amazing-story-of-hate-street-dialogue/

The other non-Rodriguez song, "Gommorah (A Nursery Rhyme)" prompted Graeme Thomson, writing in the **London Observer** in August 2008, to observe: "Gomorrah is as darkly spacey as anything Arthur Lee and Love ever did." This reference to Arthur Lee and Love is an interesting one. Rodriguez wasn't interested in Love or Lee. But, like Love, his music struck a distinctive chord. When Gary Harvey wrote the two songs, he emulated the Sugar Man's style. "I consciously wrote them to sound like it was coming out of his mouth and feeding into the morose feeling that I got from Rodriguez about life." That said Rodriguez didn't care for someone copying his style.

The length of time that it took Rodriguez to write a song is one of the unexplored questions in his career. By all accounts, he was a slow, tedious writer, who looked to every word, every subtle nuance and every phrase with care. He remains this way to the present day. He is also secretive or somewhat insular about his songwriting. He doesn't want to talk about it. He prefers to write and let the final result do his talking.

COFFEY-THEODORE'S PRODUCING AND MIXING MAGIC

While Rodriguez wrote great songs, he also had a sense of what he wanted to accomplish in the studio. "We really didn't trust the mixdowns we were getting out of the Detroit studios," Dennis Coffey said. The Dennis Coffey-Mike Theodore team took the final tapes to New York where Clarence Avant told them that they had an unlimited budget. He wanted to make **Cold Fact** right. Theo-Coff did.

Ray Hall was hired to complete the mixing at New York's RCA studio. Hall, an engineer, is noted for his work with Carol King, Sam Cooke, the Monkees, Nina Simone and John Denver among others. He was selected for his jazz influenced mixing. What Coffey and Theodore envisioned was an album with Bob Dylan type lyrics complimented with soft jazz sounds mixed with a pop direction. This combination guaranteed a hit LP. It did become a chart hit forty plus years later.

Dennis Coffey: "I think some of the studios had the equipment really punched up so that when you heard them in the control booth, they sounded great, but when you got them home, they didn't sound so good."

THE COLD FACT ALBUM COVER AND
EARLY COPYRIGHT QUESTIONS

The **Cold Fact** cover was unique. This was due to a commercial photo studio, Ransier and Anderson, who hired renowned photographer, Bob Flath. He conceived the seated pose that was used on the cover. There were also many experiments with Flath attempting to use the dive bars that Rodriguez played for a cover shot. Eventually, they conceived the crystal ball, which added an element of mystery with Rodriguez sitting in the center of it.

Flath drove over to the Sewer By the Sea and shot some pictures. He couldn't believe the place. What a dump! He shot Rodriguez in the club. He took some photos on a motorcycle. Finally, it was Rodriguez who came up with the idea of shooting him sitting in front of a crystal ball. The problem was finding a crystal ball in Detroit. They went all over the Motor City. They found a Woolworth's five-dollar crystal ball with snow inside. They let the snowfall down the crystal ball, and then shot a photo of it. Flath then manipulated the photo by enlarging it so that Rodriguez appeared to be sitting in the crystal ball.

Once **Cold Fact** was completed and ready for release the commercial potential didn't materialize. Somewhere along the line Rodriguez and **Cold Fact** got lost. There was still the talent equation. Rodriguez' album had more lyrical beauty than sales.

Sussex had a release that was ready for the singer-songwriter market. They printed the lyrics on the back sleeve, they sent out promo copies to the burgeoning FM stations. Sussex did attempt to bring disc jockeys into the fold. The minimal promotion failed. The talent equation remained strong, if unrecognized, until 2012.

When he finished recording **Cold Fact**, Rodriguez had the songs in place for **Coming From Reality**. A look at the talent equation tells one a great deal about Rodriguez' music and its artistic, if not commercial, future.

REFLECTING ON WHY COLD FACT DIDN'T SELL

No one can answer this question: "Why didn't **Cold Fact** sell? Dennis Coffey provides the best answer. "I don't think Sussex was prepared to handle him." Mike Theodore has a similar comment: "At the time he was avant garde. They weren't ready to buy what he was saying even though it was true."

There were other reasons for **Cold Fact's** dismal sales. Avant didn't press many copies. Coffey and Theodore went on to other projects. The Detroit music scene moved away from Rodriguez' sound. Everyone left for Los Angeles. **Cold Fact** was an undiscovered masterpiece that took more than four decades to reach the general public. The music remains timeless and the story is far from its conclusion.

The lack of U. S. sales for **Cold Fact** made it even more of a mystery. As Rodriguez said: "It's the music business. " The South Africans had it right as Abba shot up the charts with their pop drivel, Rodriguez' **Cold fact** ruled the South African listening public. They knew something the rest of us didn't and that was about the magnificent, if undiscovered, talent of Sixto Rodriguez. The legend continued to obscure the reality but that would change when Steve Rowland produced **Coming From Reality** and Malik Bendjelloul would produce **Searching For Sugar Man**.

No one could believe that **Cold Fact** was not a chart hit. Everyone praised Rodriguez' talent equation. The competitive nature of the music business prompted everyone to move on to new projects. Soon Rodriguez was forgotten but over time a cult audience embraced his music. When he became a recording and touring icon in 2012 many of his more fervent followers rued the day he went mainstream. They wanted Rodriguez' talent equation to remain in the midst of a small cult following.

chapter

TWELVE

THE TALENT EQUATION, RODRIGUEZ AND HIS MUSIC

"IT STARTED OUT SO NICE." SIXTO RODRIGUEZ

"MAKE IT NEW." EZRA POUND

"LEARNED, REPSECTABLE BALD HEADS, EDIT AND ANNO-
TATE THE LINES, THAT YOUNG MEN, TOSSING ON THEIR
BEDS, RHYMED OUT IN LOVER'S DESPAIR." W. B. YEATS

Sixto Rodriguez had a musical vision. He believed in writing original songs, and he also listened to and performed a wide variety of cover tunes. The Frank Sinatra, the Nina Simone, the Sarah Vaughan and the Etta James songs that he heard as a young man were instrumental in forming his songwriting persona. The Sugar Man's talent was that of a hybrid. He was a private 60s hippie with a musical connection to a nostalgic time.

These classic singers impacted his persona. The Rodriguez cool came from these concert legends. Why would the Sugar Man cover these artists? The answer is a simple one. He is not a person one can categorize. The talent equation is one established by a brilliant contrarian. He blends Cole Porter and Bob Dylan.

At some Rodriguez concerts, there is grumbling when he covers a Sinatra song. The minions want his original tunes. But some audiences appreciate the cover tunes. When he appeared at San Diego's North Park Theater in early June 2014, the audience and reviewers were ecstatic about his cover of Sinatra's "I'm Gonna Live Until I Die." The poignant lyrics were not lost on the crowd.

There is another side to Rodriguez' listening persona. He also performs classic rock songs "Blue Suede Shoes," "Good Golly Miss Molly," or the doo-wop standard the Flamingos' "I Only Have Eyes For You." Other Rodriguez in-concert covers include a Little Willie John influenced "Fever," a Roy Hamilton infused "Unchained Melody," a Jackie DeShannon inspired "What The World Needs Now Is Love" and a Lou Rawls styled "Dead End Street." What is obvious is that the Sugar Man can't be categorized. He remains a musical contrarian. That is his charm.

Rodriguez can write a romantic ballad, a hard-edged political song, a personal tune or a folk song with ease and precision. How did he come by this talent? It was in the small Detroit clubs that he perfected his craft. He immortalized these clubs in esoteric lyrics that are never dated. He was a Motor City musical apprentice training for bigger and better things.

The apprentice period was an important one. He learned to please an audience. He is also a wellspring of information on Detroit's musical-political past, the classic rock music era, the singer-songwriter syndrome, and, unfortunately, the vagaries of the record business. These experiences created writing methods that allow the Sugar Man to blend his disparate elements into song.

The lyrics, the talent equation, Detroit's influences and his quirky persona are evident in Rodriguez' songwriting. There are three bonus cuts on **Coming From Reality** that explain a great deal about Rodriguez and his music. These tunes offer a glimpse into his psyche.

THE CLUBS, THE MOTOR CITY AND
THE THREE BONUS SONGS

Rodriguez' apprenticeship in a wide variety of Motor City clubs created a cache of tunes with gritty realism. The three bonus songs that are included on the reissue of **Coming From Reality** explain Rodriguez' talent. "I'll Slip Away," originally a Harry Balk production, is typical of the Sugar Man as he writes: "And I'll forget about the girl that said no. Then I'll tell who I want where to go. And I'll forget about your lies and deceit. And your attempts to be so discreet." Rodriguez details a failed relationship in a sensitive manner. As he said, he will slip away without rancor or anger. This is typical of the Sugar Man's demeanor.

Another bonus cut from **Coming From Reality**, "Can't Get Away," is a gritty look at Detroit during Rodriguez' formative years. "Schooled on the city sidewalks. Coldness at every turn. Knew I had to find the exits. I never ever would return." This youthful sketch of what he didn't value about Detroit turns into admiration. There is also a life lesson in this song.

"Street Boy" is an autobiographical window into the Sugar Man's early life. Those who describe Rodriguez as "quirky or eccentric" don't understand him. He has seen the street, he is not interested in what that life has to offer. He simply reflects on it in song.

Cold Fact's myriad influences celebrate the Detroit landscape, as the songs offer a window into his life. His lyrics often reflect an everyday life that is a philosophical tome to blue-collar values.

RODRIGUEZ AND THE DRAMA OF EVERYDAY LIFE

While his lyrics are idiosyncratic, they also delve deeply into the American soul. Rodriguez' clarity of observation disregards clichés and rules. He pierces the heart of American hypocrisy with a lyrical beauty seldom seen in rock music. His philosophical openness runs like a surrealistic thread through his songs.

Rodriguez offers a range of experiences from the real world. The more substantial and deep moving songs include "Crucify Your Mind" and "Forget It." They describe the inner workings of his intellectual life. There is an oblique Dylanesque lyrical direction. He is a writer and a teacher, who is a Shaman with a gentle philosophical bent. His songs speak of a lost America, as in "Heikki's Suburbia Bus Tour."

While Rodriguez' lyrics define his talent, his music is equally inspiring. The myriad influences make his songwriting simplistic. What were Rodriguez' favorite books? What inspired him? There are clues.

Rodriguez read J. R. R. Tolkien's **The Hobbit** and **Lord Of The Rings**. There were lessons in the use of Tolkien's imagery that the Sugar Man employs in his writing. **Lord of The Rings** is so obtuse that it is open to any interpretation. That is the reader could use it to formulate ideas.

Both of Rodriguez' albums contain elements of Tolkien. These elements include Rodriguez' view that evil, race and social class differences are the main parameters in his writing. There is one song that reeks of Tolkien. The song: "It Started Out So Nice."

IT STARTED OUT SO NICE: TOLKIEN
AMONG OTHER INFLUENCES

There are songs on the second album, **Coming From Realty**, that reflect Tolkien's influences. "It Started Out So Nice," is not only inspired by J. R. R. Tolkien's **Lord Of The Rings**, it suggests Rodriguez' philosophical bent. He also employs real people as inspirations for his songs. "Heikki's Suburbia Bus Tour" sees Rodriguez borrowing the name of a friend, Heikki, to write a song that is Beatles influenced. Heikki despite the name is a tall blonde friend with a wife and two bulldogs. He is also a contrarian who talks at length about the suburban malaise overtaking American society. Heikki is a biker. He is also a brilliant mathematician with engineering skills. When one of Heikki's friends dies, there is a motorcycle funeral. When the funeral ends, the mourners ride to the suburbs. The long hairs and hippies endured stares from the suburbia. Now they turn the imagery around, as the freaks travel to the burbs to view what they consider the real freaks, the suburban dwellers. Like many of Rodriguez' songs, Heikki breaks convention and challenges stereotypes. The funeral makes a statement concerning suburban boredom and its deleterious impact. One wonders was the funeral imaginary or real?

While history is integral to Rodriguez' songs, there is an inherent philosophical bent buried within the Sugar Man's writing. After four decades out of the limelight, Sixto Rodriguez burst onto the entertainment world in 2012 with a vengeance.

The mystery continues. Where was he for more than forty years? He wasn't where Malik Bendjelloul suggested in **Searching For Sugar Man**. He was easy to find according to the Australian band, Midnight Oil, as they toured the U. S. Rodriguez was writing and performing, albeit at insignificant venues. His wife, Konny, said, that he often performed for free. She pointed out that people took advantage of him.

When Light In The Attic reissued **Cold Fact** and **Coming From Reality,** Rodriguez was still relatively unknown. It didn't matter to his fans. The Sugar Man's supporters were drawn to his character, as well as to his music. To Matt Sullivan, the Sugar Man is humble and agreeable. When Sullivan flew from Seattle to Detroit to convince Rodriguez to let

Light In The Attic release his two albums, he wanted to make sure that the Sugar Man was treated equitably.

Matt Sullivan: "We didn't want to re-release the LPs if Rodriguez was not on board."

The Rodriguez phenomenon was as much about the songs, as it was about his mysterious story. The everyman nature of Rodriguez' tale is explained in "A Most Disgusting Song." Rodriguez revisits the bucket of blood bars that he played with guarded enthusiasm. These small clubs prompted him to bring along a drummer, John Gentile, and with Rodriguez' classical guitar it made for a sophisticated sound. It was at a gay club, the In-Between, that Rodriguez initially turned his back to the audience as he sang "Crucify Your Mind." Why? No one knows! Those who saw him in the Detroit clubs remarked that the back to the audience performances were few and far between. It could be another urban myth associated with the Rodriguez story.

Steve Rowland: "Rodriguez' songs were about his friends, his life, his influences and his family. No one knows what they mean except Rodriguez."

Why did Rodriguez turn his back to the audience? He explained: "I was more concerned about them listening to the songs," Rodriguez continued. "I was just really trying to deliver that tune." When Dennis Coffey and Mike Theodore saw Rodriguez at the Sewer By The Sea, he was facing the club wall. They stood in awe. His lyrics and music were too sophisticated for the bar denizens. They knew they had to target him in the recording studio.

Sixto Rodriguez: "We were trying to do clubs, because that's where you could get work."

Rainy M. Moore booked some of the worst clubs in and around Detroit. She had connections with the bar owners, the nightclub moguls, the press, the heads of recording studios, local musicians and the managers looking for new acts. She exposed the Sugar Man to all aspects of the Detroit music scene. She helped to broaden Rodriguez' songwriting.

Rodriguez got out and about in Detroit. He listened to a wide variety of local sounds including the Detroit Emeralds, Bob Seger, the Amboy Dukes, Iggy Pop and the Stooges, Question Mark and the Mysterians, the MC5 and an early version of Grand Funk. The blues, rhythm and blues and classic rock influences coalesced to help form Rodriguez' lyrical magic. There were some obscure musicians that he favored. One in particular stands out.

HOW T. J. FOWLER IMPACTED RODRIGUEZ

T. J. Fowler, a blues-jazz Detroit musician, influenced Rodriguez. Fowler, much like Rodriguez, played the gutbucket clubs. He led a jazz-blues organ combo. Like most musicians in Detroit, he went to work for Berry Gordy Jr for a brief Motown stint. In the 1970s, as Rodriguez emerged, Fowler left the music scene for the business world. Not only was Fowler a jump blues musician, he held a day job most of his life, he was an under the radar Detroit performer. Rodriguez identified with him.

What was Fowler's influence? Because of the difficulty finding good paying gigs, Fowler always had a stripped down horn section. Rodriguez employed this sound when he could. The horns impacted his writing. Calvin Frazier, the guitarist in Fowler's band, had riffs influencing the Sugar Man. These adventurous musical pieces prompted Rodriguez to stretch his music. It was the manner in which Fowler blended blues, pop and jazz sounds that found their way into the Sugar Man's writing.

The key songs that Fowler recorded include the slow blues "Little Baby Child" and "Got Nobody To Tell My Troubles." These tunes spoke to Rodriguez' creative muse. They were the type of songs that the Sugar Man replicated. Fowler's urban blues style appealed to Rodriguez' innate songwriting talent. As the leader of an obscure blues band, T. J. Fowler, provided a window for Rodriguez into the Detroit musical world. He also unwittingly created a blueprint for Rodriguez' future.

INFLUENCES ON RODRIGUEZ' SOUND:
COMMERCIAL SONGS

In numerous interviews, Rodriguez remarked that Bob Dylan's "Masters of War,'" Neil Young's "Ohio," Paul Simon's "I Am A Rock" and Barry McGuire's "Eve of Destruction" were key influences. It is not surprising that Rodriguez favored commercial hits; despite his hippie persona he was serious about producing chart hits. These mainstream songs highlight Rodriguez' clear understanding of what it took to chart on the **Billboard** Hot 100.

When Detroit's **Metro Times** interviewed the Sugar Man they asked about Phil Ochs. Rodriguez said: "Well…he's another one. I question how he passed; I saw him in Detroit as a matter of fact, and he was a really healthy guy." Then Rodriguez went on to speculate about events in American history. There is a conspiracy tone to his political thought.

There is a streak of paranoia brought out by the cataclysmic events in his life. But Rodriguez can still call up history with precision and accuracy.

In this interview, Rodriguez said that he was born at 831 Michigan Avenue, right by the Kosciusko statue. There is a casino there now. As he talked about his youth, there is no doubt of the Sugar Man's love for the Motor City. He always had mainstream intellectual and musical interests that reflected Detroit.

In the early 1970s, while Rodriguez still had aspirations for his musical future, he was a quiet musical scholar. Rodriguez listened to a great deal of pop music. Carol King's **Tapestry** album and a number of early Elton John releases intrigued him. They accentuated the commercial side of his writing. In the mid-1970s, he listened intensely to Fleetwood Mac's **Rumours** LP. Why? Sales! Rodriguez remarked: "There was a lot of beautiful music out there." One common misconception is that Rodriguez is a protest-folk music writer. He can write a pop song, a love song or a commercial song. The problem is that no one heard his music. This **Metro Times** interview is a rare insight into his brilliant, if peripatetic, mind. The photo of a young Rodriguez holding a guitar with his foot atop a fire hydrant was the perfect setting for his in-depth comments. When Rodriguez began the interview, he demonstrated his vast intellectual interests.

Sixto Rodriguez: "Mexicans are indigenous people. They have a lot of history there, the Olmec culture, 1200 B.C. There's a drug war on the borders of America, but they only cover Iraq and Iran and Afghanistan. I asked a journalist down there [Mexico] I heard there were 40,000 killed there, and he said, 50,000, and you don't hear boo about it in certain Rupert Murdoch columns. And the scandal in the media over there in England will include Tony Blair, and will eventually include the Bush administration. I have to remind everyone that California produces Arnold Schwarzenegger, produces Ronald Reagan and Richard Nixon. So that kind of is who owns the media."

Rodriguez believes that most proclamations from the various levels of government are pure nonsense. He makes no bones about the deception and dishonesty he believes drives governmental policy. Some of his friends describe him as paranoid. Others say that he is realistic. Those inside the music business have abused Rodriguez, and this is enough to make anyone paranoid. Or perhaps this is realistic. Who knows!

The Sugar Man believes that yellow journalism is ruining the search for the truth. He referred to the Kennedy assassination, and how the Zapruder film influenced the times. This piece of film showing President John F. Kennedy's assassination is another small, but significant, window into the Sugar Man's mind. He is a firm believer Kennedy was assassinated by government officials. The Kennedy assassination is an event Rodriguez believes proves the conspiracy folks have it right. He sees numerous government conspiracies in domestic politics.

When Corey Hall concluded the **Metro Times** interview, there is no doubt that Rodriguez' life has strong political beliefs. When he mentioned the Zapruder film again and speculated on the Kennedy assassination, once again, he suggested that there is a great deal of American history that didn't make sense. This explains why his close friends describe him as "loveable but paranoid."

The talent equation didn't immediately translate into commercial success. It is ironic that it took forty years before America and the world fell in love with his music. Thank God for Stephen "Sugar" Segerman, Craig Bartholomew-Strydom, Brian Currin, Andy Harrod, Steve Rowland, Dennis Coffey, Mike Theodore, Matt Sullivan, Simon Chinn and Malik Bendjelloul. They provided us with a story that is so amazing that it is almost fictional. Fortunately, as Rodriguez might say, "it is coming from reality."

FAME, FORTUNE AND SONGWRITING AT 70 PLUS

To achieve fame at seventy is a rare feat. It is improbable but explainable. Rodriguez has enormous talent. Not even the capricious nature of the music business dims his talent.

The snowy Detroit winters fall like a blanket over Rodriguez' continual search for intellectual truth. The artist in middle age is rediscovered. It is like a fictional portrait, as he wanders on stage more than ninety nights a year. Is it due to the talent equation? Is it due to nostalgia? Is it due to the original songs? Rodriguez doesn't know the answers. He is simply happy to be back on the road. It is Rodriguez' emotional, but passionate, persona that allows his talent to shine through the show business abyss.

Rodriguez is a songwriter that works in isolation. If his work isn't promoted, it remains obscure. There are many other Rodriguez' with a similar talent. The talent equation is one that maintains the creative process. Fortunately, for Rodriguez, **Searching For Sugar Man** brought the music to the fore.

SOME HINTS ON HOW RODRIGUEZ MADE HIS MUSIC

Sixto Rodriguez is a private person. He is humble. He is introspective. To analyze how he made his music, it is necessary to examine his thoughts. When he was young, he hung out at the Detroit clubs. He met the musicians. He had a plan. He hoped to become a professional musician. He did. It was just a little later than most performers.

Rodriguez isn't a mainstream personality. This leads to esoteric lyrics that highlight his personal thoughts. His songs often have a pop, commercial tone. While others, like "Crucify Your Mind," are in the singer-songwriter mold that is much like Bob Dylan. He was so multi-talented and diverse; it was difficult to categorize him. His **Cold Fact** producers, Dennis Coffey and Mike Theodore, were perfect for the first song cycle. Steve Rowland, the **Coming From Reality** producer, gave him enormous studio freedom for the later songs as well as adding "Sandrevan Lullaby-Lifestyles" to create a romantic interlude in a batch of personal songs.

Steve Rowland: "I realized early on that he had to be himself. I gave him free rein and then I added the necessary production touches. He didn't need anyone to tell him how to record, he had it down."

In **Cold Fact** the talent equation is one that blended the Theo-Coff production team with the elusive and often unpredictable Rodriguez. His daughter, Regan, commented to many people that they tried to change his songs and in the tug of war **Cold Fact** emerged. By the time that he recorded **Coming From Reality**, Rodriguez was adept at studio production. Steve Rowland recognized his talents and carefully worked them into the final production.

THE INDUSTRY KILLED RODRIGUEZ

The changes in the music landscape from 1970 to 1975 curtailed Rodriguez's career. When he recorded **Cold Fact**, there were more than sixty constantly booked Detroit recording facilities. By 1975, less than twenty studios were still in business. Motown, Clarence Avant, John Rhys, Dennis Coffey and Mike Theodore moved to California, and so did much of the recording business.

In the 1970s, pop music was in a slump. The Doobie Brothers "Black Water" with its syrupy pop tone and John Denver's "Thank God I'm A Country Boy," were far from Rodriguez' sound. The rise of bubble gum, glam, progressive, soft rock, disco and teenybopper music obscured serious artists like Rodriguez.

Suddenly, Detroit's rusting remains indicated the Motor City was on its last legs. Hitsville U. S. A., which became Motown, soon evolved into a museum. In 1970, when **Cold Fact** was released, the nail was driven into Rodriguez' commercial coffin. The state of the music business in 1970 was moving into a disastrous direction. As he made an appearance in the wake of **Searching For Sugar Man's** success in 2012, Rodriguez had some thoughts about the industry.

When Sixto Rodriguez appeared at Zulu Records in Vancouver, British Columbia in the aftermath of **Searching For Sugar Man's** success, he was relaxed. He was also unusually candid. The appreciative capacity audience cheered during the interview. The results led to rare insights into the Sugar Man's mind. He made it clear that he harbored no ill will against anyone in the industry. He also emphasized that he was looking forward to receiving his past royalties.

WHERE DOES RODRIGUEZ FIT IN THE PANTHEON OF MODERN SONGWRITERS?

Sixto Rodriguez is the new breed of songwriter. He is a gifted iconoclast whose words burrow deep into the American consciousness. Until the success of **Searching For Sugar Man**, Rodriguez had a cult following and many critics considered his music quirky. The Sugar Man is quirky; the music is mainstream, hit oriented as well as Tin Pan Alley brilliant. He creates songs with the panache of earlier standards by Cole Porter. It is not surprising that Porter is one of his favorite composers. He is the foremost singer-songwriter contrarian to emerge in recent years.

Rodriguez, who gives us hope that the Great American Songbook has taken a new direction, is in the forefront of the writing revolution. On the Sugar Man's fairy tale saga, Larry Rohter, writing in the **New York Times**, summed up Rodriguez' timeless quality: "Because of an odd confluence of circumstances it is also a story unlikely ever to occur again."

chapter

THIRTEEN

THE STATE OF THE MUSIC BUSINESS IN 1970 AS COLD FACT IS RECORDED AND RELEASED

"THE MUSIC INDUSTRY IS A FAST-PACED BUSINESS, BUT IT IS NOT ALL ABOUT THE MONEY. THAT'S NOT THE REASON YOU DO THINGS, THERE IS MORE BEYOND THAT, ANOTHER KIND OF REWARD – SELF-EXPRESSION. ANYWAY, YOU CAN'T TAKE MONEY WITH YOU WHEN YOU GO." RODRIGUEZ ON THE MUSIC BUSINESS

As 1970 dawned, the rock music world was undergoing fundamental changes. Bob Dylan moved back to New York, the folk rockers and psychedelic musicians had their day, and the rise of progressive rock brought free form songs. It also inaugurated song cycles that had little to do with positive social change. Nor for that matter did the songwriting improve. The early 1970s artists and bands had little to offer in the way of creativity, one critic suggested that rock music in the early 1970s suffered from "confusion and an excess of bad ideas."

What the industry suffered from was mediocre glam rock, progressive rock, and heavy metal. Then eventually disco emerged to further cloud the picture. These musical directions fragmented the marketplace. Then punk came along late in the decade to rescue rock and roll. The problem for Rodriguez is that he was closer to Joni Mitchell than Led Zeppelin. As a result, there wasn't much of an audience for his music.

In 1979, Rodriguez re-emerged in Australia, and he continued to be popular in South Africa. "There is no information on the singer known as Rodriguez," one South African remarked. As the myths grew and persisted, the Sugar Man personally remained under the radar. His mythical importance increased in South Africa. The rest of the world ignored him.

The mystery surrounding Sixto Rodriguez continued into 1996 when a letter to London's **Mojo** magazine inquired: "Any information about U. S. singer Rodriguez, who wrote all his work in prison and shot himself onstage after quoting from his song 'Forget It." This single line, "Thank Your For Your Time?" prompted those who speculate to wonder what to make out of the song. They continually mused what had Rodriguez intended? This letter was typical of the obsessed Sugar Man fans. There was no reply to this **Mojo** letter. The mystery was out there. There really was no mystery, as he never had a chance at stardom. The story of how Rodriguez brought his music to the mainstream in **Searching For Sugar Man** at times obscures his earlier talent. As the Sugar Man looked to Bob Dylan, he realized that they had a symbiotic relationship.

BOB DYLAN AND RODRIGUEZ: THE SIMBIOTIC RELATIONSHIP

Nothing was more indicative of the changes in rock music in 1970 than the release of Bob Dylan's **Self Portrait**. The irony is that Dylan released material that he believed was non-commercial. Dylan wanted some time off from the acclaim and fanfare. He purposely put out non-commercial albums. Not surprisingly, they sold spectacularly. In 1969, Dylan's albums **John Wesley Harding** and **Nashville Skyline** peaked at number 2 and 3 on **Billboard**. The following year the **Self Portrait** album reached number 4 and sold more than three million copies. What does this have to do with Sixto Rodriguez? Plenty! Dylan had enormous promotion. Rodriguez' LPs languished. The Sugar Man had an equally good product. It didn't matter the sales Gods weren't listening.

Anything Dylan turned out sold well. It was as much to do with Columbia Records publicity, as it was with Dylan's enormous talent. He had a songwriting persona. He had a mythical and mystical aura. Rodriguez had the same mantra without promotion. The result was no sales.

The point is that Rodriguez' original talent was hurt by being compared to Dylan. He is not an artist who knowingly apes the Dylan songwriting structure. Like Dylan, he finds fame a double-edged sword. Alec Baldwin warned Rodriguez that the fame game was an excruciating one. Rodriguez never forgot his 2012 conversation with Baldwin. It was a portent of things to come.

Like Dylan, Rodriguez loves to experiment. His playful way with words, his intricate music and the obscure Detroit message gives Rodriguez a special place in the songwriter's pantheon.

In 1970-1971, the rock and roll industry was not friendly to Rodriguez' original songs. His lyrical brilliance was closer to the Dylanesque protest songs than to the droll lyrics of the Age of Aquarius. Somehow Rodriguez couldn't envision writing the libretto to Jesus Christ Superstar. He wondered if the music industry had lost its way. It had.

The other problem with the lack of commercial success came from the small record labels. They were dying out, going bankrupt and being swallowed up by corporate conglomerates. Sussex Records was on the ropes before it got off the ground. Unfortunately, Rodriguez was with a small label run by industry insiders who didn't understand his talent.

Steve Rowland: "I was in London and I couldn't believe the people in the publishing companies. They didn't see the new talent. Rodriguez was that talent but no one would listen to me."

RODRIGUEZ' COLD FACT: THE 1970 ROCK
INDUSTRY KILLS HIS MUSIC

In 1970, as **Cold Fact** was released, the rock and roll industry entered a soft, safe place. What was obvious is that there wasn't a breakout album. There was no one with a gift for newly developed lyrics. The lack of idealism, the inability to write convincing lyrics, and the musical underachievement did not augur well for **Cold Fact**. Rodriguez was the new talent who lacked promotion and publicity. As much as Clarence Avant believed in Rodriguez, he did little to further the Sugar Man's career. This irony and contradiction was one Avant never addressed.

Rock music executives settled into safe marketing. The pop acts were given the best promotion. When Van Morrison asked for better marketing, Warner Brothers told him he was a cult artist. They would spend a few dollars on FM radio, a few more dollars with an ad or two in **Rolling Stone** and then depend upon Morrison's phalanx of cultish fans to purchase his albums. Fortunately, for Van, he released **Moondance** in February 1970. When **Moondance** peaked at twenty-nine on **Billboard**, Warner executives were ecstatic. They told Van that albums sold not through advertising but word of mouth. This began a confrontational relationship that didn't end until Van left Warner for greener pastures.

What did this have to do with Rodriguez? Plenty! Clarence Avant, like Warner executives, believed that heavy promotion didn't work. It also cost money. The industry was redefining its business model. Rodriguez was caught in the middle of this transformation.

There were other musical changes that doomed **Cold Fact**. The arrival of Led Zeppelin, Black Sabbath and Deep Purple brought a thundering rock sound quickly labeled heavy metal. But this was only one side of the musical changes in 1970-1971. Don MacLean's "American Pie" released in November 1971 became an anthem to rock and roll's classic past. This was another trend that placed Rodriguez' music into Woolworth's cut out bin. The force of rock and roll history was not kind to the Sugar Man.

In the early 1970s, the list of innocuous and insignificant hits went on forever. Chart songs like Paper Lace's "Billy Don't Be A Hero" and Vanity Faire's "Hitchin' A Ride," took rock music into a new commercial and artistic low. Then things got worse.

As Elton John and Rod Stewart popularized a rocking, but bland, mainstream music, Rodriguez' songs were lost. The Beatles went solo, record labels signed fewer acts, and there was a decline in the number of albums released. Singer-songwriter's were fewer and less significant. Everything in the industry pointed away from the Sugar Man.

Harry Balk: "Rodriguez didn't play the game. He didn't agree to do the disc jockey interviews, sock hops were anathema to him, and he wasn't interested in smoozing with industry types. He refused to honor the time tested standards on the road to a hit record."

This is, of course, blatant nonsense. Balk didn't like the Sugar Man because he challenged him to think differently. Rodriguez also told Harry to stop acting like all of the other industry types. The challenge for Balk was to think differently. He didn't. The industry types interviewed never blamed themselves for Rodriguez' lack of commercial success.

Steve Rowland: "The record executives were looking for the next big thing. He was under their nose. His name was Sixto Rodriguez."

WHY THE INDUSTRY SIGNED RODRIGUEZ
AND DIDN'T UNDERSTAND HIM

In the late 1960s, before he recorded **Cold Fact**, Rodriguez was considered the embodiment of the singer-songwriter. He fit the economic model that major record labels desired. He wrote the songs. He allowed the label a share of the songwriting and publishing. He didn't complain about the lack of promotion. He didn't peruse his contracts closely. He recorded quickly and in a fiscally conservative manner. He was simply elated to have a record deal. That was a mistake.

The problem with the early 1970s singer-songwriter syndrome was dreadful lyrics punctuated by pompous and arrogant intellectual allusions. When Neil Young sang: "I'd rather head for the ditch than the middle of the road," he reminded listeners how insipid lyrics were in the midst of the changes in the record business. Young, one of the most creative forces in the industry, often had to write lyrics quickly to meet the commercial demand. When Young rewrote Del Shannon's "Runaway" as "Like A Hurricane," he demonstrated one of the problems with the music business. You can't use the past for present day hits.

As the singer-songwriter syndrome declined in 1973, Seals and Croft were typical of the hits of the day with "Summer Dreams," which indicated the genre's dreadful nature. As soft rock replaced the topical singer-songwriter, Rodriguez went back to work rehabbing homes. He had no regrets. He recorded two excellent albums. He didn't mention this to anyone until 1998 when he triumphantly restarted his career in South Africa.

WHERE IS RODRIGUEZ IN THE 1970s?

As Rodriguez recorded **Cold Fact**, the music business transition continued. There was so much money in rock music that super groups like Led Zeppelin were given their own label. The changes in production were enormous. The new system prompted artists to take months, or even years, rather than days, to record an album. There was an unbridled sense of creative freedom due to money flowing into the labels like a water faucet that couldn't be turned off.

Another change in the 1970s was the rise of bootlegging or pirating. Bootlegs were often concert albums, pirating was simply copying a commercially released LP. There were also numerous bootlegged VHS tapes of concerts. The Grateful Dead fans were the forerunner of this phenomenon. Rodriguez' albums in South Africa and Australia were consistently bootlegged. Someone was making a great deal of money. It wasn't the Sugar Man.

THE RISE OF COUNTRY ROCK IMPACTING RODRIGUEZ

There were other trends counter to Rodriguez' sound. When the country rock revolution took place in the early 1970s, Gram Parsons created a group, the Flying Burrito Brothers, who are still playing in various incarnations. From San Francisco, the New Riders of the Purple Sage and Commander Cody and His Lost Planet Airmen emerged to take country-rock into a new direction. Then Nashville got in the act with the Nitty Gritty Dirt Band. In Austin, Asleep At the Wheel reinvented Bob Wills and the Texas Playboys. These sounds were contrary to the Sugar Man.

The old hippie subculture vanished in the wave of mandolins, banjos and steel guitars. Even Ricky Nelson came back with his country rock group, the Stone Canyon Band. This helped to bring an end to the musical direction that could give Rodriguez an audience.

For Rodriguez, there was still hope. As he recorded **Cold Fact**, Detroit was a traditional rock and roll town. Cobo Hall featured the Doors and the Who in concert. The Grande Ballroom had Arthur Lee and Love as well as Iggy Pop and the Stooges. Somewhere John Sinclair was shouting obscenities and calling his pieces poetry. No one else thought much about Sinclair's words. They didn't compare to the Sugar Man's poetic use of language. Rodriguez looked and sounded good in this atmosphere. He was also at ease with the times.

It was not uncommon to see Rodriguez walking near the Grande Ballroom with a guitar on his back. He was a walker who appeared to most people to have a mission. What that mission was, no one knew.

By 1974 there was no room for Rodriguez in the music business. He continued to perform where and when he could and he continued to write songs. But the changes in the music business in 1970 began the long road to obscurity as he raised his family. When **Searching For Sugar Man** stormed the big screen in 2012 no one was more surprised than Sixto Rodriguez.

chapter

FOURTEEN

COLD FACT RECONSIDERED

"IN SOUTH AFRICA, 'COLD FACT' WAS THE ALBUM THAT
GAVE PEOPLE PERMISSION TO FREE THEIR MINDS AND
START THINKING." CRAIG BARTHOLOMEW STRYDOM

"THEY WERE FOLKY BUT NOT EXACTLY FOLK-ROCK AND
CERTAINLY NOT LAID BACK; SOMETIMES PISSED OFF BUT
NOT FULL OF RAGE ALIENATED BUT NOT INCOHERENT,
HIS SONGS JAMMED WITH A GENTLE STREAM OF CON-
SCIOUSNESS." RICHIE UNTERBERGER REVIEWING COLD
FACT

In March 1970 few people paid attention to Rodriguez' debut album **Cold Fact**. For detectives hoping to reconstruct a picture of the
Sugar Man, it is a hit and miss affair. Rodriguez had thoughts and ideas
about how his music should sound. He didn't always communicate these
notions. His daughter, Regan, has mentioned many times that were dif-

ferences in the studio. Mike Theodore described the recording sessions as "relaxed and informal." If there were differences it was because Rodriguez wanted a sparse sound. He wasn't keen on strings and horns. Later, he reflected that the added instrumentation made **Cold Fact** a work of art. In August 2002, **Mojo** agreed the album was "buried treasure."

COLD FACT RECONSIDERED AND STEVE ROWLAND EMERGES

Cold Fact's completion was a carefully conceived process. It created a cult feeling among musicians, producers, engineers and assorted industry people. The critics spoke glowingly of the songwriting. The strong reviews for **Cold Fact** paved the way for the second album **Coming From Reality**. It was different from Rodriguez' debut album. It is a romantic, highly personal, picture of his life and those around him. **Coming From Reality** was the blueprint for another sound and a romantic, nostalgic adventure.

Not many artists who sell virtually no albums on their first try get a second chance. Rodriguez did because of his enormous talent. He also had a super producer, Steve Rowland, in his corner. Rowland realized that the folk fad obscured his talent. He reinvented Rodriguez into a contemporary artist with careful production. He crafted half a dozen potentially chart friendly hits.

Steve Rowland: "I don't understand to this day what went wrong in 1971? Rodriguez' talent was beyond the folkies of the day. He was the next big thing. No one saw it."

After **Cold Fact** failed to sell, Sussex Records gave up on Rodriguez. When Steve Rowland heard **Cold Fact**, he systematically pointed out Rodriguez' commercial potential. Steve hadn't met him. Rowland told anyone who would listen that his talent was as good, if not better, than any of Bob Dylan's songs. Clarence Avant agreed. He funded a second LP.

The aloof, alienated persona that Rodriguez projected didn't help record sales. He was friendly to most people, but Rodriguez had little interest in promoting his songs. He looked at the corporate big wigs with disdain.

THE COLD FACT ALBUM MYSTERY

In March 1970 Rodriguez' **Cold Fact** was released to tepid sales. Everyone was surprised. No expense was spared in recording **Cold Fact**. The finished product was an undiscovered masterpiece. The making of the album enlisted Detroit's best session musicians. The producers provided the basic structure for the session musicians. The Detroit Symphony's conductor, Gordon Staples, brought in the string section to make "Crucify Your Mind" a Dylanesque song with classical overtones. Telma Hopkins, a member of Tony Orlando And Dawn, added her signature vocal on "Gommorah." This song also featured a children's choir. The production costs were high as somewhere in the neighborhood of $30,000.

During the recording sessions, Rodriguez was shy about working on the floor with the other musicians. "He's a little bit too eccentric for that," Coffey remarked. Rodriguez prepared his songs at home and brought them into the studio. The instrumental tracks were already recorded. They simply recorded the vocals and added the instrumental tracks.

As **Cold Fact** hit Detroit record stores, it was played regularly on the Motor City's FM station, WABX. There was also a hippie type magazine, **Big Fat**, that had Jimi Hendrix on the cover, and the magazine was a **Cold Fact** booster. The **Big Fat** issue had an ad advertising Rodriguez running for common council. Politics were more important to the Sugar Man than fame and fortune. The irony is that Detroit's counterculture press praised Rodriguez as much for his political activism as his music.

Sixto Rodriguez: "Politics superseded music. Nothing beats reality."

As **Cold Fact** was released, Rodriguez spent his time running for public office. He watched in frustration as civic corruption, the waste of funds as well as ignoring the ideas of the average citizen sunk the Motor City into a financial abyss. He hoped to be elected to the Common Council and help solve these problems. This is Detroit's version of the City Council. He worked. He was politically active. He was a community organizer. He also raised a family. It was a busy life. The only problem is that his music was ignored. He had everything except a hit record.

In the U. S. **Cold Fact** was relegated to the cut out bin. In South Africa, it sold triple platinum. In Australia it was five times platinum. It charted at twenty-three in Australia. It remained on the charts there for fifty-five weeks. It wasn't until Seattle's Light In The Attic reissued the album in 2008 that it found an American audience. What were the forces shaping Rodriguez' songs?

THE FORCES SHAPING RODRIGUEZ' SONGS

The **Cold Fact** album is one of genius. The lyrics, the soft, calm music and the sense of floating from the late 1960s into the early 1970s creates a listening euphoria. The LP is a mini-history of Detroit, and its surrounding pop culture. There are many personal songs. When Rodriguez sings about meeting a girl in Dearborn, he uses real life experiences to paint a picture of the changing Motor City landscape. Perhaps his lyrics were too sophisticated. This may have been due to his education. His philosophical references were toned down, but he still employed cutting edge phrases.

His writing was influenced by his time at Wayne State University. The honors college, Monteith, searched through their records, and they revealed that he spent a decade working on his philosophy degree. He had A grades in his courses. The main focus during the Sugar Man's lengthy education was to understand and emulate the existential philosophers. In the process, he became one of them. Like many college students, the cafe-bars around Wayne Sate University became his philosophical workshop.

The barometer for his writing often took place at the Decanter, a small student restaurant, near Wayne State University. When the students heard that Rodriguez liked and listened to Henry Mancini and Frank Sinatra, they were amazed. Then it was, as Rodriguez remembered, playing "little parties, drinking parties." It was from these experiences that **Cold Fact's** songs took shape. The multi-layered college life was a paean to his writing brilliance.

Long before he was a public figure, Rodriguez performed around Detroit, while continually shaping his writing skills. It was at places like Morey Baker's on Livernois Avenue that Rodriguez not only learned his craft, but the famous line in "Inner City Blues:" "met a girl from Dearborn, early six o'clock this morn, a cold fact" epitomized his Motor Town experiences.

THE DETROIT COFFEE HOUSE SCENE AND RODRIGUEZ

Sixto Rodriguez has never talked about the coffee shops in and around Wayne State University. During the interviews for this book, there were fleeting references to the Sugar Man wandering into these 1960s-1970s establishments and how they influenced his songwriting. Everyone agreed that the fertile intellectual atmosphere in and around the coffee shops and small clubs, particularly the Living End, the Wisdom Tooth and the Poison Apple impacted his lyrical imagery.

The coffee houses established the live music scene. It was because of these venues that Rodriguez found small, intimate clubs to perform. One of these was the Chessmate along Livernois near the 6 Mile Road. In 1963 this acoustic-folk club, which started as a coffee house for chess players, began to book musical acts. Joni Mitchell, Tom Rush and Linda Ronstadt among others performed at this intimate club. The characters who came in inspired Rodriguez' "ditty bop pimp" characterization and provided him with the visual stimulus for his lyrical direction. **Cold Fact**'s lyrics embraced the coffee shops turned into the small folk performing venues that exploded around Wayne State University.

In 1968 the Chessmate began to book rock music and electric acts, and by this time Rodriguez had written the songs that made up **Cold Fact**. Without the Detroit coffee houses turned music venues, he might not have had the impetus for his songs.

COLD FACT: FINISHED AND RELEASED

When **Cold Fact** was completed, it was released by A & M in South Africa. The remaining Sussex LPs were warehoused in New York. Little effort was made to publicize or distribute the LP. Neil Bogart was too busy with other projects. A & M was working on new artists and five years after the LP was completed A & M's New York warehouse was cleaned out. The remaining four hundred **Cold Fact** LPs were shipped to Australia. From 1976 to 1979, they became collector's items down under. This resulted in two Australian tours, and the development of a strong fan base.

The pulping of **Cold Fact** is a much-neglected subject. What is pulping? It is destroying an album that doesn't sell to make room for others. It degrades the artist. It allows for a tax write off for the record company. It is one reason that some artists never cut another album. Pulping is an excuse for failure. Real or imagined.

To understand **Cold Fact** is to realize that Rodriguez is rebelling against the nefarious practices of the record business. He did that by turning his back on the industry until his genius was recognized. Now he can pursue his career on his terms.

No one in the U. S. noticed when **Cold Fact** charted for fifty-five weeks in Australia. It rose to a peak position of twenty-three. Matt Sullivan's Light In The Attic label understood the demand. When LITA released **Cold Fact** in 2008 the label also pressed a thousand limited edition virgin vinyl LP releases. These albums sold out in a few weeks. One wonders if Rodriguez had Light In the Attic's promotional genius in 1970-1971 what might have been in the U. S. market?

REFLECTING ON COLD FACT FORTY YEARS LATER

Cold Fact has some specific thoughts. On "Hate Street Dialogue" he sang: "The inner city bothered me." The song went on to describe everything that was wrong with Detroit. The fact that Rodriguez didn't write the song made it one that he was ambivalent about. He doesn't like to talk about it. He never performs it. The lyrics, however, remain true to the album.

"Sugar Man" has a similar theme. It is an anti-drug song describing the disillusionment with the local drug dealer. On "Sugar Man," Rodriguez said: "It was fun doing that song. It's more like a prayer. I stretched it out from a short song to a long song." The ten songs that Rodriguez wrote on **Cold Fact** were ones he spent a decade crafting.

"I really thought **Cold Fact** was going to make it," Rodriguez continued. "But it didn't happen." He talked about being twenty-nine and raising two daughters. The third one, Regan, was not yet born. He simply went to work doing home restoration and demolition. Family came first.

"I continued to play," Rodriguez recalled. "It's something that I don't think I can stop." When he toured Australia in 1979 and 1981, Rodriguez observed: "It was a nice escape from reality." He also reminisced about his triumphant 1998 South African tour. "Never in my life did I think something like that would have happened!"

There were a number of good guys in Rodriguez' rediscovery, but none is more important than producer David Holmes. He loved "Sugar Man." He covered it with his group, the Free Association. Light In The Attic has re-released most of the Free Association material.

Holmes flew Rodriguez to New York City to put down backing vocal tracks for a new single release of "Sugar Man." From that day, when Rodriguez was still unknown, Holmes championed his music, as well as the Sugar Man in concert. Like most followers, Holmes believes that Rodriguez' writing is amongst the best in the last forty years.

Sixto Rodriguez: "I think it's the lyrics that kids still appreciate. We all have the same thoughts about things. I feel very contemporary."

HOW DID COLD FACT CHART IN 2013?

After the success of **Searching For Sugar Man**, **Cold Fact** charted forty-three years after its release. Surprisingly, it was on the Danish charts that **Cold Fact** achieved its first top ten hit. It was a number four position. Did Rodriguez celebrate or care after all the rejection and frustration? He has never said. One can only speculate. Then a ten ranking in Sweden attested to filmmaker Malik Bendjelloul's genius. It was followed by a seventeen position on the Spanish charts. In Finland, a fifty rating was achieved. This was supplemented in Belgium with an eighteen position. The fifty-four slot on the Dutch pop chart was an indication of **Cold Fact's** popularity throughout Europe.

In New Zealand, the album charted at twenty, and it was thirty in Australia. The sales continued to be strong for **Searching For Sugar Man**. By 2014, Rodriguez had three Australian chart LPs. His popularity continued to grow after **Searching For Sugar Man's** Oscar victory.

When Steve Rowland came along extolling the Sugar Man's virtues as a singer-songwriter, his comments added credibility. For a time, Rowland was like a voice in the wilderness. He would tell anyone who would listen that Rodriguez was the next big thing. Rowland was right. It simply took more than forty years for his prophecy to ring true. "He is singularly the best person I have ever worked with in the studio," Rowland concluded.

AMONG INDUSTRY PEOPLE: STEVE ROWLAND SAVES THE DAY

Rodriguez' enormous talent amazed industry insiders. He had much more than lyrical brilliance. He was also a first rate guitarist. He had a sense of arranging, as well as an in-concert persona. Steve Rowland said repeatedly that Rodriguez' songs were the best tunes of 1971. Unfortunately, no one was listening until 2012.

It was in his approach to recording where Steve Rowland differed from other producers. He hired the best London session musicians. They were musicians who worked with Rowland on numerous projects. The engineers were used to complete a master tape and that was the beginning of Rowland's genius. "I had a special engineer who prepared the tapes," Rowland concluded. Then Steve completed the final mix.

Steve Rowland: "If I had a dollar for every asshole who didn't think a record I completed was a hit, I would retire. No one congratulated me for **Coming From Reality**."

What this quote suggests is that Rowland not only has a special touch with artists. He is on the same page. Rowland learned his production techniques from a wide variety of studio experiences in Los Angeles, Madrid and London. He was also known for producing mega hits for groups or artists who needed their albums placed into a commercial mode.

In 1971, Rodriguez' creative life took a turn toward more in-depth personal songs. He had a greater degree of artistic freedom. Rowland knew how much leeway to give the Sugar Man. The result was quite a different LP from **Cold Fact**. The **Coming From Reality** album was a blend of the romantic, the topical and the personal. Rodriguez was full of new music.

If there is a holy grail for record producers, Rowland is a founding member. He is still well and alive in his seventies in Palm Springs. The California sun is a tonic for Rowland who continues to work on a television series, new music, reconstituting his vast catalogue and getting ready to go back in the studio.

He ranks Rodriguez as one of the top five acts that he has worked with in his career. He discovered the Herd with Peter Frampton. He convinced Peter Frampton to sing and then to go solo. He brought Sarah Brightman into the record business. He was the driving creative force behind the cult band, the Family Dogg. The albums he produced for P. J. Proby and the Pretty Things attest to his ability to take an artist into the hit record charts. He was awarded a gold record for producing **Jerry Lee Lewis: The London Sessions**. Rowland won the ASCAP Award for best country song of the year for "Drinkin' Wine-Spo-Dee-Oh-Dee."

He discovered and signed the Cure, the Thompson Twins and he managed Boney M. Rowland was in the midst of creating one hit after another when he produced **Coming From Reality**.

As disco moved in the music business, Clarence Avant didn't pick up Rodriguez' option. There is an irony to Rodriguez ending his Sussex Record's career. He was told that there would be no third album. One of the songs from **Coming From Reality** had a line: "Cause I lost my job two weeks before Christmas." That is exactly when Avant fired Rodriguez. Rowland was devastated, as was Rodriguez. But the Sugar Man took a philosophical view. He went on with his life. He was never angry. He was never petty. He was never prone to name-calling. The suits in the record business should have taken note. They didn't.

The two Rodriguez albums were in the cut out bin in Woolworth's by 1972 as no one paid attention. Rodriguez was another singer-songwriter destined for obscurity.

THE REALITY OF RODRIGUEZ' COLD FACT ALBUM:
THE CASE OF THE PHILIPPINES

No one realized that **Cold Fact** sold well in Australia and South Africa. In the Philippines, **Cold Fact** was a brief hit. In Manila, the songs began playing on two rock and roll stations. It was 1971, and the Philippines were embroiled in political turmoil with dictator Ferdinand Marcos and his shoe-hoarding wife, Imelda, taking away the Filipino's constitutional liberties. One of the freedoms that the Marcos' despised was the right to listen to decadent American rock and roll.

A single of "I Think of You" with a b-side "To Whom It May Concern" was released as a Philippine bootleg. It sold well. The rumor was that Rodriguez was part Filipino. The two major Manila radio stations DZRJ and DZUW played Rodriguez daily. He was a bigger star in 1971-1972 than any other American or British act. The Manila press published the picture of Rodriguez from the **Cold Fact** cover. Whoever released the records in the Philippines made a fortune. To this day there is no reliable report of record sales in the Philippines.

When **Coming From Reality** received inordinate airplay, there was talk of bringing Rodriguez to Manila. It didn't materialize. The Marcos regime imposed martial law. The radio stations were controlled. Sixto Rodriguez was not played on the radio in Manila until 2012.

In 1996, I was a featured speaker at the 100th celebration of Philippine Independence. My four books on Filipino farm labor and their George Washington, Jose Rizal, brought an invitation from former Philippine Vice President Salvador Laurel. After I spoke, Mr. Laurel took me to dinner. He asked me about Rodriguez. I had never heard of Sixto Rodriguez. It doesn't get any stranger. For Rodriguez to be played on Manila radio in the present day is a testimony to his continued genius. It is also a testimony to how the myths surrounding Rodriguez' life have created legends in the Philippines.

The next volume, **Rodriguez: Coming From Reality**, continues to microscopically examine Steve Rowland's career, his contribution to the second album, and his enduring friendship with the Sugar Man. He is not the only person in the story to not act with self-interest. Matt Sullivan, Mike Theodore and Dennis Coffey also lacked self-interest. They were in Rodriguez' corner from day one. After wandering into the creative wilderness from 1975 to 2012, Rodriguez emerged in 2012 with the Oscar winning **Searching for Sugar Man**. Finally, the documentary brought his talent to the consumer.

SOME UNRESOLVED THOUGHTS ON COLD FACT

When the A and M label released **Cold Fact** in South Africa the murky royalty story took shape. It remains an unresolved issue. The album copies in a New York warehouse shipped to Australia is another part of the story, as the Sugar Man became popular down under. Another intriguing aspect of the story took place in 2014 when the French Deep House and Electro music producer featured "Hate Street Dialogue" in an album "The Avenger Featuring Rodriguez." This release charted in

France but Rodriguez' involvement remains murky. Did he ever receive royalties? That remains the key question. There is no answer so far.

Although "Hate Street Dialogue" charted at only 103 in France, it provided a window into how producers continue to use music from **Cold Fact**.

The chart positions for **Cold Fact** indicate its wide appeal.

Chart (2013–2014)	Peak Position
Australian Albums (ARIA) [9]	11
Belgian Albums (Ultra top Flanders) [10]	50
Belgian Albums (Ultra top Wallonia) [11]	180
Danish Albums (Hit listen) [12]	4
Dutch Albums (Mega Charts) [13]	54
Finnish Albums (Seamen viral linen list) [14]	18
French Albums (SNEP) [15]	81
New Zealand Albums (Recorded Music NZ) [16]	20
Spanish Albums (PROMUSICAE) [17]	17
Swedish Albums (Sverigetopplistan) [18]	10

There were no musicians credited on the original album sleeve, but Rodriguez and Mike Theodore have filled in the gaps:[5]
- Rodriguez – vocals, acoustic guitar
- Dennis Coffey – electric guitar
- Mike Theodore – keyboards, brass and string arrangements
- Andrew Smith – drums
- Bob Pangborn – percussion
- Bob Babbitt – bass
- Detroit Symphony (Leader Gordon Staples) – strings
- Leader Carl Reatz – horns (trombones, baritone sax)
- Friends and family of Joyce Vincent and Telma Hopkins – children's choir on "Gommorah"
1. Recorded in Detroit in August and September 1969.
2. Arranged and produced by Mike Theodore and Dennis Coffey.
3. Engineering by Mike Theodore at Tera-Shirma Studio, Detroit.
4. Ray Hall at R.C.A. New York – remix
5. Ransier and Anderson – photography
6. Nancy Chester (See / Hear! & How!) – cover design

chapter

FIFTEEN

SIXTO RODRIGUEZ'S BUSINESS MOVES

"FOLKS CAN MAKE A LOT MORE MONEY WITH SKILLED MANUFACTURING OR THE TRADES THAN WITH ART HIS-TORY." BARACK OBAMA

"RODRIGUEZ IS STILL KEENLY INTERESTED IN FIND-ING OUT WHAT HAPPENED ALL THOSE YEARS AGO AND WHERE THE MONEY WENT." MARK A. LEVINSOHN, RODRI-GUEZ' ATTORNEY

"I'M READY FOR THIS AND I WILL PURSUE THE LEGAL PART OF IT. I WILL LET EVERYBODY KNOW THE OUT-COME AND I'LL BE DONE WITH THAT AND I'LL MOVE ON." RODRIGUEZ COMMENTING ON HIS LEGAL ISSUES, OCTOBER 2014 AS HE TOURS AUSTRALIA

After he signed a contract with Harry Balk in July 1966, it was a typical beginners recording deal. The two percent royalty, the one dollar signing bonus and the lock that Gomba Music had upon Rodriguez' future songwriting tied him up as a writer until late July 1971. Why would Rodriguez sign such a contract? The answer is a simple one. Harry Balk had a reputation for making hits. If you listened to Harry, you had a future in the record business.

A case in point was Jamie Coe and the Gigolos. They were Michigan's most popular bar band. Coe had the looks, the songwriting skills and the best back up band in the area. But he wouldn't move beyond the local nightclub circuit. The reason was that Coe wouldn't go on the road; he was difficult to work with in the studio and in the clubs. He also refused to take Harry's advice. Balk cut him loose. Coe remained a Detroit legend. That was it.

Rodriguez watched, as dozens of great acts couldn't secure a record contract. Rodriguez felt fortunate to have signed with Balk. He was the producing legend who guided Little Willie John, Del Shannon and Johnny and the Hurricanes to fame and fortune.

THE MYRIAD LAWSUITS FURTHER
CONFUSE THE ROYALTY QUESTION

After Balk arrived at Motown, he forgot about Sixto Rodriguez. The Sugar Man was just one of many artists who made records that didn't sell. What Balk had was a five-year songwriting contract binding Rodriguez to his company, Gomba Music. Rodriguez reasoned that Balk was neither selling his product nor was he licensing it. The Sugar Man never received a statement of record sales from Balk. He believed that he was free to negotiate and sign with any record label.

When Rodriguez signed the deal with Avant, he did so in good faith. Then in 2014 Balk sued Avant alleging that he had coerced Rodriguez into changing the copyrights on songs that were in Gomba Music's domain.

After Balk sued Avant, the story took another strange twist. Avant sued Rodriguez alleging fraud. The end result is that there were two lawsuits for royalties no one paid Rodriguez prior to **Searching For Sugar Man**. It is a mess. Harry Balk's attorney's differed with Rodriguez. They allege that he changed the copyrights on some songs using the songwriting name Sixth Prince or Jesus Rodriguez to avoid paying Gomba royalties. Rodriguez responded that this is nonsense. He pointed out that his music languished, no one licensed it, and no one had an interest in promoting him. For these reasons he believed his copyrights returned to the public domain. That belief gave Rodriguez the right to renew the copyrights with new songwriting names. This reasoning is the basis of Clarence Avant's May 2014 legal action.

They blame Avant for the royalty mess. Avant responded that this is nonsense. The story remains convoluted. A publisher handles the copyright in the music business. Gomba Music was Rodriguez' first publisher and they buried the songs. There are many types of publishing deals and none of Rodriguez' were acceptable ones. Some people say that he is paranoid. Not really, if you have been duped twice there is no paranoia. You have simply signed bad business deals. That is what the Sugar Man did. No question!

The evidence indicates that the disco era swallowed up Rodriguez' royalties. This is with help from record company executives in South Africa and Australia, as well as the high living Neil Bogart. When you ask around, no one is at fault. At Rodriguez' has said: "It's the music business." The royalty battle has taken more turns than a NASCAR driver.

The lost Rodriguez royalties are largely the result of business deals that Clarence Avant made with Neil Bogart. He made them in good faith. There is also evidence some South African and Australian labels allegedly did not report full royalties. There was allegedly Bogart's London post office box where royalties may have been sent. No one can confirm the rumors. The only confirmable fact is that Sixto Rodriguez wasn't paid. The rest is speculation. Now the myriad lawsuits involve everyone. The last person sued for past royalties is Rodriguez. How weird is that? He was sued for royalties he never received.

When Avant sued Rodriguez, he did so citing the contracts third party clause. What the hell was going on? Avant began paying Rodriguez royalties in 2008, and he has licensed his material intermittently since 1970. What happened in the thirty-eight years before Light In The Attic released **Cold Fact**? No one knows. Then in May 2014 the barrage of lawsuits brought the royalty question to the public's attention.

HARRY BALK'S GOMBA MUSIC FIRES
THE FIRST LAWSUIT SALVO

In early May 2014, Harry Balk's Gomba Music filed a lawsuit in Michigan's federal court against Clarence Avant and Interior Music. The basis of this legal action was Balk's five-year songwriting contract with Rodriguez that expired in late July 1971. The lawsuit accused Clarence Avant of attempting to circumvent the agreement by attributing his songs to other songwriters. Those writers Jesus Rodriguez and Sixth Prince were pseudonyms. Gomba cited copyright infringement. Avant denied the charges countersuing Rodriguez. He also vented his frustrations in a lengthy interview.

The **Detroit Free Press** interviewed Avant: "I think I've really been painted as the bad guy...it really bugs me that I have to go through this, when I'm the one guy who believed in Rodriguez," Avant continued. "I wish him nothing but the best, because I think he deserves it."

By late May 2014, after Clarence Avant sued Rodriguez alleging that he "concocted a scheme to fraudulently conceal the writing of compositions by Sixto Rodriguez, attributing most of the songs on **Cold Fact** to the name Jesus Rodriguez." The ensuing controversy revived the royalty question.

CLARENCE AVANT'S LAW SUIT

Avant's Interior Music in a third-party complaint against Rodriguez pointed to a clause in the Interior contract. This clause stipulated his songs had to be free from other licensing concerns prior to a royalty payment. The Sugar Man's legal team was incensed.

"Rodriguez provided a sworn affidavit, written notice of his rescission from the Gomba contract," one of Rodriguez' attorney's remarked. Avant's lawyers argued that it took forty-three years for Gomba Music to contact Interior and claim ownership of songs on **Cold Fact**. They did so because of royalties. Gomba Publishing had no interest in his music until the money train rolled into the bank.

Interior Music responded accusing Rodriguez of a failure to cooperate. After a summons was issued for a court appearance the matter stalled in the courts. The attorney's for all sides were not talking, and it was suddenly a private matter.

Rodriguez' contract with Balk's Impact label began his musical-business education. When he was in Tera Shirma recording **Cold Fact**, Rodriguez watched musically headstrong young performers who cared little about royalties. He vowed not to be one of them. He was. He signed the wrong agreement. That initial contract with Balk was not only an unmitigated error, it has fueled the recent legal wrangling.

HARRY BALK IS AN HONEST MAN

Unlike many record executives, Harry Balk is an honest man. This doesn't mean he isn't a hard ass businessman. He is. He has a tough reputation. His contracts were often one-sided and at times they paid the artist a minimal royalty. That said, Harry did pay royalties. Balk saw the potential in Rodriguez' music. Rodriguez reminded Balk of Del Shannon. Like Shannon, Rodriguez was a superb songwriter.

Harry Balk: "On the royalty question, no one talks about all the money that you lose. They only scream about the artist not being paid. It's bullshit. Look at the whole fucking package."

When Rodriguez signed with Clarence Avant, he was happy to get a second chance in the record business. Avant said that he wasn't aware of the contract with Harry Balk's Gomba Music. By signing a five-year deal with Gomba, Rodriguez legally was not entitled to write songs for Interior Music. The courts will decide the issue. That is unless it is settled out of court. This is a rumored possibility.

WHAT DID THE RODRIGUEZ CONTRACT PROVIDE?

The Sussex contract was a standard one. Rodriguez received a two per cent royalty, Sussex had an option for two more albums. They could terminate the contract at any time. The two percent royalty was paid on the wholesale price with numerous deductions for packaging, albums given away for promotion, sales of discounted product, storage, media promotion and unspecified commercial inducements. One wonders if anything was left for the artist? There usually wasn't.

Sussex Records was obligated to cover recording costs, including studio musicians, and they were liable for all remixing and other production costs. The Sussex contract read that all money spent by the company had to be recovered prior to a royalty payment. This is the crux of the matter. Clarence Avant remarked that the South Africa and Australia sales were bootlegs. Rodriguez' management disputes this claim. The matter remains unresolved.

THE PRESS REACTS TO THE ROYALTY QUESTION 2014

The enduring mystery in the Sixto Rodriguez story is the royalty question. The background to the continued royalty controversy took place when Rodriguez' New York attorney, Mark Levinsohn, and a veteran New York record label auditor, Gary Cohen, contacted Avant concerning royalties. This took place in May 2013, and for the next year the royalty question took on a new life. Then Avant countersued.

The irony is that Rodriguez' attempt to secure royalties led to a protracted legal battle. Harry Balk and Clarence Avant are attempting to make the Sugar Man the bad guy. He isn't. He hasn't been paid from the early days. The legal situation is complex. When I interviewed half a dozen people about the law suit they said "no comment" or "stay away from this issue." They were pissed. One said: "This is none of your fucking business."

Rodriguez' attorney asked: "Where were the royalties?" They certainly didn't vanish. Levinsohn wanted immediate action. In a statement employing innuendo, as well as facts, Levinsohn called out Avant for his nasty behavior on the royalty question.

This brought an angry reaction from Clarence Avant. "Even when I tried to give his masters away, nobody wanted to take them," Avant remarked to Brian McCollum of the **Detroit Free Press**. Egos were being stomped on as the lawsuit wound its way through the courts. The worst was yet to come and the legal beagles did what they could to make Rodriguez look like the bad guy. It sounded like another fictional story.

In late May 2014, the issue came to a head in a series of lawsuits. The London press weighed in on the issue when Sean Michaels in the **London Guardian** observed: "The star of **Searching For Sugar Man** has been dragged into a legal battle between two companies over the rights to his songwriting royalties." That said it all. As the battle raged between Harry Balk's Gomba Publishing and Clarence Avant's Interior Music, Rodriguez was a sideline observer. He cared. He had an attorney. He wasn't a participant.

That all changed when Gomba Music contacted Interior Music and claimed ownership of the **Cold Fact** songwriting. That led Balk to allege collusion with Avant. That claim is allegedly nonsense. The indignity that Sixto Rodriguez faced is that in late May 2014 he was accused of "breaching warranties and representations, plus a failure to cooperate." What this means is that he was issued a summons, and he is now a part of the legal proceedings. Rodriguez' attorney said that he had no comment at the time.

These lawsuits are within the domain of the music industry. The irony is that Clarence Avant and Harry Balk are well to do businessman. This is not about the money, it is about two music moguls in their eighties trying to prove which one is the biggest kid on the block. This is disgraceful behavior on their part, and once again Rodriguez finds himself in the middle of music industry brouhaha.

The bottom line is that Sussex Records claims there were no royalties prior to licensing Rodriguez' albums to Light In The Attic. When I interviewed someone close to Rodriguez, they requested anonymity. This person said: "The royalties have been so small as to be virtually nonexistent. Is this possible? This doesn't make sense. There has to be a royalty trail. Somewhere. There are a lot of people out there who are like a lying sack of shit." Ouch! Then this industry insider said: "You figure it out." He left the Motor City Casino and I think he said: "Have a nice day." I wasn't sure he meant it.

There is another problem. No one knows what the payment terms were in the original Sussex contract. There are other key questions. What were the overseas distribution deals? How clear are the bookkeeping records? Until these questions are answered, the mystery of unpaid royalties will continue to swirl around the Sugar Man.

"Everybody's received royalties since our reissue," Matt Sullivan remarked. "I have received my royalties punctually," Steve Rowland observed. That said there were royalties from 1970 to 2007 that remain unpaid. That is the crux of this complex case. Federal law provides for legal avenues by active artists to ensure proper royalty payments. When I asked a former Sussex Record's employee if this worried Clarence Avant, she laughed and replied: "Do you really think there are books from a company that went bankrupt in 1975? Are you stupid?" I asked her: "What went wrong at Sussex Records?" She kicked me out of her place of employment. Told me to "have a nice day." Somehow I didn't think she meant it.

WHERE DID SUSSEX RECORDS GO WRONG?

Sussex failed because it lacked adequate distribution. The independent record distributors avoided paying for records shipped. They went out of business quickly and shady gangsters often ran them. The mega record stores, like Russ Solomon's Tower Records in Sacramento, California, demanded bigger discounts, a one hundred eighty day credit period with full return rights and all shipping was paid by the label. Solomon also demanded free advertising and special in-store promotional material. Solomon wasn't a criminal. He was a good businessman. He was also typical of the record milieu. Rodriguez was swimming with sharks.

Another reason that Sussex failed is that they didn't have a top tier artist roster. The label also suffered from its connection to Buddah and A & M Records. After Buddah Records made a deal to distribute Sussex, it was the kiss of death. The distribution money wasn't paid, records languished in warehouses and no one heard **Cold Fact**.

There was another part of the Buddah deal that caused problems. Sussex assigned all international distribution rights to Buddah and A & M. This turned out to be a disastrous financial move. There is little knowledge about what went on, but whatever it was it cost Rodriguez a great deal of money. It also cost Clarence Avant money. South Africa, because of apartheid and an international boycott, was not considered a major market. As everyone ignored South African royalties, Rodriguez' albums were flying off the shelves.

There is no evidence that the South African companies paid Buddah royalties. In **Searching For Sugar Man**, executives from Cape Town based labels said that the money went to Clarence Avant. Maybe! Maybe not! The matter has never been properly clarified. No one was eager to go to South Africa to search for lost royalties. There is no way to determine the amount of bootlegging but Rodriguez' albums were pirated in Australia, New Zealand, Zimbabwe, South Africa, the U. K. and the Philippines. There was a world market. No one could find out what was going on. There were unresolved legal problems. These problems remain.

THE PROBLEM WITH INTERIOR MUSIC

Clarence Avant's company, Interior Music, collected royalties domestically. There is no apparent record of what was or what wasn't collected.

The majority of Interior Music royalties were collected from Bill Withers and the SOS Band. Rodriguez' songs were published by Interior on a standard industry deal. There was a 50/50 split between the songwriter and the music publisher. "Since Interior didn't have U. S. sales there were no royalties," a former Sussex employee commented and continued: "You have to realize things were loose, no one was in charge."

There was another problem with Rodriguez' royalties. The payment for mechanical royalties is set by statute. At that time the mechanical royalty was two cents a song played on the radio or twenty cents for a ten-track album. The mechanical royalty was paid directly to Sussex Records. There appears to be no public record of what was paid.

Since Interior Music was affiliated with BMI, Rodriguez should have been able to collect his royalties directly from BMI. He didn't. Clarence Avant didn't act in a criminal matter. There was limited radio airplay, there was virtually no promotion, and there were few performance royalties reported or collected. Avant pointed out that since no money was in the coffers, there were no royalties sent to Rodriguez.

THE GREAT RODRIGUEZ ROYALTY SEARCH CONTINUES

When Sony Legacy released the **Searching For Sugar Man** soundtrack, there was an explicit statement on the CD that Rodriguez was paid royalties. This is, of course, a red flag for not receiving royalties from past sales.

In an attempt to pry his music away from the industry sharks, Rodriguez organized a series of businesses. "Motown Records said that everything that Harry Balk owned now belonged to them," Rodriguez continued. "Well that was questionable to me so what I did was start a corporation." In fact, Rodriguez licensed two companies, Sandrevan and Sixth Prince, to product his copyrights. He was looking not only to license his product, but also to collect past and current royalties. He had no idea that in South Africa he was a major artist until 1998. He received royalties from Australia and New Zealand. How much he collected from down under is unclear.

How and why he named his publishing companies tells one a great deal about the personal Rodriguez. Since Rodriguez was the sixth son in the family, the Sixth Prince Company was a fitting company celebrating his family lineage. Sandrevan Publishing is a tribute to the instrumental break in **Coming From Reality**, and it is a reminder of how much he loves his daughters, Eva and Sandra. Regan was born in 1979 and she quickly fit into the family. When they traveled to South Africa in 1998, she was nineteen years old and she got her first taste of big time show business.

Sixto Rodriguez: "I had my brother say that he wrote the songs and we put him under contract to our corporation." Jesus Rodriguez was the perfect front man because Balk had tied Rodriguez to a five-year contract. Jesus Rodriguez became the songwriter of record. There was only one problem. Jesus Rodriguez didn't exist. He was a fictional brother.

Why did Rodriguez file incorporation papers in Michigan? It was to challenge past contracts. He wanted to be free to collect his royalties. Rodriguez never received royalties for his two albums or his Impact single. It was at this point that Rodriguez retired. The sharks beat him in the music business.

As filmmaker Malik Bendjelloul was interviewed in December 2012, he said that Rodriguez was not interested in money. "He never started to consume," Bendjelloul continued. "And when you don't consume there are a lot of sacrifices." When Rodriquez filed the incorporation papers, it was an attempt to protect his product. He told close friends his business plan was to free his songs from Balk and Avant. He knew exactly what he was doing. This was typical Sixto Rodriguez. It was more abut his integrity than money. That is what Sixto Rodriguez is all about, integrity, compassion and talent.

When questioned about royalties, Rodriguez said: "I have my past contracts and those are currently being resolved. I'm going to go into my next one with three attorneys. I'm going to have one who handles international law, one in entertainment law and one just for contracts. Hopefully everything will work itself out. At the moment I'm with Light In The Attic and everything is going good."

Light In The Attic is the only label to treat Rodriguez equitably. They featured his material in their publicity long before **Searching For Sugar Man** created the mainstream Rodriguez phenomenon.

The business dealings with Harry Balk, Clarence Avant and Sussex Records taught Rodriguez a great deal about business. The Sugar Man actively promoted the documentary, as he envisioned potential future album sales. As **Searching For Sugar Man** was about to open, Rodriguez sat in a New York hotel telling reporters that the film would open in eighty-four theaters. He was concerned about the business side of the industry, as well as he was aware of not being paid. Rodriguez emphasized that the Late Night With David Letterman appearance where he performed "Crucify Your Mind" was a boost to his career as was **Esquire** selecting "I Wonder" as the song of the month. Suddenly after forty years Rodriguez' music was a hot item. The business end still needed resolution. Rodriguez was aware of fame's pitfalls. He sought out advice from those who battled with celebrity.

Rodriguez talked with Alec Baldwin, Michael Moore and Sir Bob Geldoff, while he was in New York. He was praised for his talent. One wonders what Rodriguez thought. He doesn't tell us how he reacts to celebrities. He also seems unaware that he is one. When he rides around New York in limousines or Cadillac SUV's, he remarks with typical Rodriguez humility: "Uncle Sony treats us good."

STEVE ROWLAND TALKS ABOUT
THE ROYALTIES THAT HE NEVER RECEIVED

Sixto Rodriguez wasn't the only one not to get paid. Steve Rowland didn't receive a statement or a penny in royalties. Then when Light In The Attic re-released **Coming From Reality**, Rowland began receiving royalties from Clarence Avant's company.

Steve Rowland: "I said wow a statement after forty years. I loved LITA's presentation of the album. The notes showed that they put a lot of care and effort into the project. It is crystal clear, his voice is out front and you could almost touch it."

On the **Searching For Sugar Man** soundtrack, Sony Legacy produced a beautiful package with four songs that Rowland produced. "Cause," "A Most Disgusting Song," "Sandrevan Lullaby-Lifestyles" and "I Think Of You." These are the tunes Rowland is paid for from the soundtrack. He is also paid for producing **Coming From Reality**.

Steve Rowland: "I never thought about the money when I produced Rodriguez. I was happy to record with an artist that I felt was credible."

RODRIGUEZ' NEW MANAGEMENT TEAM

Once he resurfaced in 2012, a new management structure took over Rodriguez's career. His financial condition improved. He gives much of his money away. He isn't interested in fortune. Fame! Maybe! His daughter, Regan, manages him, and she is doing an excellent job. In March 2013, after grossing $700,000 for five shows, he returned to Detroit oblivious to the money.

He has shown some signs of spending his money. A new fence is built around his house on Avery Street. There is an orange cone on the cement stairway leading to the front door. It looks like some cement work is about to commence. He still doesn't have a computer. He doesn't own a car. The rumor is that he has a cell phone. He lives in the same house that he bought during a federal land auction in the mid-1970s. "He lives a very Spartan life," Regan Rodriguez commented. His youngest daughter told **Rolling Stone** that he gave most of his money away. She wishes he would spend some on himself. He tips everyone very well in the bars and restaurants in and around the Cass Corridor. For decades without fame, Rodriguez was treated royally. He is returning the favors.

There is some good news on the royalty front. The Sony Legacy soundtrack and the two Light In The Attic albums have paid Rodriguez substantial royalties. What does this mean in terms of money? **Cold Fact** remained in Amazon's Top 30 for over a year. Since Rodriguez gets paid from the soundtrack, it is a princely sum, as the CD has sold close to 400,000 units. The **Coming From Reality** LP exceeded 250,000 units and the soundtrack sold well in excess of 350,000 units. The million units sold worldwide made Rodriguez a legitimate star.

In the midst of these lawsuits, rumors circulated in **Rolling Stone**, and other publications, that Rodriguez was considering recording a third album. Business problems and lawsuits have delayed this project.

Rodriguez' business affairs are complicated by the lawsuits. When Clarence Avant sued the Sugar Man for "fraud," the lawsuit brought cries of disbelief. It seemed he was suing Rodriguez for royalties that he hadn't paid. That is not the case. So far there is no word from Avant's high-powered Beverly Hills legal team about the specifics of the action against Rodriguez. There is no doubt that Avant's four lawyers are the priciest among those involved in this confusing legal action.

What the 2014 lawsuit does is to take Rodriguez off the road at a time that he is making big money. There is an irony to the legal action, if not a blatant sense of unfairness to an artist who deserves respect.

Sixto Rodriguez is a visionary who loves music. He has been at the behest of mercenaries who have taken his money at every turn. Those days have not only ended, but the Sugar Man controls his economic destiny.

RODRIGUEZ: FOLLOWING THE MONEY VIA RECORD RELEASES

1966: SIGNED A DEAL WITH HARRY BALK FOR FIVE YEARS. A PUBLISHING AND SONGWRITING AGREEMENT WITH GOMBA ENDING IN LATE JULY 1971-CONTRACT WAS FOR ONE DOLLAR. NO ROYALTIES PAID.

AUGUST 1967: "I'LL SLIP AWAY" (IMPACT 1031) BACKED WITH "YOU'D LIKE TO ADMIT IT" RELEASED AS A SINGLE CREDITED TO ROD RIGUEZ. NO ROYALTIES PAID.

1969: SIGNED A DEAL WITH CLARENCE AVANT AND SUSSEX RECORDS AND AVANT'S PUBLISHING ARM INTERIOR MUSIC. NO SUBSTANTIAL ADVANCE OR ROYALTIES PAID.

MARCH 1970: COLD FACT IS RELEASED BY SUSSEX RECORDS IN AMERICA. NO ROYALTIES PAID.

APRIL 1970: "INNER CITY BLUES" BW "FORGET IT" (SUX 204) IS A 45 RELEASED IN THE USA BY SUSSEX. NO ROYALTIES PAID.

JULY 1970: "TO WHOM IT MAY CONCERN" BW "I THINK OF YOU" (SUX 234) RELEASED IN THE USA BY SUSSEX. NO ROYALTIES PAID.

1970: AVANT SIGNS A DISTRIBUTION DEAL WITH NEIL BOGART. A AND M RECORDS COMES IN AS A PARTNER AND THE MOST

POPULAR SOUTH AFRICAN RELEASES WERE ON THE A AND M LABEL. NO ROYALTIES PAID.

NOVEMBER 1971: COMING FROM REALITY IS RELEASED IN THE U. S. NO ROYALTIES PAID.

1972: "SUGAR MAN" BW "INNER CITY BLUES" (AM45031) IS RE-LEASED IN ITALY BY A AND M RECORDS IN ASSOCIATION WITH SUSSEX. NO ROYALTIES PAID. THIS IS A SEVEN-INCH VINYL RE-LEASE WITH JESUS RODRIGUEZ LISTED AS THE SONGSWRITER FOR "SUGAR MAN" AND SIXTH PRINCE AS THE SONGWRITER FOR "INNER CITY BLUES." THE CLARENCE AVANT LAW SUIT IS BASED ON THIS RELEASE ALLEGING THAT HE WAS DUPED BY THE SONGWRITING CREDIT.

1972: "TO WHOM IT MAY CONCERN" BW "I THINK OF YOU" (A & M 7SX-1008) IS RELEASED BY A AND M IN BRAZIL. NO ROYALTIES PAID.

1973: "HALFWAY UP THE STAIRS" BW "IT STARTED OUT SO NICE" (A & M ASK-5164) IS RELEASED IN AUSTRALIA BY A & M. NO ROYALTIES PAID.

1977: AT HIS BEST IS A RODRIGUEZ COMPILATION LP WITH THREE UNRELEASED TRACKS RELEASED IN AUSTRALIA AND NEW ZEALAND. ROYALTIES MAY HAVE BEEN PAID.

1977 "SUGAR MAN" BW "INNER CITY BLUES" (BGMS 002) IS RE-LEASED BY THE BLUE GOOSE LABEL IN AUSTRALIA. ROYALTIES PAID.

1977-1978: BUDDAH RECORDS SIGNED A DEAL WITH A LONDON BASED HOLDING COMPANY TO LICENSE SUSSEX RECORDS AND THIS INCLUDES THE RIGHTS TO THE TWO RODRIGUEZ ALBUMS. NO ROYALTIES PAID.

1978: "CLIMB UP ON MY MUSIC" BW "TO WHOM IT MAY CON-CERN" (BGMS 309) IS RELEASED BY THE BLUE GOOSE LABEL IN AUSTRALIA. PERHAPS ROYALTIES PAID.

1979: A LIVE AUSTRALIAN LP BY RODRIGUEZ IS RELEASED. HE LICENSED IT FOR ONE YEAR. ROYALTIES PAID.

1981: A LIVE ALBUM RECORDED IN 1979 IS RELEASED IN AUSTRALIA AND NEW ZEALAND. IT APPEARS THAT RODRIGUEZ LICENSED THIS LP. THERE WAS AN UPFRONT FEE AND ROYALTIES PAID FOR THE ALBUM. THE ALBUM WAS RECORDED LIVE AT THE REGENT THEATER ON MARCH 17 AND 18, 1979.

1982: THE BEST OF RODRIGUEZ IS RELEASED IN SOUTH AFRICA. POLYGRAM LICENSED THE ALBUM TO SOUTH AFRICA'S RPM LABEL. THIS IS A RE-ISSUE OF THE AUSTRALIAN ALBUM. THERE IS NO WORD ON ROYALTIES.

OCTOBER 1996: AFTER THE FACT/COMING FROM REALITY IS RELEASED IN SOUTH AFRICA WITH STEPHEN "SUGAR" SEGERMAN'S LINER NOTES. AGAIN NO WORD ON ROYALTIES.

1998: LIVE FACT IS THE ALBUM RELEASED DURING RODRIGUEZ' TRIUMPHANT SOUTH AFRICAN TOUR. THERE MAY HAVE BEEN ROYALTIES PAID ON THIS RELEASE.

APRIL 2002: AMP RECORDS: THIS IS A SMALL LONDON BASED RECORD LABEL THAT RELEASED A RODRIGUEZ SINGLE "SUGAR MAN" ON ONE SIDE AND MUDDY WATERS PERFORMING "TOM CAT" (AMP 7001) ON THE B-SIDE. IT IS A BUDGET LABEL WITH A LOW LEVEL REPUTATION. THIS RECORD IS COLLECTIBLE AS ONLY 500 COPIES WERE PRESSED. NO ROYALTIES PAID.

SEPTEMBER 2005: SUGARMAN: THE BEST OF RODRIGUEZ IS RELEASED. NO WORD ON WHETHER OR NOT ROYALTIES WERE PAID.

2005: ALL THE FACTS. THIS IS A 3CD SET MARKETED AND DISTRBUTED BY SONY MUSIC. IT CONTAINS RE-ISSUES OF COLD FACT AND AFTER THE FACT. ROYALTIE PAID.

2008: LIGHT IN THE ATTIC RELEASES COLD FACT. ROYALTIES PAID TWICE A YEAR THROUGH CLARENCE AVANT'S COMPANY, AVANT GARDE.

2009: LIGHT IN THE ATTIC RELEASES COMING FROM REALITY. ROYALTIES PAID TWICE A YEAR FROM CLARENCE AVANT'S COMPANY.

APRIL 2009-2010: LIGHT IN THE ATTIC RELEASES "INNER CITY BLUES" BW "I'M GONNA LIVE UNTIL I DIE" (LIVE) (LITA 45-018) ROYALTIES PAID THROUGH CLARENCE AVANT'S COMPANY.

JULY 2012: THE SEARCHING FOR SUGAR MAN SOUND TRACK IS RELEASED BY SONY LEGACY. ROYALTIES PAID FROM SONY LEGACY THROUGH CLARENCE AVANT.

RODRIGUEZ AND THE QUESTION OF INTELLECTUAL PROPERTY

The money in the music business is in the huge revenue generated by record companies, music publishers and songwriters. Intellectual property is the term used to denote a song. The question of who owns it is the road to royalties. A common practice in the industry is for a label owner, a manager, or an industry insider to share songwriting credit. Rodriguez avoided this trap. What he didn't escape was airtight one-sided contracts. That is a part of the basis of the multiple lawsuits filed in 2014.

The problem with the music business is that the labels often secure the publishing rights for a song. The collection and payment of royalties is a resulting problem. Whatever the reason, Rodriguez was not paid royalties until 2008. That is the first statement and payment he received for **Cold Fact**. Who is responsible for the lack and royalties? Why weren't they paid? These questions remain a mystery. Perhaps the recent slate of lawsuits will answer that perplexing royalty soap opera.

The royalty question remains a bone of contention with the Rodriguez family. While the Sugar Man has little or no concern with things monetary, his family and advisers want justice. That is a laudable goal, as there are royalties. Somewhere!

Shortly after the success of **Searching For Sugar Man**, Kaleem Aftab of the **London Independent** interviewed Rodriguez. When the talk turned to money, Rodriguez was unusually forthcoming. This July 24, 2012 article saw Rodriguez speculate on his royalties or lack of them. He wasn't sure that any existed. "I don't believe the story that there were no royalties," Rodriguez observed. This 2012 comment festered. He came to believe that there were in fact substantial royalties. But in talking with the London journalist, Rodriguez made it clear that he disdained money. "There are a lot of rewards, not just the recognition and the 'oxygen money'; I call money 'oxygen.' Everyone needs oxygen but that's not my goal."

As Rodriguez speculated on his sudden success, he had some positive comments about performing in South Africa in 1998: "It was a culture shock at first. The country is beautiful." He told Aftab: "I was just happy to play there." That sums up Sixto Rodriguez. He doesn't know he is a legend. He doesn't want to be one. Humility is still his foremost personality trait. While he talks about his lost royalties, it is as an existentialist not a businessman. The Sugar Man wouldn't have it any other way.

STEVE ROWLAND IN A HOLLYWOOD WESTERN

chapter

SIXTEEN

STEVE ROWLAND'S EARLY YEARS

"AS A RECORD PRODUCER I HAVE PRODUCED A LOT OF GOLD AND PLATINUM ARTISTS. RODRIGUEZ IS THE BEST. NO ONE WRITES SONGS LIKE HIM." STEVE ROWLAND

"WRITING IS THE BEST RUSH I'VE EVER FOUND. I'M UT-TERLY, HOPELESSLY ADDICTED TO IT. I GOT INTO A KIND OF A DREAM EVERY DAY." T. C. BOYLE

While growing up in Hollywood, Steve Rowland was an actor who became the lead singer in a number of rock and roll bands. He had no idea that he was on the way to becoming one of the U. K.'s major re-cord producers. The story of how he evolved from a television actor, to a screen personality to a lead singer in some of the most popular club bands in the U. S. and Europe gives some clues as to how and why he evolved into an acclaimed record producer. The forces early on shaping Rowland put him unwittingly in this direction.

FORCES SHAPING STEVE ROWLAND

There is a complexity to Steve Rowland. He has had many careers, beginning as an actor in television, evolving into motion pictures. He entered the music business as a singer and eventually emerged as an acclaimed record producer.

Steve Rowland: "As a kid growing up I wasn't particularly popular. It was only after I started winning diving championships that people clustered around me. That made me realize that people never seem to like you unless they think you are a somebody. Somebody they can benefit from perhaps."

What does this have to do with Sixto Rodriguez? Plenty! Rowland visualized himself as an outsider. He views himself the same today. After Steve listened to **Cold Fact** and met Rodriguez, he realized that here was the ultimate sensitive outsider. They developed a rapport and a bond that continues to the present day. When Steve listened to Rodriguez' "The Establishment Blues," one line caught his attention. "The mafia's getting bigger, like pollution in the river." This lyric prompted Rowland to think about his father. That memory drove Steve toward success.

Steve Rowland: "As a twelve year old kid in New York's Hell's Kitchen my dad was a bag man for the mob. He picked up earnings from the slot machines, jukeboxes and he delivered the cash to the boys. The reward was a couple of bucks in change, which coming to a poor family helped out."

By 1943, Roy Rowland was making Hollywood feature films. In the 1950s and 1960s Rowland was a hard working and in demand director known for such films as "Our Vines Have Tender Grapes," "Meet Me In Las Vegas," "Rogue Cop," "The 5000 Fingers of Dr T" and "Two Weeks With Love."

How did his father's experiences impact Rowland? His father was his hero. Roy Rowland was an accomplished movie director, as well as an astute businessman. Steve followed in his father's footsteps.

After Rowland discovered that Mafia money was behind many of Hollywood's productions, he was worried. He wasn't a moralist, but he wanted to control his creative destiny. He believed he could do this only by leaving Hollywood. He had made his mark in television and films. Now it was time to move on. A four-picture movie deal was his ticket to Europe. In 1963, Rowland left for Spain to make movies. After the Beatles and Rolling Stones broke worldwide, Rowland moved to London.

He hoped to get into the music business as a singer. He had a decade of experience in the music business in Los Angeles and Spain.

Steve Rowland appeared in 1950s television shows and acted extensively in movies. He also moonlighted as a lead singer in several Los Angeles club bands. Rowland is a tough individual who never took any guff from anyone. This helps to explain his multiple careers. How many people are motion picture and television actors, columnists, athletes, record producers, songwriters and lead singers? Not many!

It was Rowland's musical apprenticeship in the Hollywood clubs that turned him into a record producer waiting in the wings to eventually produce Rodriguez' second album **Coming From Reality**. No one in the acting profession realized that music was Rowland's first love. He proved it in London from the mid-1960s by producing one hit single and album after another. His Palm Springs home has a room where his gold and platinum records hang in triumph. Like Rodriguez, Rowland is humble and most visitors have to ask him about the Wall of Gold. Rowland is proud of his producing awards. He simply doesn't like to brag. He should.

STEVE ROWLAND: WAITING IN THE WINGS

In Los Angeles, Steve was a keen observer of the vibrant music scene. Although he moved to Spain in May 1963 to appear in films, he was aware of the British Music Invasion. Few people in America had heard of the Beatles. In 1963 Rowland not only knew about the Beatles, he listened to their records. He watched them perform in Madrid in 1965 at the Plaza De Toros de Las Ventas. It was their only appearance in the Spanish city. The crowds' reaction to the Beatles' concert influenced Rowland so much that he decided to move to London. He hoped to begin a solo career as a singer.

Steve Rowland: "When I saw the hysteria over the Beatles, I envisioned my own future. There was room for young singers and I hoped to fill that role. I had been training for a solo music career in Los Angeles and Spain for a decade."

Although he didn't realize it at the time, Rowland was completing his musical apprenticeship in Spain. Once he settled into Spanish life in 1963, he pursued a dual career for the next few years. By day Steve made movies, by night he was a lead singer in a Spanish rock band, Los Flaps. Rowland quietly made the transition into the music business.

The Los Flaps were a Spanish garage and pop-rock band whose cover of the instrumental "Pennsylvania 6-5000" remains a classic. Rowland was the lead singer who took them toward the Spanish charts.

Steve Rowland: "In order to supplement my income between films, I answered an ad in a free English language magazine in Madrid. I was looking to make some extra money, rather than just depend on the film industry for my livelihood. I answered the ad and got the gig."

When Steve arrived in London, he began planning a group, which became the Family Dogg. He had listened to the Mamas and Papas, and the Fifth Dimension, and he believed that their harmonies, combined with superior songwriting and production, could bring hits to a like-minded English group.

Steve Rowland: "I met Albert Hammond in Spain during a concert at Circo Price in Madrid. Both our bands were on the bill. Albert was a member of Los Diamond Boys. During our conversation, Albert mentioned that he was going to London and as I was also, we discussed the possibility of us getting together and possibly forming a band."

At this point, Rowland had no idea that he would become a legendary British record producer earning gold and platinum singles, as well as million selling albums. He also earned an ASCAP Award for producing Jerry Lee Lewis' "Drinking Wine Spo-dee-oh-dee." Steve was simply trying to make a living. He didn't realize that he was headed for a musical career rather than continue acting. But music had always been in his life. It was also his first love.

It was during his acting career that Steve learned to persist. As Steve grew up in a motion-picture family, he watched the production end of the movie industry. He saw what made a film commercially viable. He always paid attention to what the public went for. His skills as a record producer are directly related to his Hollywood years.

It was in Hollywood in the 1950s and early 1960s that his lengthy apprenticeship in the entertainment industry began the education that made Rowland a multi-talented actor, musician and eventually a record producer. He was training to produce Rodriguez' **Coming From Reality**. He had other things on his mind acting and singing. There were a number of lessons he learned in Hollywood.

AUDITIONING FOR A 1950s HOLLYWOOD MUSICAL: THANKS. NEXT!

One of his earliest show business lessons came after Steve Rowland graduated from high school. It was the 1950s and Steve had begun going to auditions for parts in various television shows and motion pictures. Universal was about to cast for a Jeanne Crain musical. A casting call went out to all the Hollywood agents to provide young guys and girls who could sing and dance. As Rowland had been singing in various bands, his agent, the Paul Small Agency, sent him to the casting. The nineteen-year-old Steve Rowland was eager to get into a musical. The Jeanne Crain vehicle seemed perfect.

Steve Rowland: "Everyone showed up at one of Universal Studio's largest sound stages. In those days you had to bring sheet music to be handed to the piano player who would accompany you. There were at least thirty people waiting to be called in."

Steve walked onto the sound stage. It was in total darkness except for a single light trained on the piano and the accompanist. Up above, about fifteen feet, was the brightly lit control booth. Obviously, the musical director, casting personnel and possibly the film's director, were in attendance. Rowland handed his sheet music to the accompanist stood in front of the microphone and prepared to sing "I've Got A Crush On You," the song he had chosen, made famous by Frank Sinatra. The accompanist went into a flourish arpeggio introduction. From above, a voice came: "Are you ready?" Steve nodded yes. The piano player asked: 'What key?' The piano player continued a flourishing arpeggio introduction.

Steve Rowland: "Perhaps I was stupid to think that I could do a Frank Sinatra number, but I figured that to do a rock and roll number wouldn't be appropriate. I started to sing. My nerves go the best of me, as I only managed to get into the song about four bars when my voice cracked. As a matter of fact, it squeaked."

Rowland recalled that at that moment, a booming voice from the control room shot out over a loud speaker like a thunderbolt. "Thank you. Next."

Steve said: "Can I try again?"

"No! Thank you. Next."

Steve Rowland: "I was completely gutted. I had fucked up badly."

Rowland realized that he wasn't going to be the next Frank Sinatra and left the audition. It is probably one of the reasons that drove him to pursue a successful rock and roll career.

For a few years in Hollywood, he was the lead singer in a twist band. First titled, the Exciters, and later to become known as the Twist Kings. They played all over Los Angeles and at many of the Hollywood functions. By 1963, he and his band mate, Budd Albright, had gained a huge following. These experiences would turn into a multi-dimensional career for Steve in London. Because of his popularity as a singer on the scene in Hollywood, Steve produced demo 45s that he shopped around to numerous small record labels in Los Angeles hoping to acquire a record contract. At the time, Rowland had no idea that he was training for a career as a major London record producer.

While in the midst of this Hollywood apprenticeship, Rowland came in touch with some of Los Angeles' most noted producers. He shopped demos to Bob Keene at Del Fi and the Bihari brothers at Modern Records. He observed their business acumen and remembered what they taught him about the business.

Before Rowland settled in London, he completed a Hollywood musical-acting apprenticeship and then he was to off to Spain to refine his acting-music talents. It is important to examine Steve's successes in Hollywood and Spain to understand how and why he became a legendary record producer.

THE APPRENTICESHIP IN HOLLYWOOD
AND ON TO SPAIN, MID 1950s-1963

As Rowland looked back upon his thirty-five TV shows in the 1950s, he was pleased with his progress as an actor. To industry observers, there was no surprise. He had studied hard for a serious acting career. He was with the West Coast version of the Actor's Studio studying the Lee Strasburg method. He was trying to get breaks. He began his career in eight to ten films as a bit player or walk on. A couple of these films were **Apache** and **The Prince**. Sometimes he received a credit and at other times he was just a stand in. It was this drive to artistic perfection that led Rowland to move into television.

When he started getting small parts on television, they quickly metamorphosed into guest spots and recurring roles. He appeared in **The Rifleman** and **Bonanza** amongst others. He had a two-year recurring role in **The Life And Legend of Wyatt Earp** starring Hugh O'Brian.

Then he got his first break in a film, **The Silver Star,** and he also appeared in **Crime In The Streets** with John Cassavetes and Sal Mineo. When Steve co-starred in the film **Gun Glory** with Stewart Granger and Rhonda Fleming, he played Stewart Granger's son, Tom Early Jr. Steve alternating making films with guest spots on the major TV talk shows.

One of his most memorable television appearances was when he appeared with Steve McQueen in **The Bill Longley Story**. This was McQueen's first television special. Right after that McQueen began the television series **Wanted Dead or Alive** and Rowland appeared in several episodes.

Before he left Los Angeles, Rowland had a cult following as an actor. In 1961, he appeared in **Wild Youth**, a teen exploitation film, that told the story of a couple of teenagers running from the law and a ruthless mobster. Rowland played Switch who was a juvenile badass kid whose name came from his switchblade knife.

Steve Rowland: "I tried to play it like Marlon Brando in James Dean's body and failed."

Once the film became a cult item, it was re-released as **Naked Youth**. The story centered on a toy doll filled with high-grade heroin in the back seat of a car. The story line is that a group of teenage criminals break out of juvenile hall and head south to Mexico. There was a lot of improvisational acting as the script was skimpy. It became a cult classic. Rowland was the only actor to survive this film, and he easily moved into a mainstream movie career. It was in Spain that he made some of his most memorable films. They included **Gunfighters of Casa Grande**, 1964, **The Thin Red Line** with Kier Dulea and Jack Warden, in 1964, the epic **Battle of The Bulge** with Telly Savalas, Henry Fonda and Charles Bronson in 1965. Then Rowland saw his future, rock music.

The technical side of the film industry had an important influence on Rowland. As he performed in various bands, he viewed rock and roll as much like a feature film. He was aware of the hooks that kept the listener interested in the music, and he saw commerciality in the movie industry. Steve was always about perfection in production, that is he asked himself how could things improve?

Steve Rowland: "When I began producing records, I examined all the production techniques as if I were making a film. I envisioned music the same as film making, or telling a story on vinyl. I had my own ideas about how a record should sound. I had numerous fights with engineers. This was because they were not used to the way I did things and they showed no respect for my methods. It was amazing. When those records that I produced became hits, they changed their tune as though they always knew the records would chart."

No one realized that Steve had produced a number of demo 45s while living in Hollywood. As he had been a lead singer, especially in the Twist Kings, he had gathered extensive experience. Other members of the Twist Kings became popular rock stars, notably Bread's David Gates, piano legend Leon Russell and the "Tequila" man Chuck Rio.

There was another important musician in Rowland's life. That is Budd Albright who worked with him at Ye Little Club on Canon Drive in Beverly Hills, where Jack Nietzsche and his jazz trio were regulars.

When the twist craze hit Los Angeles, Steve Rowland's band was one of the most popular twist aggregations. When the early Twist Kings played the Encore Room on La Cienega, there were lines outside the club waiting to get in. Out of necessity, because of the Twist Kings popularity in the clubs, Steve began producing demo 45s in Hollywood to play for the various label owners interested in recording Rowland's group. He saw big money in rock and roll records.

Steve Rowland; "All the time, I was trying to get a record deal. I had many attempts to come up with the right demo. I heard many demos that others had made. I though they were awful."

No one paid any attention to Steve's interest in record production. He was doing it to make the Twist Kings a commercial band. They were already legendary as a live band in and around the Sunset Strip. Steve had a vision. He wanted them to have a hit record.

The people that were helping Steve record his demos weren't able to capture his sound, so he turned to making his own. After Steve played his demos, Intro Records signed him. The label was an Aladdin subsidiary. In 1961, Imperial purchased Aladdin and Intro was a forgotten part of the business process.

Steve Rowland: "Those at Intro thought that I could be a teen idol. I didn't like the idea and I didn't like the songs that they selected for me to sing. So I wrote an instrumental 'Out Ridin,' I went in to a Santa Monica recording studio and recorded with Earl Bostic on sax. I was the drummer, the writer and the producer. I got lots of radio play on KFWB. Word had it that the guys who represented me at the time were connected, if you know what I mean."

When the "Out Ridin" single was released it was a picture 45 with Steve sitting in a small Go-Kart racer with three good-looking girls surrounding him. The band was listed as Steve Rowland And the Ring Leaders. The b-side was "Here Kum The Karts" and this 45 is a rare collectible.

STEVE ROWLAND'S RARE 45 ON THE CROSS COUNTRY LABEL.

As Steve explained his rare picture 45, he smiled. There was something he wasn't telling me about the people who had his best interests at heart.

I asked Steve: "Where these mob guys?"

Steve smiled: "No comment."

Steve's friends asked: "How come your record got played so much on KFWB?"

Steve said: "Word had it that my management spoke to the staff at the radio station and alluded to the fact that there could possible be a teamsters strike."

STEVE ROWLAND'S EARLY PRODUCTION SKILLS DEVELOP

Steve Rowland: "I knew the basics of musical production because in Los Angeles, at the time, you had to make your own demos. Sam Cooke and J. W. Alexander helped me with the early demos. Hal Blaine, Jack Nietzsche and various other session guys worked with me on my early productions. I learned a lot from them."

The 45s that Rowland produced were not hits. But he learned a great deal about the music business and how it works. During this period, he honed his production skills.

Steve Rowland: "I discovered that the three most important things in making a record are: number one, the song. Number two, the vocal, and number three, when producing a record, less is more."

The search for show business gold was the central theme to Rowland's life. Thus was created a multi-layered career that was influenced by the lessons he learned in 1950s Hollywood.

Steve Rowland: "I had on the job training as an actor, a writer and a singer/musician before I was thirty. I loved all parts of the business. The crass, brutal and selfish Hollywood lifestyle was what prompted me to want to leave Hollywood. Lucky for me, I was cast in a western to be shot in Spain. I was thrilled to get out."

THE MUSICAL, TV, MOVIE APPRENTICESHIP
IN HOLLYWOOD, 1958-1963

The Los Angeles club scene was changing. The jazz groups were fading. Folk music was not for the drinkers. Rock and roll began appearing in the major Hollywood clubs. The rockers brought in gorgeous girls, heavy drinkers and a party atmosphere. It didn't take long for a host of bands to form up and down the Sunset Strip.

Steve Rowland: "I look back at how it all started at P. J.'s club on Santa Monica and Crescent Heights, Budd Albright and I were sitting at the bar throwing a couple of drinks in our head. Trini Lopez was a major attraction at P. J's entertaining three or four nights a week. We knew Trini, and this particular night we asked him if we could sing a number with him. He said: 'Sure guys, let's do it.' Trini played, Budd and I sang. The reaction from the gathered clientele was crazy, screaming 'more, more!' We were literally bowled over. It was from that casual appearance that we got the idea to form a band together."

There were so many excellent musicians looking for work, that Rowland had no trouble hiring band mates. It was the day of the young musician coming to Hollywood looking for fame and fortune. The bars opened up their rooms to bands that played and excited people for a small fee.

Steve Rowland: "When we set up at the Encore Room for our opening night, the manager, Jack Chambers, started hollering at us as only a few bar fly's were sitting at the long wooden topped bar. It was a quarter to ten. Chambers threatened to not pay us because the big crowd that we had predicted had not arrived. Then, almost on the dot of ten o'clock, Robert Mitchum, Mitzi Gaynor, Martha Hyer and many other stars walked in, filling the place. We rocked out and it turned into a two-hour long show. We almost tore the building down."

Rowland and Albright signed to play there three nights a week to sold out crowds. The throngs at the Encore prompted talent scouts from the Thunderbird Hotel in Las Vegas to waive a lucrative contract at Steve Rowland's group. At the time, Steve had no idea that the Thunderbird was a mob-backed hotel. They would have paid well and they were promised every imaginable amenity. Rowland and his Twist Kings were too busy in Hollywood to accept the Thunderbird's offer.

Steve Rowland: "In 1962 to 1963 the Thunderbird Hotel wanted to give us a long term residency. However, we just couldn't get out of Hollywood to make the gig. Nevertheless, we were riding high and were playing all over Hollywood and Los Angeles. David Gates, Leon Russell and Chuck Rio had joined the group and we were fast becoming a much sought after twist band."

They had changed the band's name from "the Exciters" to "the Twist Kings," and they ruled the Hollywood club circuit. They had a bit of a rivalry from the Whiskey A Go Go, but it really didn't matter because all the clubs were making money. The night that the Cuban Missile Crisis came down, the Twist Kings were booked for their opening night at the Doll House on Ventura Boulevard in Encino. The club that night had a ghostly atmosphere. They played to two waitresses, a bar tender and the club owner. This proved to be a single appearance. As Rowland remarked: "It showed me the fickle nature of show business."

When they played the Carolina Lanes at the L. A. Airport they drew huge crowds. This turned into a three nights a week stint that drew standing room only crowds. The drinkers lined up three deep at the bar. A doorman was hired to control the ever-expanding crowd.

There was a big party when the Twist Kings made a special appearance at the trendy and private, Deauville Club, on the Pacific Coast Highway at the Beach in Santa Monica. This three-story building contained a restaurant and nightclub. Rowland and Albright performed there to a raucous one-night crowd.

When Rowland and Albright performed at the Peppermint Lounge West, there was a huge line outside waiting to get into the club. As the Twist Kings played to adoring throngs, there were record scouts in the audience at all times. The Peppermint Lounge was the catalyst to Rowland developing his ability to make demo 45s. The other members of the Twist Kings signed recording contracts and Rowland left for Spain.

Steve Rowland: "We usually got mobbed by the girls. (I could dig that because I was addicted) It was a hard gig, but a rewarding one, as Chuck Rio who was in the band was known for playing sax on 'Tequila."

Connie Stevens, Ed "Kookie" Byrnes, Vince Edwards and Jim Mitchum hung out with Rowland. Mitchum brought his friend, Jett Powers, and when Powers moved to London and changed his name to P. J. Proby, he had Rowland produce one of his albums. It was a night of rock and roll that continued for months as the Twist Kings moved from club to club enhancing their reputation. Steve spent his days doing parts in films.

When Robert Mitchum wandered in to see the guys perform his favorite rock and roll hits, he must have thought about the calypso album that he had recorded along with the hit "Thunder Road." Mitchum loved the music end of his career, as much as acting. Once in awhile, Mitchum wandered unannounced into the club to see young Steve perform. Mitchum was impressed and during the intermission, he reminded Steve that he had watched him sing as a young boy.

Steve Rowland: "When I was eleven years old I sang 'Darling Clementine' in a scene in my father's film, **Boys Ranch**."

This 1946 film was based on the actual boys ranch in Oldham County, Texas northwest of Amarillo and the movie was a long running one that contained a feel good message as America was recovering from World War II. For young Steve Rowland it was an inspiration for an acting career.

Steve Rowland: "The performing bug bit me right there and then in **Boys Town**. However, my father wanted me to get an education, so I hung up the idea of being a singer until I got to high school. All through high school, I kept thinking about trying to become a rock star. So, after graduation, I formed a band with H. B. Barnum called the Four Shades of Blue. I was the drummer. I was terrible."

But Rowland was training for bigger things. He played with Barnum at MGM Studio parties. And in the daytime, he worked in the mailroom. The band got paid fifty dollars for each of three small appearances.

THE MAGIC TIME OF THE EARLY 1960s

The early 1960s was a magic time for Steve Rowland. His twist band had more gigs than they could play. He was still busy as an actor, and he was expanding his already formidable musical knowledge. He was also learning about the music businesses intricacies.

Steve Rowland: "The guy who managed Budd and I owned and managed Ye Little Club on South Canon Drive in Beverly Hills. The place was known as a major jazz venue. It was always a jazz club but now rock and roll was creeping into the mix. Marshall Edson saw dollars in rock and roll and immediately turned his club into a gold mine. In doing so, he was responsible for launching our career. The shows Budd and I did at Ye Little Club were legendary."

Rowland's band performed cover versions of "Whole Lot of Shaking," "Good Golly Miss Molly," "Linda Lu," "Johnny B. Goode," "Sweet Little Sixteen" and "Roll Over Beethoven" among others. When Rowland was in Spain he recorded "Linda Lu" for the Hispovok label. Ray Sharpe's 1959 hit version of "Linda Lu" intrigued Rowland, but he put his own spin on it. He received a great deal of Spanish radio play.

Edson told Rowland and Albright that they had a future in the rock and roll music world. Steve watched the financial end of the music business closely and quietly educated himself.

The club scene soon got out of hand. Every evening there was standing room only in the clubs. There were always people milling around outside. From time to time the Los Angeles Police Department showed up to see if something was going down. There usually was. The various Rowland bands were part of a rock and roll revolution.

There was a great deal that Rowland learned from his Hollywood years. He received an extensive education in television, the movies, the early rock and roll revolution, and he became a student of the entertainment business. He was still a young man, but he had an understanding of the vicious nature of the corporate entertainment industry. He was a young man in his thirties, he was already a show business veteran. Steve had some memories about his early Hollywood years.

Steve Rowland: "I have always gotten along with most people. Especially, those that I worked with in films and television. However, I couldn't stand Stewart Granger. As I had been featured quite heavily in the fan magazines when the **Hollywood Reporter** and **Variety** listed the films to begin shooting at MGM Studios, many kids stood outside MGM's gates and came up to me for autographs. For some reason, this made Granger furious. He hated rock 'n' roll and loudly stated so. Nevertheless, I played it loudly in my dressing room. He then told me not to take my shirt off in one of the scenes in the film. I ignored him. He did everything he could to undermine me with all those on the set. I guess he resented me."

What Rowland experienced in his youthful Hollywood years impacted his career. From television and feature films, he learned about the essence of drama. When Steve settled in London a few years later to become a legendary record producer, he set up his own production company. He understood the commercial aspects of the entertainment industry, and this went a long way to guarantee his future artistic and business success.

ON TO SPAIN TO MAKE MOVIES AND MUSIC WITH LOS FLAPS: HOW IT INFLUENCED ROWLAND'S RECORD PRODUCTION

Steve Rowland: "I went to Spain with the four movie deal but I wasn't making very much money. So once again to enhance my income, I checked out a free American magazine that advertized a band looking for an English or American singer. The band was called Los Flaps. I auditioned and got the gig. We became quite successful. From that, an idea struck me that maybe I should go to England and try to get a record deal. I didn't want to depend on acting anymore, so the idea of going to London appealed to me."

Los Flaps were a successful Spanish band. Together with Rowland, they made a record. It was after cutting four tracks with Los Flaps that Rowland's future producing credentials were influenced. But there was no guarantee of a long term recording contract. Rowland reminisced about those four tracks.

Steve Rowland: "Los Flaps' and I, however, did get a record deal in Spain with the Hispovok label. We cut four tracks, which were released as a 45. The producer was having trouble communicating and was a little mental and at one point got so frustrated he slammed a glass of whatever he was drinking down on the recording desk and obviously all recordings came to a stop. Since nobody came forth, I volunteered to take over the production. 'I Got A Woman,' 'Mucho Mas,' 'Dancing Shoes' and 'Linda Lu' were four tracks that I produced for Los Flaps 1964 record release. I might as well as well have saved my energy as the record died a death."

Los Flaps eventually cut sixteen songs but only two 45s were released. They remain a highly collectible 1960s cult band. The blend of American and Spanish rock and roll made Los Flaps one of Spain's earliest cult bands. The sixteen tracks that they recorded included instrumental versions of "Washington Square" and "Pennsylvania 6-5000," and they became club hits. This material is available from the Rama Lama label; **Una Saga Del Rock Madrileno 1964-1967** in a two disc set combined with other cult bands that celebrate Madrid's garage rock era. Steve Rowland left Los Flaps, but he had fond memories of how professional and popular the group was until they broke up in 1968. Rowland was on to London with a new career direction in mind.

The music business was still in the far recesses of Steve Rowland's ambition. He continued to make movies and appear on television in Spain. It was at this time, while he was in Spain, that the music bug germinated. He had entered the Spanish record business as the lead singer of Los Flaps, who earlier had had brief chart success. They always say the opportunities come out of the blue. Steve made the most of it. As he always says, "luck is opportunity meeting preparation."

Rowland's calculating mind took over. He saw success beyond the club circuit. He realized that the Beatles and the Rolling Stones created opportunities for producers in the music business, and he saw a bigger concert scene. He decided to pursue a rock and roll career. He left the film business. When Steve Rowland decides on a career path, he pursues it full speed ahead.

Steve Rowland: "As a group, Los Flaps and I were minimally successful. Therefore, I decided to pick up and go to England to try to make it in the music business there."

The time with Los Flaps in Spain defined his early music career. The Los Flaps interlude was an interesting one. The original band was organized by a group of aeronautical engineering students who loved American rock and roll. They were a Madrid based group in 1964-1965 that charted five hits. They also served as Rowland's backing band, as he performed in and around Spain during the time he was making movies. There was a rival group on the scene made up of four American servicemen. The name of the band was Joe and The Jaguars. Mickey Hart, the future Grateful Dead drummer, was one of the members. Rowland loved their sound and shortly after, he was asked if he would like to join them as one of their lead singers. This he did for a brief time. This is only one of the many bands that Rowland's superb vocals graced.

The Mickey Hart band, billed as Joe & The Jaguars, were stationed at the American military base of Torrejon. Their lead singer, Joe Bennett, was previously in a rockabilly band, The Sparkletones; they had a hit, "Black Slacks."

Steve Rowland: "I played with Joe and the Jaguars a few times before I left for London. They were great guys playing American rock and roll. I had to do it their way. But I loved that. Joe Bennett was a great guy and a wonderful singer."

Los Flaps and the Jaguars provided Rowland with one more notch on his rock and roll career. He realized that in order for these bands to be successful, they needed to have their songs crafted in a more professional manner. He was becoming a producer and he didn't realize it. Discounting the Jaguars, the best of the Spanish bands, with Steve Rowland as lead singer, was Los Flaps. In the press, the Jaguars were ranked number two behind Los Flaps. The popularity of both bands was due to American lead singers as Joe Bennett gave the Jaguars an American presence, as did Rowland with Los Flaps.

After Rowland did a few shows with the Jaguars and left for London, Joe Bennett signed a deal with Hispovok. This led to eight songs recorded and released on two EPs. Hispovok is a subsidiary of Polydor Records, and it gave Bennett a great deal of European exposure. His American chart hits with the Sparkletones while he attended Cowpens High School in Spartanburg, South Carolina included not only the Top Forty hit "Black Slacks" but "Penny Loafers and Bobby Sox" which charted at forty-two on **Billboard** early in 1958. Bennett's rock and roll career in the U. S. was behind him but Hispovok revitalized his old songs.

After Los Flaps disbanded, the group had their 45s re-released on RCA. This brief period of success on the Spanish charts turned into long-term cult recognition. Steve Rowland was at the heart of this achievement.

MAY 23, 1963 CHANGES ROWLAND'S LIFE:
WHAT MADRID DID FOR HIS CRAFT

On the morning of May 23, 1963 Rowland left Los Angeles for Madrid. He was flying there to co-star in a movie, **Gunfighters of Casa Grande**. Steve loved living in Madrid. It reminded him of life back home in Southern California. One day he picked up an entertainment newspaper and read a story about the emerging British music scene. The article was alive with praise for a then unknown group named: "The Beatles."

However, Rowland put it in the back of his mind as he was in Spain with a four-picture movie deal.

Rowland didn't drink, he didn't smoke and he didn't do heavy drugs. While on the set between takes, he had some time on his hands. He read and listened to the wave of music crashing on the U. S. charts. He couldn't escape the vibration of the new sound. While in Hollywood. Steve's band, the Twist Kings, had been a number one attraction in the clubs, but others, like Johnny Rivers, had arrived and were taking over. Inside Rowland's head the music was now buzzing louder and louder.

His Los Angeles musical apprenticeship had honed in on every aspect of the recording business. He became a songwriter; he learned about sound technique and engineering. He could produce. He had a sixth sense about what made a hit record. Perhaps this was because Steve had spent many hours with his motion picture director father, Roy Rowland, talking about what made successful films. At the time no one realized that Steve was more than just an actor. He was an aspiring musician, as well as a fledgling record producer. However, the music business was put on hold while he took a detour for filming in Spain.

ROWLAND'S ROAD TO LONDON WAS
LONG AND ACCIDENTAL

The road to London was both planned and accidental. He had thought for some time about relocating to London's music scene. There was another reason to travel to London. His parents were living there at the time, and he could visit while considering his future career options.

After spending time visiting with his parents and hanging out at some of the trendy London clubs, Rowland began to analyze his career. Music was now his first choice. Acting was the back up.

For the next three years, Rowland continued to refine his production techniques. He was trained differently than London based record producers. There was a sense of drama to the rock songs that Steve produced. He viewed them much like a movie with a beginning, an exciting mid-point and a climax. This was not typical of late 1960s rock music producers. Rowland was waiting in the wings for the perfect artist to make the perfect album. He would have to wait until he found Rodriguez and carefully produce **Coming From Reality**.

HOLLYWOOD HEAT: UNTOLD STORIES
OF 1950S HOLLYWOOD

What is obvious is that no one realized the extent of Steve Rowland's skills. It is also as a writer that Steve Rowland excels. His writing career is not as well publicized as his acting, singing and producing skills. He is an exceptional writer who authored columns for 1950s fan magazines, and he has collected the material on his life in the 1950s in a book published in England, **Hollywood Heart: Untold Stories of 1950s Hollywood**.

He has recounted his early acting experiences. The best part of the book is Rowland's prose. "Nosing my Corvette into an empty slot near the top of the hill on La Cienga Boulevard I cut the engine and sat for a long moment watching little rillets of rainwater hurry bits of paper and discarded cigarette butts along the gutter toward their final journey." This is excellent writing and it sets the stage for Steve's visit to the Club Renaissance where he listened to jazz that didn't resonate. "For some reason I just couldn't catch the beat." (p. 93) Then Steve looked around and saw Robert Blake, Dean Stockwell and Dennis Hopper among others hanging out with a group of young starlets. He wondered if there was more to life. What this book chapter suggests is that he had a serious side as a young man. Steve recovered from these thoughts, talked to Tony Curtis, before leaving the club with a beautiful young girl.

The Club Renaissance was located across the street from Ciro's, which catered to the Hollywood elite. The Club Renaissance was as Rowland described: "Hollywood hardcore-a discreet watering hole for the new centurions." (p. 92) The chapter on the Club Renaissance has a surprise for the reader. Steve describes the club in a dream. Then he awakens from the dream and actually drives down to the club. The image of the Club Renaissance is a wonderful piece of creative fiction that recalls fact. When Steve does go down to the club that night, he does meet Tony Curtis. The only sad part of the story is that he didn't go home with the beautiful blonde in the story. It was a redhead. He doesn't write about what really happened. That might tell more than Rowland wants us to know. He uses a marvelous literary device to make a lot of key points about Hollywood.

The most interesting part of Rowland's book is a chapter on a Hollywood hit man. Steve goes into a club meets a young girl, takes her home, listens to records and then the boyfriend comes home. He enters the apartment hollering: "Dina I'm back." Her boyfriend is mob connected. Steve ran out of the bedroom, out to the balcony in his underwear and down an overgrown hillside. He was holding his pants and shirt. Life in Hollywood was interesting for Rowland.

Hollywood Heat: Untold Stories of 1950s Hollywood, which came out in 2008, is filled with the inside story of Steve Rowland's life and the Hollywood that he grew up in during the 1950s. The book is an exceptional literary marvel that goes beyond what the usual gossipmongers write about Tinseltown.

Rowland's book suggests that he was ready to make movies in Spain, to go to England to perform and produce and to expand his talents in the entertainment business. He did just that. Not even Steve Rowland realized that he was waiting in the wings to become the producer of Sixto Rodriguez' legendary **Coming From Reality** album. Rowland thought that by settling in London, he was beginning a brief production career that would lead him back to Hollywood. He was in for a surprise. It was a forty-year run for Steve producing legendary rock albums with a wide variety of artists.

Steve Rowland provided the framework, the relaxed studio atmosphere, the session musicians and the formula for what became a cult album and then one of the blockbuster sellers of recent years. The LP title, **Coming From Reality**, was apocryphal. It predicted what would happen in forty plus years. When an album hits the charts that long after it is completed it tells the story of a creative songwriting genius and Hall of Fame production skills. Sixto Rodriguez and Steve Rowland were on the same page. Thank goodness.

MATT SULLIVAN AND STEVE ROWLAND IN PALM SPRINGS

chapter

SEVENTEEN

STEVE ROWLAND: WAITING IN THE WINGS

"THERE IS NO SILENCE WITHOUT A CRY OF GRIEF, NO FORGIVENESS WITHOUT BLOODSHED." HARUKI MURAKAMI
"PEOPLE SAY YOU ARE LUCKY IF YOU ACCOMPLISH SOMETHING. LUCK IS OPPORTUNITY MEETING PREPARATION." STEVE ROWLAND

The lackluster sales of **Cold Fact** made Rodriguez' musical future questionable. In 1971, nobody knew his music and few people cared. **Cold Fact** vanished into the mist, unless you count the few copies that showed up in Woolworth's cut out bin. The record business was undergoing a transition. The singer-songwriter faded, the rise of soul, funk, pop and the disco craze caused Sixto Rodriguez to fall by the wayside. Although Rodriguez had a contract for a second album, Sussex Records was not interested. They needed to be persuaded that Rodriguez had commercial potential.

THE LONDON MUSIC BUSINESS AND THE ROLE OF
ROWLAND'S DEPORTATION THAT CREATED
HIS RECORD PRODUCING CAREER

When Steve Rowland landed in London in December 1966, he had no idea that he would live there for the next forty years. When he arrived in the U. K., Rowland had a visitor's visa. He didn't pay close attention to the expiration date on the government document. When Home Office officials showed up at the flat that Rowland was staying in, he was shocked. They began the process of deporting him to Spain. In a few days, he was back in Barcelona. It was this trip that paved the way for Rowland to emerge as a legendary British producer. Looking back, Steve explained those early London days.

Steve Rowland: "I decided to pay a visit to my parents who at the time were living in London. My father had been in Spain making films and had just finished directing a move set in Barcelona. While spending time in London, as a first time visitor, I took the opportunity to take in as much of the London music scene as possible. The English rock scene was beginning to take over the world. Records by the Beatles, the Rolling Stones, the Animals, Sandy Shaw, the Springfield's featuring Dusty Springfield seemed to be blaring from every shop on Oxford Street. Carnaby Street in particular was the fashion and music center at the time. One day, while I was walking up Oxford Street, I ran into a guy. We stopped and we began talking. Our conversation was mostly about the London music scene. He asked me what I did and how come I was in London? I said I had been making movies in Spain and had also recorded a few records. His eyes seemed to widen with a bit of astonishment. He asked me if I would allow him to manage me if he was able to get me a recording contract in England. His name was Georgie Rave. He persuaded me to come with him to the Fontana Record Company, where he said that he had a 'special in.' He introduced me to a fellow by the name of Dick Leahy who in turn introduced me to Jack Baverstock, the CEO of Fontana Records. It just happened that I had a bunch of my demos with me and I was anxious to play them for anyone who would listen. Dick Leahy was the assistant to Mr. Baverstock and as it happened he had a few minutes to spare. He would listen and report to Baverstock. He put the demos on and after hearing the first one (one of the recordings I had made with Los Flaps), he immediately picked up the phone and called upstairs to Baverstock's office. Leahy had been impressed and was anxious for Jack Baverstock to hear what he had heard. Baverstock was a very staid Englishman. After listening intently to the demos, he re-acted with a few words, one of which was 'interesting.' He then told me to come back in a couple of days at which time he would have made a decision whether or not to offer me a recording deal. I eagerly returned a couple of days later and was offered a recording contract."

Then came the visit from the Home Office. The deportation cri-sis turned into a nightmare. Rowland believed that he was done in the U. K. and he prepared to resume his acting and music career in Spain. He thought of returning to America. Then a series of events took place due to his English friends and Fontana Record mogul Jack Baverstock's determination to hire him as a lead singer. The only way to bring Steve back to London was as a producer. This soon took place. Steve recalled those hectic days.

Steve Rowland: "But as luck would have it, the Home Office sent officers to the flat where I was living with instructions for my deporta-tion back to Spain. They only gave me forty-eight hours before I had to leave. I had unwittingly over stayed my entrance Visa. However, while I had been in London, I had met a young lady named Sue, who later married Lionel Blair, a top British entertainer. She and I had become good friends. Before I left I spoke to her on the phone and told her my situation. "

Sue said: "Don't worry Steve; I think I have an idea of how to sort it out. So don't worry. While you're back in Barcelona, I will set up a meeting with Jack Baverstock, who Lionel and I know very well. I will try to set up a meeting for you and Jack to speak on the phone to sort out the problem. Hopefully, you'll be able to return to England on a work permit."

Steve Rowland: "This she was able to do. The only rock in the road was that the Home Office was not going to give me a work permit as a singer. Jack Baverstock came up with the idea for the Home Office to grant me permission to re-enter the country as a record producer. The trigger was that I was to produce U. K. artists for possible better sales in the U. S. The Home Office fell for it and the very first group that Jack Baverstock turned over to me to produce was Dave Dee, Dozy, Beaky, Mick and Tich. My first production was successful, the record sold over 250,000 copies, and I was awarded a silver disc for sales. The title was 'Hold Tight.' Not only was I over the moon, but also my record produc-tion career was launched in England. I owe everything to Jack Baver-stock, Dick Leahy and that strange fellow that I met on Oxford Street, Georgie Rave."

The Home Office drama, the deportation and the return to London brought Rowland back into the U. K. music business. When Jack Baverstock of Fontana Records brought Steve into London on a work permit as a record producer, the results were immediate. What the Fontana Record mogul didn't realize is that Rowland had served a ten-year apprenticeship in the music business.

The grey haired Baverstock was reserved, soft spoken but his outward appearance hid the calculating mind of a shrewd and demanding businessman. The forty three year old Baverstock ran Fontana with an iron fist. It was his way or the highway.

The Fontana Record label was important to the London music business. This was largely due to a legendary American music mogul, Freddy Bienstock, who came to the U. K. to expand his business interests.

THE HIDDEN ROLE OF FREDDY BIENSTOCK ON THE ROAD TO RECORDING RODRIGUEZ' SECOND ALBUM

Although Bienstock was an American businessman, he relocated to London, where he was the principal partner in Carlin Music. His career in the music business is a legendary one. He worked at in New York's songwriting factory, the Brill Building, while still in his teens. He also was employed at New York's Chappell Music where his cousins Jean and Julian Aberbach were high-level executives. Bienstock made his reputation when Col. Tom Parker agreed to allow Hill and Range to publish classic Presley's classic early hits "Jailhouse Rock," "Love Me Tender" and "Don't." In 1957, Bienstock left New York and moved to London. He purchased Hill and Range's London subsidiary, Belinda Music, in 1966 to handle the Aberbach catalogue and expand his business into the United Kingdom. This was the same year that Rowland spent his 1966 Christmas in London. Their paths never crossed but the result was the road to Sixto Rodriguez' **Coming From Reality** LP.

The first time that Rowland met Freddy Bienstock was a year later when he formed the rock band the Family Dogg. The band's publishing company, Samsong, was made up of the first names of Steve Rowland, Albert Hammond and Mike Hazelwood, and they were set up with Carlin Music.

Bienstock changed the name of Belinda Music to Carlin Music in 1966. The Bienstock-Baverstock conglomerate pushed Carlin Music's song title collection to over 100,000 tunes.

Steve Rowland: "I got along great with Freddy, who was a terrific guy, a short time later he introduced me to, Marty Machat, who became my manager."

Marty Machat was a show business lawyer who also managed Leonard Cohen, and he had dealings with everyone from Frank Sinatra to Michael Jackson. Although he didn't work closely with Freddy Bienstock, Rowland was in the midst of the record business as Bienstock's successes led to millions of dollars. Some of that success was directly related to the product that Rowland produced.

FREDDY BIENSTOCK LOOKS AT HIS SUCCESSES

Freddy Bienstock: "I didn't think we had much of a chance when we started. But I can't resist a challenge." This comment was made after Bienstock paid one hundred million dollars to purchase Chappell and Company in 1984. It was the world's largest music publisher at the time. After he founded Carlin Music, he continued to collect millions from music royalties. It was his success from 1966 that allowed Bienstock to purchase Chappell and Company and Steve Rowland's production profits helped to amass Bienstock's fortune.

Bienstock, a committed family man, talked to his children, Roger and Caroline, about his new company. He told them that he would name it Carlin by combining their names.

Freddy Bienstock: "I was not enamored with rock and roll but I changed after a while. By listening to the songs that were submitted to me for Elvis, I soon had a good idea what he wanted."

Steve Rowland was another influence. His production techniques convinced Bienstock that rock and roll had a long-term financial future. Nothing appealed to Bienstock more than the thought of continual profits.

In 1969, Bienstock made a series of business moves that flooded Carlin Music with money. He left his employer, Hill and Range, to set up the Hudson Bay Music Company with Jerry Leiber and Mike Stoller. He acquired two music firms, Koppelman and Rubin, and this led to the publishing rights to Bobby Darin, Tim Hardin, John Sebastian as well as the catalogue of the King and Starday Record labels inventory. By the time that Steve Rowland came into the mix there was an enormous amount of production money.

During his time in London, Rowland had limited contact with Bienstock. He dealt with Fontana Record head, Jack Baverstock, most of the time.

THE STEVE ROWLAND BUSINESS MODEL

Once Rowland had his immigration papers in order, it was time to set up a business model. When he arrived back in London, Rowland established his own company, Double R Productions. He rented a London office at NO. 6 Denmark Street across from Carlin Music. "I shared an office with Peter Meisel and Trudy of Hansa Records when they first came over from Germany to break artists in the U. K. market," Rowland said.

Rowland's early successes prompted him to relocate to a larger and more prestigious office behind the West End Central police station, one street west of trendy Seville Row. His continued success prompted Steve to set up Family Circle Productions with his partner Robert Oppenheimer. Rowland was perpetually busy and in the midst of his hectic schedule he discovered Sixto Rodriguez' music. It was Rowland's business plan, as well as his producing talent, that made him an important player in London record production. Had he not established a solid reputation, as a producer, he would not have been able to convince Clarence Avant to fund a second Rodriguez album.

By 1971, Rowland had acquired a strong track record. His reputation as a producer from 1967 to 1970 was mind-blowing. He had produced thirteen top ten records with the group Dave Dee, Dozy, Beaky, Mick and Tich, including a number one, "The Legend of Xanadu."

STEVE ROWLAND WALKS INTO CARLIN MUSIC AND DISCOVERS RODRIGUEZ

Steve Rowland's circuitous road to record production was due not only to his latent talent; it was also due to the fact that he had been a rock and roll person since the early 1950s. No one knew of Rowland's well-developed production talents. He was considered an actor and a singer. Like Rodriguez, myths and legends that grew up around Rowland hid his long training in the music industry. He could do it all. He could write songs, he could arrange songs, he could mix tunes he could produce and he could front a band.

After Baverstock circumvented the Home Office by signing Rowland as a producer, it allowed him to return to London. He was surprised that the Home Office was still interested. Officials from the Home Office arrived at Fontana demanding to see Rowland's production schedule. Baverstock was pissed. He immediately brought in a group for Rowland to produce.

Fontana assigned Rowland a group with no hits and a strange name, Dave Dee, Dozy, Mick and Tich. They were considered quirky and non-commercial. Baverstock told Steve to make some hits. The result was thirteen top ten U. K. hits and a number one with "The Legend of Xanadu." Steve Rowland was on his way as a British record producer.

From his rented office space in London's West End, Steve walked daily across the street to Carlin Music where he had carte blanche run of the office. Rowland had an ear for a new sound. He didn't follow the trends like the English, as he looked for unique performers. Jack Baverstock was a brilliant businessman who knew a producer when he saw one. After he talked with Rowland a few weeks earlier, he realized that he had a double-edged talent-a singer who also was a producer.

The Kinks, Ray Davies, said it best when he remarked that Baverstock had "a tremendous ear." So did Rowland. That is one reason they had a symbiotic relationship.

Steve Rowland: "I owe my London producing career to the faith that Jack Baverstock had in a young kid who wanted badly to be a singer, but ended up being a record producer."

Steve Rowland built the firm foundation of pop music in the late 1960s that paved the way for the progressive rock of the 1970s. He also helped to make the Carlin Catalogue one of the worlds most profitable.

Jack Baverstock took the Fontana label to the bank. From 1966, he either produced, wrote the liner notes, assigned songs and producers to artists like Wayne Fontana and the Mind Benders, Blossom Dearie, the Cocteau Twins, Lulu, Manfred Mann, the Walker Brothers and Scott Walker among others.

But there was a dark side to Baverstock. He had opinions on records that didn't always square with sales. Baverstock was an over the top critic. When Rowland finishing producing "Hold Tight" for Dave Dee and the group, Baverstock had a fit. He didn't think it was a hit. He threatened to fire Rowland. Steve remarked: "Fine."

There was another problem. Baverstock placed his name on "Hold Tight" as the producer. Rowland was livid. He stormed into Baverstock's office. Steve was ready to quit. Baverstock was headstrong, but he wasn't stupid. He realized that Steve knew the business, and he placed Rowland's name on subsequent pressings of "Hold Tight."

Early on, Baverstock found that he couldn't bully or intimidate Rowland. There were a number of times Rowland threatened to quit. Baverstock was too smart to let his hit maker go elsewhere.

Their differences ended quickly when the record became a Top Ten hit. Baverstock never admitted he was wrong. But he didn't fire Rowland, and they continued to work together.

It was Baverstock who was responsible for Steve Rowland's emergence as a producer. Once they unleashed him, he worked night and day, and the results were impressive. He eventually became the producer who brought the second Rodriguez classic, **Coming From Reality**, into the commercial marketplace.

THE EMERGENCE OF STEVE ROWLAND

For almost five years, Rowland worked on his producing skills. He didn't know anything about Sixto Rodriguez, and he hadn't heard his music. Then one day he walked into Carlin Music, and noticed a pile of new albums. As he viewed the pile of new albums on a desk, there was one that stood out. He picked it up, puzzled by the unusual album design. The album was titled **Cold Fact**. The artist was Rodriguez. He immediately went into one of the listening rooms and put the record on. He was instantly transfixed by the poetic lyrics. Rowland had never heard more sophisticated lyrics surrounded by such beautiful music. He wondered. Who the hell is Rodriguez?

ROWLAND BROUGHT IN TO STRAIGHTEN
OUT THE PRETTY THINGS

Jack Baverstock called Rowland into his office for a special assignment. He had what the Fontana Record chief considered a near impossible task. He wanted Rowland to update the Pretty Things sound.

"Those damned kids think they know the record business. They don't know shit," Baverstock told Rowland. He said that the Pretty Things were beating a dead horse by continually making Chicago blues type records. They weren't from Chicago. They were from Essex, just outside of London and their recordings lacked the rawness of the true genre. Baverstock told Rowland to solve the problem.

Rowland came aboard, as the Pretty Things' producer, to get them on the charts. He began working on their 1967 album **Emotions**. They didn't like the songs on their new LP even though they wrote most of them.

The Pretty Things realized that Rowland was their last chance at commercial success. They listened. They cooperated. Things went well during the recording sessions. Rowland had no idea that they didn't like the material. As a matter of fact, he had a lot of respect for Phil May and Dick Taylor who were also very talented commercial artists. The band had a plan. They would adhere to recording a commercial album and then sign with another label.

Rowland produced a single, "Progress," which featured a commercial brass section accompanied by strings. Although it was hard edged, the record entered the tale end of the charts. The irony is that it became a cult single that continues to have a lengthy life. It did, however, alter the Pretty Things' sound, and there was a great deal of publicity in the London music magazines, **Disc**, the **New Musical Express** and **Melody Maker**. Although the buzz in the industry didn't translate to heavy commercial sales, the Pretty Things were no longer viewed as the copycat Chicago blues band. Rowland helped them develop a sound that broke the band in the U. K. market. Rowland's productions also increased the band's awareness and sales in America. What the song did was to make the Pretty Things one of the premiere cult English rock bands.

The Pretty Things were much publicized for criticizing their music. They didn't care for the new sound on the **Emotions** album. They refused to perform "Progress" in concert. They systematically ignored all of the tunes on the album. Some have interpreted this as criticism of the song. The truth is that they had difficulty performing it. It was too complicated. Another problem was that the group was breaking apart before they recorded **Emotions**. The constant changes in the Pretty Things musical structure was a challenge for record producer Steve Rowland. He met the challenge and conquered it.

Steve Rowland: "Jack ran the show with an iron fist. He knew a great arranger who just happened to be a friend of his. The arranger's name was Reg Tilsley. He had a reputation as an outstanding musician/arranger. As I left Jack Baverstock's office his parting words were 'make the songs God-damned commercial.' When Jack talked you listened and tried to do as he asked."

Baverstock told them they needed to develop a pop sound. This sound intensified when Reg Tilsley began to write and conduct the orchestral arrangements for many of the tracks. The band hated the results, as a matter of fact they hated everything about the album. The revelation surprised Steve Rowland: "I never had any trouble with the boys in the studio. Dick Taylor and Phil May and the others were totally cooperative. I think it was a good album, it is what it is." The album survives as a cult classic.

There are many things that shaped Rowland's producing genius. Some of the influences took place early in his life. He had experiences that shaped his character and eventually turned up on his record productions. Rowland grew up in a motion picture family. He was privileged to see how films were made and what ingredients it took to make them commercially successful. Rowland always thought outside of the box. His motto was: "If you don't take chances, you'll never be original." These influences included merging lush orchestral arrangements into a raw rock/pop sound. Or creating musical simplicity for a heart-rending lullaby. Rowland's ability to mix an instrumental arrangement into a simple lush sound is personified in Rodriguez' track "Sandrevan Lullaby-Lifestyles."

ROWLAND THE PRODUCER, 1967-1970

Steve Rowland: "In 1967 to 1970 I had 13 top ten hits with Dave Dee and a number one hit with their record 'The Legend of Xanadu.' At the time, I had formed the Family Dogg. We had four hit records including a number five on the British charts, 'A Way of Life.' At that time I had no idea who Sixto Rodriguez was. I didn't know anything about his album **Cold Fact** until one day I saw that album lying on a desk at Carlin Music. At that time, three of my productions were in the charts. They included Dave Dee, The Family Dogg and the song "Progress" by the Pretty Things. After listening to the Rodriguez album, **Cold Fact**, I told the powers that be that more than anything I wanted to produce the next Rodriguez album, should there be one."

What Rowland didn't know was that there were no plans for a second album. Rodriguez was difficult. He didn't handle the teen dances well. He was polite to a fault but personally remote with the disc jockeys. He had a counterculture life. To him, the record business was just that, a business.

It was Clarence Avant who gave the go ahead for the second album. Avant spent some time researching Steve Rowland, and he believed that he was the producer to bring Rodriguez into the commercial mainstream. Avant was also one of Rodriguez' biggest fans.

WHY STEVE ROWLAND WAS PERFECT TO
PRODUCE COMING FROM REALITY

The relationship between Steve Rowland and Sixto Rodriguez was perfect. They saw his music as one, and Steve believed that in order to get the best out of Rodriguez, he would not mess with the man's music. A meddling producer had ruined many artists. Steve was determined to have Rodriguez' voice and lyrics as close to his artistic direction as possible. Rowland saw a talent in Rodriguez that was perfected. He simply needed great production. Steve was up to the task.

Steve Rowland: "Rodriguez was suspicious of what could possibly come down on him and ruin his songs. I saw that anxiety in Rodriguez' body language. I told him not to worry, that anything that he didn't like that he recorded, we would redo to his satisfaction."

I asked Steve what he had to change in the album while recording **Coming From Reality**?

Steve Rowland: "I didn't change anything, I just added drama in the instrumental backing."

Why was Rowland the perfect producer for **Coming From Realty?** It was simple. He understood Rodriguez, his lyrics, his music and his studio techniques.

Steve Rowland: "The content of his lyrics, the social comment that he expounded upon got right to me. I could feel the pain."

Steve felt that the song, "Like Janis," spoke about many of the girls that Rowland had once dated. But he was cautious about interpreting Rodriguez' lyrics. That infringed on the Sugar Man.

Steve Rowland: "Once I heard that song, that was it. That was the one that really got me. I could feel the pain."

I asked Steve why he was so concerned about having a certain type of atmosphere when recording. I didn't think it mattered.

Steve Rowland: "I created a relaxed atmosphere for Rodriguez because I could tell when I first met him that he was a sensitive soul. I know how easy it is to upset someone if you try to override their wishes. I wanted to bring out the truth in the best way that I could."

STEVE ROWLAND ON RODRIGUEZ

As Rowland listened to Rodriguez first album **Cold Fact**, he had his own vision before he started producing **Coming From Reality**. Steve had firm convictions. But he listened carefully to Rodriguez. Steve's suggestions always were ones that he discussed with Rodriguez. A good example of this is how they worked closely to make "Sandrevan-Lullaby-Lifestyles" a dreamy, romantic song. He gives the Sugar Man all the credit. That is Rowland's way. He is humble.

Steve Rowland: "Before we went into the studio, I told anyone who would listen that Sixto Rodriguez was sure to be the next big thing. No one listened to me. They thought I was off my rocker."

Comments like: "He's a poor man's Bob Dylan," indicated the level of insensitivity between London's supposedly trendy, hip and knowledgeable music executives. No one envisioned Sixto Rodriguez' original talent. That is no one except Steve Rowland.

As Steve Rowland looked back upon his days in London as the producer of **Coming From Reality**, in an interview with the **New York Times'** Larry Rohter, he said: "I've produced a lot of big name artists with big hits, like Peter Frampton and Jerry Lee Lewis, but I've never worked with anyone as talented as Rodriguez."

chapter

EIGHTEEN

COLD FACT IN RETROSPECT

"RODRIGUEZ'S MUSIC AND STYLE HAVE A WARM AND
WEARY AND CARING AND RESIGNED AIR THAT JUST
SEEMS TO WRAP YOU IN ITS COCOON AND MAKES THE
WORLD SEEM A SLIGHTLY BETTER PLACE."   STEPHEN
"SUGAR" SEGERMAN

"ORIGINALITY IS BEING DIFFERENT FROM ONESELF, NOT
OTHERS." PHILIP LARKIN

"TURN MY BACK TO THE EAST,
FROM WHENCE COMFORTS HAVE INCREASED;
FOR LIGHT DOTH SEIZE MY BRAIN
WITH FRANTIC PAIN."
WILLIAM BLAKE (MAD SONG)

When Rodriguez' **Cold Fact** was released, the album didn't enter the commercial marketplace. Changing musical tastes, lack of promotion, the wrong label, the inability to secure the right concerts, as well as a Mexican-American singer in an Anglo dominated singer-songwriter's market, were factors that prompted **Cold Fact's** descent into obscurity. That descent doomed Sixto Rodriguez' career and those in the know in the music business didn't believe that there would be a second album.

One of the intriguing aspects of **Cold Fact** is the album cover. As Stephen "Sugar" Segerman commented in **Searching For Sugar Man**, Rodriguez appeared as a Shaman, a mystic, a hippie type, a man of mystery and this fueled the South African legend.

THE HEROIC AND HOPELESS NATURE OF COLD FACT

There is something heroic and hopeless about **Cold Fact**. Everyone agrees about the album's literary merits. What is the reason **Cold Fact** was neglected? Perhaps it was the Sugar Man's soft, low-key approach to life. He was polite, deferential and gentlemanly to a fault. The rock music business is filled with hustlers, egomaniacs and self-promoters. Rodriguez is none of these. He doesn't like to talk about himself. Like Van Morrison, his lyrics spoke to the intelligent listener. The novelist Ford Maddox Ford opened his 1917 novel, **The Good Solider**, with a sentence that described Sixto Rodriguez: "This is the saddest story I have every heard." That was the case until Stephen "Sugar" Segerman and his gang from South Africa helped to bring Rodriguez roaring into the commercial mainstream.

Why was **Cold Fact's** brilliance ignored? There is no simple answer. There are some clues. The first clue is inside the industry. Steve Rowland spent weeks at London's Fontana Records office attempting to get people to listen to **Cold Fact**. He went into the listening booth a half a dozen times and came out crying out the Sugar Man's praises. Fontana's employees looked at him like he was nuts. The listening booths at Fontana were for previewing new albums. Rowland spent so much time listening to **Cold Fact**, that the imperious Brits kidded him that he was lonely for America. When he discussed Rodriguez' musical genius, the Fontana staff ignored him. They wondered why he would listen to an obscure Mexican-American singer. "They wanted the next big thing," Steve Rowland continued. "It wasn't **Cold Fact**."

Steve Rowland: "I never understood the Brits, they didn't see the beautiful lyrics or the gritty Detroit street scenes. It still baffles me."

CULTURAL THEMES AND DETROIT INFLUENCES

One of the hallmarks of **Cold Fact** is Rodriguez' use of urban cultural themes. He has a talent for describing ironic situations with a touch of lyrical poetry. His keen eye is demonstrated in "Only Good For Conversation." Rodriguez writes: "My pockets don't drive me fast. My mother treats me slow. My statue's got a concrete heart. But you're the coldest bitch I know." Dennis Coffey's understated fuzz guitar adds a great deal to tune that laments a bitter romance with an unhappy ending.

As Steve Rowland remarked: "Rodriguez' songs are personal ones. They are about things that happened to him." Another example is "Jane S. Piddy" as Rodriguez writes: "Now you sit there thinking feeling insecure. The mocking court jester claims there is no proven cure. Go back to your chamber, your eyes on the wall. Cos you got no one to listen, you got no one to call." This song is another window into Rodriguez' relationships. Only he knows what they mean. This doesn't obscure the lyrical poetry that is Sixto Rodriguez. These lyrics make his debut album a special one. But where did these tales originate?

It was at the local watering holes around the blue collar Wayne State University that Rodriguez was inspired. From spots like the In Between, the Sewer By The Sea and Anderson's Garden, he took copious mental notes for his poetic lines. These phrases became unforgettable songs.

Sixto Rodriguez: "The Decanter was on Palmer and Cass. A lot of people would get together there. It was right by the school. There would be working people and artists, musicians, and so things would just take off from there. Detroit was a very diverse city then."

The influences from the Cass Corridor also included the anarchist publication, **Fifth Estate Tribe**, which reported on the problems of the Vietnam War, racism and malignant suburban growth. In 1969, **Creem** emerged as a monthly rock and roll magazine that put Detroit on the map.

Some years later the long bar at the Cass Café was home to Rodriguez, while he basked in obscurity. He never told anyone that he recorded two albums. That is Rodriguez; he is modest to a fault. This bar-restaurant features a gallery with paintings by local artists; it has an eclectic menu and one of the best selections of beer and wine in the Motor City. I chatted up the bar tender and the waiter who love talking to Rodriguez. "He still comes in but things have gotten crazy since **Searching For Sugar Man**," the waiter remarked. In 2014, the Cass Café Gallery had a portrait series dedicated to writing Detroit's history through art.

As Rodriguez sat at the bar, prior to **Searching For Sugar Man**, he read the **Metro Times**. He brought in whatever philosophy book he was reading, and he talked at length about politics. His humility prevented him from talking about his music or nascent career. Why does he love the Cass Café? It is simple. He loves the people and the fraternal atmosphere.

There was an article proclaiming that the Cass Café bar was the best for in-depth conversation in the Motor City. He read the story. He laughed. No one bothered Rodriguez, as he furtively scribbled his notes for new songs. Then 2012 arrived and Rodriguez had to hide out. Fame and fortune is a mixed blessing.

In 1970, the term Indie music meant very little. In 2008, when Light In The Attic released **Cold Fact**, Rodriguez was fast becoming a darling of the Indie crowd. The twisted electronic sound on "Sugar Man" is contemporary. It is Coffey's fuzz guitar on "Only Good For Conversation" that prompted later critics to laud the album. Mike Theodore provided the full sound that sets the song apart from others. Theodore also arranged the horns on "Crucify Your Mind," as Rodriguez invoked a Dylanesque persona. While some critics label **Cold Fact** pop-psych and others psych-folk, everyone agrees, Theo-Coff produced a masterpiece.

Rodriguez is an accomplished acoustic musician. But 1970 wasn't the right time for an acoustic psych-folk album. The genius of Coffey and Theodore was to blend in soft instrumental accompaniment while accentuating the lyrics. They also maintained the style and direction of the Sugar Man's music. Mike Theodore was intrigued by and worked assiduously with the music. Not surprisingly, it was the lyrics that Theodore loved. He told Kevin "Sipreano" Howes: "He was talking about the streets, where he lived, the drug dealers, and hookers."

THE SONGS ON COLD FACT

Cold Fact opens with "Sugar Man." The haunting vocal, with images of drugs and Detroit's deprivation, gives the LP an eerie feeling. Dennis Coffey's magnificent fuzz guitar makes "Only Good For Conversation" take a much different musical direction, the beauty of Rodriguez' writing and his sophisticated music is showcased.

The lyrics project poetic truths. These truths are evident in "Crucify Your Mind." It is also a song about a lost relationship. Most of Rodriguez' writing centers on people he knew, loved or hung out with in Detroit. "Crucify Your Mind" suggests that he is delaying gratification with a young lady to provide chemical stimuli. "Was it a huntsman or a player that made you pay the cost, that now assumes relaxed position and prostitutes your loss...." That says it all. When he wonders if you are "Tom the curious" or "James the weak," he intensifies the message.

One of the problems with Rodriguez is that his most commercial songs suffer from lengthy titles or personal diatribes. "This Is Not A Song, It's An Outburst: or, The Establishment Blues" takes its cue from one of Bob Dylan's lengthy titles. What makes "The Establishment Blues" unique is the stream of consciousness vocal style. The themes in this political song are a reminder of his intellectual focus. He has the interest of the blue-collar working class, the college student, the minority community and the disenfranchised in his lyrics, as well as in his daily pursuit of happiness. He lives and breathes his art.

As "Hate Street Dialogue'" skewers San Francisco's 1967 Summer of Love, it fits into the album's context. One wonders what Rodriguez thinks of Mike Harvey's lyrics? Perhaps one day we will find out. This is an excellent song well produced by Coffey and Theodore in the Rodriguez mold.

"Forget It" is one of the Sugar Man's classic tunes. According to a close friend, it is about a failed relationship. It could also be interpreted as Rodriguez' reaction to local dive bar audiences that might have ignored his music for the pool table or a young lady with big breasts. Either way, he let the listener know that if you didn't like his music, you could "Forget It."

The second side of **Cold Fact** begins with "Inner City Blues." It is a paean to Marvin Gaye and Motown. Then "I Wonder" has the greatest bass line intro, courtesy of Bob Babbitt, of any Rodriguez song. It is an anthem of sexual awakening and coming of age. When Rodriguez croons, "I wonder when was the last time you had sex," it sounds more like an invitation than a condemnation.

"Like Janis" considers the travails of the rock and roll lifestyle. Or more likely it is about one of his girl friends. When he sings: "And you measure for wealth by the things you can hold," Rodriguez lets the listener know his Bohemian inclinations. He continues: "And you want to be held with highest regard.... It delights you so much if he's trying so hard." No doubt one of his girl friends gave him trouble. He answered her in lyrical form. When Rodriguez says: "So don't try to impress me, you're just pins and paint. And don't' try to charm me with things that you ain't," he speaks for everyone who has had a rocky relationship.

"Gommorah (A Nursery Rhyme)" is a head scratcher. The song has it's own unique appeal. It is not one of the songs written by Rodriguez. But it fits the **Cold Fact** context. The last two tunes "Rich Folks Hoax" and "Jane S. Piddy" continues anti-establishment themes. The imagery in "Rich Folks Hoax" is brilliant with lines like: "The moon is hanging in the purple sky" and "the priest is preaching from a shallow grave." These phrases suggest the depth of his songwriting wizardry. "Rich Folks Hoax" brought praise from the psych-folk critics who recognized the diversity of the Sugar Man's songs.

THE ROYALTIES QUESTION, THE QUESTIONING CRITICS AND AUDIENCES

The **Cold Fact** album and **Searching For Sugar Man** intensify the discussion of where Rodriguez' royalties went. No one knows. For more than two years, the convoluted explanations, the arguments and the disagreements have come no closer to solving the problem. Then Harry Balk sued Clarence Avant who then sued Sixto Rodriguez, and by early 2015 the royalty issue remains unsolved.

Another problem that **Searching For Sugar Man** never mentioned is that Rodriguez was performing for large audiences in Australia and New Zealand in 1979 and 1981. This was the first time that the Sugar Man played arenas or larger venues. He was an opening act for Midnight Oil at the larger venues. When he played solo in Australia, he regularly sold out 5000 seat auditoriums. This was not part of the documentary nor should it have been. What it suggests is that the Rodriguez mystery was the product of South Africa's isolation in the world of apartheid.

One of the tragedies of the Rodriguez story is the **London Guardian** questioning the documentaries authenticity. This is typical of British journalism. The British believe that they invented rock and roll, and that any artist who comes back from the depths of obscurity is due to U. K. influences. The story that Stephen "Sugar" Segerman and Craig Bartholomew-Strydom tell is one that remains not only a wonderful tale but a true one. The **Guardian's** attempts to impugn the documentary lack veracity. It is typical British journalism. Just ask Van Morrison.

There is one other mystery to the Sugar Man tale. Clarence Avant may not be the dragon that **Searching For Sugar Man** suggests. He was ambushed on camera. This was not easy to do. He is a major figure in the music industry, as well as in the television, radio and movie fields. The albums that Sussex produced employed the top people in the field, no expense was spared and the end result was that thirty thousand dollars was spent on each album. In the next book on Steve Rowland's production of **Coming From Reality**, the expenses for a fancy apartment in one of the wealthiest areas of London for Rodriguez and Rainy M. Moore and the studio musicians employed suggests how much money Avant spent. His return was zero. Then in 2012 he cashed in. Avant promptly paid royalties.

Another mystery is the vanishing master tapes. When South Africa and Australia released Rodriguez material, they didn't always have master tapes. The culprit here is Buddah Records. When Buddah was in tough financial times they signed with a British holding company to license Rodriguez' material. The master tapes vanished. When Craig Bartholomew-Strydom began tracing the money, he was told to begin looking for the money in London. He was given a number. Craig called. There was no answer. The number was disconnected the next day. The mystery remains.

Although **Cold Fact** sold well in South Africa, it was a country with limited record sales. The vinyl collecting population was small, and there was little contact with the outside world. This ended in the early 1990s and Rodriguez' triumphant series of 1998 concerts would not have been possible without the end of apartheid.

While Rodriguez has given his substantial royalties away, that doesn't excuse the lack of payment. Someone is responsible. It is just that no one admits to holding back the Sugar Man's funds.What must not be forgotten is that Malik Bendjelloul's sensitive and beautifully told story provided incredible insight into the music business. It reminds us of how little integrity there is in the industry. Even more significant, **Cold Fact** is the perfect record.

For those who listened to **Cold Fact** non-stop and watched **Searching for Sugar Man** multiple times, there is a sense of relief that Sixto Rodriguez is recognized at seventy plus as a legitimate rock star. No one is happy that a good portion of the money has vanished. That is the mystery of the Sixto Rodriguez story.

COLD FACT AS BURIED TREASURE

There are some interesting trivia points surrounding **Cold Fact**. The original title of "Sugar Man" was "Sugar Man on Prentis." Not surprisingly, this is a Detroit street where Rodriguez observed Volkswagen Frank the drug dealer. He was an urban legend who made "Sugar Man" infamous. **Rolling Stone** listed "Sugar Man" as number thirty-four in the list of "100 Greatest Drug Songs." "Like Janis" and "Jane S. Piddy," "Sugar Man" had a similarity that the critics noted but they are quite different songs.

When he wrote "Only Good For Conversation," Rodriguez revealed some clues into his psyche. His wives and girl friends had money concerns. In the song, he addressed these issues. "My pocket doesn't drive me fast," Rodriguez continued. "You've nothing I would care to own." That said it all about the people who attacked Rodriguez' laid back counterculture lifestyle.

In August 2002 **Mojo** featured the album as a "buried treasure." There were some attempts to advertise **Cold Fact**. An ad in the March 28, 1970 **Billboard** used the phrase: "Word From The City." In the April 4, 1970 **Billboard**, it was noted that Sussex was a beginning label and **Cold Fact** was recommended listening. When the April 18, 1970 **Billboard** awarded the album a four star review, things looked bright for **Cold Fact's** future. They weren't.

There was one good business move. Festival Records bought four thousand albums for sale in Australia. The Rodriguez cult was on its way. The bootleggers were ready to make **Cold Fact** a continuous seller down under.

Things got strange in 1976 when two thousand copies of **Cold Fact** were sold from a New York warehouse to an Australian importer. Then the album hit the Australian album charts and remained there for fifty-five weeks. Rodriguez was a cult star for most of the 1970s down under.

In 1978 Blue Goose Music leased the album from RCA. In May 1978 it was released with a new catalogue number and then re-issued in 1986 by BMG. The point is that Rodriguez had a small, but loyal, following down under. He was not under the radar. His albums sold in respectable numbers. He also had major label releases. Where was the money?

In April 1991 the South African company, Teal Trutone, re-issued **Cold Fact** in CD, LP and cassette format. The use of an orange circle on the CD cover let the listener know that the CD featured the hits: "I Wonder," "Sugar Man" and "Inner City Blues."

The reissues continued in the mid-1990s when **Cold Fact** was released with the ubiquitous moniker "Made In The UK."

The Rodrigologists went nuts. The albums in their various formats were filled with mistakes, wrong track listings, and incorrect musicians. You name it and the mistake was made. Brian Currin, one of the original Rodrigologists, stepped in to correct these travesties. Currin contacted

Mike Theodore who provided key information, he used one of his concert photos from 2001 and all mistakes were rectified. In the **South African Rock Digest**, number 165 for August 5th 2002, Currin explains the process. It is another example of the thanks everyone owes the South African Rodrigologists.

Much of Rodriguez' success is due to collectors. The record geeks who searched for other Rodriguez type artists found Jeff Becoat, Jeff Monn, Paul Martin, Vashti Bunyon and Karen Dalton among others. The CD releases of these artists created small cult followings. There are many other Rodriguez' out there," psych music critic, Neil Skok remarked. "I can give you a list. There is a never-ending supply of singer-songwriters/ underground acts that never got their due. There are a thousand Rodriguez.'" This is the beauty of the Rodriguez story. His musical genius was discovered allowing him to go back on the road where and when he desires. While a third album is a possibility, it will be at his discretion with his total control. This is the power that **Searching For Sugar Man** has upon his art and career. In South Africa, when he arrived for a series of concerts, he was not only alive but still talented, Konny Rodriguez said: "Dead men don't tour." A South African television station produced an hour special, "Dead Man Walking," that looked deeply into the Rodriguez story.

What makes the South African TV special important is that it lays out much of the material that was not a part of **Searching For Sugar Man**. There is more of Sixto Rodriguez in this TV show than in the documentary. The viewer is able to listen as the Sugar Man's articulates his frustrations with being ignored for forty years in the music business. There is a graciousness, a sense of humor and a self-deprecating tone to Rodriguez' comments. Dead Man Walking highlights the Sugar Man as not only an exceptional human being but one of most interesting writers in the rock music realm.

CAMPAIGN POSTER FOR MAYOR, 2013

chapter

NINETEEN

THE MYTH AND REALITY OF DEAD MAN WALKING

**"THE ONE DUTY WE OWE OUR HISTORY IS
TO REWRITE IT." OSCAR WILDE**

"DEAD MEN DON'T TOUR." KONNY RODRIGUEZ

When Sixto Rodriguez walked out on stage in Cape Town in 1998 his wife, Konny, remarked: "Dead men don't tour." The myth and realities of Sixto Rodriguez shone brightly for a time in South Africa. Then it was back to rehabbing Detroit homes. It took another fourteen years for international fame and fortune to be bestowed upon Rodriguez. There is a myth and a reality to dead man walking. The term comes from a South African TV show "Dead Men Don't Tour," which premiered on July 5, 1998 on SA television. It was fifty-two minutes of exquisite Rodriguez music interspersed with commentary.

IN LONDON: DEAD MAN WALKING SPECULATION

In a July 2012 article by Jonathan Dean, in the **London Sunday Times**, the ubiquitous title: "Dead Man Walking," suggested the continued myths surrounding Sixto Rodriguez. Dean speculated on how important it was for the Sugar Man to perform his songs: "He had waited half his life to tell that to people who will listen....He's more alive than he has ever been. That's the madness."

Like most U. K. aficionados, Dean was intrigued by the story. "They all thought he was dead," Dean wrote. "That's the madness, he was in Detroit all along, gutting houses when he should have been playing stadiums." That says it all. There was no mystery. The reality was that Sixto Rodriguez was a hard working single father raising three children. That was the story but no one could forget the music.

As **Searching For Sugar Man** brought Rodriguez into the media eye, he was asked why he hadn't been heard from in forty years. He replied: "In the music business there are no guarantees, there's a lot of rejection, criticism and disappointment."

When Dean met Rodriguez in London at the height of the publicity blitz over **Searching For Sugar Man**, he found Rodriguez calm, rationale and puzzled by the acclaim. When he asked the Sugar Man about his South African fame, Rodriguez characteristically replied: "It was a surprise."

SOUTH AFRICANS ON DEAD MAN WALKING

The catalyst to dead man walking came from Stephen "Sugar" Segerman's hardwork. Without Segerman's persistence, the Sugar Man might be a forgotten Detroit musician.

The half million **Cold Fact** albums sold in South Africa is a major miracle. The white South African populations increased from 3.8 million in 1970 to almost five million by 1990. Rodriguez' sales were an unprecedented achievement in a nation just opening its commercial arms to rock and roll.

The interview with London reporter, Jonathan Dean, took place with Konny Rodriguez standing next to her husband. She received virtually no press mention, but she was in the mix.

When Dean remarked that Clarence Avant appeared "threatening," Rodriguez smiled. He said: "Good one. Yeah! All right man." Then as the interview ends Konny asks Dean to stand with Rodriguez for a picture. The Sugar Man and his wife were still reacting to the newfound fame.

On his sudden fame, Rodriguez remarked to Dean: "I didn't feel lost, I knew exactly where I was." That is a good lesson for all of us.

RODRIGUEZ AND BOB SIMON SIT DOWN FOR 60 MINUTES

When 60 Minutes' host, Bob Simon, sat down with Rodriguez, the Sugar Man's eloquence was spellbinding. When Simon asked about how Rodriguez felt about his albums not selling, he replied: "I was too disappointed to be disappointed." Rodriguez sat strumming his guitar on a bar stool in the Old Miami. Simon looked comfortable, if a bit detached. Rodriguez does that to you.

Then Simon talked about Rodriguez' songs labeling these tunes the soundtrack for the South African anti-apartheid revolution. The Sugar Man was visibly uncomfortable. He doesn't like talking about himself. He doesn't like praise. He doesn't consider himself a pathfinder. If the songs found success, Rodriguez has told people, it is due to the words. He is simply the person who channels those thoughts onto paper. He suggests that there is a higher authority guiding his work.

On the subject of day laboring and subsistence living, Rodriguez had some thoughts. "Poor doesn't mean dirty and poor doesn't mean stupid." Rodriguez said. The Dead Man Walking had firm opinions. The October 7, 2012 60 Minutes interview with Bob Simon was a catalyst to Rodriguez' increased economic wellbeing. He was finally making money. The interview continued.

His daughter, Regan, remarked that he was giving his money away. She said it made him feel good. Simon asked: "You don't think he's gonna go out there and buy a Ferrari?" Regan responded: "I don't see him buying a Ferrari—if anything, I'm hoping he will get a new pair of glasses."

When the 60 Minutes interview concluded, Bob Simon watched with abject curiosity as the locals greeted Rodriguez. It was 2012, and he still had a small degree of anonymity. That would soon end. The Dead Man Walking was alive hiding out from hoards of well-wishers. Everyone wanted a piece of Rodriguez.

The South African television program "Dead Men Don't Tour," explains the amazing parameters surrounding Rodriguez' career. This 1998 TV documentary shown in South Africa on July 5, 2001 on SABC 3 at 9:30 p.m., directed by Tonia Selley, is a tribute to his artistry, as well as his gracious personality.

His daughter, Eva, used the phrase, "Dead Men Don't Tour," as did his wife, Konny, to emphasize that Sixto Rodriguez was well and alive. He was far from a dead man either personally or artistically.

The myths and realities of Rodriguez' career continue to play out. He is a mysterious and Shaman type personality who remains humble and oblivious to his superstar status. There is still a great deal to come from Sixto Rodriguez. There is talk of a third album, and perhaps a live album. The soundtrack for **Searching For Sugar Man** continues to sell in large numbers. As Rodriguez prepared to tour Australia in late 2014, he had three songs on the charts down under. Not bad for a guy who hasn't released an album in forty-plus years.

THE DEAD MEN DON'T TOUR TV SPECIAL: ANOTHER SIDE OF RODRIGUEZ

The South African TV special, "Dead Men Don't Tour," is a fifty-five minute documentary with musical accompaniment from Big Sky. The numerous interviews and concert footage suggests the triumphant level of the Sugar Man's initial South African concerts.

The choice of Big Sky to back Rodriguez was a brilliant one. The band, organized by Steve Louw, had three South African hits in their debut album, **Waiting For The Dawn**. They could play American style rock and roll better than any South African group. They are featured in the documentary giving the viewer a sense of the Sugar Man's dramatic South African concerts. To the locals, he was: "The Dead Man Walking."

The interviews with Stephen "Sugar" Segerman and Craig Bartholomew-Strydom provide insight into the Rodriguez phenomenon. There is live footage from concerts in Durban, Pretoria and the Blues Room in Johannesburg. There is a younger Rodriguez in this beautiful South African countryside. Some of the footage from this South African documentary found its way into **Searching For Sugar Man**.

During the interviews, while the 1998 tour was ongoing, there was a great deal of comment about the past. Stephen "Sugar" Segerman talks of discovering the music while he was serving in the military in Pretoria. Mad Andy Harrod pointed out that he wanted Rodriguez' material re-released in South Africa. It was. He was instrumental in that process.

Craig Bartholomew-Strydom, remarked: "I spent nine months trying to get hold of Rodriguez, I called PolyGram and they had no idea how to get hold of him." When Roger Armstrong heard about Craig Bartholomew-Strydom, he instructed management at his company, Ace Records, to release Mike Theodore's phone number. When Bartholomew-

Strydom called Theodore that ended the Rodriguez mystery. He was well and alive in Detroit. The first phone call to Rodriguez appears to be from Bartholomew-Strydom. Then Segerman talked to Eva Koller Rodriguez. She had her father call Segerman. That paved the way for the triumphant 1998 South African concerts.

"I was expecting eight hundred seaters," Rodriguez remarked of the tour. His daughter, Sandra Kennedy Rodriguez, observed: "It was shocking." His family couldn't believe the reception. Neither could Rodriguez. He said that he had trouble putting his opinions in words. "I consider myself a writer, I try to write to the core of it," Rodriguez said.

"I owe them so much," Rodriguez said of his 1998 South African audience. One of the benefits of his South African tour was his back up band, Big Sky. The band had played his music for decades. They were exquisite and effortless. The lead guitar riffs were the best in his show complimenting Rodriguez' excellent guitar work.

Big Sky is made up of the best South African musicians. Willem Moller's electric guitar filled in all of Rodriguez' original lines. Russel Taylor on keyboards displayed a controlled Jerry Lee Lewis swagger, Reuben Samuels, drums and percussion, provided the understated sound that made the songs from **Cold Fact** and **Coming From Reality** sound like they were recently recorded. Graeme Currie's electric bass on "I Wonder," made it as good as the original. The band's final member, Tonia Selley, provided backup vocals and percussion. Big Sky is a rare band. They are an in the front headliner who quietly backed the Sugar Man.

During the documentary, Segerman talks at length about the myths. They were retold with a veracity few could believe. Fortunately, Stephen "Sugar" Segerman was on the case.

SIXTO AND KONNEY IN SOUTH AFRICA

Konny Rodriguez: "He had played for too many people in Detroit for free. He was taken advantage of."

During the South African tour, he met some construction people. The Sugar Man was in his element. He pointed out the pride that he had in rehabbing homes. This humble man, who they worshipped, stunned the South Africans. He was a hero to them. Rodriguez let them know that he was just a guy.

Sixto Rodriguez: "Now that this is happening in 1998, it is incredible."

When Rodriguez went on stage, he stood for ten minutes staring at the audience. He was happy. They were ecstatic. He told the audience: "Thanks for keeping me alive."

Sixto Rodriguez: "I am a musician, I am political in a sense that these issues are not going to disappear unless something is done about it."

On his South African concerts, Rodriguez said: "It's the international language. It's amazing that in the four rehearsals, each time we played it improved. In Durban the band was fine we jammed. When Martin Luther King said he went to the mountain, I've been to the ocean."

Big Sky performed some jazz jams that Rodriguez loved. In "Climb Up On My Music," Big Sky's jazz instrumentals took the song to new heights. The piano solo had a mild Jerry Lee Lewis touch that created a new version.

"He's Gandhi with a guitar, " Craig Bartholomew Strydom continued. "His lyrics were a precursor to Generation X."

Sixto Rodriguez: "I write new music. I go to shows. I see other artists. Am I the same person who came from the airport? I don't think so."

In one of the TV clips he is wearing a tuxedo. This is a South African show at the elegant Blues Room. Not only does Rodriguez have a tuxedo on, he is resplendent in a bow tie. The blue tux sets off his voice in a romantic manner. This is a Rodriguez no one has seen, he is comfortable with it. This is the beauty of Sixto Rodriguez. He can adjust to anything, anywhere, anytime. He can fit into any situation. It is a revealing clip.

The Dead Men Don't Tour analogy is one of the most creative myth making devices. The problem is that with Sixto Rodriguez there is an elusive element of reality. The 1998 South African tour benefitted from Brian Currin's tour diary. I have rewritten it here. But the greater bulk of the material can be viewed on http://sugarman.org/tourdiary.html#tour1

The highlights from the 1998 South African tour were many. The list below suggests some of the important ones.

Early February 1998: The final negotiations for a two-week South African tour are completed. In conversation with Stephen "Sugar" Segerman either before the tour or while on tour, Rodriguez revealed that he did not own a CD player. He did have a reel-to-reel player and he used that to play **Cold Fact**.

11th February 1998: Segerman telephones his fellow Rodrigologists Brian Currin and Craig Bartholomew-Strydom that Rodriguez is on his way. They are ecstatic. They also begin the preparations for his arrival and the concerts. The most important aspect of the South African Rodrigologists is that they want him to be comfortable as well as having a positive concert experience.

12th February 7.20 A. M.: Radio Good Hope almost shouts out: "Rodriguez is coming to South Africa!" "I Wonder" fills the airwaves. Listeners flood the station with every form of communication. The interest in Rodriguez' appearance is more than anyone expected. It is like he is coming back from the dead. When a limousine pulls up to pick up the Sugar Man and his family at the airport, he smiles. Times have changed.

16th February: There is still skepticism. Is this the real Rodriguez? The Cape Town press confirms the local concerts. There are still those who doubt it.

17th February: When an article appears in **The Star** in Johannesburg, there is some reasonable assurance that the real Rodriguez has arrived. There is still skepticism from the local media and record executives. Tickets sell out in hours.

19th February: Rainbow Productions turns out the key publicity. It appears that there was some help from Londoners associated with Rodriguez. Posters are tacked up in cities outside of Cape Town where Rodriquez is scheduled to appear. They vanish and some are put up for sale. Most of the posters are brought to the concerts to be signed.

20th February: There is an excellent and rather lengthy Interview in the **Mail & Guardian** by Craig Bartholomew-Strydom. He spoke with Rodriguez by phone and the revelations were important to the growing Sugar Man's following. There is a certain amount of humor in the early stages of the interview as Rodriguez takes charge by asking many questions. Finally, Bartholomew-Strydom says: "Hey, who's doing this interview?"

25th February: The posters advertising the Cape Town concerts around Cape Town quickly disappear. They are taken down by Rodriguez' fans who bring them to the concerts for the Sugar Man to sign.

28th February: The Old Mutual District welcomes Sixto Rodriguez and his music to South Africa. Source: **The Saturday Paper**, Natal, 28th February 1998 and **The Star** Johannesburg.

2nd March: Stephen "Sugar" Segerman contacts the press, radio and television and anyone else who will listen. He explains that Rodriguez and his family have left Detroit for a two week, six concerts South African tour. In a press release, Zev Eizik is described as Rodriguez' manger. Zev is also a family friend. A close acquaintance of Midnight Oil, Eizik is also a respected, highly trained, manger working for more than thirty years for Australian Concert Entertainment. Rodriguez, along with his wife, Konny, and his daughters were in their guesthouse in Camps Bay. Stephen "Sugar" Segerman was invited to interview them. When he walked in the door, Rodriguez put out his and said: "Hello Sugar." It was a magic moment. The respect and admiration that Segerman accorded Rodriguez impressed the Sugar Man and they quickly became close friends.

3rd and 4th **March**: The Milestones Studio in Cape Town is the site of Rodriguez' rehearsals. The Milestones Studio opened in 1987 and it is the premier recording facility in South Africa. The number of rehearsals is not announced. The shows are so tight that one can guess there were a number of rehearsals.

5th **March:** This is a busy day for the Sugar Man. It is a press day beginning with a 7 A. M. interview on the Breakfast Club TV Program on SABC 2. During that evening at 7:30 P.M. Rodriguez is the guest of Front Row TV (MNET). He performs a beautiful acoustic version of "I Wonder."

6th March: After a noon rehearsal at the Velodrome in which Rodriguez sings some of the lyrics from "A Most Disgusting Song," they rehearse "Sandrevan Lullaby-Lifestyles." It is not known how the band or Rodriguez reacted to rehearsing this song. He did not perform it at the concert. At 9:30 P. M. Rodriguez strides out on stage. The tour has begun to resounding applause and a media coronation. It is at the Bellville Velodrome that Rodriguez rekindles his long dormant career.

- **7**[th] **March:** The second show at the Bellville, Velodrome is much tighter than the opening performance. The previous night the crowd was pleased and then it turned to resounding applause for the second show. The set list for Rodriguez' first South Africa appearances Cape Town included: (This set list is on the Internet from Big Sky)
- I Wonder
- Only Good For Conversation
- Can't Get Away
- Crucify Your Mind
- Jane S. Piddy
- To Whom It May Concern
- Like Janis
- Inner City Blues
- Street Boy

- Halfway Up The Stairs
- I Think Of You
- Rich Folks Hoax
- Climb Up On My Music
- **ENCORES:**
- Sugar Man
- Establishment Blues
- Forget It

Note: This set list was the major one, there were some minor variations to some shows.

9th March: The Standard Bank Arena in Johannesburg was the site of the third concert with Big Sky's leader, Steve Louw, creating the tightest set of the tour in a show that drew the loudest applause. Big Sky also performed their hits "Waiting For Dawn," "Another Country" and "Get Down Mr. Green."

10th to 13th March: The fourth concert continues at the Standard Bank Arena in Johannesburg. Then Rodriguez has something of an itinerant schedule. He appears briefly at the Allenby Campus in Bramley where he practiced for forthcoming shows. Then he arrived for a student question session. He answered a wide variety of intriguing questions, and he performed three songs. He also does a second show at the Standard Bank Arena on March 11. He also performs at the Carousel in Pretoria. The Village Green in Durban on March 13th completes the 1998 South African tour.

15th March: The tour ends and Rodriguez is lauded in the press, on radio and television and most significantly in the raucous reception from the sold out concerts. He enjoys himself and can't believe the reception.

23rd March: Rodriguez writes from Detroit that he is home and he is thankful to South Africa. He is particularly thankful to the Rodrigologists led by Stephen "Sugar" Segerman and Craig Bartholomew-Strydom. They made the Sugar Man's trip the highlight of his life.

See Brian Currin's tour diary for a complete run down on the 1998 tour at http://rodriguezandbigsky.com/category/tour-diary/

The work of Brian Currin and Stephen "Sugar" Segerman to archive Rodriguez' 1998 South African tour keeps alive historical material that otherwise might have been lost to posterity.

THE 1998 SOUTH AFRICAN SHOWS AND WHAT THEY TELL US

The South African TV special contains clips of the local shows. They are an example of his continued stage presence. They also explode the Harry Balk myth that Rodriguez didn't perform very well. He was dynamite on stage. The audiences listened with rapt attention.

The clip of his daughters talking about how happy they were for their father suggests the sweet moments that took place during the concerts. When he performed "Sugar Man" the South African audiences were alive and singing the words with him.

As Stephen "Sugar" Segerman talks about the myths, he recalls that people weren't sure that it was Rodriguez appearing in South Africa. Until the day of the first concert he assured everyone it was the real Rodriguez. Konny Rodriguez is featured in the TV documentary, and she points out his rehabbing in the housing industry is a job he enjoyed. There is a marvelous clip of Rodriguez talking with home rehab workers.

During the course of the documentary, Konny points out how she met Sixto on campus at Wayne State University, and she talks about how little the Sugar man cared for money. "He is not at all materialistic," Konny continued. "He places his values on other things."

Konny appears to be as thankful as the Sugar Man for this 1998 brief career resurgence. He goes into a native neighborhood with his guitar and while talking to the people he performs a few songs. He loves South Africa. The young people in the audience from sixteen to twenty three sing along with the Sugar Man. They know the lyrics. There is no generation gap with his music.

The number of album signings and autograph sessions in 1998 would have tired out any artist. Rodriguez embraced it. "I'm an everyday person, I'm a musician," Rodriguez continued. "Whatever is wrong with the system can be corrected."

His children have also learned from their father. Sandra Kennedy Rodriguez: "He taught me how to fight for my rights." Another daughter, Regan, is a bright, forward thinking young girl now with a family, but she retains all of the Sugar Man's positive values. She also manages his career with panache.

Sixto Rodriguez: "Stop the violence, accept peace." This was a statement from the stage in South Africa, as he began "The Establishment Blues."

Big Sky is featured in the TV special and Rodriguez said he was amazed that with just four rehearsals they were flawless. They were because they had played his material from the beginning of their careers. One band member wears a Ramones t-shirt and remarks that Rodriguez was "a precursor to Generation X's music."

A clip of "Climb Up On My Music," with Rodriguez wearing a tuxedo, is a rare insight into his ability to perform in any venue. Once again Harry Balk and the naysayers are wrong, Sixto Rodriguez is a consummate professional and seasoned performer. One observer remarked: "Rodriguez was a South African cult and that was fortunate." Whatever South Africans thought, none of it altered the Rodriguez persona. He was the same person. Humble! Articulate! Intelligent! Thoughtful! A poet!

Sixto Rodriguez: "Am I the same person that came here?" He isn't. He sees the future. It would just take another fourteen years for the acclaim to come rolling in like a ball of thunder. The 1998 TV documentary closes with "Forget It" and shots of Rodriguez in a tuxedo at the upscale Blues Room. It is a fitting tribute to an enormous talent that was on the precipice of rediscovery.

THE RODRIGUEZ ALBUMS RESULTING
FROM THE 1998 SOUTH AFRICAN TOUR

One of the byproducts of the 1998 South African tour was a new, limited edition Rodriguez album. On March 19th 1998, he recorded **Live Fact** with Big Sky. This LP suggests that Rodriguez was eager to get back into the studio. The problem is that he didn't have new songs. Prior to his South African tour, he made an abortive attempt to record a third album. Mike Theodore has the musical tracks. They are waiting for the words. But the South African album was an immediate fan favorite. The **Live Fact** LP helped to erase Rodriguez' frustration of not having songs for a third LP.

The "Dead Men Don't Tour" comment by Konny Rodriguez tells it all. The mystery of Sixto Rodriguez continued after his 1998 South African tour. The TV special "Dead Man Walking" goes a long way toward pointing out how much popular culture depends upon myth. Reality is not a welcome part of the rock and roll equation. The next volume in this Rodriguez biography concentrates on the **Coming From Reality** album and the seminal role of Steve Rowland. He brought the Sugar Man into another producing dimension.

WATCHING DEAD MEN DON'T TOUR

The **Dead Men Don't Tour** TV special broadcast on South African channel SABC 3 offers some insights into the Rodriguez mystique as the special begins with a marvelous rendition of "I Wonder." The fifty-six year old Rodriguez is handsome, beautifully dressed and in top form on stage. It is almost tragic to watch this brilliant entertainer and realize that he has been in Detroit with limited success.

What this documentary demonstrates is that Sixto Rodriguez not only had his talent intact, but his 1998 South African tour was a major triumph. The question is: Why did it take fourteen more years for the Rodriguez phenomenon to take hold? The trademark Rodriguez hat, the cool boots, the easy stage manner suggests a consummate professional. Where was the music industry?

There is almost a rap cadence to Rodriguez' vocals but they are so effortless and professional it is amazing. "I was expecting eight hundred seaters," Rodriguez said of the South African shows. Tonia Selley directed the special and the music also included a version of "Inner City blues" recorded on the Paris streets on June 12, 2009. This documentary is almost as eye opening as **Searching For Sugar Man** and it is another example of his enormous talent. The best is yet to come.

chapter

TWENTY

RODRIGUEZ ON RODRIGUEZ: THE YOU TUBE MUSICAL AND INTERVIEW HISTORY

"ONE MUST LIVE LIKE A BOURGEOIS AND THINK LIKE A DEMIGOD." GUSTAVE FLAUBERT

"I LIVE IN MY IMAGINATION." JAMES ELLROY

"THE ACTOR TONY CURTIS ONCE TOLD ME THAT FAME IS AN OCCUPATION IN ITSELF." BOB DYLAN

Sixto Rodriguez lives a private life. He is at home in the Cass Corridor. He emerges predominantly through his art. That art is his music. Much of the controversy surrounding Rodriguez' life and career centers around the notion that he was a major writer of significant rock songs. His two albums remain legendary. Some critics see him as a phenomenon created by a documentary. Others view the Sugar Man as an icon. The truth is probably somewhere in the middle.

Unlike many rock musicians, Sixto Rodriguez never allowed his writing, his performing and his career to take precedence over his family. He remains a strong family man. He continues to be tied to the intellectual perks of the Cass Corridor. He remains true to his personal vision of art and music.

THE SUGAR MAN SHOULD HAVE THE FINAL WORD

The final word on Sixto Rodriguez should come from the Sugar Man. In the aftermath of the success of **Searching For Sugar Man**, he gave out a number of candid, insightful interviews. By 2015 those media events came to an end. The fame, the money, the power and the constant media attention didn't change the Sugar Man. What happened is that fame intruded upon Rodriguez' privacy. With grace and humility, he retreated from the media fishbowl.

There are dozens of Rodriguez performances caught on camera prior to **Searching For Sugar Man**. These video clips celebrate his performing genius. They also demonstrate that he can hold an audience in the palm of his hand.

There are some interviews and musical spots prior to the thunderous popularity of **Searching For Sugar Man**. The laid back, charismatic laced interviews were prominent once Rodriguez signed with Light In The Attic. They provided the forums, the publicity and the atmosphere that began his comeback.

On June 23, 2009 a video clip from Seattle's Triple Door featuring Rodriguez performing "I Wonder" suggests his stage presence and performing genius. This was prior to the fame generated by **Searching For Sugar Man**. There was by 2009 the cult of Sixto Rodriguez.

Jonathan Zwickel of the **Seattle Times** pointed out Rodriguez' career revival was due to LITA. At the same time, major media outlets, NPR, **Spin** and **Rolling Stone** mentioned Rodriguez. Zwickel interviewed Rodriguez by phone from his home in Detroit, and like everyone else marveled at the music. When he asked the Sugar Man about his strange journey back to musical prominence, Rodriguez said: "There's no blueprint for music-rock 'n' roll, my rags to riches story kinda stuff. But I must say, it's better that it wasn't riches to rags, because that would be an even worse story."

As Zwickel continued his phone conversation, Rodriguez veered away from music for a moment. He reflected on the event that influenced his writing and his career. One event stood out the assassination of President John F. Kennedy.

Sixto Rodriguez: "The background at the time was My Lai, Kent State, the assassination of Kennedy, the Zapruder film. I consider myself a political musician, as opposed to boy-girl love songs. I have a lot of confidence in the creative part of it."

That extensive explanation goes a long way to understanding the Sugar Man's writing and the content that is included in his ubiquitous tunes. After a series of appearances in 2009, Rodriguez was asked about his future. He replied: "If you have a sock, and it's of one color, and it gets a hole and you're sewing it with a thread of another color, and it gets so many holes that it's completely covered with other colors, the question is, 'is that the same sock?" Rodriguez would find out three years later when **Searching For Sugar Man** created a mini-industry for his music. The Zwickel interview demonstrated that he was back as an entertainer.

In June 2009 a clip of Rodriguez at London's Barbican presents a vision of the Sugar Man before fame intruded on his privacy. "I'm not old, I'm ancient," Rodriguez said. "Either you're alive or you are not. I am not getting old. I am not getting dead," Rodriguez joked. His patter ends and he performs a cover of Frank Sinatra's "I'm Gonna' Live Until I Die." It is a rare insight into a non-Rodriguez composed song, as he performs an encore for an enthralled London audience.

The notion that Rodriguez didn't perform until **Searching For Sugar Man** burst on the scene is another myth. He was performing in and around Detroit for almost four decades. A good example is when he appeared at Donovan's Pub on November 2, 2009 in a benefit concert. There is a marvelous video of "Forget It" on You Tube from the Donovan's Pub show, as well as a heart felt acoustic "I Think Of You." He was also a regular at the Detroit Street Fair performing there in 2009.

A TELLING INTERVIEW WITH A LONDON JOURNALIST

In July 2012 in the wake of **Searching For Sugar Man's** success, Rodriguez sat down for interviews with a number of journalists. One interview stands out for its insight into the Sugar Man. Rodriguez was in London in the Sony offices. The **London Guardian** sent over Killian Fox for an in-depth profile.

As Rodriguez sat down, Fox noticed his stylish black suit, his black-rimmed jeweled glasses and his slumping shoulders holding a guitar. She decided that he was the archetypical cool musician. He surprised her by asking everything about her life. Rodriguez disarmed and charmed her.

"It's just a typical rags to riches story," Rodriguez continued. "Better that way than riches-to-rags." This is typical Sixto Rodriguez self-effacing humor. He was easy to interview. He also had a strong commitment to touring. "We're going to LA after London, and we got a call to do Australia next spring," Rodriguez concluded.

When Fox asked about his future, Rodriguez said: "I haven't reached the plateau yet. I feel fit and ready." He was as for the next two and a half years he was regularly on the road. The nice thing is he is able to perform where and when he wants. It just took forty years to get to that position.

THE 2012-2014 INTERVIEWS AND PERFORMANCES

The 2012 to 2014 interviews offer rare insight into Rodriguez warm and humble personality. He is a marvelous entertainer and an even better interview.

Rodriguez was forthcoming with the media. When he appeared on a Detroit TV show in July 2012, The Weekly Comet, he performed "Sugar Man" accompanied by his acoustic guitar. It was a laid back and friendly interview with Malik Bendjelloul sitting next to him smiling.

The Hollywood Reporter presented a behind the scenes look at **Searching For Sugar Man** with Rodriguez and Bendjelloul talking at length about the Oscar winning documentary. The use of clips set the tone for intense media interest. Rodriguez talks about his discussion concerning celebrity with Alec Baldwin and how it impacted his privacy. Soon, Baldwin informed Rodriguez, he would experience the same phenomenon. He did. There is continued myth about Rodriguez and his escape from reality. The best way to analyze Sixto Rodriguez is with his own words. There are a number of interesting You Tube interviews that are sincere and forthcoming from the Sugar Man. It is also his moments with reporters when he relaxes that his personal genius shines through. The list below is not scientific; it is simply my favorite You Tube interviews and music. From these you will see the essence of an artist with integrity, humility and a caring personality.

INTERESTING SIXTO RODRIGUEZ YOU TUBE INTERVIEWS AND MUSIC

1. **"RODRIGUEZ AND THE RIGORS OF FAME AT SEVENTY."** THIS FEBRUARY 2013 INTERVIEW IS THE RESULT OF **SEARCHING FOR SUGAR MAN'S SUCCESS**. IT IS CANDID AND FORTHCOMING.

2. **"OSCAR WINNER MALIK BENDJELLOUL AND SIXTO RODRIGUEZ ON THE WEEKLY COMET."** THIS IS A RELAXED INTERVIEW ON A DETROIT TV PROGRAM. RODRIGUEZ PERFORMS "SUGAR MAN."

3. **"RODRIGUEZ INTERVIEW."** THIS A MARCH 2013 INTERVIEW FROM, "SWAY IN THE MORNING," A NEW ZEALAND TV SHOW. RODRIGUEZ GRACIOUSLY MEETS AND SHAKES HANDS WITH A GROUP OF SOUTH AFRICAN FANS WHO NOW LIVE IN NEW ZEALAND. THE RECEPTION IS AMAZING, AS EVERYONE IN NEW ZEALAND KNOWS HIS MUSIC. THE LENGTHY INTERVIEW IS A TRIBUTE TO HIS TALENT. HE IS GRACIOUS AND HUBMLE IN THIS REVEALING FOUR MINUTE INTERVIEW. HE WAS ASKED ABOUT THE MONEY AND RODRIGUEZ COMMENTED WITH A SLY SMILE: "I THINK I COULD USE IT." THAT IS SIXTO RODRIGUEZ.

4. **"TIME OUT INTERVIEW: RODRIGUEZ (SUGAR MAN)."** THIS INTERVIEW FROM THE **NEW ZEALAND HERALD** USES A GREAT DEAL OF THE **SEARCHING FOR SUGAR MAN** MATERIAL. RODRIGUEZ IS COMFORTABLE AS HE TALKS ABOUT HIS LIFE AND CAREER.

5. **"SIXTO RODRIGUEZ IN BIRMINGHAM."** THIS IS A MARVELOUS THREE SONG CLIP FEATURING "RICH FOLKS HOAX," "STREET BOY" AND "SUGAR MAN."

6. **"RODRIGUEZ GLASTONBURY FESTIVAL 2013."** THIS IS FROM THE ENGLISH FESTIVAL AND THE RODRIGUEZ SONGS "ONLY GOOD FOR CONVERSATION," "CRUCIFY YOUR MIND/ LIKE JANIS," "I WONDER" AND "DEAD END STREET" ARE GREAT VIEWING AND LISTENING. BUT THAT IS JUST THE WARM UP, THE SUGAR MAN CONTINUES ON WITH A FULL SET OF THIRTEEN SONGS AND BY THE TIME HE ENDS WITH "FORGET IT," HE HAS MESMERIZED THE U. K. AUDIENCE. THIS IS AN HOUR OF RODRI-GUEZ YOU CAN'T GET ANYWHERE ELSE. DON'T MISS IT.

7. **"LIKE A ROLLING STONE"** THIS VERSION OF BOB DYLAN'S SONG IS THE BEST COVER EVER.

8. **"CRUCIFY YOUR MIND"** THIS IS THE LIVE VERSION WITH A TWENTY-FIVE PIECE ORCHESTRA FROM THE DAVID LETTER-MAN SHOW. AT THE END OF THE SHOW, LETTERMAN IS OBLIVI-OUS TO THE SUGAR MAN'S STORY. AS RODRIGUEZ OBSERVED "UNCLE SONY" KNEW HOW TO PUBLICIZE **SEARCHING FOR SUGAR MAN**.

9. **"I WONDER"** THIS IS A LIVE VERSION FROM SEATTLE WHICH WAS ON KEXP. THIS CLIP IS FROM A LIGHT IN THE ATTIC SHOW AT THE TRIPLE DOOR IN 2009. THE SUGAR MAN IS IN FINE VOICE.

10. **"CRUCIFY YOUR MIND"** THIS IS A LIVE VERSION FROM AUSTRALIA. IT SUGGESTS THAT THE SUGAR MAN STILL HAS IT IN CONCERT. IT IS FROM A SOLD OUT SHOW WITH A DIFFER-ENT CADENCE FOR THIS SONG AT THE FACTORY THEATER IN SYDNEY.

11. **"INNER CITY BLUES"** THIS IS A THREE MINUTE TWEN-TY-SECOND LIVE VERSION RECORDED JUNE 12, 2009 IN PARIS. IT IS A MARVELOUS PREQUEL TO SEARCHING FOR SUGAR MAN.

12. **"I'M GOING TO LIVE UNTIL I DIE"** THIS LIVE CLIP FROM AUSTRALIA DURING THE 2013 TOUR FEATURES RODRIGUEZ INTRODUCING THE SONG TO A RAUCOUS AND APPRECIATIVE CROWD. AT TIMES THE AUDIENCE IS LOUD AND UNWIELDLY. HE HANDLES THEM BEAUTIFULLY. THE UNUSUAL PART IS THAT RODRIGUEZ TALKS FOR MORE THAN TWO MINUTES BEFORE GO-ING INTO THE SONG. THE STRANGE PART IS THAT HIS VOCAL IS SUBDUED BUT THE CROWD IS NOT. THEY DO QUIET DOWN AS HE GETS INTO THE SONG. THE DRUNKEN CROWD MADE THIS A STRANGE YOU TUBE VIDEO. IT IS ONE THAT DEMONSTRATES

RODRIGUEZ IS A SHOW BUSINESS VETERAN WHO CONTROLS THE CONCERT VENUE.

13. **"THE ESTABLISHMENT BLUES"** THIS VERSION OF RODRIGUEZ' MOST POLITICAL SONG IS VERY UNIQUE AS IT IS FILMED INSIDE A BRICK STRUCTURE WITH A GREAT VIDEO OF RODRIGUEZ SINGING INTO AN OLD STYLE VERY DATED BUT COOL MICROPHONE WITH JUST AN ACOUSTIC GUITAR.

14. **"DEAD MEN DON'T TOUR-RODRIGUEZ IN SOUTH AFRICA 1998 (TV DOCUMENTARY)"** THIS IS A TV SPECIAL FROM SOUTH AFRICA'S SABC TV FOR A PROGRAM SHOWN ON JULY 5TH 1998. IT WAS UPLOADED BY ONE OF THE BAND MEMBERS WHO BACKED RODRIGUEZ. SHE IS TONIA MOLLER. SOME OF THE FOOTAGE FROM THIS SPECIAL WAS USED IN BENDJELLOUL'S DOCUMENTARY. THIS IS NOT ONLY A BRILLIANT DOCUMENTARY, IT PROVIDES THE FOUNDATION FOR **SEARCHING FOR SUGAR MAN.** THE INTERVIEWS WITH STEPHEN "SUGAR" SEGERMAN, CRAIG BARTHOLOMEW STRYDOM, ANDY HARROD AND A HOST OF OTHERS MAKES THE DOCUMENTARY A GOLD MINE. THE LIVE FOOTAGE IS INCREDIBLE. SIXTO IN HIS LATE FIFTIES IS A MONSTER LIVE ACT.

15. **"I WONDER"** THIS LIVE VERSION AT SAN FRANCISCO'S AMOEBA RECORD-CD STORE ON NOVEMBER 23, 2008 SHOWCASES THE SUGAR MAN'S TALENT BEFORE FAME AND FORTUNE CHANGED HIS LIFE.

16. **"I THINK OF YOU"** THERE IS NOTHING SPECIAL VISUALLY HERE. BUT IT IS NICE TO LISTEN TO THE TRACK WITH THE VIOLINS AND THE GREAT MIKE THEODORE ARRANGMENTS.

17. **"I WONDER"** THIS IS A VERSION FROM THE ROOTS & BLUES & BBQ FESTIVAL IN COLUMBIA MISSOURI WITH BACKING MUSICIANS FROM MEMBERS OF THE EDWARD SHARPE AND MAGNETIC ZEROS BAND. THE LARGE STAGE AND GIANT VIDEO SCREEN PROJECT RODRIGUEZ' TALENT TO A YOUNG, ENERGETIC AUDIENCE. THIS IS ONE OF THE MORE INTERESTING AND UNIQUE RODRIGUEZ PERFORMANCES. ONE GENERATION MEETS ANOTHER IN CONCERT AND THINGS GO SMOOTHLY. THIS TOOK PLACE ON SEPTEMBER 21, 2012.

18. **"I WONDER"** THIS IS A VERSION FROM LOS ANGELES' EL REY THEATER ON SEPTEMBER 28, 2012. STEVE ROWLAND WAS IN THE AUDIENCE AND BACK STAGE. HE RECALLED THE AUDI-

ENCES RAPT ATTENTION. THIS WAS ONE OF THE TENTH ANNI-
VERSARY CONCERTS FOR RODRIGEUEZ' LABEL LIGHT IN THE
ATTIC.

19. **RODRIGUEZ LIVE AT ZULU RECORDS** THIS WAS AN
APPEARANCE AT A VANCOUVER B. C. RECORD STORE. "SUGAR
MAN' PLAYED AS RODRIGUEZ CAME ON CAMERA. HE IS INTER-
VIEWED FOR A MOMENT AS HE SMILES AND ACKNOWLEDGES
THE AUDIENCE. THIS IS A RARE TEN-MINUTE CLIP. THE RODRI-
GUEZ PERSONA COMES THROUGH WITH CHARM AND GRACE.
HE CONNECTS AS ALWAYS WITH THE RAPT CROWD. HE IS ALSO
CANDID ABOUT INFLUENCES, HIS PAST AND THE FUTURE.

There are many You Tube Rodriguez clips and the number of his
appearances increases daily. It is a tribute to his talent and persistence
that his songs remain a part of the American cultural folklore. The best
is yet to come for Sixto Rodriguez.

Q MAGAZINE TALKS TO ARTISTS
ABOUT ALBUMS THAT CHANGED THEM

In April 2015 Q magazine published a short piece on the albums
that changed people's direction. Paolo Nutini remarked "I think I was
seventeen when I first heard music that really spoke to me and it was by
Sixto Rodriguez." Nutini, how a platinum selling solo artist, talked of
the "fantasy created" by the Sugar Man's music. Mike Theodore's string
arrangements caught Nutini's attention and said that they seemed to be
"hanging from a star."

Paolo Nutini summed up **Cold Fact:** "The record is like a painting. You see the Mona Lisa and hundreds of people see hundreds of
different things." That says it all about **Cold Fact**. Nutini is one of many
performers who have taken their cues from the Sugar Man.

EPILOGUE

"TELL US IN PLAIN WORDS." MOLLY BLOOM IN JAMES JOYCE'S ULYSSES

"I AM A SLAVE OF MY CHARACTERS. BUT NOT OF MY-SELF." GEORGES SIMENON

"OH! OH! SAYS THE LITTLE CRICKET, I AM NO MORE SORRY.
IT COSTS ME TOO DEAR TO SHINE IN THIS WORLD.
HOW MUCH I AM GOING TO LOVE MY DEEP RETREAT.
TO LIVE HAPPILY, LIVE HIDDEN."
JEAN-PIERRE CLARIS DE FLORIAN, 17TH CENTURY FRENCH POET

The French novelist Georges Simenon remarked that he was "a slave of my characters....But not of myself." Unwittingly, he could have been describing Sixto Rodriguez' songwriting. No one has analyzed why and how Rodriguez composed those beautiful, lyrically sophisticated songs that no one listened to in 1970-1971. Then suddenly in 2012 **Searching For Sugar Man** makes him a songwriting icon. Why did Rodriguez toil in obscurity for more than forty years? There are other concerns over royalties, songwriting copyrights, his mysterious family ties and his shy personal demeanor.

THE PERPLEXING QUESTIONS IN THE AFTERMATH
OF SEARCHING FOR SUGAR MAN

In the aftermath of **Searching For Sugar Man**, questions remain about Sixto Rodriguez. The most persistent one is the royalty issue. It is still unanswered. This is the first of two books on Sixto Rodriguez. What happened during the **Cold Fact** album didn't take place in a vacuum. The Sugar Man had a happy, productive life. One that was just fine without fame and fortune.

How did Detroit influence Rodriguez' art? How did his wives and family nurture his creativity? What role did his brief encounter with the music business play in his decision to leave the industry? What did the royalty question do to his psyche? Only the Sugar Man can answer these questions definitively. This book addresses those questions.

The irony is that **Cold Fact** is an album that didn't just flop commercially; it disappeared from the music radar. What does this tell us about the music industry? The answer is obvious. Without promotion an artist is doomed. It doesn't matter if you have a beautifully crafted set of songs. Your records sell platinum in South Africa and Australia. You never receive royalties. You don't know that you are famous. Then you find out these facts. When he did Rodriguez hired a lawyer who articulated his thoughts on past royalties.

Mark A. Levinsohn, Rodriguez' lawyer, said the Sugar man is "still keenly interested in finding out what happened all those years ago and where the money went."

One of the problems with the Rodriguez story is that virtually everyone interviewed is territorial. That is Rodriguez is their man, they created him, they provided the story, and they helped to bring him to international prominence. Segerman and Bartholomew-Strydom have written a book **Sugar Man: The Birth, Death And Resurrection of Sixto Rodriguez** from Bantam books in Australia. The books September 15, 2015 release comes as the authors are rumored to be writing, a Broadway stage play, as well as a feature film script. They are territorial about the Sugar Man and they don't like others who write about him. This is understandable; they brought him back to international acclaim.

This is a natural reaction from those close to Rodriguez and his music. They love him. They want to protect him. What I found is that everyone wants to segment the story. Some of his friends believe that South Africa and London is the apex of the tale. Others point to the Australian counterculture. Some suggest that his Detroit roots are all that is needed to understand the Sugar Man.

Rodriguez is neither pompous nor presumptuous. He is a private person with little concern about money. He often refuses to take credit for his brilliant songwriting. He is uncomfortable with praise. Those around him, particularly his daughters, have done a good job protecting him from the media hordes. Regan has his best interest at heart, and she deflects those who blow smoke at him. When he performed in New York at the Barclay Center in Brooklyn and later at New York's Radio City Music Hall, Rodriguez had to take Steve Rowland into the bathroom for a private discussion because a bilious Sony Record's executive wouldn't stop talking. Rodriguez is polite and suffers fools very well. But there is a limit. He is tired of people telling him he is the next big thing. He knew that forty years ago.

ASPECTS OF RODRIGUEZ' LIFE THAT NEED WORK

What was his Mexican family like? How did 1950s rock and roll influence his 1960s songwriting? His wives, his family and his friends know the answers. He needs to write a book as the numerous questions about his life and his art are intriguing ones. His daughter, Eva, is reportedly working on one about her father.

The role of Rodriguez' education has never been fully explored. He is an honors graduate of the Wayne State University philosophy program. He finished his degree taking classes in Colorado. That is another mystery that needs an in-depth explanation.

The work of producers Dennis Coffey, Mike Theodore and Steve Rowland is the key to the Sugar Man. These legendary producers need a future voice in his career. That remains a concrete cold fact.

THE RODRIGUEZ MYSTERY REMAINS

The Rodriguez mystery is the key element in understanding and interpreting **Searching For Sugar Man**. But does a Rodriguez mystery remain? It does. The few minutes that Rodriguez appears in Bendjelloul's documentary are like magic bullets. He lights a wood-burning stove. The eerie light shines off his face. One sees an artist. One sees a great man. One sees mystery.

There is no mystery about Sixto Rodriguez' talent. It is a unique one. When Bruce Springsteen said: "We learned more from a three minute record than we ever learned in school,' he unwittingly described Rodriguez. It is as if Rodriguez provides a secret or invisible history of America.

No one has written about Rodriguez' cover songs. In some concerts, when he interrupts the flow of tunes from **Cold Fact** or **Coming From Reality**, the audience screams for his signature album favorites. What do the cover songs tell us about Rodriguez? When he sings "Blue Suede Shoes," he pays tribute to Carl Perkins not Elvis Presley. As he covers "Whole Lot of Shakin' Going On," it is the Big Maybelle version, not Jerry Lee Lewis' that influences him. What does this tell us about Rodriguez? Plenty! He is a musical contrarian. He loves the obscure or unknown. This fits into his musical persona.

The mystery of the artists who cover Rodriquez is another intriguing aspect of his tale. Reggae musicians cover his songs; rappers can't get enough of his lyrics and music. The romantic performers love his words. The Indie crowd is mesmerized by his lyrical magic.

Rodriguez' music skewers the pompous and pretentious. He also has a way of cutting through the show business milieu that reduces many artists to a caricature of their sound. As Gary Puckett sang one song after another that sounded the same, other artists are encouraged to follow up with like sounding tunes. Their careers end prematurely. Rodriguez ignored this industry ploy. The Sugar Man loses himself in his music.

In June 2014 **The Hollywood Reporter** posed the question: "Where Is Sixto Rodriguez Today?" The answer, according to **THR**: "He lives in the same rundown Detroit neighborhood and even plays his trusty old, out of tune guitar." Nice writing. The problem is that it is not close to the truth. He has a number of guitars. Rodriguez' neighborhood is being gentrified. He has put up a new fence. He is fixing the dilapidated concrete steps leading into his house. Rumor has it that he is adding conveniences to the inside of his home. Heaven forbid! He is rumored to have a cell phone. He might even have cable TV. He has money. He has a happy life. He had all this before **Searching For Sugar Man** The media can't leave him alone. This explains his reluctance to conduct interviews and or have pictures taken. He no longer has his privacy.

The ream of newsprint devoted to Rodriguez is a mixed blessing. There is no end to the public fascination with the Sugar Man. This craft or the art that Rodriguez practices needs to be examined and understood in light of the times. Becoming a hit musician is a difficult process and somehow Rodriguez made the transition to stardom.

RODRIGUEZ THE POLITICIAN

In 1979, the Czech playwright, Vaclav Havel, was elected the president of his country. It seemed an impossible task for a poet-scholar to lead a nation. Rodriguez has conducted unsuccessful campaigns for Mayor of Detroit, and the City Council, as well as campaigns for state-wide electoral positions. He always had the right ideas about Detroit's future. He wants people to engage in philosophical and political reflection. He is adamant about reforming the corrupt bureaucracy. Like Havel, he could lead.

What makes Rodriguez politically significant is that his statements on issues impact Detroit politics. His music questions police authority, politicians who deceive, and he praises the blue-collar working class attempts to end Detroit' pillage by politicians. While he hasn't been successful running for public office, he has made a difference. He attacks the issues and people listen. That is the Sixto Rodriguez way.

Rodriguez is an existentialist employing images in his music embracing political reform. When he praised John Sinclair's risqué poetry, Rodriguez railed against censorship. When he sings of "young bloods" marching in the streets, he gives his support to youth politics. Long after the political values of the counterculture faded, Rodriguez continues to embrace this ethos. As the South African and Australian counterculture developed, his music was their guiding light. Rock music within the counterculture produced a softer, more sympathetic, South African democracy. In Australia, it freed the youth down under from the shackles of conformity. While Rodriguez won't take credit for the changes, his music was a contributing factor.

As a global counterculture emerged, the legend of Sixto Rodriguez grew. He became a symbol of the struggle against oppression. That is a symbol everywhere but in the United States. That is the tragedy of his career.

ANTI-APARTHEID AND RODRIGUEZ

One of the curious criticisms of Sixto Rodriguez is that he wasn't as strong an opponent of apartheid as **Searching For Sugar Man** suggested. This is, of course, nonsense. Education is one area that is used to enslave the native population. Rodriguez was critical of this ploy. From the first time that he performed in South Africa and appeared on various television and radio outlets, Rodriguez talked of education's importance. For every dollar spent on a black South African's education, there was six spent on a white South African. While Rodriguez didn't address this statistic, he did talk of equality in education. He made the case that apartheid enslaved.

In 1983, as South Africa's white government passed a new apartheid constitution, the seeds of discontent and revolution continued the inevitable march toward change. His music was an inspiration to protesters. By the time that white music protesters began to challenge apartheid, Rodriguez' music was two decades old.

RODRIGUEZ: THE PERSONALITY AND
THE GIGS SUCH AS THEY WERE

Unlike many celebrities, Sixto Rodriguez is frighteningly normal. While he has a reclusive side, he doesn't cut himself off from society. He has developed a phalanx of friends. He reads. He is political. He has a structured day-to-day lifestyle. He is also a musician who has remained working since 1971. He never left the business. Contrary to the message in **Searching For Sugar Man**, he continued to work when and where he could find a gig.

From the mid-1970s until 2012, Sixto Rodriguez sporadically performed Then surprisingly, **Searching For Sugar Man** brought fame and fortune. He remained the Sugar Man. He is conventional in an unconventional manner.

Located just a few blocks from the Cass Corridor, Rodriguez' Avery Street home is a warm place where he can hide from prying journalists and obsessed fans. It was not always this way. His interest in music and politics sustained his personality into his early seventies.

RODRIGUEZ' UNLIKELY INFLUENCE ON ROCK STARS

Since Sixto Rodriguez came to America's attention in 2012, he has had a whirlwind-touring schedule. Ironically, long before fame and fortune set in, Rodriguez influenced a number of rock stars. Dave Mathews grew up in South Africa listening to "Sugar Man." Now the Dave Matthews band is one of America's most popular acts.

Ironically, Matthews lives in Seattle's Fremont District not far from Light In The Attic's office. His band covers "Sugar Man" in concert. The large number of artists covering Rodriguez are diverse and multi-talented. These diverse artists include half a dozen reggae acts, Steve Rowland's Family Dogg, Susan Cowsill, Paolo Nutini and David Holmes among others.

When David Holmes recorded "Sugar Man" in April 2002, with the Free Association, Rodriguez was flown to New York to provide back up vocals for the lead singer Petra Jean Phillipson. It was Holmes' way of paying tribute to Rodriguez' talent.

Then the British press in 2003 jumped onto the Rodriguez bandwagon. Ben Thompson in the **London Telegraph** noted: "The growl backing vocals come from the song's author, the enigmatic and extravagantly talented singer-songwriter Sixto Rodriguez...." The remainder of this 2003 review recounts Rodriguez' inability to achieve commercial recognition. That is until David Holmes paid one hundred dollars for a copy of **Cold Fact** at London's Camden Town flea market. He listened and recorded "Sugar Man." The London journalist, Ben Thompson, was so smitten with Rodriguez' music that he called him in Detroit. Thompson and Rodriguez talked about the influence of drugs on Samuel Taylor Coleridge's **Rime Of The Ancient Mariner**. Thompson had never talked this deeply about literature with a rock artist. He was flummoxed by Rodriguez' intellect.

The Scottish rock star, Paolo Nutini, counts Rodriguez amongst his biggest influences. Since bursting onto the music scene in 2003, Nutini rose from performing at London's Bedford Pub to international stardom with the fourth best selling CD in 2014 and acclaim from all over the world.

Nutini knew of Rodriguez' music as early as 2002 and he appeared with him in 2007 at St. Andrews Hall in Detroit. They perform a version of "Sugar Man" with Nutini taking the lead vocals resplendent in a brown leather jacket. Why this clip wasn't used in **Searching For Sugar Man** remains a mystery. Nutini was on board the Rodriguez bandwagon long before his improbable fame and fortune.

In 2009 Nutini said: "He is my musical hero. Rodriguez stands alone. His voice is so moving it takes you to another place, and he has a gracefulness to his arrangements that I try to achieve when I write. We have met a few times and he said he bought my record and loved it. And when I got to sing with him in Detroit it was incredible."

When Nutini saw **Searching For Sugar Man** and listened to "I Wonder" Rodriguez' music became part of his act. The Sugar Man also performs Nutini's "Last Request."

Paolo Nutini: "Basically every person I spoke to about music, the second thing I would say would be about Rodriguez. Somehow that seemed to get back to him and we hung out a few times."

Then Rodriguez' management sent Nutini a video of Rodriguez on a train singing "Last Request." In 2012, when he was in London, Rodriguez asked Nutini to perform some songs with him at a small private members only club. After this experience, Nutini reflected on it.

Paolo Nutini: "The man is incredible, he really has heart. Everything about his music is amazing and really speaks to me. The beauty of it is the mystery of the man."

MUSICAL PHRASES AND A BIOGRAPHICAL LEGACY

One wonders why Sixto Rodriguez couldn't get rock and roll music out of its early 1970s rut? As Mike Theodore speculated, after watching him at the Sewer By the Sea: "When we walked in and heard the songs he was singing, and what he was writing. We had to record him. We had to make a deal for him. He's great. We said, this is it." Nothing happened. Then forty-two years later Theodore shows up in **Searching For Sugar Man**, perplexed as to why the Sugar Man wasn't a star. He was. It just took forty plus years for his musical phrases to establish his biographical legacy.

Detroit was a hotbed of musical experimentation and Rodriguez' lyrical brilliance attests to this influence. The Sugar Man's lack of lyrical inhibition is an important aspect of his talent. In "Sugar Man," Rodriguez sings: "Silver magic ships you carry. Jumpers, coke, sweet Mary Jane." That sums up a part of the 1960s in a few brilliant words. So powerful is the effect of the songs that the bookings remain constant and the demand for a third album is a part of the Sugar Man's daily life. Time will tell.

RODRIGUEZ AND THE CONSCIOUSNESS OF ADJUSTMENT

What is consciousness? It is the awareness of one's surroundings, shared feelings and beliefs, as well as an awareness of issues. Rodriguez in his early years talked at length about consciousness. He learned about consciousness in a philosophy course. He realized that consciousness was about his brain's functions. That intrigued the Sugar Man.

It is this concern with consciousness that has prompted Rodriguez' skeptical view of organized religion. He is a religious man who doesn't practice. He sees organized religion as one of the world's great problems. That is the beauty of the Sugar Man. He is strong in his beliefs and firm in his convictions. That is what doomed his music. He is independent. He will do it his way. That is Sixto Rodriguez' consciousness. Despite some paranoia over the blows that the music industry dealt his career, he remains true to his original vision. There is a reason. His mind is one of continual consciousness, and this helps the Sugar Man cope with his surroundings.

Consciousness to reach new intellectual heights can stimulate a person. That is the case of Rodriguez. Fame and fortune have been a mixed blessing. There is a raging paranoia within Rodriguez. He has been taken advantage of for half a century and now he is in control. The paranoia is justified. People want to get next to him. He is shy. He is private. He is justifiably skeptical when people show up with schemes to create hits. He has been there. He has done that. He doesn't need the strife, the turmoil, the lies and the deception. He needs to be left alone. This has proven to be a virtually impossible task.

Sixto Rodriguez' story has more parameters than one can imagine. As the shy man dressed in black walks down dank Detroit streets with a guitar slung over his back, he is oblivious to fame and fortune.

As a street poet he has few peers. Charles Bukowski comes to mind but Rodriguez has a lyrical sophistication that goes beyond Hollywood's decadent bars that Bukowski portrayed.

Sixto Rodriguez' rise to fame and fortune is a Cinderella story. There is one problem. The risk of overexposure. The Sugar Man can tour wherever and whenever he pleases. But his daughter, Regan, realizes that too much Rodriguez will dim or water down the product. The complex intertwined record business welcomes Rodriguez. He will let them know when and where he will perform.

RODRIGUEZ AND THE CASE AGAINST BIOGRAPHY

Sixto Rodriguez is an extraordinarily private person. He needs solitude to create. He is happy at home with family. When the awards flooded in for **Searching For Sugar Man**, he wanted no part of the big stage. Then came the concert offers. He has gone on the road to become a rock legend in his post seventy years. He has glaucoma and his body shows the abuse of years working in the home rehab industry. At times, he flies first class to his concerts. His daughter, Regan, explained that everything she does is to make him comfortable. He travels in an air-conditioned tour bus. He stays in the best hotels. According to those close to him, he would be just as happy driving around in an old van. He continually remarks: "Uncle Sony is good to us."

Flaubert and the French symbolist poets believe that biography is unnecessary. They argue that a person's art, their works, their writings, their thoughts; their intellectual contributions are elevated above the world. This is an interesting notion but not the correct one. It is impossible to understand Sixto Rodriguez without examining Detroit, the corrupt music business, the history of pop and other forms of music and the ups and downs of his volatile life. The Sugar Man's story didn't happen in a vacuum. It was the product of American forces that shaped his magical lyrics. But to Rodriguez, he wouldn't want a biography. He prefers the music to do his talking. That is the Sugar Man's case against biography.

The Sixto Rodriguez story tells a tale of brilliance, obscurity and ultimate redemption. The irony is that the Sugar Man ignored or perhaps purposely placed the success that he received late in life in the recesses of his mind. He lives a good life. Fame and fortune will not change him. That is a good thing.

APPENDIX

I

A RODRIGUEZ TIME LINE: KEY POINTS

JULY 10, 1942: RODRIGUEZ WAS BORN IN DETROIT ON MICHIGAN AVENUE ABOUT FIVE BLOCKS FROM THE CENTER OF TOWN. THIS IS PROBABLY AN UBRAN MYTH AS A NUMBER PEOPLE CLOSE TO HIM ALLEGE THAT HE WAS BORN IN A SUBURBAN DETROIT AREA. PERHAPS DEARBORN. THEN DURING OTHER INTERVIEWS, RODRIGUEZ REMARKED HE WAS BORN AT 831 MICHIGAN AVENUE IN DETROIT.

LATE 1945: HIS MOTHER DIES WHEN HE IS THREE YEARS OLD.

1945-1946: HE MAY HAVE SPENT SOME TIME IN AN ORPHANAGE.

1948-1949: HE RETURNS TO THE FAMILY HOME NEAR DOWNTOWN DETROIT.

1950s: RODRIGUEZ' FATHER MAKES FOREMAN AT GREAT LAKES STEEL. RODRIGUEZ MAY HAVE ATTENDED THE HOLY REDEEMER CATHOLIC CHURCH AND WATCHED MOVIES AT THE ALAMO THEATER.

1955: WPAG BECOMES THE FIRST SPANISH RADIO STATION IN DETROIT AND RODRIGUEZ IS PROBABLY A LISTENER.

1958: RODRIGUEZ DROPS OUT OF HIGH SCHOOL TO JOIN THE ARMY. HE FAILS THE PHYSICAL AND GOES TO WORK IN DETROIT.

1958: HIS DAD BUYS HIM HIS FIRST GUITAR.

JULY 1964: EVA RODRIGUEZ IS BORN. THAT SAME YEAR HIS FATHER GIVES HIM A BIRTDAY GIFT. IT IS THE BEATLES FIRST ALBUM.

JULY 25, 1966: RODRIGUEZ SIGNS A CONTRACT WITH HARRY BALK'S GOMBA PUBLISHING. IT IS AN EXCLUSIVE FIVE-YEAR DEAL TAKING EFFECT JULY 25, 1966 AND CONCLUDING JULY 25, 1971.

JANUARY-MARCH 1967: PRODUCER HARRY BALK HEARS SOME RODRIGUEZ DEMO TAPES COURTESY OF RAINY M. MOORE.

APRIL 1967: HE RECORDS SIX SONGS FOR HARRY BALK'S IMPACT LABEL. SOME OF THESE TUNES ARE LATER RE-RECORDED FOR THE COLD FACT AND COMING FROM REALITY LPs.

APRIL 20, 1967: HARRY BALK'S GOMBA MUSIC COPYRIGHTS "I'LL SLIP AWAY," "YOU'D LIKE TO ADMIT IT," "TO WHOM IT MAY CONCERN," "FORGET IT" AND "THIS DISCOTHEQUE." THESE SONGS WERE RECORDED BY RODRIGUEZ WITH DENNIS COFFEY ON GUITAR AND PROBABLY MIKE THEODORE ON KEYBOARDS. BALK WAS THE PRODUCER. WHEN THESE SONGS WERE RECORDED. THERE WERE TWO VERSIONS OF "TO WHOM

IT MAY CONCERN." ONE WAS A VOCAL AND THE OTHER AN IN-STRUMENTAL VERSION.

AUGUST 1967: IMPACT RECORDS RELEASES "I'LL SLIP AWAY" AS A SINGLE WITH HARRY BALK PRODUCING. THE SONG IDENTIFIES ROD RIGUEZ AS THE SINGER. THE B-SIDE IS "YOU'D LIKE TO ADMIT IT."

SEPTEMBER 23, 1967: THE SINGLE "I'LL SLIP AWAY" IS RE-VIEWED FAVORABLY BY CASHBOX. THE REVIEWER STATES: "ROD RIGUEZ COULD MAKE A NAME FOR HIMSELF WITH THIS BLUESY MID TEMPO ROCK BALLAD."

SEPTEMBER-OCTOBER 1967: HARRY BALK SPENDS SOME TIME PROMOTING THE IMPACT SINGLE.

JANUARY 1968: RODRIGUEZ PERFORMS AT THE SEWER BY THE SEA FOR FOUR WEEKS. THERE WERE FOUR SETS A NIGHT FROM EIGHT UNTIL TWO IN THE MORNING.

JULY 1969: RODRIGUEZ SIGNS A CONTRACT WITH SUSSEX RECORDS AND CLARENCE AVANT. THE DEAL ALSO INCLUDES A PUBLISHING AGREEMENT WITH AVANT'S SONGWRITING COM-PANY, AVANT GARDE.

AUGUST-SEPTEMBER, 1969: COLD FACT IS RECORDED AT TERA SHIRMA STUDIO IN DETROIT. THERE ARE THIRTY RE-CORDING SESSIONS.

MARCH/APRIL 1970: SUSSEX RECORDS RELEASES THE AMERICAN VERSION OF COLD FACT.

APRIL 18, 1970: BILLBOARD AWARDS COLD FACT A FOUR STAR REVIEW.

LATE 1970: STEVE ROWLAND BEGINS PREPARATION TO TAKE RODRIGUEZ INTO THE RECORDING STUDIO TO RECORD COMING FROM REALITY.

APRIL 1971: COLD FACT IS RELEASED IN SOUTH AFRICA. SOME SOURCES SAY 1972 IT WAS AVAILABLE ON A BOOTLEG IN 1971.

NOTE: THE TIME WILL CONTINUE IN VOLUME 2 RODRI-GUEZ: COMING FROM REALITY.

APPENDIX

II

KEY FACTS ABOUT RODRIGUEZ

1. THE COLD FACT ALBUM IS LISTED AS NUMBER 60 IN THE BEST ALBUMS OF 1970. IT WAS AWARDED A PLATINUM DISC IN SOUTH AFRICA IN 1988.

2. THE COLD FACT LP IS LISTED AS THE 449TH BEST ALBUM OF THE 1970s BY ROLLING STONE.

3. SUPER GUITARIST CHRIS SPEDDING WHO PLAYS ON THE SECOND LP COMING FROM REALITY IS ONE OF ENGLAND'S BEST SESSION GUITARISTS. HIS SOLO WORK AND COLLABORATIONS WITH ROBERT GORDON ARE SUPERB. IN 2015 HE CONTINUES TO RELEASE SOLO MATERIAL.

4. IN 2O12 COLD FACT WAS ON THE SWEDISH ALBUM CHART AT 60. AT THE SAME TIME IT WAS ONLY 86 IN THE U. S.

5. IN OCTOBER 2012 RODRIGUEZ' 1970 COLD FACT DE-BUTED BUBBLING UNDER AT 113 ON THE U. S. BILLBOARD ALBUM CHART. THIS WAS THE FIRST ALBUM IN BILLBOARD CHART HISTORY TO HIT THE CHARTS MORE THAN 42 AND A HALF YEARS AFTER ITS RELEASE.

6. THERE WERE TWO SONGS ON THE COLD FACT ALBUM THAT RODRIGUEZ DID NOT WRITE. THEY WERE "HATE STREET DIALGOUE" AND "GOMMORAH (A NURSERY RHYME)" WITH THE MUSIC WRITTEN BY MIKE THEODORE AND DENNIS COF-FEY AND LYRICS BY GARY HARVEY. RODRIGUEZ HAS NEVER PERFORMED EITHER SONG IN CONCERT.

7. WHEN RODRIGUEZ APPEARED ON THE LATE SHOW WITH DAVID LETTERMAN ON TUESDAY AUGUST 14, 2012, HE PERFORMED "CRUCIFY YOUR MIND." A SYMPHONY STRING SECTION AND HORNS WERE HIRED BY SONY LEGACY.

8. RODRIGUEZ IS STOIC AND HE SELDOM MENTIONS THAT HE IS PART NATIVE AMERICAN. HE HAS PERFORMED WITH GUI-TARIST JOE PODORSEK AT A NUMBER OF NATIVE AMERICAN EVENTS. PODORSEK WAS A DETROIT GUITARIST WHO OWNED CAPITOL MUSIC. HE SOLD EQUIPMENT TO FLEDGLING MU-SICIANS. HE SOLD DENNIS COFFEY ALL HIS EARLY GUITARS. PODORSEK ATTENED MACKENZIE HIGH WHERE HE PLAYED IN THE HIGH SCHOOL ORCHESTRA.

9. RODRIGUEZ' FIRST AUSTRALIA PERFORMANCE WAS AT MELBOURNE'S BROOKS HALL ON MARCH 15, 1979. AN AUSTRA-LIAN LABEL LICENSED COLD FACT AND RENAMED IT RODRI-GUEZ ALIVE WHILE RELEASING IT TO SOLID SALES.

10. THE REVIEWS FOR THE 1979 AUSTRALIAN SHOWS WERE MIXED ONES AS RODRIGUEZ HAD TROUBLE PERFORMING IN THE LARGER VENUES. HE WAS SIMPLY UNCOMFORTABLE. THE SMALLER VENUES LED TO STRONG SHOWS AND VERY POSITIVE REVIEWS.

11. THE SOUTH AFRICAN BAND, BIG SKY, WAS CONTRACT-ED TO BACK RODRIGUEZ IN SWEDEN IN 1998 AND WHEN RO-DRIGUEZ THOUGHT HE MIGHT NOT BE ABLE TO COMPLETE THE TOUR, THE BAND'S TICKETS WERE CANCELLED, THEN RO-DRIGUEZ DID THE SWEDISH SHOWS. BIG SKY WAS REPLACED BY A GROUP OF SWEDISH MUSICIANS WHEN RODRIGUEZ FINALLY COMPLETED THE SWEDISH TOUR.

12. RODRIGUEZ HAS HAD SOME TEACHING EXPERIENCE AS WELL AS WORKING AS A SOCIAL WORKER.

13. ON JANUARY 11, 2013 WHEN RODRIGUEZ APPEARED ON THE TONIGHT SHOW, HE RECEVIED SOME GOOD NEWS. THIS WAS THE SAME DAY THAT THE OSCAR NOMINATION FOR SEARCHING FOR SUGAR MAN BEGAN ANOTHER PHASE IN HIS CAREER AND THAT OF THE DOCUMENTARY FILM MAKER MA-LIK BENDJOUELL.

14. RODRIGUEZ RAN FOR THE MICHIGAN HOUSE OF REP-RESENTATIVES TWICE, THE STATE SENATE ONCE AS WELL AS DETROIT'S MAYOR AND CITY COUNCIL A NUMBER OF TIMES. HE IS HIGHLY POLITICAL. HE IS AN ISSUE ORIENTED POLITI-CO.

15. THE NAME JESUS RODRIGUEZ WAS USED TO ATTEMPT TO PROTECT HIS SONG COPYRIGHTS. ONE OF HIS BROTHERS IS NAMED JESUS. THE ONLY PROBLEM IS THAT THERE IS NO JESUS RODRIGUEZ.

16. SIXTH PRINCE IS A TERM COINED BY RODRIGUEZ TO IDENTIFY HIS BIRTH ORDER AND HE USED IT IN ATTEMPTS TO PROTECT SONG COPYRIGHTS. HE RE-REGISTERED THE SONG COPYRIGHTS USING THIS NAME. CLARENCE AVANT WHO AL-LEGED FRAUD SUED HIM.

17. IN 1991 WHEN COLD FACT WAS RE-RELEASED IN SOUTH AFRICA, IT SOLD HALF A MILLION COPIES.

18. THE AUSTRALIAN MOVIE CANDY FEATURED RODRI-GUEZ' "SUGAR MAN" ON THE SOUND TRACK.

19. IN LONDON IN 2005 IT APPEARS THAT LAUREN LA-VERNE OPENED FOR RODRIGUEZ. SHE IS A BRITISH RADIO DJ, TELEVISION PRESENTER AND SINGER. SHE HAD A HIT RECORD PROVIDING THE VOCALS ON THE MINT ROYALE'S "DON'T FAL-TER."

20. THERE ARE REFERENCES TO THE TOILKIEN BOOKS IN "IT STARTED OUT SO NICE."

21. HEIKKI IS A MALE MOTORCYCLE ENTHUSIAST WHO IS ALSO AN ENGINEER. HE WAS THE INSPIRATION FOR THE SONG "HEIKKI'S SUBURBIA BUS TOUR."

22. THE LYRIC "EAST LAFAYETTE WEEKEND SLUTS" IS THE CORRECT LYRIC TO "A MOST DISGUSTING SONG." IN THE AL-BUM RODRIGUEZ SINGS THE LINE AS "SLOPPY-AT-WEEKEND SLUTS...."

23. THE COVER PHOTO FOR THE COMING FROM REALITY WAS SHOT BY THE NOTED PHOTOGRAPHER ATIZHAL WILSON.

24. MILTON SINCOFF DESIGNED THE COVER FOR COMING FROM REALITY.

25. "AND THAT'S A CONCRETE COLD FACT." THIS IS A LINE FROM THE "ESTABLISHMENT BLUES." BUT "INNER CITY BLUES" ALSO CONTAINS THE PHRASE "COLD FACT."

26. RODRIGUEZ' SONGWRITING HAS BEEN PRAISED FOR ITS EVEN HANDED AND BRILLIANT LYRICS. HE CAN TAKE ANY SUBJECT AND TREAT IT WITH INTELLIGENCE AND HONESTY WHILE MAINTAINING A POETIC DIRECTION.

27. HE TOURED AUSTRALIA IN 1979, 1981, 2007 AND 2010 BE-FORE FAME CAME WITH SEARCHING FOR SUGAR MAN. IN OC-

TOBER 2014 HE SOLD OUT EVERY VENUE DURING ANOTHER
TRIUMPHANT TOUR.

28. HE SIGNED WITH LIGHT IN THE ATTIC, A SEATTLE LA-
BEL. THEY BROUGHT HIM TO APPEAR AT SEATTLE'S TRIPLE
DOOR. THE RE-RELEASE OF COLD FACT AND COMING FROM
REALITY CREATED A RENEWED INTEREST IN HIS CAREER.
THANKS TO MATT SULLIVAN FOR THE RE-RELEASES. SULLIVAN
PERSONALLY WENT TO RODRIGUEZ' DETROIT HOME TO MAKE
SURE THAT HE WAS OKAY WITH THE RE-RELEASES. HE WAS. THE
REST IS HISTORY.

29. EACH WINTER LIGHT IN THE ATTIC SENDS RODRIGUEZ
SOME FIRE WOOD FOR HIS STOVE.

30. WHEN HE ARRIVED TO TOUR SOUTH AFRICA IN 1998
RODRIGUEZ DIDN'T HAVE A GUITAR. HIS SOUTH AFRICANS
FRIENDS QUICKLY PURCHASED HIM ONE.

31. RODRIGUEZ HAS THREE DAUGHTERS EVA, SANDRA
AND REGAN. HIS TWO WIVES RAYMA AND KONNY LIVE IN THE
DETROIT AREA.

32. RODRIGUEZ' OLDEST DAUGHTER, EVA, IS AN AQUARI-
US.

33. IN MARCH 2015 WHILE AT THE PEAK OF HIS FAME, RO-
DRIGUEZ TOOK TIME TO TESTIFY AGAINST A WATER RATE IN-
CREASE BEFORE THE DETROIT WATER BOARD. THIS IS AN INDI-
CATION OF HIS CONTINUED POLITICAL INVOLVEMENT.

APPENDIX

III

RODRIGUEZ QUOTES

1. "THERE'S NO GUARANTEES IN MUSIC, AND I KNEW THAT FROM THE BEGINNING. I THINK IT'S BETTER IF THESE HEART-BREAKS HAPPEN TO YOU EARLY THAN WHEN YOU'RE LATER IN YOUR YEARS. I THINK IT'S BETTER THAT YOU GET THE BUMPS EARLY."

2. "AS I UNDERSTAND IT, A LOT OF PEOPLE THERE EX-CHANGED CASSETTES OF MY MUSIC. I THINK THE ISOLATION OF SOUTH AFRICA AT THE TIME, AND THE ERA OF MILITARY CONSCRIPTION AND GOVERNMENT REPRESSION, FOSTERED THE APPRECIATION FOR MY SONGS." THIS IS RODRIGUEZ COMMENTING ON THE POPULARITY OF HIS MUSIC IN SOUTH AFRICA AND ITS INFLUENCE UPON HIS LIFE. THIS QUOTATION ANSWERS THE QUESTION OF WHETHER OR NOT HE WAS A STRONG VOICE AGAINST APRTHEID. HE WAS.

3. "I'VE MET AND SPOKEN WITH MY AUDIENCES THERE, SO I KNOW FROM THEIR ACCOUNTS HOW IT HAPPENED. BUT WHY MY HOMETOWN AND HOME COUNTRY DIDN'T NOTICE ME BACK THEN, I DON'T KNOW. LIFE IS NOT LINEAR, NOT REAL LIFE. I HAVE TO CREDIT THE HEROES WHO MADE 'SEARCHING FOR SUGAR MAN' AND ALSO THE INTERNET."

4. "THERE'S NO BLUEPRINT FOR SUCCESS."

5. "I LIKE TO MEND ROOFS, BUILD WALLS, I WORKED IN A GAS STATION...."- RODRIGUEZ, 1998

6. "THIS SYSTEM'S GONNA FALL SOON, TO AN ANGRY YOUNG TUNE-AND THAT'S A CONCRETE COLD FACT."

7. "WE WENT SWIMMING IN GRAND BEND AND TO POW-WOWS (A MAGICAL INDIAN CEREMONY) THROUGHOUT MICHI-GAN. AS FAR BACK AS 1974 I WAS INVOLVED IN ORGANIZING AN AMERICAN-INDIAN POW-WOW AT THE WAYNE STATE UNIVERSI-TY CAMPUS."- RODRIGUEZ, 1997

8. "I'VE DONE A BIT OF THIS, A BIT OF THAT. I'M SOLID WORK-ING CLASS. I FINISHED A BA IN PHILOSOPHY AT WAYNE STATE UNIVERSITY. I JOINED IN INDIAN POW-WOWS THROUGHOUT MICHIGAN. I STAND UP FOR THE AMERICAN INDIAN IN JAIL, FOR JUSTICE AND I RAN FOR ELECTION."- RODRIGUEZ, MARCH 1998

9. "I'VE BEEN WORKING ON MY CONSCIOUSNESS FOR THE PAST 20 YEARS, AND ON AN ARTS DEGREE (MAJORING IN PHILOSOPHY) FOR THE PAST DECADE. IT TOOK ME SO LONG (FOR THE DEGREE) BECAUSE I WAS BUSY WITH OTHER THINGS IN BETWEEN. I'VE BEEN MAINLY BASED IN DETROIT, WHICH IS WHERE I WAS BORN AND RAISED. I RAN FOR MAYOR TWICE, FOR STATE REPRESENTATIVE TWICE AND FOR THE CITY COUN-CIL THREE TIMES." — RODRIGUEZ, MARCH 1998

10. "I THOUGHT THAT THE HIGH POINT IN MY LIFE HAS BEEN AUSTRALIA." RODRIGEUZ TO JOURNALIST ANDREW WATT

11. "I SAW SOME THINGS I THOUGHT PEOPLE SHOULD BE MADE AWARE OF, BUT I WAS UNABLE TO DO THAT WITH MY MUSIC." THIS IS AN EXPLANATION OF WHY HE RAN FOR POLITICAL OFFICE.

12. "THE SYSTEM'S GONNA FALL SOON, TO AN ANGRY YOUNG TUNE-AND THAT'S A CONCRETE COLD FACT." THIS IS A LINE FROM THE SONG "COLD FACT" WHICH REFLECTS HIS VIEW OF THE LATE 1960S.

13. "I DIG BOOKS AND I AM INTO COMMUNICATION." THIS IS RODRIGUEZ IN CONVERSATION WITH AUSTRALIAN WRITER GLEN BAKER WHO WROTE THE LINER NOTES FOR THE ALIVE LP.

14. "I TAPPED INTO THE WRITER'S POETIC LICENSE." THIS IS A REFERENCE TO THE LYRICS AND IMAGERY OF THE SONG "JANE S. PIDDY."

15. "DON'T BOTHER TO BUY INSURANCE CAUSE YOUR'RE ALREADY DEAD." A TYPICAL LYRIC CRITICAL OF THE MIDDLE CLASS FROM THE SONG "CAUSE."

16. "AND YOU MEASURE YOUR WEALTH." A LINE FROM JANE S. PIDDY ABOUT SOME OF THE YOUNG LADIES HE MET IN HIS DATING DAYS.

17. "IT HAS A LONG HISTORY OF PROBLEMS BUT THERE'S A LOT OF STRONG PEOPLE FROM DETROIT. THEY'RE WORKER BEES. JUST LIKE MYSELF." THIS IS RODRIGUEZ COMMENTING ON THE REASONS FOR DETROIT'S HISTORICAL ECONOMIC MESS IN CONVERSATION WITH THE NEW MUSCIAL EXPRESS.

18. "BUT KNOWLEDGE IN ITSELF IN NOTHING; IT'S WHAT YOU DO WITH THAT INFORMATION."

19. "I HOPE TO PLAY TO SOUTH AFRICANS, AND ALSO TO COMMUNICATE TO AMERICA WHAT IT SOUNDS LIKE ON THIS SIDE OF THE GLOBE. I FEEL LIKE MARCO POLO, MAN." A COMMENT MADE IN 2004.

20. "TELL THE PEOPLE NOTHING, TELL THE PEOPLE ANY-THING, TELL THE PEOPLE *EVERYTHING*. AND SO NOW THROUGH THE INTERNET, THE TECHNOLOGICAL WONDER OF THE AGE, IT'S A VERY AMERICAN INVENTION, VERY FREE." RODRIGUEZ IN CONVERSATION FOR AN ARTICLE IN DETROIT'S METRO TIMES.

21. "IT'S STILL A QUESTION OF THE HAVES AND HAVE-NOTS. AND SO TO SLICE IT SO THINLY IS TRUE, UNFORTU-NATELY." RODRIGUEZ IN CONVERSATION WITH COREY HALL OF THE DETROIT METRO TIMES.

22. "I'M CONTEMPORARY. I READ THE NEW YORK TIMES. MY MATERIAL KEEPS SURFACING. IT'S REAL SIMPLE STUFF, WHICH ENDURES. ALL I NEED IS A COUPLE OF DAYS REHEARS-ING WITH MY SOUTH AFRICAN BAND (STEVE LOUW'S BIG SKY)." THIS IS FROM A GRAHAM HOWE INTERVIEW, MARCH 1, 1998.

23. "I'VE ALWAYS CONCENTRATED ON SOCIAL ISSUES, BECAUSE I'VE ALWAYS FOUND IT EASIEST TO WRITE ABOUT THINGS THAT UPSET ME. BUT I CAN (AND HAVE) EXPLORED THE BOY-GIRL THEME IN MUSIC AND I ENJOY WRITING BAL-LADS TOO." FROM AN INTERVIEW WITH KAREN RUTTER.

24. "WHAT I DO LIKE IS RAY CHARLES AND BB KING, THOSE CATS. I'M JUST AVERAGE AS A GUITAR PLAYER. I'M JUST AVER-AGE, BUT THE THING IS: I'M REAL LUCKY. I'VE BEEN ABLE TO GIVE HERE, YOU KNOW. I'VE HAD LUCK. THAT'S THE ONLY WAY I'M ABLE TO ACCOUNT FOR ALL THIS STUFF. (LAUGHS.) HERE IN CAPE TOWN, HERE IN SOUTH AFRICA, THERE WERE 20,000 AT SIX CONCERTS (FOR MY 1998 SA TOUR)." THE CONCERT AT-TENDANCE WAS ACTUALLY WELL OVER 30,000.

25. "I LIKE WRITERS, MUSICIANS AND PERFORMERS, ALL IN ONE Y'KNOW, IT'S LIKE THAT. I THINK YOU'RE DOING MORE TO THE ART FORM."

26. "WELL WHEN YOU WRITE YOU GET IT OFF YOU...IT'S LIKE LETTING OF STEAM...IT BECOMES SOMETHING OUTSIDE OF YOU...."

27. "WHAT SONG DO I LIKE? I LIKE 'A MOST DISGUSTING SONG.' I TRY TO COMPARE IT TO JOHN LENNON'S 'ROCKY RACCOON.' I WROTE IT IN THAT KIND OF LIGHT. EVERYBODY AFFECTS EVERYBODY ELSE MUSICALLY." RODRIGUEZ WASN'T AWARE THAT PAUL MCCARTNEY WAS THE PRIMARY WRITER ON THE SONG.

28. "I CAN'T IMAGINE IT GETTING MUCH BUSIER. THIS IS PRETTY BUSY. YOU GOTTA STAY BALANCED AND NORMALIZED, PACE YOURSELF. AT THIS LATE DATE I HAVE A NEW PERSPECTIVE ON THINGS BECAUSE OF THE SUCCESS OF THE MUSIC NOW." RODRIGUEZ COMMENTING ON HIS APPEARANCE WITH JAY LENO ON THE TONIGHT SHOW.

29. "IT'S AN EXTRAORDINARY TRIP. IT FEELS LIKE PICASSO, MONET. ALL THESE EXCITING NEW THOUGHTS COMING AT ME. IT'S GLOBAL. I'M LUCKY TO HAVE THIS SECOND CHANCE. IT'S VERY REAL AND TOTALLY UNEXPECTED."

30. "THERE WERE A LOT OF SOLDIERS AND THEY TOLD ME HOW THEY WERE IN SERVICE, THEY HAD CONSCRIPTION THERE, AND THEY'D TRADE CASSETTES AND THAT WAS HOW IT CIRCULATED, IN PART, AT THAT TIME." RODRIGUEZ ON HIS FIRST TRIP TO SOUTH AFRICA AND WHY HIS MUSIC BECAME SO POPULAR.

31. "AS A RESULT OF TECHNOLOGY I'M ALMOST A NEW ACT."

32. "MUSICIANS WANT TO BE HEARD. SO I'M NOT HIDING. BUT I DO LIKE TO LEAVE IT THERE ONSTAGE AND BE MYSELF, IN THAT SENSE. BECAUSE SOME PEOPLE CARRY IT WITH THEM." RODRIGUEZ IN CONVERSATION WITH ROLLING STONE, JANUARY 2013.

33. "I WENT BACK TO SCHOOL, AND I WENT TO WORK, MOSTLY MANUAL LABOR, TO TRY TO MAKE A LIVING. IT TOOK ME TEN YEARS TO GET A FOUR-YEAR DEGREE, BUT I GRADUATED. I ALSO RAN FOR OFFICE IN DETROIT. IT'S ALL VERIFIABLE." THIS QUOTE IS FROM RODRIGUEZ IN CONVERSATION

WITH BRAD WHEELER FROM THE CANADIAN GLOVE AND MAIL ON WHAT HE DID WHEN HE LEFT MUSIC.

34. "UNCLE SONY'S BEEN GOOD TO US."

35. WHEN ASKED ABOUT THE SUICIDE RUMOR, RODRIGUEZ REMARKED OF HOW THIS STORY STARTED: "I DON'T HAVE ANY IDEA. I THINK THAT'S KIND OF THE DISTORTION THAT HAPPENED."

36. "THERE WAS AN ELEMENT OF MAGIC IN THE WHOLE THING." THIS IS RODRIGUEZ COMMENTING ON HIS FIRST SOUTH AFRICAN TOUR IN 1998.

37. "I AM A MUSICAL POLITICAL. IT'S HARD TO SEPARATE THE TWO FROM ME."

38. "I MET ALEC BLADWIN AND I TOLD HIM, 'YOU'RE A FAMOUS MAN,'AND HE SAID: 'THAT'S A DOUBLE EDGED SWORD.' I KIND OF AGREE WITH HIM."

39. "I LIVE BELOW MY MEANS. I THINK THAT'S A GOOD DISCIPLINE BECAUSE YOU NEVER CAN TELL. I'M NOT AN ESCTHETIC. I JUST THINK THAT'S WISER."

40. "YOU CAN KEEP YOUR SYMBOLS OF SUCCESS AND I'M NOT CHOOSING TO BE LIKE THEM." FROM LYRICS TO "I'LL SLIP AWAY."

41. "I'M HAPPY WITH THE FILM IDEA." RODRIGUEZ APPEARING ON DETROIT'S WEEKLY COMET SHOW JULY 20, 2012 DESCRIBING SEARCHING FOR SUGAR MAN.

42. "YES I SUPPOSE IT DOES HAVE A MAGICAL TWIST TO IT. BUT I WAS NEVER ASLEEP." RODRIGUEZ COMMENTING ON HIS NEW FOUND FAME.

43. "WHEN I WAS WRITING THESE SONGS, IT SEEMED LIKE A REVOLUTION WAS COMING IN AMERICA. YOUNG MEN WERE

BURNING DRAFT CARDS, THE CITIES WERE ABLAZE WITH AN-GER."

44. "THERE WON'T BE A REVOLUTION, THE SYTEM WILL SIMPLY COLLAPSE UNDER THE WEIGHT OF ITS OWN GREED, CORRUPTION AND BIGOTRY." THESE ARE TYPICAL POETIC AND IN YOUR FACE RODRIGUEZ LYRICS.

45. "YOU CAN KEEP YOUR SYMBOLS OF SUCCESS...I'M NOT CHOOSING TO BE LIKE THEM."

46. "I WAS READY FOR THE WORLD, BUT I DON'T THINK THE WORLD WAS READY FOR ME." RODRIGUEZ INTERVIEWED IN LONDON IN 2012.

47. "WHEN I COME TO TOWN, THEY BUILD A BAND AROUND ME. IT'S A GREAT FEELING." RODRIGUEZ ON HIS RECENT SUC-CESSES IN CONCERT APPEARANCES IN THE U. S., AUSTRALIA, EUROPE AND THE U. K.

48. "ALTHOUGH THE MATERIAL IS OLD...I DO CONSIDER MYSELF CONTEMPORARY AND THERE'S A NEW LEASE OF LIFE FOR THE MATERIAL."

49. "BARRIERS ARE BEING BROUGHT DOWN BY TECHNOL-OGY THROUGH THE INTERNET," RODRIGUEZ CONTINUED. "THE FILM, *SEARCHING FOR SUGAR MAN*, HAS EXCITED MY MU-SIC CAREER. SO WE ARE TOURING."

50. "THERE'S SO MUCH POTENTIAL HERE STILL. THE MID-TOWN IS GROWING NEAR THE CAMPUS AND IT'S STABLIZED. IT'S LIKE ANY URBAN CENTER...IT'S GOING TO TAKE OFF AGAIN." RODRIGUEZ ON DETROIT AS HE SEES IT AND HE COMMENTS ON THE WAYNE STATE UNIVERSITY CAMPUS NEAR HIS HOME.

51. "THE SOCIAL REALISM IN DETROIT...YOU KNOW I TALK ABOUT POLICE BRUTALITY. THE WORD BIGOT-COPS NON-FIC-TION. I THINK YOU CAN HAVE IT IN ORANGE COUNTY CALIFOR-NIA...ANAHEIM...RODNEY KING, WASN'T THAT A TRAFFIC VIOLA-

TION? THEY USED TASERS WHEN THEY APPREHEND. ISN'T THAT PUNISHMENT EVEN BEFORE THE CHARGE? THERE ARE SERIOUS QUESTIONS LIKE GOVERNMENT REPRESSION, CENSORSHIP, THOSE KINDS OF ISSUES, THE WARS. YOU KNOW SYRIA, 60,000 DEAD THERE, TWO MILLION MOVED OUT OR MIGRATED OUT OF THERE. WE HAVE THESE ISSUES AND THE THING IS...AND NOW WE'RE LEARNING MORE FROM NATIONAL PUBLIC RADIO ABOUT THE VIETNAM WAR AND IT'S PRETTY REVEALING AS TO WHAT WENT ON. AND CALIFORNIA, YOU KNOW RICHARD NIXON, RONALD REAGAN, ARNOLD SCHWARZENEGGER, YOU KNOW. I'M A POLITICAL...MUSICAL, POLITICAL, SO MAYBE I USE THE PROTEST SONG AS A VEHICLE, AND FOLK MUSIC, TO DESCRIBE THESE THINGS."

52. "EVERY TWO YEARS THERE ARE ELECTIONS. I FEEL MORE WOMEN SHOULD RUN FOR PUBLIC OFFICE. IT'S PROVEN THAT THEY ARE SMARTER AND THEY MATURE FASTER. THE GUYS THAT ARE IN CONGRESS CAN'T DO IT BEYOND A CERTAIN POINT. WHAT WE HAVE IS POLITICAL STAGNATION. SO I THINK THAT IS THE PARADIGM ABOUT THE NEW CENTURY, IT SHOULD BE PUT IN EFFECT. ACTIVISM...CHANGE THE WHOLE THING. TURN IT RIGHT OVER. IT'S OBSOLETE. I FEEL THAT IN WASHINGTON THAT'S WHAT'S HAPPENING, SO EVERY TWO YEARS. AND IF I WOULD RUN...I HAVE ENCOURAGED OTHER PEOPLE TO RUN AND I'VE WORKED ON THEIR BEHALF. I LOVE MICHAEL MOORE FROM MICHIGAN BECAUSE HE'S A POLITICAL FILMMAKER. HE BRINGS UP ISSUES AND HE BROUGHT UP COLUMBINE AND HERE IT IS AGAIN THIS ISSUE ABOUT VIOLENCE AND AGGRESSION. AGAIN, THESE ARE THE SAME ISSUES THAT ARE HAPPENING. AND I'M A SOLID 70 SO I USE THAT HINDSIGHT TO SAY, "HEY, THERE'S OTHER WAYS."

53. "IN CONTRACTS THERE'S AN AREA CALLED 'UNJUST ENRICHMENT.' AND THESE BOOTLEGS ARE LICENCED BOOTLEGS SO IT'S NOT LIKE THERE'S NOT A TRAIL HERE. I THINK THAT WILL BE RESOLVED. I REALLY THINK IT WILL BE BECAUSE IT'S SO PUBLIC NOW. AND THE TRAIL LEADS TO CLARENCE

AVANT SO I DON'T WANNA...IT'S PRETTY MUCH IN HIS CORNER AS TO WHERE IT STANDS. THE DIRECTOR DIDN'T WANT TO GO INTO ANY ONE PARTICULAR PART OF THE FILM AS TO...HE WAS JUST PRESENTING THE WHOLE STORY. THAT'S WHAT MALIK BENDJELLOUL TOLD ME. HE'S NOMINATED FOR AN OSCAR AND THAT'S PRETTY AMAZING...SOMEBODY WHO DIRECTED HIS FIRST FILM." RODRIGUEZ COMMENTING ON CLARENCE AVANT SEE THE INTERVIEW http://13thflooroffice.files.wordpress.com/2013/02/rodriguez-interview.pdf

54. I WAS RECOMMENDED TO WORK UNDER HIM BY A PERSON NAMED NEIL BOGART." RODRIGUEZ COMMENTING ON HOW HE WAS BROUGHT TOGETHER WITH PRODUCER STEVE ROWLAND.

55. "I KNOW DETROIT. IT'S GOT HISTORY."

56. "THEY WANT TO USE VIOILINS AND I DIDN'T KNOW IF I SHOULD LOOK SO ACCOMPLISHED." A REMARK RODRIGUEZ MADE BEFORE APPEARING ON LATE NIGHT WITH DAVID LETTERMAN PERFORMING "CRUCIFY YOUR MIND."

57. "I PREFER TO KEEP MY PERSONAL LIFE TO MYSELF. BUT I WANT TO SHARE MY MUSIC ITH EVERYONE."

58. "THAT WILL BE RESOLVED ONE WAY OR ANOTHER." RODRIGUEZ' COMMENT ON THE MISSING ROYALTIES.

59. "NOW I THINK I'M MORE GROUNDED THAN I WOULD HAVE BEEN THEN. MAYBE IT'S FOR THE BETTER THAT THIS KARMA HAS WORKED THIS WAY." RODRIGUEZ REMARKING ON HIS SECOND CHANCE FOR FAME AND FORTUNE.

60. "I TRY TO KEEP MYSELF SEPARATE FROM WHAT I DO, LIKE ANYONE, I THINK."

61. "ALTHOUGH I BELONG TO THE OLD CENTURY, I LIKE TO FEEL THAT I'M CONTEMPORARY."

62. "IT'S BEEN A MUSICAL ODYSSEY. IT'S EDUCATIONAL AND IT'S ALSO ENLIGHTENMENT. AND THE THING IS, I NEVER DREAMED IT WOULD GET AT THIS LEVEL....I WAS GONNA MAKE SOME RECORDS, I WAS GONNA SELL SOME RECORDS AND PLAY BIGGER ROOMS. YOU KNOW WHAT I MEAN UP THE FOOD CHAIN....BUT THIS IS LIKE, THE JUMPS ARE SO HUGE." RODRIGUEZ IN COVERSATION WITH EDD HURT.

63. "I'M NOT THE ONLY ONE WHO GOT BURNED, BUT THAT WAS NOT THE STORY." RODRIGUEZ COMMENTING ON THE DOCUMENTARY SEARCHING FOR SUGAR MAN.

64. "I DIDN'T BELIEVE THERE WERE ROYALTIES, BECAUSE I DIDN'T BELIEVE THE FIRST PART: THAT I WAS ANYTHING IN SOUTH AFRICA." RODRIGUEZ COMMENTING TO EDD HURT ON HIS RELUCTANCE TO BECOME INVOLVED IN THE SEARCHING FOR SUGAR MAN DOCUMENTARY.

65. "YOU'VE GOT TO BE FROM SOMEWHERE." WHAT RODRIGUEZ SAYS WHEN HE IS ASKED WHETHER HE LIKES LIVING IN DETROIT.

66. "I DIDN'T FEEL LOST, I KNEW EXACTLY WHERE I WAS." RODRIGUEZ ON HIS YEARS OF OBSCURITY AND WORKING DEAD END JOBS.

67. "WE ALL HAVE HISTORIES AND OUR COUNTRIES HAVE THEIR HISTORIES. BUT ENOUGH IS ENOUGH. THERE ARE THINGS TO GET DONE, AND NO MATTER HOW LOFTY OUR IDEAS. YOU ONLY GET SO MUCH TIME TO FIGURE THIS OUT. THE IMPERMANENCE OF LIFE, THE MYSTERY OF LIFE-YOU'VE GOT TO DEAL WITH WHAT YOU CAN. I FEEL PRIDE."

68. "IT'S TOO LATE TO GO BACKWARDS. FORWARD IS THE WHOLE DEAL."

69. "I'VE NEVER EVEN PLAYED A GIG IN AMERICA, MY HOME COUNTRY. I'VE JAMMED INFORMALLY WITH FRIENDS, YES, BUT NEVER A FORMAL CONCERT. NOBODY WAS EVER INTERESTED

IN MY MUSIC." THIS COMMENT IS FROM AN INTERVIEW WITH NILES VAN DER LINDEN. IT APPEARS THAT RODRIGUEZ WAS TALKING ABOUT STADIUM OR BIG VENUE CONCERTS.

70. "I WAS SKEPTICAL ABOUT IT. I THOUGHT HE HAD ENOUGH FOOTAGE BY JUST THE PEOPLE IN THE FILM. HE HAD DENNIS COFFEY WHO'S A WELL-KNOWN GUITAR PLAYER. HE'S INTERNATIONAL, HE'S ON THE GERMAN STRUT LABEL. AND THEN STEVE ROWLAND, HE'S AN ACTOR TURNED MUSIC PRODUCER. HE BUNKED WITH ROBERT MITCHUM, HE DATED NATALIE WOOD, HE GOT PICKED UP BY ELVIS IN HIS CADILLAC." THIS IS A QUOTE THAT RODRIGUEZ GAVE IN A FILM FESTIVAL SUGGESTING WHY HE WASN'T NEEDED IN THE DOCUMENTARY. IF THERE IS A DEFINITION OF HUMILITY IT IS THIS QUOTE.

71. "IT'S MOSTLY MUSICIANS I HANG OUT WITH, CREATIVE GUYS AND GIRLS, ARTISTS. WE SEE EACH OTHER AT THESE EVENTS-BUT BASICALLY I WAS DOING HARD LABOR." RODRIGUEZ ON HIS LIFE PRIOR TO THE FAME AND FORTUNE BROUGHT ON BY SEARCHING FOR SUGAR MAN.

72. "MUSIC IT'S A CURSE, IT FOLLOWS YOU AROUND. IF YOU WANT IT, IT'S THERE, IT'S NOT SOMETHING YOU ABANDON. AT LEAST I DIDN'T, AND I WOULDN'T. I'M IN FOR THE DURATION. I'M GOING LONG TERM FOR THIS MUSIC THING THAT'S WHAT I LOVE TO DO."

73. "I WASN'T AWARE OF ROYALTIES," RODRIGUEZ IN A FEBRUARY 2013 INTERVIEW IN SOUTH AFRICA.

74. "IT'S HARD NOT TO FEEL THE EXHILIRATION." RODRIGUEZ COMMENTING IN FEBRUARY 2013 ON HIS RECENT CONCERT SUCCESSES AND WHAT THIS MEANS TO HIM.

75. "I SEE IT AT DIFFERENT LEVELS." RODRIGUEZ ON HIS POST SEARCHING FOR SUGAR MAN SUCCESS.

76. RODRIGUEZ SAID: "AUSTRALIA PICKED UP ON ME WAY BACK THEN, SO I WAS HAPPY WITH THAT. AFTER I WENT THERE

IN '79, I LOVED EVERYTHING AUSTRALIAN. EVEN THE BRIS-BANE BALLET CAME TO DETROIT AND I WENT TO SEE THEM. I'D CATCH EVERYTHING AUSTRALIAN. ANYWAY, IT TURNS OUT THAT AUSTRALIA IS VINDICATED, YOU KNOW WHAT I MEAN?" IN CONVERSATION WITH JOURNALIST ANDREW WATT.

77. "I LEFT THE MUSIC SCENE IN '74 AND, EXCEPT FOR THE AUSTRALIAN TOUR, I DIDN'T RE-ENTER IT UNTIL '98," RODRIGUEZ CONTINUED. "I PRETTY MUCH STAYED PLAYING THE GUITAR, BUT NOT IN A COMMERCIAL SENSE."

78. "BUT MUSIC STAYS WITH US, WE CARRY THAT WITH US. THERE'S STUFF YOU CARRY WITH YOU - YOUR CULTURE, YOUR LANGUAGE, YOUR MUSIC."

79. "I THINK IT'S PRETTY PHENOMENAL IN THE SENSE THAT IT'S A ROCK 'N' ROLL FAIRYTALE IN A WAY. THERE'S A CERTAIN ELEMENT OF MAGIC IN IT."

80. "MIDNIGHT OIL WAS A MAGIC BAND, THEY WERE A HIGH-POWERED BAND, SO THEY ARE TONING DOWN FOR MY PERFORMANCES. IT'S A LIVING ART, MUSIC, SO WE'LL DEVELOP SOME KIND OF CHEMISTRY." THIS COMMENT WAS MADE IN AUSTRALIA WHEN MEMBERS OF MIDNIGHT OIL BACKED THE SUGAR MAN ON TOUR.

81. "I WAS READING SOME POETS WHEN I WROTE THEM," HE SAYS OF HIS EARLY SONGS. "I CARRIED A DICTIONARY. I TRIED TO PUT A PHRASE TOGETHER."

82. "I DIDN'T DO IT IN A DELIBERATE WAY THAT MAYBE IT WOULD READ AS POETRY. BUT I'D DO VOCALS WITH GUITAR KIND OF THINGS, SO THE LYRICS ARE IMPORTANT TO ME."

83. "I WAS HOPEFUL THEY WOULD BE HEARD. YOU DON'T DO IT ON THE ASSUMPTION THAT YOU KNOW THE OUTCOME. BUT I DIDN'T THINK THEY WOULD LAST THIS LONG ACTUALLY, SO THAT'S BEEN A SWEET SURPRISE."

84. "I UNDERSTAND THAT IT WAS SOLDIERS WHO DEFEND-ED THEIR COUNTRY. THEY HAVE CONSCRIPTION IN SOUTH AFRICA, AND THEY HAD SOLDIERS IN NAMIBIA AND ANGOLA AS WELL. THEY WOULD TRADE CASSETTES OF MY MATERIAL. I'VE MET PEOPLE IN THE AUDIENCE AND THERE ARE A LOT OF SOLDIERS." IN CONVERSATION WITH KEN SHANE.

85. "IT'S A NEW CENTURY. WE HAVE TO END THE VIO-LENCE, WE HAVE TO SAVE SOCIAL SECURITY SO THE YOUNG-BLOODS DON'T HAVE TO WORRY ABOUT THAT PART OF IT." THIS IS RODRIGUEZ IN CONVERSATION WITH KEN SHANE.

86. "I DO WRITE. I DO WRITE IDEAS AND DO GUITAR RIFFS. IT'S A LIVING ART, AND I'M CONSTANTLY TURNING SOME-THING NEW UP. BUT RIGHT NOW WHAT'S IN FRONT OF ME IS THIS FILM. SONY LEGACY AND LIGHT IN THE ATTIC HAVE PUT ME ON THE MAP. THESE YOUNGBLOOD STRANGERS HAVE EX-CITED MY MUSICAL CAREER."

87. "DON'T BE A SECRET PARTNER." A QUOTE FROM RO-DRIGUEZ ON THE SUBJECT OF LOVE. HE REPEATED THIS QUOTE TO AN AUDIENCE AT THE HIGHLINE BALLROOM.

88. "I WAS SKEPTICAL ABOUT THE WHOLE IDEA OF MY BE-ING IN A FILM." RODRIGUEZ' COMMENT WHEN HE MET MALIK BENDJELLOUL.

89. "WELL, YOU NEVER THROW AWAY YOUR WORK CLOTHES, BUT THIS THING IS LIKE A MONSOON." RODRIGUEZ ON HIS FUTURE AND THE POSSIBILITY OF RETURNING FROM ARTISTIC AND FINANCIAL OBSCURITY TO SUCCESS AND THEN BACK AGAIN TO OBSCURITY. THIS ARTICLE WAS AN INTERIVEW WITH LARRY ROHTER IN THE NEW YORK TIMES.

90. "EVEN WITHOUT THE MONEY, THERE HAVE ALREADY BEEN REWARDS JUST FROM THE OPPORTUNITY TO DO ALL THIS. I GUESS WE ALL WANT TO GET THERE RIGHT AWAY, BUT I BELIEVE IT'S NEVER TOO EARLY, NEVER TOO LATE." RODRI-

GUEZ ANSWERING A QUESTION ON WHETHER OR NOT THE LACK OF MONEY BOTHERS HIM.

91. "I CHOSE THE FOLK SONG AS A GENRE IN MUSIC TO TALK ABOUT THIS SOCIAL REALISM. THERE WAS A LOT OF TURBULENCE IN AMERICA. THE VIETNAM WAR. THERE WERE A LOT OF THINGS HAPPENING." RODRIGUEZ DURING AN INTERVIEW WITH THE NEW ZEALAND HERALD, JANUARY 21, 2013.

92. "I DON'T TRUST A MAN WHO DRINKS. AND I DON'T TRUST A MAN WHO DOESN'T DRINK." RODRIGUEZ ON MONDAY APRIL 27, 2009 COMMENTING TO THE AUDIENCE AT THE BEACHLAND BALLROOM IN CLEVELAND OHIO.

93. "I DID LETTERMAN WITH A 25-PIECE ORCHESTRA; IT WAS A POWERFUL PERFORMANCE EVEN WITHOUT ME. I DIDN'T HAVE ANYTHING TO DO WITH THE ORCHESTRATION. THE ORCHESTRATION STOLE THE SHOW. BUT I'LL BE TOURING SOLO EVEN THOUGH I GOT ABOUT 12 BANDS. I HAVE A FULL BAND IN ENGLAND. I HAVE A SWEDISH BAND. I HAVE A SOUTH AFRICAN BAND. I HAVE BRITISH BANDS. I'VE BEEN DOING THAT FOR A WHILE NOW SINCE 1998. SOMETIMES I'M AT A LACK OF WORDS BECAUSE I'VE LED SUCH AN ORDINARY LIFE AND THERE'S NOT MUCH TO SAY ABOUT HARD WORK BEYOND THAT IT'S HARD WORK. I'M JUST ENJOYING THIS TIME." THIS IS FROM AN INTERVIEW WITH JEFF NIESEL.

94. "I CONTINUED TO PLAY. IT'S SOMETHING THAT I DON'T THINK I CAN STOP. I WENT TO WORK AND DID RESTORATION AND DEMOLITION OF BUILDINGS. I LEARNT ANOTHER TRADE. THAT'S THE PATTERN OF MY CAREER. IT'S KIND OF ALL MISMATCHED, BUT THAT'S THE WAY IT WENT. LIFE ISN'T CHRONOLOGICAL. SOME PEOPLE ARE OLDER AT A YOUNGER AGE."

95. "THE MYSTERY OF LIFE IS YOU DON'T KNOW WHEN IT WILL END." RODRIGUEZ REMARKING IN THE OLD MIAMI BAR WHILE 60 MINUTES FILMED A SPOT WITH BOB SIMON.

96. "I'M TRYING TO STAY IN GOOD SHAPE HERE, BECAUSE I'D LIKE TO GET OUT AND MEET THE PEOPLE, AND PLAY THEM MY SONGS. I'M NOT OLD - I'M ANCIENT. BUT THERE'S ONLY ONE AGE: EITHER YOU'RE ALIVE OR YOU'RE NOT." RODRIGUEZ IN CONVERSATION WITH STEVE CHICK, THE LONDON GUARDIAN, AUGUST 7, 2008

97. "I KNOW IT'S ALL BULLSHIT, BUT KEEP IT COMING." RODRIGUEZ REMARKING TO A LONDON AUDIENCE AT THE ROYAL FESTIVAL HALL IN LONDON, NOVEMBER 2012.

98. "I FELT I WAS READY FOR THE WORLD, BUT THE WORLD WASN'T READY FOR ME. I FEEL WE ALL HAVE A MISSION - WE HAVE OBLIGATIONS. THOSE TURNS ON THE JOURNEY, DIFFERENT TWISTS - LIFE IS NOT LINEAR." IN A FEBRUARY 2013 INTERVIEW WITH MICHELLE FAUL AND JEFF KAROUB.

99. "IT'S A ROCK AND ROLL MYSTERY NOW. WHO WOULDA THOUGHT." RODRIGUEZ IN CONVERSATION WITH JEFF KAROUB AND MICHELLE FAUL

100. "FREE LOVE IS TOO EXPENSIVE." RODRIGUEZ COMMENTING ON STAGE AT USHER HALL, EDINBURGH, NOVEMBER 2102.

101. "THE LITTLE MAN GETS SHAFTED, SONS AND MONEYS DRAFTED...." RODRIGUEZ "THE ESTABLISHMENT BLUES."

102. "I READ SOME POETS WHEN I WROTE THEM," HE SAYS OF HIS SONGS. "I CARRIED A DICTIONARY. I TRIED TO PUT A PHRASE TOGETHER. I DIDN'T DO [IT] IN A DELIBERATE WAY THAT MAYBE IT WOULD READ AS POETRY. BUT ... THE LYRICS ARE IMPORTANT TO ME." RODRIGUEZ ON HIS METHOD OF SONGWRITING. THIS IS A VARIATION OF AN EARLIER QUOTE.

103. "I THINK OMISSION IS A SIN. WITHHOLDING EVIDENCE IS UNETHICAL TO SAY THE LEAST, BUT I'LL RESOLVE THAT," RODRIGUEZ SAID IN AN INTERVIEW WITH THE ASSOCIATED PRESS IN A DETROIT BAR.

104. "AND YOU CAN KEEP YOUR SYMBOLS OF SUCCESS, THEN I'LL PURSUE MY OWN HAPPINESS." RODRIGUEZ USING SONG LYRICS TO SUGGEST HIS VIEW OF MONEY AND ITS IMPORTANCE. OR PERHAPS ITS LACK OF IMPORTANCE.

105. "IT'S BEEN A MUSICAL ODYSSEY," RODRIGUEZ SAYS. "IT'S EDUCATIONAL AND IT'S ALSO ENLIGHTENMENT. AND THE THING IS, I NEVER DREAMED IT WOULD GET AT THIS LEVEL — I WAS GONNA MAKE SOME RECORDS, I WAS GONNA SELL SOME RECORDS, AND PLAY BIGGER ROOMS. YOU KNOW WHAT I MEAN: UP THE FOOD CHAIN, LIKE THAT. BUT THIS IS LIKE, THE JUMPS ARE SO HUGE." FROM AN ARTICLE BY EDD HURT.

106. "I DO DEMOLITION, THAT SORT OF THING," RODRIGUEZ COMMENTING IN THE DOCUMENTARY.

107. "YOU GO HOME BUT YOU CAN'T STAY," RODRIGUEZ LYRICS IN THE SONG "STREET BOY."

108. "YOU COULD HEAR THESE RADIO STATIONS LATE AT NIGHT AND DISC JOCKEYS WERE BECOMING MORE IMPORTANT, PLAYING JIMMY REED, THE SINGING GROUPS, ALL THE DOO-WOP GROUPS." RODRIGUEZ IN AN INTERVIEW WITH KEVIN "SIPRANO" HOWES ON HIS EARLY MUSICAL INFLUENCES.

109. "I LOVED THE WOODY GUTHRIE TRADITION OF SPEAKING ABOUT WHAT'S HAPPENING TO THE COUNTRY." FROM A SCOTT FEINBERG INTERVIEW.

110. "I'M A FORTUNATE MAN, QUITE FORTUNATE. IT'S HAPPENED. IT'S PRETTY AMAZING." SCOTT FEINBERG INTERVIEW.

111. 'NEVER BE ASHAMED OF HARD WORK, THE STRUGGLE NEVER ENDS." RODRIGUEZ

112. "HATE IS TOO STRONG AN EMOTION TO WASTE ON SOMEONE YOU DON'T LIKE." RODRIGUEZ

113. "THE MYSTERY OF LIFE. WHEN ARE YOU GOING TO DIE?" RODRIGUEZ

114. "CAUSE MY HEART'S BECOME A CROOKED HOTEL FULL OF RUMORS." RODRIGUEZ LYRICS FROM "CAUSE."

115. "SOON YOU'LL KNOW I'LL LEAVE YA, AND I'LL NEVER LOOK BEHIND, CUZ I WAS BORN FOR THE PURPOSE OF CRUCIFYING YOUR MIND." RODRIGUEZ' LYRICS FROM CRUCIFY YOUR MIND.

116. "I HAD TO LEARN HOW TO WORK THESE SMALL ROOMS AND GET MORE CONFIDENCE," RODRIGUEZ IN AN APRIL 11, 2013 ROLLING STONE INTERVIEW.

117. "I DON'T EYEBALL MY AUDIENCE, LIKE THE WAY A RAP ARTIST DOES WHO IS MORE CONFRONTATIONAL. I GET MORE IN TUNE WITH MY EYES CLOSED, AND I LISTEN TO THE SONG SO THAT I CAN RE-CREATE IT." RODRIGUEZ IN ROLLING STONE APRIL 11, 2013.

118. "I DON'T KNOW IF IT MEANS I'M SMART OR I'M EDUCATED, BUT IT'S QUITE AN HONOR." RODRIGUEZ COMMENTING ON DETROIT'S WAYNE STATE UNVIVERSITY AWARDING HIM AN HONORARY DOCTORATE IN HUMAME LETTERS, MAY 20, 2013

119. "DOES THE PRESSURE CONCERN ME? YEAH, I THINK SO. I THINK THAT NOW, BECAUSE OF THE SPACE OF TIME, AND IN MY PARTICULARLY CASE, IT'S AN UNUSUAL CAREER." RODRIGUEZ TO UNCUT WRITER MICHAEL BONNER, JULY 2013

120. "I'M BORN AND BRED OUT OF DETROIT." RODRIGUEZ TO BONNER. IN THE BRITISH MAGAZINE UNCUT, JULY 2013

121. "I FEEL A LOT OF MUSICIANS ARE LISTENING TO ME RIGHT NOW."

122. "THIS IS WHAT I ALWAYS WANTED, TO MAKE SOMETHING OF MYSELF THROUGH MUSIC. HAS IT CHANGED ME? IT

STARTED OUT WITH PERSONAL SUCCESS, BUT NOW IT'S MUCH LARGER THAN THAT." QUOTE TO BONNER, UNCUT, JULY 2013

123. "THERE'S NO SHAME IN HARD WORK." SIXTO RODRIGUEZ

124. "I'VE ALWAYS BEEN HAPPIER IN THE CITY," RODRIGUEZ IN AN INTERVIEW IN 2010.

125. "MY CAREER HAPPENED THROUGH INTRODUCTIONS." RODRIGUEZ IN A 2010 INTERVIEW.

129. "YOU'VE GOT TO BE FROM SOMEWHERE." A COMMENT WHEN ASKED WHY HE LIVED IN DETROIT BY RODRIGUEZ WHEN SEARCHING FOR SUGAR MAN OPENED AT THE L. A. FILM FESTIVAL.

130. "THE THING WITH ALL THIS IS THAT I UNDERSTAND NOW ABOUT SOUTH AFRICA, WHICH I DIDN'T KNOW MUCH ABOUT AT THE TIME. THERE WAS APARTHEID AND GOVERNMENT SUPPRESSION AND POLICE BRUTALITY." RODRIGUEZ IN CONVERSATION WITH JEFF NIESEL.

131. "I CALL IT A DESCRIPTIVE SONG AND NOT A PRESCRIPTIVE SONG," RODRIGUEZ COMMENTING ON SUGAR MAN.

132. "A GUY STARTED PLAYING ME ON MIDNIGHT RADIO IN AUSTRALIA, AND WE HAD ENOUGH ATTENTION THAT WE COULD SELL OUT THE CONCERTS." RODRIGUEZ ON HIS 1979 AND 1981 AUSTRALIAN TOURS.

133. "THERE ARE NO GUARANTEES IN THE MUSIC FIELD. THERE'S A LOT OF REJECTION, A LOT OF CRITICISM AND A LOT OF DISAPPOINTMENT." RODRIGUEZ IN CONVERSATION WITH BRAD WHEELER.

134. "IT'S LIKE HAVING TWO LIVES. BIZARRE IS A WORD YOU COULD USE." RODRIGUEZ IN CONVERSATION WITH SOUTH AFRICAN WRITER RIAN MALAN.

135. "I WAS READY FOR THE WORLD, BUT I DON'T THINK THE WORLD WAS READY FOR ME." RODRIGUEZ COMMENTING ON THE FAILURE OF HIS TWO ALBUMS TO A LONDON JOURNALIST.

136. "VOLTAIRE SAID THAT THE PEN WAS MIGHTIER THAN THE SWORD, BUT TODAY MAYBE THE JOURNALIST AND THE CAMERA ARE MIGHTIER THAN THE PEN." RODRIGUEZ IN CONVERSATION WITH DAVID SEGAL.

137. "MY FATHER SAID TO ME...I TRY TO REMEMBER EVERYTING HE SAID. HE'S MY ROLE MODEL." RODRIGUEZ IN CONVERSATION WITH DAVID SEGAL.

138. "MUSIC GENERATES OXYGEN AND MONEY. IT RAISES THE CONSCIOUSNESS OF THE AUDIENCES." IN COVERSATION WITH DAVID SEGAL.

139. "I LISTEN TO OTHER BANDS AND WRITE DOWN THOUGHTS AND LYRICS. THERE ARE PLENTY OF INSPIRATIONS." TALKING TO DAVID SEGAL ABOUT SONGWRITING.

140. "YOUR MIND CAN GET SHARPER IN YOUR OLD AGE BECAUSE YOU HAVE THE HISTORY." RODRIGUEZ TALKING TO DAVID SEGAL.

141. "I'M NOT A VISUAL GUY. I'M AUDIO." IN CONVERSATION WITH DAVID SEGAL.

142. "FAME IS A DOUBLE EDGED SWORD."

143. "THE ONLY REASON MY ALBUMS WERE REISSUED WAS BECAUSE OF THE SEATTLE LABEL LIGHT IN THE ATTIC. THE ONLY REASON THEY GOT INVOLVED WAS THROUGH DAVID HOLMES." RODRIGUEZ IN CONVERSATION WITH DAVE SEGAL.

144. "MUSIC IT'S MAYBE 80 PERCENT BOY/GIRL THEMES, BUT THERE ARE OTHER SOCIAL THINGS THAT ARE VERY IMPORTANT." RODRIGUEZ IN CONVERSATION WITH DAVID SEGAL.

145. "THE GUYS IN CONGRESS PROVED THAT THEY CAN'T DO THE JOB OF FIXING SOCIAL SECURITY, SO IT'S TIME FOR THE WOMEN TO TAKE OVER." RODRIGUEZ IN CONVERSATION WITH DAVID SEGAL.

146. "THEY SAID, 'I HEARD YOU WERE DEAD.' WHAT DO YOU SAY TO THAT?" RODRIGUEZ COMMENTING ON THE MYTHS SURROUNDING HIS LIFE TO THE LONDON TIMES JONATHAN DEAN.

147. "LET'S BE CLEAR. BOB DYLAN HAS WRITTEN MORE THAN 500 SONGS. I'VE WRITTEN 30-BUT THE COMPARISON IS SWEET, THANKS A LOT." RODRIGUEZ TALKING TO THE LONDON TIMES JONATHAN DEAN.

148. "POOR PEOPLE CAN'T AFFORD AN INCREASE IN WATER RATES." RODRIGUEZ TESTIFYING BEFORE THE DETROIT WATER BOARD, MARCH 2015

149. "I STILL DON'T KNOW WHAT HAPPENED TO THAT MONEY. IT WOULD TAKE YEARS. BUT THE BASIS OF MUSIC IS PUBLISHING AND NOW WE HAVE INFORMATION WE DIDN'T BEFORE." RODRIGUEZ IN CONVERSATION WITH THE LONDON TIMES JONATHAN DEAN.

150. "I DON'T TRUST HISTORY."

151. "I WAS DECADES IN THE MUSICAL WILDERNESS. I DON'T FEEL LOST I KNEW EXACTLY WHERE I WAS." RODRIGUEZ IN CONVERSATION WITH JONATHAN DEAN.

152. "THERE ARE THINGS TO GET DONE, AND NO MATTER HOW LOFTY OUR IDEAS, YOU ONLY GET SO MUCH TIME TO FIGURE THIS OUT. THE IMPERMANENCE OF LIFE, THE MYSTERY OF LIFE-YOU'VE GOT TO DEAL WITH WHAT YOU CAN. I FEEL PRIDE." RODRIGUEZ IN CONVERSATION WITH JONATHAN DEAN.

153. "DON'T TRUST WOMEN. YOU KNOW WHY? BECAUSE YOU CAN'T TRUST MEN." RODRIGUEZ COMMENTING DURING

AN APRIL 8, 2007 SHOW AT THE CORNER HOTEL IN AUSTRA-LIA.

154. "THE ZEROES ARE THE HEROES." RODRIGUEZ COMMENTING ON PEOPLE BORN IN 2000. THIS COMMENT WAS MADE APRIL 8, 2007 AT THE CORNER HOTEL.

155. "I'VE BEEN CHASING MUSIC SINCE I WAS SIXTEEN." THE HOLLYWOOD REPORTER

156. "IT'S ALL PRACTICE. A STUDENT IS ALWAYS A STUDENT." THE HOLLYWOOD REPORTER

157. "I ONLY HAVE TO COME UP WITH A THREE MINUTE SONG." A COMMENT TO THE HOLLYWOOD REPORTER

158. "WE DO MUSIC FOR THE MONEY. WE ALSO DO IT FOR THE FUN." THE HOLLYWOOD REPORTER

159. "MUSIC HAS A LOT OF VALUE." THE HOLLYWOOD REPORTER

160. "I GAVE IT UP AFTER 1974. I WASN'T SEEING IT GOING ANYWHERE." THE HOLLYWOOD REPORTER

161. "IT'S A SMALL GROUP OF PEOPLE WHO RUN THE MUSIC SCENE." THE HOLLYWOOD REPORTER

162. "IT BLEW MY MIND, YEAH IT WAS MIND BLOWING TO SEE ALL THAT AUDIENCE AND YOUNG BLOODS. AFRICANS ARE MY FAN BASE, WE HAVE A GLOBAL AUDIENCE AND AUSTRALIA TO ME AUSTRALIA IS FIRST AND IT WAS ALL WELL AND GOOD." RODRIGUEZ REMARKING TO THE HOLLYWOOD REPORTER

163. "I WAS KIND OF RELUCTANT IN GETTING INOLVED IN IT." RODRIGUEZ COMMENTING ON MEETING MALIK BENDJEL-LOUL AND COOPERATING ON SEARCHING FOR SUGAR MAN." YOU TUBE EYEWITNESS NEWS IN SOUTH AFRICAN DURING HIS FEBRUARY 2013 TOUR http://www.youtube.com/watch?v=49pCAiev8h4

164. "THE ONLY OTHER TIME I FELT SO YOUNG WAS WHEN I WAS IN CAPE TOWN." RODRIGUEZ BEING INTERVIEWED IN SOUTH AFRICA, FEBRUARY 2013.

165. "YOU CAN'T HELP BUT BE PERSUADED BY HENRY MANCINI." RODRIGUEZ QUOTED IN KEVIN HOWES' LINER NOTES TO COLD FACT.

166. "I GUESS LOOKING OUT THAT WINDOW WERE SOME OF THIS VISUALS, LIKE KENT STATE, THE ASSASSINATIONS OF SO MANY PEOPLE IN THE 60S, UNREST, THE RESISTANCE AGAINST THE WAR." RODRIGUEZ IN CONVERSATION WITH SAUL AUSTERLITZ, BOSTON GLOBE, SEPTEMBER 21, 2008.

167. "DO YOU WANT TO KNOW THE SECRET TO LIFE? YOU BREATHE IN AND THEN YOU BREATHE OUT." RODRIGUEZ COMMENTING IN 2008 WHILE PERFORMING IN NEW YORK AT JOE'S PUB.

168. "I'VE WAITED THIRTY YEARS TO MEET MY FANS. I WANT TO MEET THEM ALL." SIXTO RODRIGUEZ TALKING TO STEPHEN "SUGAR" SEGERMAN, 1998.

169. "IT'S A PRIVILEGE TO PLAY MUSIC, A REAL JOY." RODRIGUEZ COMMENTING TO AN AUSTRALIAN REPORTER OCTOBER 2014.

170. "I'M A SOLID 72, SO THERE'S THE POLITICAL, THE MEDICAL, THE LEGAL IN WHAT I DO, BUT WE WANT TO KEEP THE MUSIC SEPARATE. THAT'S THE THING I ENJOY." RODRIGUEZ COMMENTING TO AUSTRALIAN JOURNALIST CRAIG MATHIESON, OCTOBER, 2014.

171. "I TRY TO STAY WITH THE ISSUES: VIOLENCE AGAINST WOMEN, A COALITION AGAINST POLICE BRUTALITY AND THE RIGHTS OF INDIGENOUS PEOPLE...I WATCH AND READ WHAT'S GOING ON, BUT I'M LIKE SOCRATES, WHO WAS ASKED IF HE WAS A CITIZEN OF ATHENS AND SAID 'I'M A CITIZEN OF THE WORLD.'" RODRIGUEZ IN COVERSATION WITH CRAIG MATHIESON.

172."AS IT GOES, WE'VE BEEN SPINNING AROUND SINCE THE FILM CAME OUT. THAT'S HELPED TREMENDOUSLY." RO-DRIGUEZ COMMENTING AS HE TOURS AUSTRALIA AND NEW ZEALAND, OCTOBER 2014.

173. "AUSTRALIA WAS THE FIRST ONE. I DID 79, 81 AND THEN NOTHING UNTIL 98 IN SOUTH AFRICA. THAT WAS MY HIGH POINT-AUSTRALIA." RODRIGUEZ COMMENTED IN OCTO-BER 2014 AS HE BEGINS A TOUR DOWN UNDER.

174. "IT WILL ALL BE FRESH STUFF, THAT'S FOR SURE. I CONSIDER MYSELF CONTEMPORARY." RODRIGUEZ SPEAKING WITH AUSTRALIAN JOURNALIST TOM CARDY, OCTOBER 2014 ON A PROPOSED THIRD ALBUM.

175. "I'VE SEEN THE FILM 35 TIMES! HAD I GIVEN UP ON EVERY MAKING IT? I THINK I PROBABLY HAD. PUT IT THIS WAY, I WAS TOO DISAPPOINTED TO BE DISAPPOINTED. BUT NOW WE'VE BEEN FOUR TIMES TO SOUTH AFRICA AND FOUR TIMES TO AUSTRALIA AND I'M FINALLY BREAKING INTO THE AMER-ICAN MARKET." RODRIGUEZ IN CONVERSATION WITH ROB HUGHES, AUGUST 16, 2012.

176. 'I'M JUST AN ORDINARY LEGEND." RODRIGUEZ IN NU-MEROUS INTERVIEWS 2012-2014.

177. "IT'S ALL AN ACT." RODRIGUEZ COMMENTING IN NO-VEMBER 2014 AS HE FINISHED A MONTH LONG AUSTRALIAN TOUR DOWN UNDER TO SOLD OUT AUDIENCES.

178. "EIGHT YEARS LATER. I CAN'T BELIEVE IT." RODRI-GUEZ COMMENTING FROM THE STAGE DURING A SOLD OUT AUSTRALIAN SHOW IN 1979. HE IS REFERRING TO HOW LONG IT HAD BEEN SINCE HE RECORDED COMING FROM REALITY.

179. "THEY HAVE A WAR EVERY FIFTEEN OR TWENTY YEARS, AND THERE'S ALWAYS A CROP OF YOUNGBLOODS WHO DON'T KNOW THIS IS HAPPENING. THEY'VE BEEN INSPIRED BY THE MEDIA. I LOVE MY COUNTRY. IT'S JUST THE GOVERNMENT I

DON'T TRUST." RODRIGUEZ INTERVIEWED BY ANDY GREENE, ROLLING STONE, MARCH 28, 2013.

180. IT'S AN OPPORTUNITY TO REACH A WIDER AUDIENCE." RODRIGUEZ COMMENTING TO ROLLING STONE'S ZACH SCHONFELD, JULY 26, 2012.

181. "I WROTE THESE PIECES UNDER THIRTY SONGS, AND THEY HAVE GOTTEN SOME LONGIVITY THAT I DIDN'T THINK WAS GOING TO HAPPEN AT ALL." IN CONVERSATION WITH ZACH SCHONFELD.

182. "IT WAS A CULTURE SHOCK AT FIRST. THE COUNTRY IS BEAUTIFUL; I REALLY THOUGHT IT WAS GOING TO BE THIRD WORLD AND FULL OF DISGRUNTLED RASTAFARI. IT TURNED OUT VERY DIFFERENT." RODRIGUEZ INTERVIEWED BY KALEEM AFTAB, THE LONDON INDEPENDENT, JULY 24, 2012 ON HIS SOUTH AFRICAN TOUR.

183. "I DON'T BELIEVE THAT STORY THAT THERE WERE NO ROYALTIES. IN THIS BUSINESS THERE ARE A LOT OF SUPERLATIVES USED, BUT IT WAS JUST SOMETHING TO BE ABLE TO PLAY THERE AND THAT I WAS ABLE TO TAKE MY FAMILY WITH ME AND SHARE THAT WITH THEM." RODRIGUEZ COMMENTING ON THE 1998 SOUTH AFRICAN TOUR AND THE ROYALTIES THAT HE MAY OR MAY NOT HAVE BEEN DUE. INTERVIEW BY KALEEM AFTAB, JUY 24, 2012.

184. "I CALL MONEY OXYGEN. EVERYONE NEEDS OXYGEN AND THAT'S NOT MY GOAL." RODRIGUEZ IN COVERSATION WITH KALEEM AFTAB.

185. "I DO WRITE STUFF DOWN. IT'S EASIER AT THE MOMENT. IT LEADS YOU TO POETRY, ALL THESE THINGS THAT HAPPENED." RODRIGUEZ IN CONVERSATION WITH KALEEM AFTAB.

186. "I BEGAN PLAYING AT 16 ON A FAMILY GUITAR AND IT ALTERED MY LIFE." RODRIGUEZ IN CONVERSATION WITH CRAIG BARTHOLOMEW-STRYDOM.

187. "CLEARLY ALCOHOL IS A MUCH MORE DESRUCTIVE SUBSTANCE. WEED IS A NATURAL SUBSTANCE. LESS HARMFUL AND HELPFUL IN SOME CASES." THIS IS RODRIGUEZ ANSWERING A CRAIG BARTHOLOMEW-STRYDOM QUESTION ABOUT HIS VIEWS OF MARIJUANA AND ALCOHOL.

188. "ANYONE HERE FROM DETROIT? MY CONDOLENCES." RODRIGUEZ JOKING WITH A SAN DIEGO AUDIENCE WHILE PERFORMING AT THE RE-OPENING OF THE NORTH PARK THEATER IN JUNE 2014 AT TWO SOLD OUT SHOWS.

189. "I KNOW IT'S THE DRINKS, BUT I LOVE YOU BACK." RODRIGUEZ COMMENTING FROM THE STAGE IN ADELAIDE IN OCTOBER 2014 WHILE ON A SOLD OUT AUSTRALIAN TOUR.

190. TAKE IT EASY ON ME. I'M A SOLID 72 YEARS OLD." THIS IS RODRIGUEZ COMMENTING TO THE ADELAIDE AUDIENCE WHILE IN AUSTRALIA, OCTOBER 2014.

191. "TO ME IT CHEAPENED THE FILM, LIKE IT WAS A PROMO FILM." RODRIGUEZ COMPLAINING TO ROLLING STONE WRITER, PATRICK FLANARY, ABOUT HIS ATTEMPTS TO HAVE REFERENCES TO A THIRD RODRIGUEZ ALBUM ELIMINATED FROM SEARCHING FOR SUGAR MAN.

192. "I'D LIKE TO COME TO PALM SPRINGS AND RECORD. IT WOULD BE RESTFUL. I LOVE TOURING BUT IT A GRIND." RODRIGUEZ IN CONVERSATION WITH STEVE ROWLAND, MAY 30, 2014.

193. "IT'S ROCK AND ROLL HISTORY NOW." RODRIGUEZ COMMENTING ON HIS IMPROBABLE JOURNEY TO STARDOM.

194. "REGAN GOT ME THE PHONE. FOR YEARS I DIDN'T HAVE A PHONE AND I'VE BEEN OUT OF CONTACT. I WAS GETTING TOO MANY CALLS AND I WAS COMING HOME TO ANSWER THE PHONE, SO I PULLED IT OUT. SO REGAN COT ME ONE." RODRIGUEZ EXPLAINING HIS LACK OF OWNING AND USING A COMPUTER AND HIS UNHAPPINESS WITH THE PHONE TO D. HOUSE IN A 2009 SEATTLE INTERVIEW.

195. "WHAT THE MULTI-NATIONALS HAVE DONE IS GET THE CHEAP LABOR AND HOW THEY RAISE THE PRICES AND TAKE THE REST. EXXON, MOBIL, THE OIL COMPANIES ARE THE ULTIMATE BENEFICIARIES." RODRIGUEZ COMMENTING TO D. HOUSE ON HIS POLITICAL CONCERNS.

APPENDIX

IV

RODRIGUEZ DISCOGRAPHY

Albums: Studio albums

1970: *Cold Fact*

Vinyl, Cassette and CD

USA: March 1970, Sussex [SXBS 7000] *South Africa:* 1971, A&M [AMLS 67000] *South Africa:* 1974, United Artists [SXBS 7000] *Australia:* 1978, Blue Goose Music [BGM 002] *New Zealand:* 1978, Interfusion [L34226] *South Africa:* 1991, Teal Trutone [KVL 5109] *USA:* August 2008, Light In The Attic [LITA036] remastered.

Cassette

South Africa: 1973, A&M [CXBS 7000] *South Africa:* 1991, Teal Trutone [KVC 5109] *South Africa:* mid-90s, Teal Trutone [MMTC 1846]

RARE RODRIGUEZ REISSUE CD

CD
Australia: 1986, BMG Arista [BGM 002] *South Africa:* late 80s, RPM [ICSXBS7000] *South Africa:* 1991, Teal Trutone [200 014-2] *Australia:* 1993, RCA Victor [VPCD 6745] *South Africa:* mid-90s, Teal Trutone [MMTCD 1846] *South Africa:* 2002, PT Music [CDA DTA 7000] *South Africa:* 2005, PT Music [CDA DTA 7000] remastered *USA:* August 2008, Light In The Attic [LITA036] remastered *South Africa:* December 2012, Sony [CDSM552]

•**1971:** *Coming from Reality.*
Live albums
•**1981:** *Rodriguez Alive* **(Australia);**

•**1998:** *Live Fact* **(South Africa);**
Compilations

•1976: *After the Fact* (reissue of *Coming From Reality*) (South Africa);

•1977: *At His Best* (Australia);

•1982: *The Best of Rodriguez* (South Africa);

•2005: *Sugarman: The Best of Rodriguez* (South Africa).

Singles

•1967: "I'll Slip Away" b/w "You'd Like to Admit It" (as Rod Riguez);

•1970: "Inner City Blues" b/w "Forget It";

•1970: "To Whom It May Concern" b/w "I Think of You";

•1977: "Sugar Man" b/w "Inner City Blues" (Australia);

•1978: "Climb Up on My Music" b/w "To Whom It May Concern" (Australia);

EDITOR'S NOTE: ADDITIONS TO BE CONTINUED IN VOLUME TWO

APPENDIX

V

QUOTES ABOUT RODRIGUEZ

1. "I WAS ALMOST AFRAID TO LISTEN TO THE MUSIC BE-CAUSE I THOUGHT, IT CAN'T BE AS GOOD AS THEY SAY. BUT IT WAS." MALIK BENDJELLOUL, THE FILM DIRECTOR OF SEARCH-ING FOR SUGAR MAN TO THE HUFFINGTON POST.

2. "I WAS LIKE, THIS IS THE BEST STORY I'VE EVER HEARD IN MY LIFE OR THAT I'M EVER, GOING TO HEAR. I WAS LIKE, NO WAY. IT WAS A BEAUTIFUL STORY." MALIK BENDJELLOUL.

3. "I WAS AFRAID BECAUSE THIS WAS THE BEST STORY I HAD HEARD IN MY LIFE, AND I DON'T EVEN WANTED TO LISTEN TO IT BECAUSE... WHAT IF IT'S BAD? I PLAYED IT TO A DYLAN FAN AND HE SAID, 'THIS IS BETTER THAN BOB DYLAN." MALIK BENDJELLOUL

4. "IT WAS LIKE ELVIS COMING BACK FROM THE DEAD." CRAIG BARTHOLOMEW-STRYDOM COMMENTING ON RODRI-GUEZ' 1998 SOUTH AFRICAN CONCERTS.

5. "I THOUGHT THAT I WOULD SEE HIM BEING BEWILDERED AT ALL THESE PEOPLE STARING AT HIM, BUT IT WAS JUST THE OP-POSITE, IT'S LIKE HE HAD ARRIVED AT THAT THING HE HAD TRIED TO FIND HIS WHOLE LIFE." CRAIG BARTHOLOMEW-STRYDOM.

6. "STUNNING. ONE OF GREATEST, AND MOST MOVING DOCUMENTARIES EVER MADE." Q MAGAZINE ON SEARCHING FOR SUGAR MAN.

7. "I REALIZED THIS IS NEVER GOING TO HAPPEN AGAIN IN THE HISTORY OF THE WORLD. IT'S A TRUE CINDERELLA STORY. IT'S BETTER THAN CINDERELLA BECAUSE CINDERELLA DIDN'T HAVE AS GOOD A SOUNDTRACK." MALIK BENDJELLOUL

8. "IT IS THE BEST STORY I HAVE EVER HEARD IN MY LIFE, AND I THINK I EVER WILL HEAR," HE CONTINUED. "I SPENT AROUND FIVE YEARS ON THE PROJECT, INSTEAD OF HIS USUAL FOUR WEEKS." MALIK BENDJELLOUL

9. "A GIFTED SONGWRITER WITH A PENCHANT FOR LYRICAL FLOURISHES INFLUENCED BY BOB DYLAN, AND ECHOING VAN MORRISON'S JAZZ-ROCK-SOUL MASTERPIECE" - LOS ANGELES TIMES

10. "EVERYONE LOVES A SHOULD-BE STAR WHO NEVER GOT THEIR SHOT," WROTE JIM FARBER IN HIS CD REVIEW OF THE SEARCHING FOR SUGAR MAN SOUNDTRACK IN THE NEW YORK DAILY NEWS (JULY 24, 2012). "....THE SOUNDTRACK...MAKES ITS OWN ARGUMENT FOR THE INJUSTICE DONE TO A SIGNIFICANT TALENT....MANY OF THE ARRANGEMENTS COME COURTESY OF PRODUCERS MIKE THEODORE AND DENNIS COFFEY (WHO PLAYED GUITAR IN MOTOWN'S STELLAR HOUSE BAND, THE FUNK BROTH-ERS)....SMALL WONDER BOOTLEGS OF RODRIGUEZ'S ALBUMS BE-CAME CLASSICS WITH WHITE SOUTH AFRICAN LIBERALS DURING APARTHEID (SOMETHING UNBEKNOWNST TO THE SINGER)....RO-

DRIGUEZ HAS HIS OWN TONE AND MELODIC CHOPS. PAIRED WITH THE SPLASHY PSYCH-FOLK ARRANGEMENTS, THEY MAKE THE CASE FOR THE LONG-MISSING 'SUGAR MAN' AS A GENUINE FIND."

11. "THE LACK OF FUNDING FORCED SOME THINGS TO BE FINISHED IN A WAY THAT INITIALLY WAS NOT INTENDED. THE FIRST YEAR OF THE PRODUCTION THERE WAS SOME MONEY COMING IN THAT WAS USED TO SHOOT WITH A SUPER 8 CAMERA. BUT THE LAST THREE YEARS THERE WAS ALMOST NO MONEY COMING IN AND IT WAS TOO EXPENSIVE TO FINISH THE SCENES WITH THE SAME CAMERA. IN THE END, IT PROVED THAT A ONE DOLLAR IPHONE SUPER 8 APP WORKED JUST AS WELL. THE BAR SCENE IN THE BEGINNING WHERE THE PRODUCERS DISCOVER RODRIGUEZ WAS, FOR EXAMPLE, SHOT WITH THAT APP." FROM A COMMENT THE SUNDANCE FILM FESTIVAL WEBSITE

12. "I SAID IT IN A REVIEW I DID OF THE RARE 'ALIVE' AL-BUM, BUT HAVING EXPERIENCED IT FIRST HAND NOW, I AM MORE CONVINCED THAN EVER THAT RODRIGUEZ WAS THE ONE WHO PUT THE AWE IN AUDIENCE. AS FOR THOSE OF YOU DOWN UNDER IN OZ WHO HAVEN'T SEEN HIM SINCE THE EAR-LY 80'S ALL I CAN SAY IS I'VE SET ASIDE A FEW GOOSEBUMPS TO SHARE WITH YOU AS I AM SURE YOUR TIME WILL COME AGAIN," JOHN SAMSON, OCTOBER 10, 2005.

13. "THIS GUY WAS LIKE A WISE MAN, A PROPHET, I'VE NEV-ER WORKED WITH ANYONE AS TALENTED," STEVE ROWLAND, PRODUCER OF COMING FROM REALITY

14. "DEAD MEN DON'T TOUR," KONNY RODRIGUEZ

15. "A LOT OF PEOPLE THOUGHT HE WAS GOING TO BE THE NEXT BOB DYLAN." MALIK BENDJELLOUL

16. "NO ONE'S REALLY GOTTEN TO THE BOTTOM OF THE MONEY YET," CRAIG BARTHOLOMEW-STRYDOM

17. "HE'S A GENUINELY HUMBLE MAN, AND HE WANTED TO STAY HOME IN DETROIT WATCHING TELEVISION," SIMON

CHINN ON WHY RODRIGUEZ DIDN'T ATTEND THE 85TH ANNUAL ACADEMY AWARDS.

18. "RODRIGUEZ IS DETROIT IN A WAY." MALIK BENDJELLOUL COMMENTING PRIOR TO THE 85th ANNUAL ACADEMY AWARDS CEREMONY.

19. "RODRIGUEZ IS AS RESERVED, CONTEMPLATIVE, PHILOSOPHICAL, ENIGMATIC, AND DEEP-THINKING AS HE COMES ACROSS IN THE FILM." STEPHEN "SUGAR" SEGERMAN.

20. "HE APPROACHED THE WORK SERIOUSLY." RICK EMMERSON ON RODRIGUEZ AS A DEMOLITION WORKER.

21. HE HAD THIS MAGICAL QUALITY THAT TRUE ARTISTS HAVE…EVEN THOUGH HIS MUSICAL HOPES WERE DASHED." RICK EMMERSON

22. "PEOPLE IN DETROIT NEED TO HEAR SOMETHING GOOD." SANDRA RODRIGUEZ KENNEDY, RODRIGUEZ' MIDDLE DAUGHTER IN SEARCHING FOR SUGAR MAN.

23. "HE WAS QUITE CONTENT TO DO MANUEL LABOR." JEROME FERRETTI

24. "WHEN I THINK ABOUT THAT NIGHT WHEN I SPOKE TO EVA ON THE TELEPHONE I NEVER REALIZED HOW OUR LIVES WOULD CHANGE." STEPHEN "SUGAR" SEGERMAN.

25. "HE TOOK ALL THAT PAIN AND TRANSFORMED IT INTO SOMETHING BEAUTIFUL." RICK EMMERSON ON RODRIGUEZ

26. "HE WAS LIKE THE INNER CITY POET PUTTING HIS WORDS TO MUSIC." DENNIS COFFEY

27. "AT THE END OF THE DAY IF YOU LISTEN TO THE STUFF NOW AT THE END OF THE DAY HE WAS RIGHT ON." MIKE THEODORE ON RODRIGUEZ' SONGWRITNG

28. "HE'S MY MOST MEMORABLE ARTIST." STEVE ROW-
LAND THE PRODUCER OF COMING FROM REALITY.

29. "THERE IS ONE IN THERE THAT IS ABSOLUTLELY A KILL-
ER, IT IS ONE OF THE SADDEST SONGS I HAVE EVER HEARD." THEN
STEVE ROWLAND PLAYS "CAUSE" AND HE COMMENTS THAT RO-
DRIGUEZ LOST HIS JOB TWO WEEKS BEFORE CHRISTMAS AS
SUSSEX RECORDS DROPPED HIM FROM THE LABEL. STEVE ROW-
LAND: "THAT IS THE LAST SONG THAT WE RECORDED AND IT
WAS THE LAST SONG RODRIGUEZ RECORDED. THEN TWO WEEKS
BEFORE CHRISTMAS SUSSEX DROPPED HIM FROM THE LABEL."
ROWLAND HAS TROUGLE MAINTAINING HIS COMPOSURE.

30. "THIS GUY DESERVES RECOGNITION." STEVE ROW-
LAND INTERVIEWED IN SEARCHING FOR SUGAR MAN.

31. "ONE OF THE STORIES I'VE HEARD IS THAT A GIRL
WHO CAME FROM AMERICA BROUGHT A COPY OF THE COLD
FACT ALBUM WITH HER." STEPHEN "SUGAR" SEGERMAN ON
HOW COLD FACT GOT TO SOUTH AFRICA.

32. "HE BECAME SOMETHING OF A REBEL ICON. WE ALL
BOUGHT HIS RECORDS. NO ONE KNEW ANYTHING ABOUT
HIM, HE WAS A MYSTERY." WILLEM MOLLER, SOUTH AFRICAN
MUSICIAN

33. TO MANY OF THE SOUTH AFRCIANS HE WAS THE
SOUNDTRACK TO OUR LIVES." STEPHEN "SUGAR" SEGERMAN

34. "TO US IT WAS ONE OF THE MOST FAMOUS RECORDS
OF ALL TIME." STEPHEN "SUGAR" SEGERMAN ON COLD FACT

35. "THIS ALBUM SOMEHOW HAD LYRICS IN IT THAT
SOMEHOW SET US FREE." CRAIG BARTHOLOMEW-STRYDOM

36. "TO A MAN THEY WILL TELL YOU THEY WERE INFLU-
ENCED BY RODRIGUEZ." STEPHEN "SUGAR" SEGERMAN COM-
MENTING ON HOW RODRIGUEZ INFLUENCED THE WHITE

SOUTH AFRICAN MUSICIANS WHO OPPOSED THE GOVERN-MENT'S APARTHEID POLICIES.

37. "I THOUGHT EVERYBODY KNEW RODRIGUEZ, AFTER ALL HE WAS AMERICAN." STEPHEN "SUGAR" SEGERMAN COM-MENTING ON HOW HE BECAME COURIOUS ABOUT RODRI-GUEZ' LIFE AND WHY HE BEGAN THE SEARCH FOR HIM.

38. "WHAT I HEARD IS THAT HE HADN'T PLAYED A CON-CERT FOR A VERY LONG TIME...THE VENUE WASN'T VERY GOOD...THE SHOW WASN'T VERY GOOD...AS THE SHOW WENT ON IT GOT TO A POINT WHERE RODRIGUEZ SAID 'THANK YOU FOR YOUR TIME AND I'LL THANK YOU FOR MINE THEN FORGET IT." CRAIG BARTHOLOMEW-STRYOM CONTINUES THE STORY BY STATING THAT HE HEARD RODRIGUEZ THEN KILLED HIM-SELF ON STAGE. THIS WAS THE MYTH THAT WAS IMPORTANT TO THE MYSTERY AND INTRIGUE OF RODRIGUEZ FOR SOUTH AFRICANS.

39. "THE FIRST WAY I TRIED TO FIND HIM WAS TO FOLLOW THE MONEY. WHERE DO DEAD MEN'S MONEY GO?" CRAIG BAR-THOLOMEW-STRYDOM ON HOW HE BEGAN HIS SEARCH FOR RODRIGUEZ

40. "MAYBE HALF A MILLION COPIES." ROBBIE MANN, RPM RECORDS COMMENTING ON THE SALES OF COLD FACT IN SOUTH AFRICA. COMMENTING ON RODRIGUEZ' SOUTH AFRI-CAN POPULARITY

41. "WE SENT TO ROYALTIES TO A AND M RECORDS." ROB-BIE MANN, RPM RECORDS

42. "HE WAS MUCH BIGGER THAN THE ROLLING STONES." STEVE M. HARRIS

43. "THAT'S HIM, THAT'S RODRIGUEZ. THAT'S MY MAN." CLARENCE AVANT INTERVIEWED IN THE SEARCHING FOR SUG-AR MAN DOCUMENTARY.

44. "IT DIDN'T SELL HERE." CLARENCE AVANT ON RODRIGUEZ' COLD FACT ALBUM SALES IN THE AMERICAN MARKET.

45. "RODRIGUEZ YOUNG MAN NEVER HAPPENED AS FAR AS I AM CONCERNED." CLARENCE AVANT IN CONVERSATON WITH MALIK BENDJELLOUL IN SEARCHING FOR SUGAR MAN

46. "AT FIRST I THOUGHT IT WAS A HOAX." LABEL HEAD ROBBIE MANN OF RPM RECORDS ON FINDING RODRIGUEZ AND THE ANNOUNCEMENT THAT HE WAS COMING TO PER-FORM IN SOUTH AFRICA.

47. "I WAS TALKING TO RODRIGUEZ THAT DEFINTELY WAS ONE OF THE GREATEST MOMENTS OF MY LIFE." STEPHEN "SUGAR" SEGERMAN ON HIS IMPRESSIONS OF THE FIRST PHONE CALL WITH RODRIGUEZ.

48. "HE READ A LOT. HE WAS INVOLVED IN POLITICS. HE WAS INVOLVED IN THE COMMUNITY. HE WAS ALWAYS A PROPO-NENT FOR WORKING FOR PEOPLE WHO DIDN'T ALWAYS HAVE A VOICE. HE HAD A LOT OF EXPERIENCE IN THAT AREA." RE-GAN RODRIGUEZ, THE YOUNGEST DAUGHTER.

49. "IN THE EARLY EIGHTIES HE WANTED TO DO SOME-THING RIGHTEOUS." RICK EMMERSON ON RODRIGUEZ' DECI-SION TO RUN FOR MAYOR OF DETROIT.

50. "HE WAS DOING WORK NO ONE ELSE WANTED TO DO. HE WOULD COME HOME AND HE WOULD BE COVERED IN DUST AND DIRT. I SAW HIM CARRY REFRIGERATORS DOWN THE STAIRS ON HIS BACK." REGAN RODRIGUEZ ON HER FA-THER'S WORK ETHIC.

51. "TO GOING FROM BEING AN OUTCAST TO BEING WHO HE REALLY WAS...A MUSICIAN ON STAGE PLAYING FOR HIS FANS." REGAN RODRIGUEZ ON THE FIRST SOUTH AFRICAN CONCERT.

52. "IT'S…THE ROUTE OF RODRIGUEZ'S ODYSSEY WHICH MAKES SEARCHING FOR SUGAR MAN SO INTRIGUING. BUT, TO BE HONEST, THE LESS YOU KNOW ABOUT IT, THE RICHER YOUR EXPERIENCE WILL BE." TIME OUT, TOKYO, MARCH 16, 2013.

53. "HE WASN'T THE MOST DYNAMIC LIVE PERFORMER AROUND, ALMOST ALWAYS PLAYING SHOWS WHILE FACING THE WALL," MIKE THEODORE COMMENTING TO ROLLING STONE, APRIL 11, 2013.

54. "HONEST TO GOD I THOUGHT THAT THIS GUY WAS GOING TO BE HUGE. HE WAS A FUCKING GENIUS." CLARENCE AVANT TO ROLLING STONE, APRIL 11, 2013.

55. "HE ONCE TOLD ME THAT HE WOULD WRITE THIRTY SONGS AND THEY WOULD TAKE HIM AROUND THE WORLD. YOU KNOW WHAT? HE WAS RIGHT." MIKE THEODORE TO ROLLING STONE, APRIL 11, 2013

56. "IMAGINE THE PRESSURE THAT HE'S UNDER NOW." MIKE THEODORE TO ROLLING STONE, APRIL 11, 2013

57. "I HAVE SOME PHOTOS HERE I WOULD LIKE TO SHOW YOU THAT I HAVE KEPT SINCE MY DAYS WITH RODRIGUEZ." STEVE ROWLAND IN SEARCHING FOR SUGAR MAN.

58.". HE'S NOT JUST A TALENT. HE'S LIKE A WISE MAN, A PROFIT, HE PROBABLY COULD HAVE DONE FANTASTICALLY WELL IF HE HAD CONTINUED." STEVE ROWLAND

59. "NOBODY WAS EVEN INTERESTED IN LISTENING TO HIM." STEVE ROWLAND ON RODRIGUEZ

60. "TO MANY OF US SOUTH AFRICANS RODRIGUEZ WAS THE SOUNDTRACK TO OUR LIVES." STEPHEN "SUGAR" SEGERMAN

61. THIS ALBUM SOMEHOW HAD LYRICS IN IT THAT SOMEHOW ALMOST SET US FREE." CRAIG BARTHOLOMEW-STRYDOM

62. "IT MAY SEEM STRANGE THAT SOUTH AFRICAN RE-CORD COMPANIES DIDN'T TRACK DOWN RODRIGUEZ." CRAIG BARTHOLOMEW-STRYDOM ON WHY IT DIDN'T HAPPEN. THE APARTHEID GOVERNMENT PREVENTED IT.

63. "I THOUGHT EVERYBODY KNEW RODRIGUEZ." STE-PHEN "SUGAR" SEGERMAN WHO WAS SURPRISED THAT AMERI-CANS DIDN'T KNOW ABOUT RODRIGUEZ.

64. "ANY MUSICOLOGISTS DETECTIVES OUT THERE?" STE-PHEN "SUGAR" SEGERMAN WRITING IN THE LINER NOTES TO THE RELEASE OF THE COLD FACT CD. CRAIG BARTHOLOMOW-STRYDOM READ THE LINER NOTES AND HE BEGAN LOOKING FOR RODRIGUEZ.

65. "AT THE TIME THE LEGEND WAS THAT RODRIGUEZ WAS DEAD." QUOTE FROM RODRIGUEZ' SOUTH AFRICAN LA-BEL

66. "THIS IS MY MAN...DON'T GET ME EMOTIONAL AGAIN." CLARENCE AVANT ON RODRIGUEZ

67. "DID IT MAKE ANY MONEY....THE ANSWER IS NO." CLARENCE AVANT ON RODRIGUEZ' FIRST ABLUM

68. "WHAT THE HELL IS THIS?" CLARENCE AVANT ON THE PERFORMANCES OF RODRIGUEZ IN 1970-1971.

69. "I WENT ON LINE TO THE WEBSITE. THERE WAS THIS MILK CARTON WITH A PICTURE. I REPLIED: 'RODRIGUEZ IS MY FATHER. I AM SERIOUS. SOMETIMES A FANTASY IS BEST LEFT ALONE." EVA RODRIGUEZ

70. "SHE EXPLAINED TO ME WHO HER FATHER WAS." STE-PHEN "SUGAR" SEGERMAN ON HIS FIRST CONVERSATION WITH EVA RODRIGUEZ.

71. "YOU WEREN'T AWARE OF SOMETHING THAT WOULD HAVE CHANGED YOUR LIFE FOREVER." REMARK OF FILM MAK-

ER MALIK BENJELLOUL TO RODRIGUEZ IN SEARCHING FOR SUGAR MAN.

72. "HE NEVER SAID ANYTHING HE JUST MOVED ON. HE READ A LOT. HE WAS INVOLVED IN POLITICS." REGAN RODRIGUEZ

73. "HE HAD A LOT OF EXPERIENCE IN THAT AREA." REGAN RODRIGUEZ ON HER DAD'S DESIRE TO HELP THE WORKING POOR.

74. "THE ARTIST IS THE PIONEER. EVEN THOUGH HIS MUSICAL HOPES WERE DASHED. HE WANTED TO MAKE A DIFFERENCE." A COMMENT FROM A FRIEND AS TO WHY RODRIGUEZ RAN FOR DETROIT MAYOR.

75. "HE DIDN'T WIN AN ELECTION EVER." REGAN RODRIGUEZ

76. "WE LIVED IN TWENTY SIX DIFFERENT HOMES. THEY WEREN'T HOMES. THEY WERE JUST PLACES THAT WE LIVED." EVA RODRIGUEZ

77. "IN SOUTH AFRICA YOU ARE MORE POPULAR THAN ELVIS PRESLEY." STEPHEN "SUGAR" SEGERMAN IN AN EARLY TELEPHONE CONVERSATION WITH RODRIGUEZ.

78. "SHE WANTED TO KNOW IF IT WAS THE REAL RODRIGUEZ." A REPORTER TALKING TO REGAN RODRIGUEZ WHEN HE ARRIVED IN SOUTH AFRICA IN MARCH 1998.

79. "IT WAS ALMOST AS IF HE DIDN'T HAVE TO PLAY. THEY JUST WANTED TO MEET HIM." REGAN RODRIGUEZ ON WHEN HER FATHER WANDERED OUT ONTO THE STAGE IN SOUTH AFRICA IN MARCH 1998.

80. "THAT WAS WHO HE WAS A MUSICIAN ON STAGE PLAYING FOR HIS FANS." REGAN RODRIGUEZ ON HER FATHER'S FIRST SOUTH AFRICAN SHOW.

81. "I SAW THIS ABSOLUTE TRANQUILITY." THIS IS A COMMENT ON RODRIGUEZ' FIRST 1998 SOUTH AFRICAN SHOW.

82. "HE GETS RECOGNIZED NOW WHEN HE GOES THROUGH AIRPORTS. THE SOUTH AFRICAN FANS ARE THE STRONGEST." REGAN RODRIGUEZ

83. "I DIDN'T REALIZE HOW PHYSICALLY FRAIL IN SOME WAYS HE WAS. BUT THEN HE TOOK OFF HIS COAT. HE WAS RIPPED. HE HAD BULDING MUSCLES AND VEINS," WYMOND MILES, OF THE FRESH AND EASY SAN FRANCISCO BAND ON THE FIRST MEETING WITH RODRIGUEZ.

85. "CHUCK ROY, THE OWNER OF THE CASS CAFÉ, WAS INTERVIEWED FOR THE MOVIE SEARCHING FOR SUGAR MAN BUT HE WAS CUT OUT OF IT." SANDY, THE BAR TENDER AT THE CASS CAFÉ.

86. THE OLD MIAMI WAS A REGULAR WATERING HOLE FOR RODRIGUEZ AND THE CENTER OF HIS 2013 CAMPAIGN FOR DETROIT MAYOR. THE DRAWING IN THE CORNER OF THE INDOOR BAR IS A REMINDER OF WHAT MIGHT HAVE BEEN. RODRIGUEZ ALSO PERFORMED AT THE OUTDOOR BAR, WHICH IS IN THE BACKYARD. 60 MINUTES SHOT ITS INVERVIEW HERE.

87. "WE HAVE A WEBSITE…AND EVERY DAY THERE ARE MESSAGES FROM AROUND THE WORLD. SOME PEOPLE ARE ONLY JUST DISCOVERING IT. THIS IS PROBABLY ONE OF THE MOST VIRAL MOVIES OF THE CENTURY." STEPHEN "SUGAR" SEGERMAN QUOTED IN THE CAPE TOWN SUNDAY ARGUS, OCTOBER 5, 2014.

88. "BENDJELLOUL AND I WENT TO THE SUNDANCE FESTIVAL, WE WATCHED AMERICAN AUDIENCES REACT TO THIS MOVIE. AT THE END THEY WOULD STAND UP AND CHEER… AND THEN CRY WHEN WE BROUGHT RODRIGUEZ OUT FOR HIS QUESTIONS AND ANSWERS." SEGERMAN QUOTED IN CAPE TOWN SUNDAY ARGUS, OCTOBER 5, 2014.

89. "HIS EYESIGHT IS VERY POOR BUT HE IS ACTUALLY IN GOOD HEALTH." SEGERMAN QUOTED IN CAPE TOWN SUNDAY ARGUS, OCTOBER 5, 2014.

90. "IT'S BEEN QUITE THE WEEK FOR SEPTUAGENARIANS PLAYING ROCK AND ROLL. THERE'S A SENTENCE I NEVER THOUGHT I'D WRITE." NATHAN DAVIES, BEAT WRITER FOR THE ADELAIDE ADVERTISER, OCTOBER 30, 2014 AFTER WATCHING RODRIGUEZ ON HIS AUSTRALIAN TOUR. THE ROLLING STONES WERE ALSO IN TOWN AT THE SAME TIME. THE REVIEWS FOR RODRIGUEZ' SHOW WERE LONGER AND MORE POSITIVE.

91. "IN SOME WAYS RODRIGUEZ IS THE ANTI-STONES-WHILE MICK AND KEITH POSED FOR MAGAZINE COVERS; RODRIGUEZ HAULED BRICKS (AND HE STILL HAS THE ARMS TO PROVE IT) WHILE THE STONES MADE MONEY AND SPENT IT, RODRIGUEZ MADE MONEY (EVENTUALLY) AND GAVE MOST OF IT AWAY." NATHAN DAVIES, ADELAIDE ADVERTISER, OCTOBER 30, 2014.

92. "HE SOUNDS MORE FIRED UP AND POLITICALLY RELEVANT THAN MOST POP STARS RECORDING TODAY." JONATHAN DEAN, LONDON JOURNALIST.

APPENDIX

VI

THE BEST OF RODRIGUEZ ON YOU TUBE

I WONDER: THIS IS A CLIP FEATURING THE SOUNDTRACK TO SEARCHING FOR SUGAR MAN AND USING THE COVER TO THE RE-RELEASED ALBUM. UPLOADED SEPTEMBER 15, 2008.

CAUSE: THIS IS A CLIP USING THE COMING FROM REALITY ALBUM COVER AS THE VISUAL. THE CLIP WAS LOADED OCTOBER 17, 2011. THIS YOU TUBE CLIP HAS ALMOST HALF A MILLION HITS.

SUGAR MAN-LIVE: THIS IS A CLIP FROM THE WEEKLY COMET. IT IS A DETROIT SHOW AND FEATURES RODRIGUEZ RESPLENDENT IN A COOL JACKET PERFORMING "SUGAR MAN" WITH A SMILING MALIK BENDJELLOUL SITTING NEXT TO HIM. UPLOADED JANUARY 24, 2012.

MALIK BENDJELLOUL: HE IS INTERVIEWED IN 2012 FOR THE BYOD PROGRAM CO-HOSTED BY ONDI TIMONER AND IT BEGINS THE PUBLICITY FOR SEARCHING FOR SUGAR MAN AS IT HAD WON THE GRAND JURY PRIZE AT THE SUNDANCE FILM FESTIVAL. THIS IS A WONDERUL INTERVIEW WHERE BENDJELLOUL TALKS ABOUT HIS DOCUMENATARY. IT WAS UPLOADED MAY 22, 2012

A MOST DISGUSTING SONG: THIS IS A CLIP USING RODRIGUEZ' RECORD AND VIDEO THAT HAS LITTLE TO DO WITH RODRIGUEZ. IT WAS UPLOADED NOVEMBER 14, 2012 AND IS A STRANGE POSTING.

LIKE A ROLLING STONE-LIVE: THIS IS A CLIP FROM RODRIGUEZ' PERFORMANCE AT LONDON'S ROUNDHOUSE ON NOVEMBER 18 2012 IN CAMDEN TOWN. HE PERFORMS THE BOB DYLAN SONG AS THE AUDIENCE SINGS ALONG. THIS WAS UPLOADED NOVEMBER 23, 2012

I'M GONNA LIVE UNTIL I DIE-LIVE: THIS IS A CLIP FROM THE ROUNDHOUSE SHOW WHERE RODRIGUEZ COMMENTS ON AGE. HE THEN COVERS THE FRANK SINATRA SONG. THE CLIP WAS UPLOADED NOVEMBER 23, 2012

CAN'T GET AWAY-LIVE: THIS IS A TRACK FROM THE 1979 LIVE ALBUM AND IT IS A RARE ALBUM. THE SONG WAS RECORDED AT THE REGENT THEATER IN SYDNEY ON MARCH 17TH OR 18TH. THEN THE CLIP CONTINUES TO PLAY THE REST OF THE ALBUM WITH "STREET BOY" CONTINUING THIS MARVELOUS LIVE PERFORMANCE. THERE IS A FLUTE ON THIS LIVE SONG THAT IS WONDERFUL. THIS AUSTRALIAN ALBUM WAS RELEASED IN 1981 AND AGAIN IN 1986. THIS CLIP HAS SOME GREAT RARE CUTS. UPLOADED JANUARY 19, 2013

CLIMB UP ON MY MUSIC: FROM LE ZENITH IN PARIS JUNE 4, 2013 ALSO CONTAINS OTHER RODRIGUEZ MATERIAL A NINETEEN PLUS MINUTE CLIP.

A TWENTY-THREE MINUTE INTERVIEW WITH THE HOL-
LYWOOD REPORTER "FINDING SUGAR MAN: RODRIGUEZ RE-
FLECTS ON A CRAZY YEAR." INTERESTING!

THERE IS A YOU TUBE INTERVIEW WITH RODRIGUEZ TALK-
ING TO THE AUDIENCE AT AN UNIDENTIFIED CLUB ABOUT AP-
PEARING ON THE DAVID LETTERMAN SHOW. HE TALKS ABOUT
VOTING, SAID HE VOTED FOR BARACK OBAMA AND THE CLUB
WAS NOT IDENTIFIED. IT IS A LOOSE AND CASUAL INTERVIEW.
HE TUNES HIS GUITAR AND THEN AT THE THREE MINUTES
NINETEEN SECONDS THE INTERVIEW ENDS. IT IS A MARVEL-
OUS LOOK AT THE PERSONAL RODRIGUEZ.

APPENDIX

VII

RODRIGUEZ COVER SONGS HE PERFORMED IN CONCERT BUT DIDN'T RECORD

1. JUST ONE OF THOSE THINGS: THIS COLE PORTER TUNE IS ONE RODRIGUEZ FAVORS IN CONCERT. WHEN RODRIGUEZ READ CATCHER IN THE RYE, HE WAS AMUSED THAT IT WAS ONE OF HOLDEN CAUFIELD'S FAVORITE TUNES. THOSE CLOSE TO RODRIGUEZ REMARKED THAT FRANK SINATRA'S VERSION INFLUENCD HIM.

2. NICE AND EASY: A GREAT FRANK SINATRA SONG THAT RODRIGUEZ ADDS HIS PERSONAL TOUCH TO IN CONCERT.

3. BLUE SUEDE SHOES: RODRIGUEZ PREFERS CARL PERKINS' VERSION TO ELVIS PRESLEY'S.

4. LIKE A ROLLING STONE: THIS BOB DYLAN SONG IS ONE OF RODRIGUEZ' FAVORITES TO COVER IN CONCERT.

5. GOOD GOLLY MISS MOLLY: A LITTLE RICHARD SONG THAT RODRIGUEZ PERFORMS A GREAT DEAL IN CONCERT.

6. LUCILLE: THIS LITTLE RICHARD COVER IS ONE OF RODRIGUEZ' FAVORITES.

7. KISS: THIS PRINCE SONG WAS PERFORMED BY RODRIGUEZ IN 2013 IN THE NETHERLANDS.

8. DEAD END STREET: THIS LOU RAWLS SONG IS PERFECT FOR RODRIGUEZ. HE PERFORMS IT FROM TIME TO TIME IN CONCERT.

9. SEA OF HEARTBREAK: THIS DON GIBSON SONG ATTESTS TO RODRIGUEZ INTEREST IN COUNTRY MUSIC. IT WAS SOMETIMES PERFORMED IN CONCERT.

10. FEVER: HIS VERSION OWES MORE TO LITTLE WILLIE JOHN THAN PEGGY LEE. ANOTHER GREAT CONCERT PIECE.

11. HAPPY DAYS ARE HERE AGAIN: RODRIGUEZ PERFORMED THIS TUNE AT KINGS PARK BOTANIC GARDENS IN PERTH, AUSTRALIA ON NOVEMBER 9, 2014. THIS IS A STRANGE COVER VERSION. THE MILTON AGER SONG WAS COPYRIGHTED IN 1929 AND IT HAS BEEN USED EXTENSIVELY IN AMERICAN POLITICS. THE SONG WAS POPULAR DURING THE GREAT DEPRESSION.

12. I ONLY HAVE EYES FOR YOU: THIS FLAMINGOS SONG SHOWS RODRIGUEZ' DOO WOP ROOTS. IT IS AT TIMES A CONCERT COVER TUNE.

13. UNCHAINED MELODY: THIS IS A ROY HAMILTON INSPIRED VERSION THAT RODRIGUEZ SOMETIMES COVERS IN CONCERT.

14. SHAKE, RATTLE AND ROLL: RODRIGUEZ OWES HIS VERSION MORE TO JOE TURNER THAN BILL HALEY AND THE COMETS. ANOTHER CONCERT COVER THAT IS A FAN FAVORITE.

15. SUBTERRANEAN HOMESICK BLUES: A BOB DYLAN SONG, HE COVERS IT LIKE HE OWNS IT.

16. REDNECK WONDERLAND: THIS IS A COVER OF THE MIDNIGHT OIL HIT. IT IS ALSO AT TIMES A CONCERT PIECE THAT HE LOVES TO PERFORM ESPECIALLY WHILE TOURING AUSTRALIA.

17. THE LETTER: IN SOUND CHECKS RODRIGUEZ HAS PERFORMED A SMALL PART OF THIS BOX TOPS SONG. HE APPARENTLY HAS NOT DONE IT IN A COMPLETE CONCERT VERSION. RODRIGUEZ WAS A BIG ALEX CHILTON AND BOX TOP FAN.

18. UNCHAIN MY HEART: THIS IS A RAY CHARLES SONG THAT HE HAS DONE DURING SOUND CHECKS.

19. WHAT THE WORLD NEEDS NOW IS LOVE: THIS JACKIE DE SHANNON HIT WAS A CLOSER AT A CONCERT THAT RODRIGUEZ PAID TRIBUTE TO THE VICTIMS OF 9-11.

20. SAVE THE BEST TILL LAST: THIS IS A VANESSA WILLIAMS SONG THAT RODRIGUEZ HAS COVERED IN CONCERT.

21. HOUND DOG: ELVIS PRESLEY IS THE INFLUENCE HERE AND HE WORKED UP A BRIEF VERSION WHEN HE FIRST WENT TO SOUTH AFRICA IN 1998.

22. AT LAST: THIS IS AN ETTA JAMES SONG THAT RODRIGUEZ HAS PRACTICED AND COVERED IN CONCERT. WHEN HE APPEARED IN 2008 AT NEW YORK'S JOE'S PUB HE RECEIVED A STANDING OVATION FOR THE SONG.

23. I'M GOING TO LIVE: THIS IS A JUDY GARLAND TUNE THAT RODRIGUEZ HAS PRACTICED WITH IN SOUND CHECKS.

24. LOVE ME OR LEAVE ME: THIS IS A SAMMY KAHN STANDARD THAT RODRIGUEZ PERFORMED IN 2013 IN BARCELONA. HE TOOK HIS CUE FROM THE NINA SIMONE VERSION. HE PERFORMED THIS SONG WHEN HE APPEARED AT THE FITZGERALD THEATER IN DETROIT.

25. WHOLE LOT OF SHAKIN' GOING ON: THIS JERRY LEE LEWIS SONG IS ONE THAT RODRIGUEZ COVERS IN CONCERT. HIS VERSION IS CLOSER TO BIG MAYBELLE WHICH WAS RECORDED TWO YEARS BEFORE THE JERRY LEE LEWIS VERSION.

26. ALL MY LOVING: THIS COVER OF A BEATLES' SONG WAS DONE IN A BRIEF THIRTY SECOND VERSION IN LIVERPOOL'S PHILHARMONIC HALL. IT WAS INTENDED AS A TRIBUTE TO THE BEATLES.

27. LEARNIN' THE BLUES: RODRIGUEZ PERFORMED THIS AT LONDON'S ROUNDHOUSE IN 2012. THE SONG, WRITTEN BY DELORES VICKI SILVERS IN 1955, WAS A FRANK SINATRA NUMBER ONE HIT.

28. LAST REQUEST: THIS IS RODRIGUEZ COVERING A PAOLO NUTINI SONG AT THE IRON HORSE HOUSE IN NORTHAMPTON MA ON SEPTEMBER 2, 2012.

29. SOMEBODY TO LOVE: RODRIGUEZ PERFORMED THIS JEFFERSON AIR PLANE COVER AND MADE THE SONG HIS OWN ON NOVEMBER 9, 2104 AT KINGS PARK BOTANIC GARDENS, PERTH, AUSTRALIA.

30. C'EST SI BON: HE PLAYED THIS FRENCH CLASSIC A NUMBER OF TIMES IN PARIS.

31. LA VIE EN ROSE: WITH A TRIBUTE TO EDITH PIAF, RODRIGUEZ PERFORMED THIS SONG IN PARIS IN 2012. THERE IS A YOU TUBE CLIP OF IT. HE ALSO PERFORMED IT AT THE L'ZENITH IN PARIS AS WELL AS AT L'OLYMPIA. THERE ARE FOUR YOU TUBE VIDEOS OF HIS PERFORMANCES.

APPENDIX

VIII

THE BEST OF RODRIGUEZ YOU TUBE MUSIC CLIPS, PART 2

1. "INNER CITY BLUES" A THREE MINUTE AND TWENTY-SEVEN SECOND CLIP FROM 2009 IN PARIS. THE SUGAR MAN PERFORMING ON THE STREET BEFORE FAME AND FORTUNE INTRUDED ON HIS LIFE. THIS VIDEO IS HIGHLIGHTED WITH FRENCH SUBTITLES.

2. "I'LL SLIP AWAY" THIS IS A WONDERFUL CLIP PRODUCED WITH MAGIX MOVIE EDIT PRO 2013 PREMINUM EQUIPMENT.

3. "CRUCIFY YOUR MIND" THIS IS CALLED A STREET SESSION AND IT IS WHILE HE WAS IN PARIS IN 2009. WELL DONE WITH A BEAUTIFUL BACKDROP. SOMEONE SHOULD GET ROYALTIES.

4. "INNER CITY BLUES" THIS VERSION IS FROM FRENCH TV CHANNEL 5 ON FEBRUARY 4, 2013.

5. "FORGET IT" LIVE AT DONOVAN'S PUB IN DETROIT ON NOVEMBER 2, 2009.

6. "CRUCIFY YOUR MIND" THIS IS LIVE AT THE FACTORY THEATRE ON APRIL 11, 2010. ONCE AGAIN THE SUGAR MAN IN ACTION BEFORE FAME AND FORTUNE. THIS IS A GREAT CLIP.

7. "CRUCIFY YOUR MIND" THIS CLIP IS FROM THE LONDON BASED JOOLS HOLLAND TV SHOW IN 2013.

8. "THE ESTABLISHMENT BLUES" THIS PERFORMANCE WAS RECORDED JANUARY 26, 2012 AND APPEARED ON THE SUNDANCE CHANNEL.

9. "I WONDER" THIS VERSION IS LIVE FROM SEATTLE'S TRIPLE DOOR NIGHT CLUB IN 2013.

10. "I WONDER" THIS IS A PERFORMANCE FROM SCHUBAS IN CHICAGO ON MAY 8, 2009. ANOTHER GREAT VIEW OF THE SUGAR MAN BEFORE FAME AND FORTUNE.

11. "LAST REQUEST." THIS IS RODRIGUEZ COVERING A PAOLO NUTINI SONG AT THE IRON HORSE HOUSE IN NORTHAMPTON MA ON SEPTEMBER 2, 2012. THIS IS SPECIAL AS NUTINI HAS COVERED RODRIGUEZ' SONGS ON RECORD AND IN CONCERT.

12. "FORGET IT" THIS IS PERFORMED IN A RECORD STORE WITH SPANISH SUBTITLES ALONG WITH A HORN SECTION AND RODRIGUEZ IS LOOKING COOL IN HIS SUN GLASSES.

13. A RODRIGUEZ CLIP FROM THE VARIETY PLAYHOUSE ON MAY 11, 2013 IS A MARVELOUS, ACOUSTIC EXPERIENCE. THE VARIETY PLAYHOUSE IS LOCATED IN ATLANTA, GEORGIA. THE CLIP HAS A SURPRISE SONG. LISTEN TO IT AND YOU WONT BE DISAPPOINTED.

14. "STREET BOY" THIS IS A FAN POSTED YOU TUBE VIDEO IN WHICH PARTS OF THE FILM ARE TAKEN TO CREATE A STORY LINE WITH THE SONG. VERY COOL.

15. "SUGAR MAN" THIS IS AN OFFICIAL CLIP ON YOU TUBE POSTED IN 2012. NICE.

APPENDIX

IX

5 MYTHS ASSOCIATED WITH SIXTO RODRIGUEZ

1. HE KILLED HIMSELF WHILE ON STAGE AFTER THE AUDIENCE IGNORED HIS SONGS.

2. HE DIED OF A DRUG OVERDOSE.

3. "HE WILL STAY IN HIS FIFTY DOLLAR DETROIT HOUSE." KONNY RODRIGUEZ IN A NUMBER 0F 2012 INTERVIEWS. IT ISN'T AND NEVER HAS BEEN A FIFTY DOLLAR HOUSE.

4. THAT HE DROPPED OUT OF THE MUSIC BUSINESS BY 1974. NOT TRUE. HE TOURED AUSTRALIA IN 1979 AND 1981 AND HE HAD NUMEROUS SMALL CLUB DATES PRIOR TO THE 1998 SOUTH AFRICAN TOUR. HE ALSO TOURED FROM 1998 TO 2011 BEFORE THE SUCCESS OF SEARCHING FOR SUGAR MAN.

5. IN 1998 THE RUMOR SPREAD THAT THE RODRIGUEZ SHOWS WERE THOSE OF AN IMPERSONATOR. AGAIN UNTRUE.

APPENDIX

X

AWARDS AND NOMINATIONS

- *SEARCHING FOR SUGAR MAN* WON THE BEST DOCUMENTARY CATEGORY AT THE 85TH ACADEMY AWARDS.[19] RODRIGUEZ DECLINED TO ATTEND THE AWARD CEREMONY AS HE DIDN'T WANT TO OVERSHADOW THE FILMMAKERS' ACHIEVEMENT IF HE CAME UP ON STAGE WITH THEM. UPON ACCEPTING HIS AWARD, CHINN REMARKED ON SUCH GENEROSITY, "THAT JUST ABOUT SAYS EVERYTHING ABOUT THAT MAN AND HIS STORY THAT YOU WANT TO KNOW."[20] HOWEVER, MALIK BENDJELLOUL ALSO SAID ON STAGE, "THANKS TO ONE OF THE GREATEST SINGERS EVER, RODRIGUEZ."[21]

7. THE FILM ALSO WON THE BEST DOCUMENTARY CATEGORY AT THE 66TH BRITISH ACADEMY FILM AWARDS ON 10 FEBRUARY 2013.
8. THE DIRECTORS GUILD OF AMERICA AWARDED THE DGA AWARD FOR BEST DOCUMENTARY ON 2 FEBRUARY 2013.

9. THE WRITERS GUILD OF AMERICA AWARDED THE WGA AWARD FOR BEST DOCUMENTARY.
10. THE PRODUCERS GUILD OF AMERICA AWARDED THE PGA AWARD FOR BEST DOCUMENTARY.
THE AMERICAN CINEMA EDITORS AWARDED THE ACE EDDIE AWARD FOR BEST DOCUMENTARY.
IT WON THE GULDBAGGE AWARD FOR BEST DOCUMENTARY AT THE 48TH GULDBAGGE AWARDS.
IT WON THE NATIONAL BOARD OF REVIEW IN NEW YORK ON 5 DECEMBER 2012.
11. THE INTERNATIONAL DOCUMENTARY ASSOCIATION (IDA) AWARDED "SEARCHING FOR SUGAR MAN" BEST FEATURE AND BEST MUSIC AT THE 28TH ANNUAL IDA DOCUMENTARY AWARDS ON 7 DECEMBER 2012 AT THE DIRECTORS GUILD OF AMERICA BUILDING, LOS ANGELES, CALIFORNIA.[22]
IT ALSO WON BEST DOCUMENTARY DURING CRITICS' CHOICE AWARDS – *SEARCHING FOR SUGAR MAN*[23]
12. THE FILM WON THE CINEMA FOR PEACE MOST VALUABLE DOCUMENTARY OF THE YEAR AWARD.
13. *SEARCHING FOR SUGAR MAN* WON THE SPECIAL JURY PRIZE AND THE AUDIENCE AWARD FOR BEST INTERNATIONAL DOCUMENTARY AT THE SUNDANCE FILM FESTIVAL. THE FILM ALSO WON THE AUDIENCE AWARD AT THE LOS ANGELES FILM FESTIVAL,[24] THE AUDIENCE AWARD AT THE DURBAN INTERNATIONAL FILM FESTIVAL,[25] THE AUDIENCE AWARD AT THE MELBOURNE FILM FESTIVAL, 2ND PLACE WINNER AUDIENCE AWARD AT THE TRIBECA FILM FESTIVAL AND THE GRAND JURY PRIZE AT THE MOSCOW INTERNATIONAL FILM FESTIVAL.[26]
14. AT THE INTERNATIONAL DOCUMENTARY FILM FESTIVAL AMSTERDAM HELD IN NOVEMBER 2012, "SEARCHING FOR SUGAR MAN" WON BOTH THE AUDIENCE AND THE BEST MUSIC DOCUMENTARY AWARDS.[27]
15. DOHA TRIBECA FILM FESTIVAL (DTFF) "SEARCHING FOR SUGAR MAN" WAS AWARDED $50,000 (US) WHERE THE FILM SHARED THE "BEST OF THE FEST" AUDIENCE AWARD WITH THE CHINESE FEATURE FILM *FULL CIRCLE*.[28]
16. BEST FILM - DÍAS DE CINE AWARDS
17. BEST FILM - IN-EDIT FESTIVAL IN SANTIAGO DE CHILE

18. THE CINEMA EYE HONORS FOR NONFICTION FILMMAKING HAS NOMINATED "SEARCHING FOR SUGAR MAN" FOR FIVE AWARDS, TYING WITH "THE IMPOSTER" FOR THE MOST NOMINATIONS. WINNERS OF THE 6TH ANNUAL CINEMA EYE HONORS WILL BE ANNOUNCED ON 9 JANUARY 2013 AS CINEMA EYE RETURNS FOR A THIRD YEAR TO NEW YORK CITY'S MUSEUM OF THE MOVING IMAGE IN ASTORIA, QUEENS, NEW YORK.

NONFICTION FEATURE FILMMAKING – MALIK BENDJELLOUL AND SIMON CHINN
PRODUCTION – SIMON CHINN
GRAPHIC DESIGN AND ANIMATION – OSKAR GULLSTRAND, ARVID STEEN
DEBUT FEATURE FILM – MALIK BENDJELLOUL
AUDIENCE CHOICE PRIZE – MALIK BENDJELLOUL[29]

SELECTED
BIBLIOGRAPHY

There were more than one hundred interviews for the book. Some people requested anonymity; others allowed their names to be used. The information from those closest to the story include Steve Rowland, Mike Theodore, John Rhys, Matt Lucas, Harry Balk, Dan Bourgoise, Roger Armstrong, Matt Sullivan, Neil Skok, John Brooks, Mitch Ryder, Barbara Lynn, Jessie Hector, Dave Williams, Sugar Pie DeSanto, George Clinton and Brian Young. There was Rodriguez material as well as reflections on Detroit and the Sugar Man's recording career from a wide variety of Detroiters.

The staffs and bar people at the Cass Café, the Old Miami and the Motor City Brewing Company were universally helpful. Special kudos to Shawn Kelly at the Woodbridge Pub for his information. The Trumbell Anarchist Collective requested anonymity but the six people interview were important to the story.

The genesis of this book began with an article, see Howard A. De-Witt, "Sixto Rodriguez: The Sugarman Returns, **Blue Suede News**, #99, Winter 2012/2013, pp. 21-26.

For some of Rodriguez' musical influences see Edward Douglas, "Interview: The Award-Winning Doc Searching for the Sugar Man," **Coming-soon.net**, July 25, 2012, http://www.comingsoon.net/news/movienews.php?id=92699 Also see Sasha Frere Jones, "Cold Facts," **The New Yorker**, August 3, 2012 for one of the best reviews of **Searching For Sugar Man**.

Also see Zach Schonfeld, "Exclusive: 'Searching For Sugar Man' Preview," **Rolling Stone**, July 26, 2012 http://www.rollingstone.com/music/videos/exclusive-searching-for-sugar-man-preview-20120726

One of the best reviews of the documentary with incisive comments on the songs is Jonah Raskin, "Searching For Sugar Man: The Sixties Surface, Again," **The Rag Blog**, December 6, 2012 http://theragblog.blogspot.com/2012/12/film-jonah-raskin-searching-for-sugar.html

For a Jewish look at Rodriguez see, David Horovitz, "In The Second Coming of Rodriguez A Passover Parable," **Times of Israel**, March 28, 2013 http://www.timesofisrael.com/in-the-second-coming-of-rodriguez-a-passover-parable/

Also see, Locke Peterseim, "Interview: Searching For Sugar Man's Star Rodriguez And Writer-Director Malik Bendjelloul," August 10, 2012 http://www.openlettersmonthly.com/hammerandthump/interview-searching-for-sugar-man-subject-rodriguez-and-writer-director-malik-bendjelloul/

An interesting look at the documentary is Poppy Harlow, "Sixto Rodriguez Becomes Superstar, Doesn't Know It For 30 Years," **KASDK. com** August 15, 2012 www.ksdk.com/news/article/333230/28/Sixto-Rodriguez-becomes-superstar-couldn't-know-for-30-years Also see the beautifully written article by Tony Karon, "Sixto Rodriguez, Secret Rock Star Behind Searching for Sugar Man," **Time Entertainment**, August 21, 2012. Also see Jonathan Crow, "Malik Bendjelloul Talks About His Oscar Nominated Movie 'Searching For Sugar Man," **Yahoo Movies**, January 24, 2013 https://movies.yahoo.com/blogs/2013-oscars/malik-bendjelloul-talks-oscar-nominate

On **Searching For Sugar Man**, also see, Rabbi Herb Cohen, "A Rabbinic Take on 'Searching For Sugar Man," **The Huffington Post**, July 6, 2013, Beth J. Harpist, "Sugar Man' Star Meets Adoring New York Crowd," **The Huffington Post**, June 8, 2013, and Penelope Andrew, "A Myth Is Replaced By A Miracle In New Doc, Searching for Sugar Man, Resurrecting Work Of Elusive Musician Sixto Rodriguez," **The Huffington Post**, October 13, 2012.

Matthew Duersten, "Spotlight On Oscar Docs; 'Searching For Sugar Man," **Los Angeles Magazine**, February 7, 2013 http://www.lamag.com/laculture/spotlight-on-oscar-docs-searching-for-sugar-man/ is an interesting piece on the eve of the 85th Academy Award ceremony.

For Konny Rodriguez' reaction to the Oscar nomination and his appearance on the Tonight Show with Jay Leno, see, Eric Lacy, "Oscar-

Nominated 'Searching For Sugar Man' Star Rodriguez, A Detroit Native To Appear On NBC's Tonight Show With Jay Leno," www.mlive.com/entertainment/detroit/index.ssf/201

Konny Rodriguez cleared up the marital mysteries surrounding her husband in an interview with Eric Lacy. The poignant and thoughtful comments of Rodriguez second wife on the late in life fame and fortune are important to the story, Eric Lacy, "Wife of Oscar-Nominated 'Searching For Sugar Man' Star Rodriguez Says He'll Stay in $50 Detroit Home," **Mlife**, January 11, 2013 http://www.mlive.com/entertainment/detroit/index.ssf/2013/01/wife_of_oscar-nominated_search.html

On Detroit, see, for example, Charlie LeDuff, **Detroit: An American Autopsy** (New York, 2013); Scott Martelle, **Detroit: A Biography** (Chicago, 2012) and Mark Binelli, **Detroit City Is The Place To Be: The Afterlife Of An American Metropolis** (New York, 2012). A brilliant look at Detroit and one song is Mark Kurlansky, **Ready For A Brand New Beat: How 'Dancing In The Street Became The Anthem For A Changing America** (New York, 2013). Also see S R. Boland and Marilyn Bond, **The Birth Of The Detroit Sound** (Detroit, 2002) Bond is a music industry insider who provide excellent material on how the Motor City influenced Rodriguez.

For the background to the Pretty Things' career prior to Steve Rowland recording the band see Hugh Dellar, ""The Pretty Things," **Shindig**, no. 45, 2015, pp. 52-63. This brilliant, in-depth article runs through 1965.

Michael Phillips, "An Improbably Happy Ending For Rodriguez," **The Chicago Tribune**, August 1, 2012 is an excellent article on how the documentary **"Searching for Sugar Man**, and how it changed Sixto Rodriguez' life. For a contrary view see Bill Cody, "Searching For Sugar Man'-True Story Or The Making Of A Myth?" January 21, 2013 http://www.ropeofsilicon.com/searching-for-sugar-man-true-story-or-the-making-of-a-myth/ This article is one of the more critical pieces on what was left out of the documentary.

Also, see the well-written, cogently argued and wonderfully researched article on Rodriguez by, Guy Blackman, "The Cold Fact Is He's Hot Again," http://www.theage.com.au/news/entertainment/music/hes-hot again/2008/09/25/1222217392243.htmI\ Also see David Malitz, "Searching For 'Sugar Man' Documentary Rediscovers Sixto Rodriguez," **The Washington Post**, July 26, 2012. For Rodriguez' reflections and in-depth comments with song analysis of the **Cold Fact** album in a telephone interview see, "Rodriguez: Return of the Sugar Man," http://www.socialstereotype.com/_/Features/Entries/2008/8/11_RO-DRIGUEZ.html

When **Cold Fact** was re-released in 2008 by Light in The Attic two reviews stood out see, Graeme Thomson, "Rodriguez, Cold Fact," **London Observer**, August 9, 2008 and Saul Austerlitz, "This Singing Sensation Was Nearly Forty Years In The Making," **Boston Globe**, September 21, 2008.

The importance of LITA to Rodriguez' career revival in 2009 and his two albums is examined in Jonathan Zwickel, "Seattle Label Revives Sixto Rodriguez's Career Four Decades Later," **Seattle Times**, June 21, 2009 http://seattletimes.com/html/musicnightlife/2009359854_rodriguez21.html

See the anonymous article, "At 70, Detroiter Rodriguez Couldn't Be Happier About His Unlikely Success," http://blog.sugarman.org/2012/11/02/at-70-detroiter-rodriguez-couldn't-be-happier-about-his-unlikely-new-fame-music-detroit-free-press-freep-com/

Also see Richard Pithouse, 'The Resurrection of Sixto Rodriguez," **The South African Civil Society Information Service**, January 23, 2013 http://www.sacsis.org.za/site/article/1550 One of the best articles on **Searching For Sugar Man** and Rodriguez' return to music prominence is Jonathan Dean, "Dead Man Walking," **London Times**, July 8, 2012.

For Rodriquez' show at the Los Angele El Rey Theater see Ernest Hardy, "Sugar Man's Rodriguez Plays Los Angeles," **Los Angeles Times**, September 29, 2012.

Also see George Varga, "Truth Stranger Than Fiction For Rodriguez," **U-T San Diego**, September 22, 2012 for San Diego's Casbah Club show. On Rodriguez politics see Corey Hall, "Free Associating With Sixto Rodriguez," **Metro Times** August 8, 2012 http://metrotimes.com/screens/free-associating-with-sixto-rodriguez-1.1355607 Also see the in-depth concert review with a favorable comment on the cover songs, George Varga, "Rodriguez, North Point Theatre A Twin Win," **U-T San Diego**, June 4, 2014 http://www.utsandiego.com/news/2014/jun/04/rodriguez-sings-at-refurbished-north-park-theatre/

On the bursting Rodriguez phenomenon see, Larry Rohter, "A Real-Life Fairy Tale, Long In The Making And Set To Old Tunes," **The New York Times**, July 20, 2012 http://www.nytimes.com/2012/07/22/movies/a-film-spotlights-the-musician rodriguez.html?smid=fb-share&_r=0, and the equally insightful article by Rachel Dodes, "A Rock 'n' Roll Mystery," **The Wall Street Journal**, July 20, 2012 http://online.wsj.com/

article_email/SB10001424052702303754904577533272231687922-lMy-QjAxMTAyMDIwMDEyNDAyWj.html?mod=wsj_valetleft_email Manhola Dargis, "Rock Musician Shrouded In Mystery Of What Might Have Been: Malik Bendjelloul's 'Searching For Sugar Man," **The New York Times**, July 27, 2012 http://www.nytimes.com/2012/07/27/movies/malik-bendjellouls-searching-for-sugar-man.html is an excellent piece.

The 1996 letter to London's **Mojo** magazine is discussed in numerous publications. At the time David Holmes was already publicizing Rodriguez.

On Craig Bartholomew-Strydom see, Mary Carole McCauley, "Ex-Baltimorean Went 'Searching For Sugar Man," **The Baltimore Sun**, April 27, 2012 http://articles.baltimoresun.com/2012-08-27/entertainment/bs-ae-sugarman-film-20120824_1_strydom-royalty-checks-music-industry

See James Delingpole, "Sixto Rodriguez Interview: The Rock 'n' Roll Lord Lucan," **London Telegraph,** August 11, 2009 for a view of Rodriguez before the documentary. This is an article that talks with Malik Bendjelloul who is in the process of making **Searching For Sugar Man**.

Also see the extremely candid interview, Irene Lacher, "The Sunday Conversation: Malik Bendjelloul," **Los Angeles Times**, February 23, 2013 http://www.latimes.com/entertainment/envelope/moviesnow/la-et-ca-mn-malik-bendjelloul-conversation-20130224,0,5383393.story

Harry Balk graciously sat down for a series of interviews, which set the record straight about his involvement with the music industry in general and Del Shannon in particular. Then I came upon the Sixto Rodriguez story and realized that Harry Balk was an unrecognized hero as he was the first person to discover, record and place Rodriguez with Dennis Coffey and Mike Theodore. Interviews with Ike Turner added a great deal to this period of rock music history. Dennis Coffey wasn't interviewed but Mike Theodore graciously provided a great deal of important information. Dan Bourgoise, the world's best copyright and song publishing guru at Bug Music, filled in many spots in the story from his long association with key figures in the music industry. Dennis DeWitt, "Harry Balk Interview," **And The Music Plays On: Del Shannon Magazine**, issue 4, summer, 1995, pp. 4-12 is an important starting point for Balk's career. It is also an insightful piece. His article is the best work done on Balk to date with great research and excellent writing.

Balk's partner Irving Micahnik is a typical music industry insider who also managed Chubby Checker. For his life see, for example, John Johnson and Joel Selvin, **Peppermint Twist: The Mob, The Music And** the Most Famous Dance Club of the 1960s (New York, 2012) and for the final word on the dance craze see Jim Dawson, **The Twist: The Story of the Song And Dance That Changed The World** (2012 Kindle edition).

For Dennis Coffey's early years, see, for example, the brilliant and exhaustively researched article by Brian C. Young, "Twirl Records and The Royaltones," http://home.comcast.net/~twirlrecords/royaltones.html

On Australia see Stevie Chick, "Detroit's Comeback King," **The London Guardian**, August 7, 2008 www.guardian.co.uk/music/2008/aug/08/popandrock3

See Adrian Mack, "Rodriguez Shows His Human Side," **Straight.com**, October 12, 2012 for his Vancouver British Columbia appearance.

When Rodriguez returned to Australia in October 2014 he was given better press coverage than the Rolling Stones and completed for his performances at seventy-two, see Nathan Davies, "Sugar Man Sixto Rodriguez Rocks Adelaide, Brings His Tunes To Town," **Adelaide Advertiser**, October 30, 2014 http://www.adelaidenow.com.au/entertainment/sugar-man-sixto-rodriguez-rocks-adelaide-brings-his-tunes-to-town/story-fni6umbp-1227107177215?nk=592373559600c8fbcb7cfee415a4f696

Howard A. DeWitt, **Chuck Berry: Rock N Roll Music** (2nd. Ed., Ann Arbor, 1985) provided background material. On the early 1960s see Howard A. DeWitt, **The Beatles: Untold Tales** (Fremont, 1985) for some essays on the early 1960s that influencing Del Shannon's career.

On the role of Johnny and the Hurricanes in Harry Balk's career, see, for example, Bill Millar, "Blowin' Up A Storm," **Melody Maker**, number 54 (March 24, 1979), p. 42: Bill Millar, "Johnny & The Hurricanes," **Goldmine**, number 57 February, 1981), pp. 10-11. For Little Willie Johnson see, for example, Lou Holscher, "Little Willie John—Fact or Fiction," **Goldmine**, number 72 (May, 1982), p. 189, Bill Millar, "Free At Last," **The History of Rock**, number 17 (1982), 336-337, Steve Propes, "Little Willie John: King of Detroit Soul Music," **Goldmine**, number 171 (February 13, 1987), p. 22.

On the royalty controversy between Del Shannon and Embee Productions see Bob Fisher, "Writs and Royalties," **And The Music Plays On**, number 1, (Fall, 1994), p. 16. ON Rodriguez' royalties see Jeff Karoub and Michelle Faul, "Rodriguez Searching For SA Royalties," **Mail And Guardian**, February 23, 2013 http://mg.co.za/article/2013-02-23-rodriguez-searching-for-sa-royalties The best article on Rodriguez' lost royalties is David Kronemyser, "What Likely Happened To Royalties For Sugar

Man?" Also see, Michael Hogan, "Rodriguez, 'Searching For Sugar Man Star, Talks Protest Songs and Politics on HuffPost Live," **The Huffington Post**, August 16, 2012.

Also see comments from a Detroit reporter, Gus Burns, "Searching For Sugarman Star Sixto Rodriguez Searching For Royalties," Mlive.com May 18, 2013http://www.mlive.com/news/detroit/index.ssf/2013/05/searching_for_sugarman_star_si.html

There were extensive interviews with musicians who were from or played in Detroit. Some knew Rodriguez others didn't, but they all helped to lay the foundation for the information that influenced Sixto Rodriguez and his music. These interviews include Jimmy McCracklin, John Lee Hooker, Solomon Burke, Charles Brown, Bob Geddins, Guitar Mac, Matt Lucas, Jamie Coe, Johnny Powers, Max Crook, Maron McKenzie and Lowell Fulson who all helped to fill in material on the African American acts and the blues from Detroit. These interviews were conducted from 1970 to 2010. This was long before I began this book but they apply to the Detroit story. No one mentioned Rodriguez, it is the Motor City that is the key.

For Rodriguez' literary side and his comparisons to John Donne see, for example, John Hayward, editor, **John Donne: A Selection of His Poetry** (London, 1950).

On Rodriguez in concert see, Sarfraz Manzoor, "Sixto Rodriguez, The Round House Review," **London Telegraph**, November 15, 2012. On William Blake, see, for example, William Blake, **The Poems of William Blake** (London, 2011). For Bob Dylan's literary side see the brilliant book by Michael Gray, **Song And Dance Man III: The Art of Bob Dylan** (London, 2000) chapter 2. Chapter 31 of this book is indebted to Gray's brilliant analysis. See David Gritten, "Sixto Rodriguez: On The Trail of the Bob Dylan of Detroit," **London Telegraph**, June 14, 2012.

See Killian Fox, "Sixto Rodriguez: It's A Typical Rags-To-Riches Story," **London Guardian**, July 14, 2012 for an interesting article in which Rodriguez basks in the positive glow and reviews for **Searching For Sugar Man**. http://www.theguardian.com/film/2012/jul/15/searching-sugar-man-sixto-rodriguez

See Jada Yuan, "Sundance: The Electrifying Search For Sugar Man," www.vulture.com/2012/01/sundance-the-electrifying-search-for-sugar-man.html for early reaction to the documentary. See the beautifully written, fact laden and cogently argued piece by a sports writer, Wright Thompson, "Searching For Sugar Man," www.grantland.com/story/_/

id/7874744/acclaimed-new-documentary-goes-hunting-lost-dylan   The role of his new found fame is detailed in Dave Hokstra, "Rediscovered By Film, Rodriguez Asks, 'How Do I Process All This?" **Chicago Sun Times**, September 20, 2012. Some critics pointed out the omissions in Malik Bendjelloul's documentary, see, for example the brilliant critique by Peter Bradshaw, "Searching For Sugar Man-Review," **London Guardian**, July 26, 2012.

On the Woodbridge section of Detroit where Rodriguez lives see, for example, Jim Zemke, "Woodbridge Pub Plants The Seeds of Community in Detroit," http://www.modeldmedia.com/features/MSH-DA201306-1.aspx On Jim Geary and the Woodbridge Pub, see Tunde Wey, "Jim Geary," May 22, 2013 http://www.uixdetroit.com/people/jimgeary.aspx

See Roger Ebert, "Searching For Sugar Man," **The Chicago Sun Times**, August 8, 2012 for a major article praising the documentary. For the Sheffield Festival see Vivian Norris, "What A Wonderful World: Documentary Is Alive And Well For Now," **The Huffington Post**, June 16, 2012.

For David Holmes cover of "Sugar Man," see Ben Thompson, "Success Is Sweet For the Sugar Man," **London Telegraph**, August 28, 2003.

On the 2005-2006 London appearances see Alexis Petridis, "The Singer Who Came Back From The Dead," **London Guardian**, October 5, 2005. Also see the review in the official website, "Rodriguez-the Music, London 2005-London 2006" at www.sugarman.org/london2005.html

For a jaded view of the Sugar Man phenomenon suggesting it is all about marketing, see Amber Hudson and Luke Sklar, "Everything Is Marketing-Live Your Sixto Rodriguez," www.sklarwilton.com/resourfescentre

For the role of Matt Sullivan and Light In The Attic on Rodriguez' career see, Joe Williams, "Label Owner Matt Sullivan Explains Why Cold Fact First Bombed And What Made Him Search For Rodriguez," **Seattle Weekly**, October 12, 2012 http://blogs.seattleweekly.com/reverb/2012/10/matt_sullivan_rodriguez_i_wond.php Also see the excellent piece of analysis and myth busting by Pete Bland, "As Myth of Rodriguez Has Blown Up, Label That Found 'Sugar Man' A Little Lost In The Shuffle," in the **Columbia Daily Tribune**, September 27, 2012 http://www.columbiatribune.com/arts_life/after_hours/as-myth-of-rodriguez-has-blown-up-label-that-found/article_f5b4afc9-8713-5ac4-200f0878bd8e.html#.UQm5lmDN5WM

On Detroit's Palmer Woods, see Christina Rogers, "Detroit Classics, Priced to Move," **The Wall Street Journal**, January 18, 2013, M 1, 6. On the Detroit reaction to the Sugar Man's re-emergence see Ben Edmonds, "40 Years Later, Rodriguez Takes His Show On The Road," **Detroit Free Press**, January 30, 2012. For a local Detroit concert see, Gary Graff, "Concert Review: Rodriguez Delivers A Sweet 'Sugar Man' Homecoming At The Crofoot," **The Oakland Press**, November 3, 2012. Also see Barney Hoskyns, editor, J. Poet, "The Rock's Backpages Flashback: Rodriguez Comes In From The Cold," http://music.yahoo.com/blogs/rocks-backpages/rock-backpages-flashback-rodriguez-comes-cold-161611729.html

See the insightful article by Stephen "Sugar" Segerman, "Rodriguez-Cult or Crap? The Cold Facts," http://sugarman.org/rodriguez/cult.html ? Also see Caryn Dolley, "The Man Who Searched For Sugar Man: Film Reels In Fame For Vinyl Store," **The Cape Times**, January 14, 2013, p. 3 and the provocative article by Iris Mann, "Ravages, Rape, Rodriguez And Real Estate," **Jewish Journal.com**, June 13, 2013 http://www.jewishjournal.com/summer_sneaks/article/ravages_rape_rodriguez_and_real_estate_2012061

An in-depth article on Segerman is Sue Segar, "The Man Who Found Sugar Man, **Cape Town Argus**, October 5, 2014.

Olivia Snaije, "France Is Sweet On Sugar Man," **The New York Times**, January 25, 2013 for a description of Rodriguez' French audience. Also see, Hannah Berk, "Mystery Singer Sixto Rodriguez Catches The Spotlight at Last, First In South Africa, Then In America," **The Urban League: The Urban School of San Francisco**, October 17, 2012 http://www.urbanlegendnews.org/arts/2012/10/17/mystery-man-sixto-rodriguez-catches-the-spotlight-at-last-first-in-south-africa-then-in-america/

Also see Alasdair Morton, "The Return Of The Sugar Man, **Facebook/tnt magazine** http://sixtorodriguez.files.wordpress.com/2012/08/tnt-magazine-rodriguez-feature-mb-quotes.pdf for an excellent interview. See Belinda Luscombe, "10 Questions for Sixto Rodriguez," **Time**, January 28, 2013, p. 56 for some interesting trivia. See Sean Michaels, "Rodriguez Set To Return to Studio After 42 Year Absence," **London Guardian**, January 30, 2013 http://www.guardian.co.uk/music/2013/jan/30/rodriguez-returns-studio-after-42-years

For Rodriguez' second chance see Kristina Puga, "Rodriguez, A Music Legend In South Africa, Gets A Second Chance At Fame," **NBCLA-**

TINO, August 14, 2012 http://nbclatino.com/2012/08/14/rodriguez-a-music-legend-in-south-africa-gets-a-second-chance-at-fame/ and Julie Hinds, "Searching For Sugar Man Gives Overlooked Icon His Due," **Detroit Free Press**, July 29, 2012. Edd Hurt, "Rodriguez Embraces Newfound Fame Through The Doc Searching For Sugar Man," **Nashville Scene, http://www.nashvillescene.com/nashville/rediscovered-singer-songwriter-sixto-rodriguez-embraces-newfound-fame-through-the-doc-searching-for-sugar-man/Content?oid=3036007**

The best description of the singer-songwriter is Bob Stanley, **Yeah, Yeah, Yeah: The Story of Modern Pop** (London, 2013), pp. 407-415. Also see Stanley on Detroit and pop music in 1975, chapter 34.

One of Rodriguez' most revealing interviews is with Andy Markowitz, "Talking To Sugar Man: A Few Words With Rodriguez," **Musicfilmweb**, June 19, 2012 http://www.musicfilmweb.com/2012/06/rodriguez-music-documentary-sheffield-docfest/

See Anthony Kaufman, "Truth Profiteer: Producer Simon Chinn Makes Good With Docs," **The Wall Street Journal**, July 26, 2012. Andrew Watt, "Rodriguez's Sweet Surprise," February 11, 2013 contains some excellent quotes on his successes and what they mean to his life and future musical career at seventy. http://www.theage.com.au/entertainment/music/rodriguezs-sweet-surprise-20130210-2e6fd.html Also see the comments on Stephen "Sugar" Segerman in Andrew Watt, "International Man Of Mystery," **The Sydney Morning Herald**, March 1, 2013 http://www.smh.com.au/entertainment/music/international-man-of-mystery-20130228-2f6vm.html

Ken Shane, "The Popdose Interview: Sixto Rodriguez," **Popdose.com**, January 11, 2013 http://popdose.com/the-popdose-interview-sixto-rodriguez/ is a revealing interview.

For the New York Highline Ballroom show see, Dino Perrucci, "Resurrecting Sugar Man: Rodriguez Comes Alive In Solo New York Show," **Rolling Stone.com**, September 4, 2012 http://www.rollingstone.com/music/blogs/alternate-take/resurrecting-sugar-man-rodriguez-comes-alive-in-solo-new-york-show-20120904

For the Cleveland appearances at Cleveland's Beachland Ballroom, see Jeff Niesel, "Sugar Man's Second Calling," **Cleveland Scene Magazine**, October 31, 2012 http://www.clevescene.com/cleveland/sugar-mans-second-coming/Content?oid=3085140

Also see the return to touring by the Sugar Man, "Rodriguez Resurfaces With Tour Behind Searching For Sugar Man," **Sound Spike**,

August 23, 2012 http://www.soundspike.com/story/4696/rodriguez-resurfaces-with-tour-behind-searching-for-sugar-man/

The first Beachland show is reviewed in Michael Galluci, "Concert Review-Rodriguez At The Beachland Ballroom, 4-24," **Scene Magazine**, April 27, 2009 http://www.clevescene.com/c-notes/archives/2009/04/27/concert-review-rodriguez-at-the-beachland-ballroom-424

Brian Howard, "Rodriguez Concert Raises The Question: What If," **Philly.com**, October 30, 2012 http://articles.philly.com/2012-10-30/news/34818514_1_1970-s-cold-fact-sugar-man-monkey is an interesting look at his career. See James Reed, "Searching For Sugar Man: Cult Musician Rodriguez," **The Boston Globe**, August 4, 2012 for a review of the documentary.

For the 23 minute interview see Scott Feinberg, "Finding 'Sugar Man': Rodriguez Reflects On A Crazy Year With A Hollywood Ending," **The Hollywood Reporter**, February 13, 2013 http://www.hollywoodreporter.com/race/finding-sugar-man-rodriguez-reflects-422022

On Dennis Coffey see his well written memoir, Dennis Coffey, **Guitars, Bars And Motown Superstars** (Ann Arbor, 2004) and Benjamin Michael Solis, "A Cuppa Joe With Motown's Dennis Coffey," **The Washtenaw Voice**, March 2011 http://www.washtenawvoice.com/2011/03/a-cuppa-joe-with-motowns-dennis-coffey/ The best in-depth Coffey interview is Peter Lewis, "Dennis Coffey The Original Guitar Hero," **Blues And Soul Music Magazine**, Issue 1067, www.lguesand 2011 http://www.bluesandsoul.com

Also see, Allan Slutsky, **Standing In The Shadow of Motown: The Life And Music of Legendary Bassist James Jamerson** (Detroit, 1989). Also see the documentaries **Standing In the Shadows of Motown** and **Radio Revolution: The Rise And Fall of The Big 8**. A brilliant book connecting Motown to more relevant Detroit political issues is Suzanne E. Smith, **Dancing In the Street: Motown And The Cultural Politics of Detroit** (Cambridge, 20001). Also see, Jack Ryan, **Recollections The Detroit Years: The Motown Sound By The People Who Made It** (Whitmore Lake, 2012) and Gerald Posner, **Motown: Music, Money, Sex And Power** (New York, 2005). Nelson George's **Where Did Our Love Go?: The Rise of Fall Of The Motown Sound** (Urbana, 2007) suggests some factors that apply to Sixto Rodriguez' career.

On labor rights and how Rodriguez' family was influenced, see, for example, Zaragosa Vargas, **Labor Rights Are Civil Rights: Mexican American Workers In Twentieth Century America** (Princeton, 2007) and

Proletarians of The North: A History of Mexican Industrial Workers in Detroit and the Midwest, 1917-1933 (Berkeley, 1993).

For a review that chides Malik Bendjelloul for leaving out the Australian part of Rodriguez' career, see Paul Byrnes, "Rodriguez Found, But Take This Sweet Story With A Grain of Salt," **The Sydney Morning Herald**, October 4, 2012. Byrnes criticizes **Searching For Sugar Man** for leaving out the Australian connection. Byrnes also talks about the rumor that there is a pot of money in Sydney waiting for Rodriguez.

On winning the Oscar for best documentary see, Mark Olsen, "Oscars 2013: 'Searching For Sugar Man' Wins Best Documentary," **Los Angeles Times**, February 25, 2013; Julie Hinds, "Searching For Sugar Man' Wins Oscar, Putting Detroit-Themed Documentary In Worldwide Spotlight," **Detroit Free Press**, February 25, 2013.

The notion of rediscovering Rodriguez and the mystery behind the story is a theme in Rebecca Davis, "Resurrecting Rodriguez," **Daily Maverick**, March 8, 20123 http://www.dailymaverick.co.za/article/2012-08-03-resurrecting-rodriguez

A marvelous article on Rodriguez' influence on South Africans is Barbara Nussbaum, "Sugar Man's Medicine For Salty Wounds: The Oscar Goes To A Cultural Healer," **The Huffington Post**, March 1, 2013 http://www.huffingtonpost.com/barbara-nussbaum/searching-for-sugar-man_b_2790787.html Also see Regina Weinreich, "Searching For Sugar Man At Guild Hall: Alec Baldwin, Honorary Chairman of the Board," **The Huffington Post**, July 7, 2012 http://www.huffingtonpost.com/regina-weinreich/searching-for-sugar-man-a_b_1656310.html For a critical look at **Searching For Sugar Man** that asks questions about the wives, see, Daniel Menaker, "Searching For Searching For Sugar Man, August 5, 2012, **The Huffington Post**, http://www.huffingtonpost.com/daniel-menaker/searching-for-sugar-man_b_1744704.html Menaker concludes that it is not a documentary but a docudrama.

See "Rodriguez Has Been Found," **Grammy.com**, January 10, 2013 for an interview prior to the Oscar's http://www.grammy.com/news/rodriguez-has-been-found

On Rodriguez' fame see Andy Greene, "Life After Sugar Man," **Rolling Stone**, April 11, 2013, pp. 20, 22. This is a particularly good article as Greene and Rodriguez walk and talk. It is one of the few later articles where Rodriguez management hasn't shut down his opinions. Also see Andy Greene, "Rodriguez: 10 Things You Don't Know About The 'Searching For Sugar Man' Star," **Rolling Stone**, March 28, 2013.

See Ruben Blades, "Whose Success?" **The New York Times Book Review**, April 7, 2013, p. 6 for the letter suggesting that label president's, like Columbia's Clive Davis, did little, if anything, to help an artist achieve success.

For Rodriguez' success see Michael Bonner, "The Sweet Taste of Success," **Uncut**, July 2013, pp. 46-50. On the abortive 2013 Mayor run for Rodriguez see David Sands, "Rodriguez For Detroit Mayor: Searching For Sugar Man Folk Star Begins Political Campaign," **The Huffington Post**, March 21, 2013 http://www.huffingtonpost.com/2013/03/21/sixto-rodriguez-mayor-detroit_n_2918080.html

To understand Steve Rowland's early music career see the Earl Palmer biography by Tony Scherman, **Backbeat: Earl Palmer's Story** (New York, 2000), Kent Hartman, **The Wrecking Crew: The Inside Story of Rock And Roll's Best Kept Secret** (New York, 2013) and Hal Blaine, **Hal Blaine And The Wrecking Crew** (Third Edition, 2003). Rowland was a drummer and he learned from key drummers.

For Freddy Bienstock's career it his eventual role in Steve Rowland's producing, see, Sandra Salmans, "New Yorkers & Co, A Song Plugger's Big Play: His Return As Boss," **New York Times**, June 4, 1985; Alan Clayson, "Freddy Bienstock: Music Publisher Whose Portfolio Encompassed Acts As Diverse As Cliff Richard and James Brown." **The London Independent**, December 15, 2014 http://www.independent.co.uk/news/obituaries/freddy-bienstock-music-publisher-whose-portfolio-encompassed-acts-as-diverse-as-cliff-richard-and-james-brown-1794329.html

Also see Mark Worth, "Cause It's The Greatest Last Song Ever Recorded," July 6, 2014, http://sugarman.org/rodwhatsnew.html This worthy piece is an unusually perceptive look at the song "Cause" due to extensive interviews with producer Steve Rowland.

Anna Hartford, "Sugar Rush: Letter From Cape Town," **The Paris Review**, February 26, 2013 is a penetrating look at the Rodriguez phenomenon in South Africa in early 2013. A brilliant piece of writing on how and why South Africa embraces Rodriguez and how fame and fortune may have blunted the message.

On the chances for a third album see, Nathan Rabin, "Searching For Sugar Man Comeback Kid Rodriguez Meets With Producers To Discuss Potential New Album," January 29, 2013 http://www.avclub.com/article/emsearching-for-sugar-manem-comeback-kid-rodriguez-91751 Also see Patrick Flanary, "Rodriguez Weights Potential Third Album,

Rolling Stone, January 29, 2013 http://www.rollingstone.com/music/news/rodriguez-weighs-potential-third-album-20130129

For Eva Rodriguez Koller's service in the Gulf War and her distinguished military career see Deborah G. Douglas and Lucy B. Young, **American Women And Flight Since 1940** (Lexington, 2004), pp. 226, 334, 350.

On Neil Bogart see, Larry Harris, Curt Gooch and Jeff Suhs, **A Party Every Day: The Inside Story of Casablanca Records** (New York, 2009) and Frederic Dannen, **Hit Men: Power Brokers And Fast Money In Music Business** (New York, 1990).

For Clarence Avant's relationship to Soul Train see Nelson George's, **The Hippest Trip In America: Soul Train And The Evolution of Culture & Style** (New York, 2014), pp. 59-62. George's excellent book gets some of the facts wrong. He claims Rodriguez sold 30,000 LPs in South Africa, when in fact, it was closer to 500,000. Avant also credits the film's editing with making him look bad. The truth is Avant's statements were broadcast verbatim. It was Avant who made himself look like a predator. But George did point out the respect, the business savvy and the sixty plus year career in show business for Avant. For Avant's role with Stax's see, Robert Gordon, **Respect Yourself: Stax Records And The Soul Explosion** (New York, 2013).

For Clarence Avant and Bill Withers see Andy Greene, "The Soul Man Who Walked Away," **Rolling Stone**, March 26, 2015, pp. 55-57, 66.

For a view of Rodriguez before the documentary and his place in South Africa, see Rian Malan, "Bizarre Is A Word For It," **London Telegraph**, October 6, 2005.http://www.telegraph.co.uk/culture/music/rockandjazzmusic/3647008/Bizarre-is-a-word-fo

Brian Currin, "Rodriguez And His Place In The Story of Rock," September 1, 2012 http://blog.sugarman.org/2012/09/01/rodriguez-and-his-place-in-the-story-of-rock/ is an unusually perceptive analysis of the Sugar Man and where he fits in the broader scope of rock and roll.

Also see the excellent review by Gervase de Wilde, "Rodriguez At The Union Chapel, Islington, Review," **London Telegraph**, December 10, 2009 http://www.telegraph.co.uk/culture/music/live-music-reviews/6780523/Rodriguez-at-the-Union-Chapel-Islington-review.html

For a brilliant examination of what Rodriguez meant to South African music and politics, see Richard Pithouse, "The Resurrection of Sixto Rodriguez," http://sacsis.org.za/site/article/1550 Pithouse is a Professor at Rhodes University, and he places Rodriguez' music and influence into the mainstream of South African history.

The influence that Soul Train may have had on Rodriguez is seen in Nelson George, **The Hippest Trip In America** (New York, 2014) and Questlove, **Soul Train: The Music, Dance and Style of a Generation** (New York, 2014). For some of the criminal elements in the music business and how they carried over into Rodriguez' day see, Joel Selvin, **Here Comes The Night: The Dark Soul of Bert Berns And the Dirty Business of Rhythm and Blues** (New York, 2014).

Although peripheral to the Rodriguez story, the Light In The Attic reissues of Betty Davis' funk albums tells us a great deal about the industry and the times. For a brilliant view of her influence see Maureen Mahon, "They Say She's Different: Race, Gender, Genre And The Liberated Black Femininity of Betty Davis," **Journal of Popular Music Studies**, volume 23, issue 2, June 2011, pp. 146-155.

On Malik Bendjelloul's tragic death see Rodriguez' reaction, Bob Gendron, "Rodriguez Pays Tribute To Director Bendjelloul," **Chicago Tribune**, May 15, 2014. Also see, Kory Grow, "Searching For Sugar Man Director Malik Bendjelloul Dead At 36," **Rolling Stones**, May 14, 2014, Bruce Weber, "Malik Bendjelloul Oscar Winner For 'Sugar' Man Film, Dies At 36, **New York Times**, May 13, 2014, Mark Olson, "Oscar Winning 'Sugar Man' Director Malik Bendjelloul Dies At 36," **Los Angeles Times**, May 13, 2014 and Xan Brooks, "Searching For Sugar Man Director Malik Bendjelloul Dies Aged 36," **London Guardian**, May 14, 2014.

For a brilliant in depth report with information from Stockholm on Malik Bendjelloul's tragic death, see Scott Johnson, "Oscar To Suicide In One Year: Tracing The 'Searching For Sugar Man' Director's Tragic Final Days," **the Hollywood Reporter**, June 11, 2014 http://www.hollywoodreporter.com/news/searching-sugarman-director-dead-thr-710882

On the dangers of success as well as the fame and fortune syndrome for Rodriguez, see George Palathingal, "Life Not So Sweet For 'Sugar Man' Sixto Rodriguez," May 29, 2013 http://www.smh.com.au/entertainment/music/life-not-so-sweet-for-sugar-man-sixto-rodriguez-20140529-zrroy.html#ixzz33OX56blU

The 2013 concerts had widely divergent reviews. See Charles R. Cross, "Concert Review: Rodriguez Charming But Disjoined and Flat," **The Seattle Times**, April 26, 2013. By 2014 the reviews were still excellent ones. See Roy Trakin, "Searching For Sugar Man: Where is Sixto Rodriguez Today?" **Billboard**, June 12, 2014 http://www.billboard.com/articles/news/6114238/searching-for-sugar-man-where-is-sixto-rodriguez-today

Steven Mirkin, "Rodriguez Turns In Erratic Set At The Greek," **Orange County Registe**r, June 3, 2014, reviews the Los Angeles Greek Theater Show in depth. Also see for the announcement of a New Jersey concert in Victoria Cepeda, "NJPC Features Mexican-American Folk Musician Sixto Diaz Rodriguez,"**Pa'lante Latino**, May 5, 2014 http://palantelatino.com/2014/05/05/njpac-features-mexican-american-folk-musician-sixto-diaz-rodriguez/

For Paolo Nutini's appreciation of Rodriguez' music see Sarah Jane Griffiths, "Discovering 'Sugar Man' Rodriguez," **BBC News Entertainment and Art**, July 25, 2012 http://www.bbc.com/news/entertainment-arts-18974892 and Colin MacFarlane, **Paolo Nutini: Coming Up Easy** (n.p. 2014), pp. 233-237.

The Voelvry Movement, led by Johannes Kerkorrel, Koos Kombuis and Bemoldus Niemand is an important musical protest against apartheid. See Albert Grundlingh, "Rocking The Boat: The Voelvry Music Movement In South Africa: Anatomy of Afrikaans Music Movement And Afrikaner Identity," (University of Stellenbosch, March 25, 2014). Grundlingh's article is the best piece on the roots of apartheid and how and why the movement triumphed. Grundlingh concludes "Voelvry did rock the boat, but more gently than often assumed." That conclusion suggests that the early native African protesters were perhaps more important then the Voelvry Movement.

See the brilliant dissertation by Taylor R. Genovese, "Get Up, Stand Up: The Role Of Music As A Driver For Political Change in Apartheid South Africa," http://www.academia.edu/3462810/

See Pat Hopkins, **Voelvry: The Movement That Rocked South Africa** (Zebra Press, 2006) for the impact of white South African musicians on apartheid. Also see R. Serge Denisoff, **Sing A Song of Social Significance** (Bowling Green, 1983). A must CD for anyone who wants to document the anti-apartheid movement is Johannes Kerkorrel's CD **Awuwa**, which came out in 1993 featuring Stef Bos who is a Dutch singer. He lived in Cape Town and he performed in Dutch and in Afrikaner. He was also a star in Belgium where he wrote the that countries 1989 entry into the Eurovision Song Contest "Door De Wind." He has a lilting, folk music vocal style. Also see, Michela E. Vershbow, "The Sounds of Resistance: The Role of Music In The Anti-Apartheid Movement," **Student Pulse**, volume 2, no. 6, 2010 http://www.studentpulse.com/articles/265/the-sounds-of-resistance-the-role-of-music-in-south-africas-anti-apartheid-movement

The Role Of Music In South Africa's Anti-Apartheid Movement," **Student Pulse: The International Student Journal**, Vol. 2, no. 6, 2010 http://www.studentpulse.com/articles/265/4/the-sounds-of-resistance-the-role-of-music-in-south-africas-anti-apartheid-movement

Johnny Clegg is an important part of the South African music movement against apartheid. He is also a respected academic, as well as a musician and he remains a seminal political figure. On Clegg see, for example, Jenny Gross, "White Father of African Rock Marks Anniversary," **Mail & Guardian**, November 7, 2010;

On the apartheid struggle see Nancy L. Clark and William H. Worger, **South Africa: The Rise And Fall Of Apartheid** (Harlow Pearson Education, 2007); Grant Olwage, **Composing Apartheid: Music For And Against Apartheid** (Johannesburg, 2008) and Lee Hirsch, **Amandala! A Revolution In Four-Part Harmony** (New

York, 2002). Amandala is a brilliant documentary film detailing the struggle of black South Africans against apartheid.

See Glenn Baker's description of **Rodriguez Alive** on **Sugarman. Org: The Official Rodriguez Website http://sugarman.org/alive.html Baker** is Australia's best known rock and roll writer and he puts Rodriguez' music into a brilliant perspective.

On the Clarence Avant law suit against Rodriguez see Keith Allen, "Searching For Sugar Man Royalty Mystery May Be Solved," **The Hollywood Reporter**, May 4, 2014 http://guardianlv.com/2014/05/searching-for-sugar-man-royalty-mystery-may-be-solved/ An interesting Rodriguez interview a few weeks after the success of **Searching For Sugar Man** cast some light on the lost royalty controversy. In this discussion, Rodriguez is not sure that there were royalties. The conversation with London journalist Kaleem Aftab was open and thoughtful. In later interviews, Rodriguez will pull back from discussing royalties.

See Kaleem Aftab, "Rodriguez: The Builder Who's Bigger Than Elvis," **The London Independent**, December 7, 2012 http://www.independent.co.uk/arts-entertainment/music/features/sixto-rodriguez-the-builder-whos–bigger-than-elvis-7966151.html

In the aftermath of the documentary there are a number of important Avant interviews the best one explaining his relationship to the Sugar Man is Brian McCollum, "Could Some Answers Finally Be On The Way For Sixto Rodriguez?" **Detroit Free Press**, May 17, 2013 https://scontent-b.xx.fbcdn.net/hphotos-xpa1/v/t1.0-9/p480x480/10650060_

10152480111363807_1868394177954855873_n.jpg?oh=3dbe253a8eec5
e596a2ddb77c8d9596c&oe=54E85C42

Also see the curious facts behind the Clarence Avant lawsuit in Kathleen Flynn, "Sixto Rodriguez Named In Lawsuit By Music Company," May 29, 2014http://www.nola.com/music/index.ssf/2014/05/rodriguez_named_in_lawsuit_by.html

For Rodriguez' Edinburgh show in 2013 see Phyllis Stephen, "Solid At 70-Sixto Rodriguez At The Usher Hall, **The Edinburgh Reporter**, http://www.theedinburghreporter.co.uk/2012/11/solid-at-70-sixto-rodriguez-at-the-usher-hall/

For a brilliant history of the Detroit music scene see David A. Carson, **Grit, Nose and Revolution: The Birth of Detroit Rock 'N' Roll** (Ann Arbor 2005). Rodriguez' connection to punk music is delineated in this volume. Also see, Lars Bjorn and Jim Gallert, **Before Motown: A History of Jazz in Detroit, 1920-1960** (Ann Arbor, 2001) is another key book written by a University of Michigan-Dearborn sociology professor. The Bjorn volume is a key to understanding the evolution of the blues, Motown and the diverse punk strains that characterized the Motor City.

For the influence of the counterculture on Rodriguez see, for example, Michael J. Kramer, **The Republic of Rock Music And Citizenship In the Sixties Counterculture** (New York, 2013).

On Rodriguez' discography and Australian popularity see, for example, Tim Forster, "Buried Treasure: From Detroit Outcast To Down Under Cult Star," **Mojo**, August 2002. Also see the official Rodriguez website SugarMan.org: Rodriguez-Discography: Albums/ Singles http://sugarman.org/rodalbums.html

The 2014 lawsuits are described in Sean Michaels, "Four Decades On, Searching For Sugar Man Singer Dragged Into Legal Battle Over His 1970s Recordings," **London Guardian**, May 30, 2014; Ben Sisario, "Now that 'Sugar Man' Is Found, Lawsuit Focuses On Missing Royalties," **New York Times**, May 2, 2014.

There are a number of key sources that were important in understanding the music business. Interviews with Roger Armstrong, Dan Bourgoise, Harry Balk, Scott Cameron, Opal Louis Nations, Dave Williams and Ronald Smith helped place the various labels and industry moves in perspective.

When Rodriguez toured Australia in October 2014 he reflected on his career as the tour began see, Craig Mathieson, "Rodriguez Brings Sugar Man To Life," **Sydney Morning Herald**, October 17, 2014. Also see the Australian article by, Tom Cardy, "Sugar Man Proves Bittersweet," **The Dominion Post**, October 15, 2014.

See the brilliant and insightful Australian radio interview with Ian Henschke on ABC Adelaide http://blogs.abc.net.au/sa/2014/10/sixto-rodriguez.html

For an interesting insight into Rodriguez from a socialist see Bryan D. Palmer, "A Life Beyond Imagination," http://www.solidarity-us.org/node/3772 This is a brilliant look at **Searching For Sugar Man** and Rodriguez' life.

For Bohemian influences on Rodriguez' life the reflections of musician Matt Lucas, Herb Gold's, **Bohemia: Where Art, Angst, Love and Strong Coffee Meet** (Mount Jackson, 2007) and those who populate the Cass Corridor helped to bring the Sugar Man's Bohemian nature to the fore.

There are many reviews stating how well Rodriguez performed after the fame and fortune of **Searching For Sugar Man**. One of the best is the review of the Sugar Man's show at Manhattan's Beacon Theater, see Beth J. Harpaz, Sugar Man' Rodriguez Plays to Adoring NY Crowd," **Yahoomusic.com**, April 8.2013 https://www.yahoo.com/music/s/sugar-man-rodriguez-plays-adoring-ny-crowd-185402015.html

This book attempts to place Sixto Rodriguez in the midst of the music industry. To do so required a great deal of information. The following books were an important part of placing the Sugar Man in the middle of the industry. See, for example, Donald Clarke, **The Rise And Fall of Popular Music** (New York, 2005), B. Lee Cooper, **Prominent Themes In Popular Songs: An Exploration of 53 Persistent Lyrical Themes** (Amazon, 2013), B. Lee Cooper, Wayne S. Haney and Frank Hoffmann **Rock Music In American Popular Culture** (New York, 1999), Clive Davis, **Inside The Record Business** (New York, 1975), Ken Emerson, **Always Magic In The Air: The Bomp and Brilliance of the Brill Building Era** (New York, 2005), Philip M. Ennis, **The Seventh Stream: The Emergence of Rock roll in American Popular Music** (Hanover, 1992). For brief mention of the English side of the music business see the captivating inside look at the business in the U. S. with insights into the man who managed Steve Rowland in the U. K. Marty Machat in a book my his son Steven Machat, **Gods, Gangsters and Honour** (London, 2009).

Howard A. DeWitt and Dennis M. DeWitt, **Stranger In Town: The Musical Life Of Del Shannon** Dubuque, 2001) contains extensive material on Harry Balk.

ABOUT THE AUTHOR AND ACKNOWLEDGEMENTS

Howard A. DeWitt is Professor Emeritus of History at Ohlone College, Fremont, California. He received his B. A. from Western Washington State University, the M. A. from the University of Oregon and a PhD from the University of Arizona. He also studied at the University of Paris, Sorbonne and the City University in Rome. Professor DeWitt is the author of twenty-three books and has published over 200 articles and more than 200 reviews in twenty-one popular and scholarly magazines.

DeWitt has also been a member of a number of organizations to promote the study of history. The most prestigious is the Organization of American Historians.

For more forty-five years he has taught full and part time at a number of U. S. colleges' is best known for teaching two college level courses in the History of Rock n Roll music. He continued to teach the History of Rock and Roll music on the Internet until 2011. Among people he brought to class were Bo Diddley, Mike Bloomfield, Jimmy McCracklin, Paul Butterfield, George Palmerton and Pee Wee Thomas. In a distinguished academic career, he has also taught at the University of California, Davis, the University of Arizona, Cochise College and Chabot College. In addition to these teaching assignments, Professor DeWitt is a regular speaker at the Popular Culture Association annual convention and at the National Social Science Association meetings. He has delivered a number of addresses to the Organization of American Historians.

He wrote the first book on Chuck Berry, which was published by Pierian Press under the title **Chuck Berry: Rock N Roll Music** in 1985. DeWitt's earlier brief biography, **Van Morrison: The Mystic's Music**, published in 1983, received universally excellent reviews. On the English side of the music business DeWitt's, **The Beatles: Untold Tales**, originally published in 1985, was picked up by the Kendall Hunt Publishing Company in the 1990s and is used regularly in a wide variety of college courses on the history of rock music. Kendall Hunt also published **Stranger in Town: The Musical Life of Del Shannon** with co-author Dennis M. DeWitt in 2001. In 1993's **Paul McCartney: From Liverpool To Let It Be** concentrated on the Beatle years. He also co-authored **Jailhouse Rock: The Bootleg Records of Elvis Presley** with Lee Cotten in 1983.

Professor DeWitt's many awards in the field of history include founding the Cochise County Historical Society and his scholarship has been recognized by a number of state and local government organizations. DeWitt's book, **Sun Elvis: Presley In The 1950s**, published by Popular Culture Ink. was a finalist for the Deems-ASCAP Award for the best academic rock and roll book.

Professor DeWitt is a renaissance scholar who publishes in a wide variety of outlets that are both academic and popular. He is one of the few college professors who bridge the gap between scholarly and popular publications. His articles and reviews have appeared in **Blue Suede News, DISCoveries, Rock 'N' Blues News**, the **Journal of Popular Culture**, the **Journal of American History, California History**, the **Southern California Quarterly**, the **Pacific Historian, Amerasia**, the **Western Pennsylvania Historical Magazine**, the **Annals of Iowa**, the **Journal of the West, Arizona and the West,** the **North Beach Review, Ohio History**, the **Oregon Historical Quarterly**, the **Community College Social Science Quarterly, Montana: The Magazine of the West, Record Profile Magazine, Audio Trader**, the **Seattle Post-Intelligencer** and **Juke Box Digest**.

For forty plus years DeWitt has combined popular and academic writing. He has been nominated for numerous writing awards. His reviews are combined with articles to form a body of scholarship and popular writing that is frequently footnoted in major work. As a political scientist, Professor DeWitt authored three books that questioned American foreign policy and its direction. In the Philippines, DeWitt is recognized as one of the foremost biographers of their political leader Jose Rizal. His three books on Filipino farm workers remain the standard in the field.

During his high school and college years, DeWitt promoted dances in and around Seattle, Washington. Such groups as Little Bill and the Bluenotes, Ron Holden and the Playboys, the Frantics, the Wailers and George Palmerton and the Night People among others played at such Seattle venues as the Eagle's Auditorium and Dick Parker's Ballroom.

My thanks to my wonderful and supportive brother and sister in law, Ken and Barb Marich, for their sane and intelligent choice of wine and food. My brothers Dennis and Duane DeWitt listened to me, and offered cogent criticism.

Marc and Gaby Magg Bristol are good friends and they publish my ranting on rock and roll music in **Blue Suede News**. Thank you Marc and Gaby for not only being critical editors but good friends. They have edited my rock, blues, country and rockabilly articles for almost thirty years. My good friend Lee Cotton published much of my ranting and raving in **Rock N Blues News** and I thank him. Neil Skok and Fred Hopkins are friends who listened to Rodriguez' music and advised me. Neil provided in depth criticism.

Paul Perry offered criticism and he helped with the title while listening to the various stage of the project. Jim Nauman offered some criticism and listened to the project as it developed. I want to thank both Paul and Jim for their forbearance.

Howard has two grown children. They both live in Los Angeles. His wife of forty plus years, Carolyn, is an educator, an artist and she continues to raise Howard. She is presently retired and vacationing around the world. The DeWitt's live in Scottsdale, Arizona That is when they are not in Paris looking for art, books and music. Howard is working on a book on Paris. That is a year away and a study of Rodriguez is next. That book is tentatively entitled **The Unreal Journey of Sixto Rodriguez Coming From Reality**

Professor DeWitt has a private detective series with the first novel, **Stone Murder**, now out and selling well. His book on the president **Obama's Detractors: In The Right Wing Nut House** is a marvelous look at the radical right. It was also the reason that his friends in Scottsdale no longer talk to him. **Stone Murder** features a San Francisco P.I. Trevor Blake III, and much of the story line will evolve around crimes that DeWitt witnessed while working four years and two days as an agent with the Bureau of Alcohol, Tobacco and Firearms. He was a street agent for the BATF and his tales of those years are in manuscript waiting for publication. He was also a key figure in the BATF Union. His second mystery novel **Salvador Dali Murder** was published in 2014.

He is currently working on a series of rock and roll mystery novels featuring Trevor Blake III, a private eye in San Francisco. The first novel **Stone Murder** can be ordered through Amazon. The sequel **Salvador Dali Murder** is also available at Amazon. He also writes fiction under another name.

Any corrections or additions to this or the subsequent volumes that will follow this study can be sent to Horizon Books, P. O. Box 4342, Scottsdale, Arizona 85258. DeWitt can be reached via e-mail at Howard217@aol.com

BO DIDDLEY AND HOWARD A. DEWITT